The Calvinism of Dispensationalism

A Historical Analysis, Positive Synthesis, and Defense of Nineteenth to Twenty-First Century Dispensationalism amid Covenant Calvinist Criticisms of Unorthodoxy in Soteriology

Dr. Keith A. Sherlin
PhD; ThD; PhD

Foreword by
Arnold G. Fruchtenbaum, ThM; PhD

Copyright, Publisher, Permissions & Cover Design

The Calvinism of Dispensationalism: A Historical Analysis, Positive Synthesis, and Defense of Nineteenth to Twenty-First Century Dispensationalism amid Covenant Calvinist Criticisms of Unorthodoxy in Soteriology
Copyright © 2023, by Keith Sherlin

ISBN: 979-8-9877278-0-5

All rights reserved. No part of this book may be reproduced in any form without permission in writing from the publisher, except in the case of brief quotations embodied in critical articles or reviews.

Published by Christicommunity, Landrum, South Carolina.
www.christicommunity.org
email: christicommunity@gmail.com

Christicommunity is a nonprofit religious educational ministry devoted to education, evangelism, & encouragement in Christlike discipleship.

Scripture quotations from The ESV® Bible (The Holy Bible, English Standard Version®), © 2001 by Crossway, a publishing ministry of Good News Publishers. Used by permission. All rights reserved.

The Scripture quotes from the NET Bible® https://netbible.com copyright ©1996, 2019 are used with permission from Biblical Studies Press, L.L.C. All rights reserved.

Scripture quotations taken from the (NASB®) New American Standard Bible®, Copyright © 1960, 1971, 1977, 1995, 2020 by The Lockman Foundation. Used by permission. All rights reserved. lockman.org .

Scripture taken from the New King James Version®. Copyright © 1982 by Thomas Nelson. Used by permission. All rights reserved.

Scripture taken from the Good News Translation in Today's English Version-Second Edition Copyright © 1992 by American Bible Society. Used by Permission.

Scripture quotations taken from the New English Bible, copyright © Cambridge University Press and Oxford University Press 1961, 1970. All rights reserved.

The theologians listed on the front cover the book are as follows by row:
Row 1: Martin Luther, John Calvin, Ulrich Zwingli, Moise Amyraut
Row 2: J.N. Darby, J.R. Graves, Lewis Sperry Chafer, Donald Grey Barnhouse
Row 3: W.A. Criswell, John F. Walvoord, J.D. Pentecost, William MacDonald
Row 4: Charles C. Ryrie, Mal Couch, Arnold G. Fruchtenbaum, Robert P. Ligntner

Book cover designed by Angelia Faith

Dedications

To Janet and Bryan Painter in memory of Danny Painter

Janet your husband Danny, and Bryan your father, graced me with investing in my educational, theological, and philosophical journey by helping to build this very library from where I work and write at this moment. Four academic degrees later, with two more in process, studies for and related to the South Carolina Criminal Justice Academy, judicial/legal studies, tests and certifications, and many hours of time writing, preparing, studying, praying, and delivering Bible teaching from this library has occurred over the years. I have also spent many hours in meditation upon God, scripture, and his providential ways through prayer and scripture reading here in this library that he graciously finished for me. He never would take a single payment for the work he did. I pray that my ministerial endeavors, accomplishments in academics and professional services for my community, state, and nation, and life overall reflects the goodness of the Lord that has developed through the many hours here that were made possible by his gracious and generous gift to me. I will always treasure the many conversations Danny and I had over the years. Danny loved me and I loved him. I will never forget the encouragement and grace he showered on me. With every accomplishment of life that stems from my studies, I praise the Lord for his life and ministry to me.

To Dr. Steve Hess and Pat Hess in memory of Dr. Bob Hess

Pat your husband, and Steve your father, took me under his wing for a season to help me understand how God's sovereignty in providence applied to both our salvation and to Israel's salvation in the future. The very first time I entered the doors of Grace Bible Church it was Dr. Bob Hess speaking and teaching that Sunday morning. As I chatted with him from that point forward he took an interest in me and would sit with me and talk to me about how a Dispensational understanding of the bible flowed consistently from a proper view of God's total sovereign providence over history, over Israel, and over the body of Christ. To this day, I still recall various statements he made to me. One of my most vivid memories was him sitting in a seat and him calling me over to him and asking me some question on Israel and the OT law. He stated, "Keith, if you misunderstand who Israel is and what laws apply to them and what laws apply to the body of Christ you will be forever confused on how the Bible harmonizes." His encouragement, kindness, and interest in me motivated me to study more and to seek diligently the proper methods to discover the beautiful harmony that exists in the scriptures when recognizing God's plan for Israel and the body of Christ. I praise the Lord for his providence in orchestrating that our paths would cross. I look forward to talking to him again in glory.

To Brannon Poore

I think you and I have modeled the triage theme in what I note here in this book, that two ministers can unify on the gospel as central while not biting and devouring each other on differences in regards to theological matters pertaining to continuity and discontinuity. I praise the Lord for the work, sacrifices, and resources you and other leaders have poured into building an elder ruled, gospel centric, and community serving ministry for the Foothills region. I praise the Lord for his providence in delivering you. I recall my dad, your father and mother-in-law, and others of us praying for the Lord to open your heart and to deliver you, themes that this book discusses. What an amazing blessing to see the fruits from those prayers and labors that have materialized in your life, family, and ministry. I pray that this book will highlight for you how much unity does and can exist among the believers that align on the precious truths of God's sovereign providence of unconditional love applied to helpless sinners. I also hope you will learn something new from this book about the Dispensational heritage that encourages your faith, gives you hope, and motivates you to great love and admiration for this rich theological stream that God birthed from within the Reformed heritage. Furthermore, I pray the gospel in your life, children's lives, any future grandchildren, and beyond continues to ring loudly that precious bell of Amazing Grace that saves sinners. Soon, quicker than we realize, we shall be standing in eternity with this glorious Savior and the believers of the ages as we rejoice over our collective labors in the Lord. Until then I pray you continue to pound the forces of hell with the greatest story ever known to world history, the story of our precious Lord Jesus who died and arose again to give hope to all who will trust in him.

THE CALVINISM OF DISPENSATIONALISM I
DEDICATIONS III
ENDORSEMENTS X

FOREWORD BY DR. ARNOLD G. FRUCHTENBAUM 1
PREFACE BY DR. MAL COUCH 3
INTRODUCTION BY DR. RON BIGALKE 5
BRIEF BOOK SUMMARY BY KEITH SHERLIN 9

CHAPTER 1. ANTITHETICAL WORLDVIEWS, DIVIDED THEOLOGIES, AND THEIR CONNECTION TO CULTURAL CONSEQUENCES 12

GOD'S PROVIDENCE IN 1776 BIRTHS A JUDEO-CHRISTIAN NATION UPON NATURAL LAW 12
    Satan's Sinister Subversions of God's Goodness 17
SATANISM: A SINISTER SEED FOR OTHER WORLDVIEWS SUCH AS HUMANISTIC LIBERALISM 18
    The Metaphysics, Epistemology, and Methodology of Satanism 20
    Satanism Masquerades in Humanistic Liberal Progressivism and Positivism 30
STATEMENT OF PROBLEM: COVENANTALISM AND DISPENSATIONALISM'S TWENTIETH CENTURY DIVISION OVER THE DOCTRINE OF SOTERIOLOGY 37
    A Failure to Apply a Theological Triage Organization Model 41
    Seven Areas Where Satanic Humanism has Undermined Human Progress 44
        Irrational Ideology of Our Origins: A Denial of Logic Needed for Liberty 45
        Involuntary Slavery: A Denial of Personal Liberty 48
        Unjustified Expulsion of Native American Indians: A Denial of Natural Personal Property Rights 49
        Women Denied Equal Rights to Vote and to Economic Equality: A Denial of Political Liberty 50
        Abortion for Convenience: A Denial of Natural Life 54
        Laws Interfering with Parental Authority: A Denial of Natural Parental Liberty 58
        So-Called Homosexual Marriages: A Denial of Natural Biological Law 59
IMPORTANCE OF THE SUBJECT: THE TWO MAIN THEOLOGIES NEED TO COOPERATE IN A THEOLOGICAL TRIAGE TO MORE EFFECTIVELY COUNTER A CRUMBLING CULTURE 63
A QUESTION TO EXPLORE: IS THERE A CONTINUITY CALVINISTIC DISPENSATIONAL 76
SOTERIOLOGY? 76
THE METHODOLOGY TO ANSWERING THE QUESTION 78
THIS BOOK'S PRIMARY POINT 80
LAYOUT OF THE BOOK 81

CHAPTER 2. THE COVENANT CALVINISTS' CRITICISMS OF DISPENSATIONALISM THAT HINDER A COALESCENT UNION 83

PERSONAL FAMILIARITY AND INTEREST WITH THIS INTERFAITH DEBATE OF THE DECADES 83
A Goal from this Work: A Hopeful Reconciliation within a Theological Triage 91

A Plethora of Historical Criticisms 93
Over Fifty Years of Criticisms from the Covenant Calvinist Tradition 94
Specific Literature with Assertions Against Dispensationalism from the Covenant
Reformed Theologian 96
    1. A.W. Pink (1886-1952) 97
    2. C. Norman Kraus (1924-2018) 98
    3. Clarence Bass (1922-2021) 98
    4. Curtis Crenshaw (b. 1945) & 5. Grover Gunn (b. 1949) 100
    6. Chad Brand (b. 1954-2023) & 7. Tom Pratt (b. 1945) 101
    8. Russell Moore (b. 1971) 102
    9. Reginald Kimbro (b. 1962) 103
    10. Donald G. Bloesch (1928-2010) 104
    11. Robert L. Reymond (1932-2013) 104
    12. John Gerstner (1914-1996) & 13. R.C. Sproul (1939-2017) 106
    14. Keith A. Mathison (b. 1967) 114
Summary of the Literature's Assertions 117

CHAPTER 3. CALVINISTIC DISPENSATIONALISTS ON GOD'S DECREE, MAN'S DEPRAVITY, ELECTION, AND/OR EFFICACIOUS GRACE 119

Thirty-Seven Dispensationalists of the Nineteenth to Twenty-First-Century who Affirmed a Calvinistic Soteriology 128
    1. John Nelson Darby (1800-1882) 128
    2. Dr. James Robinson Graves (1820-1893) 131
    3. Dr. Lewis Sperry Chafer (1871-1952) 134
    4. Dr. Herbert Lockyer (1886-1984) 144
    5. Dr. Alva J. McClain (1888-1968) 148
    6. Dr. Donald Grey Barnhouse (1895-1960) 150
    7. Dr. Merrill F. Unger (1909-1980) 155
    8. Dr. W.A. Criswell (1909-2002) 159
    9. Dr. John Walvoord (1910-2002) 161
    10. Dr. J. Dwight Pentecost (1915-2014) 166
    11. William MacDonald (1917-2007) 169
    12. John A. Witmer (1920—2007) 172
    13. Dr. Charles C. Ryrie (1925-2016) 174
    14. Dr. Earl D. Radmacher (1931-2014) 179
    15. Dr. Norman Geisler (1932-2019) 182
    16. Dr. Rolland McCune (1934-2019) 190
    17. Dr. Paul Enns (b.1937) 195
    18. Dr. Mal Couch (1938-2013) 198
    19. Dr. John F. MacArthur Jr. (b.1939) 201
    20. Dr. Erwin Lutzer (b.1941) 204
    21. Dr. Arnold G. Fruchtenbaum (b.1943) 207
    23. Dr. Robert P. Lightner (1931 - 2018) 216
    24. James Quiggle 219

25. Dr. Kenneth Keathley 223
26. Dr. Tony Evans 225
27. Dr. Danny Akin 228
28-37. Ten More Calvinistic Dispensationalists Briefly Noted 231
    28. Dr. William Baker 231
    29. Steven Ger 232
    30. Dr. Woodrow Kroll 232
    31-32. Dr. Mike Stallard & Dr. Tom Constable 233
    33-35. Dr. Stanley Toussaint, Dr. Harold Hoehner, & Dr. Roger Raymer 234
    36-37. Dr. Michael G. Vanlaningham & Dr. Gerald Peterman 234
CHAPTER SUMMARY: DISPENSATIONALISM IS CLEARLY NOT AN ARMINIAN MOVEMENT 235

CHAPTER 4. DIVERSITY AMONG DISPENSATIONALISTS AND COVENANT THEOLOGIANS ON THE ATONEMENT OF CHRIST 237

FOR WHOM DID CHRIST DIE? A PROPOSED SOLUTION FROM A REFORMED DISPENSATIONAL MODEL 242

CHAPTER 5. A DISPENSATIONAL CONTINUITY PERSPECTIVE ON THE GODHEAD'S UNIFIED WORK OF REDEMPTION IN THE O.T. & N.T. 254

THE COVENANT CRITICISM RESTATED: DISPENSATIONALISM DENIES THAT OLD TESTAMENT SAINTS ARE IN CHRIST & BY THAT TEACHES O.T. WORKS SALVATION 257
TRUTHS FOR A UNIFIED TRANS-DISPENSATIONAL FAMILY OF GOD IN CHRIST THAT ALSO DISTINGUISHES N.T. SAINTS FROM O.T. SAINTS 261
    1. The Importance of a Literal Hermeneutic & Its Application to Colossians 1:17-18: A Foundation to a Trans-dispensational Christological (Yahweh) Focus of History & Eternity 261
    2. God's Single Doctrine of Election for All People Creating One Redeemed Family 279
    3. The Trans-dispensational Atonement of Christ Magnified in Each Dispensation 281
    4. Pre-Cross Saints Provisionally in Christ's Grace Died and Went to Paradise until Actually Experiencing the Full Righteousness of Christ by His Death 287
    5. The Holy Spirit Dwelt With but Did Not Permanently Indwell the Old Testaments Saints 289
    6. Both Old and New Testament Saints Experienced Regeneration 291
    7. Baptism into Christ and his Grace Occurs for All Saints; Baptism into the Body of Christ Only Occurs for those Alive from Pentecost to the Rapture 293
        Does an "in Christ" Trans-dispensational Position Undermine the Pre-Tribulation Rapture Doctrine for N.T. Saints? 294
CONCLUSION: ALL SAINTS ARE IN CHRIST EVEN THOUGH NOT ALL SAINTS HAD EXPLICIT FAITH IN CHRIST AS WE WOULD TODAY 296

CHAPTER 6. A DISPENSATIONAL VIEW OF FOREKNOWLEDGE AND A SYNTHESIS OF GOD'S OMNISCIENCE WITH MAN'S WILL 299

GOD'S ETERNAL FOREKNOWLEDGE: A REJECTION OF THE OPEN THEISM PERSPECTIVE AND THE ARMINIAN PRESCIENT VIEW THAT GOD LEARNS THE FUTURE 299

AN EXEGETICAL STUDY ON GOD'S ABSOLUTE OMNISCIENCE FROM A LITERAL HERMENEUTIC: THE BIBLE TELLS US WHEN GOD KNOWS THE FUTURE 306
GOD IS NOT OMNI-OBSERVANT BUT OMNISCIENT FROM HIMSELF 308
THE BIBLE DOES NOT SAY GOD LOOKED INTO THE FUTURE AND SAW THE FUTURE SO HE COULD THEN MAKE HIS PLAN 309
GOD DID NOT CHOOSE THE GREEK WORDS FOR LOOK AND SEE. LUKE USED THESE WORDS IN OTHER PLACES BUT NOT IN DESCRIBING GOD'S FOREKNOWLEDGE 309

    Luke 21:1: Jesus Looked and Saw/Observed 309
    Luke 17:14: Jesus Responds After Looking and Seeing Their Actions 310
    What Then Does the Difference Between the Words Look and See and Foreknow Mean? 310

A Biblical Diagram of God's Mind/Knowledge in Contrast to a False View of God's Mind/Knowledge from the Open Theist and Mere Foresight View *311*
A PROPOSED DISPENSATIONAL SYNTHESIS OF GOD'S INFALLIBLE OMNISCIENCE & FOREKNOWLEDGE WITH MAN'S RESPONSIBILITY 313

CHAPTER 7. CONCLUSION: DISPENSATIONALISM AND COVENANT REFORMED THEOLOGY CAN HARMONIZE AS A "HAND IN A GLOVE" UNION 329

A FINAL PLEA: THE EVIDENCE PROVES DISPENSATIONALISM OFFERS A CALVINISTIC AND PRACTICAL SOTERIOLOGY 329
FURTHER OPTIONS FOR EXPLORATION: A CALVINISTIC MOLINISTIC DISPENSATIONALISM? 335

APPENDIX A: THE WIDESPREAD INFLUENCE AND GLOBAL PERMEATION OF DISPENSATIONALISM 343

Dispensationalism's Global Evangelistic Emphasis *349*
Dispensationalism's Submission to Scripture as the Supreme Authority *349*
    The Heart & Essential Emphasis of Dispensationalism: God's Glory and Grace in Christ for Faith, Hope, and Love 352
Dispensationalism's Love for Education Has Birthed Major Educational Centers *353*
Dispensationalism's Influence in Global Politics *356*
    A Brief Historical Journey to President Truman's Stand for the Israel State 358
    President Truman Embraced a Literal Reading of the Bible's Promise to Israel .. 362
    Summary of an Introductory Analysis of Dispensationalism 365

APPENDIX B: EVANGELICAL DISPENSATIONALISM: A CHRIST CENTERED STREAM OF THEOLOGY THAT DIFFERS FROM FUNDAMENTALISM 367

INTRODUCTION: MULTIPLE STREAMS FEEDING ONE BODY OF HOLY WATER 367
DOES DISPENSATIONALISM CAUSE DISUNITY? DEFINING EVANGELICALISM IN CONTRAST TO FUNDAMENTALISM 369
JESUS CHRIST'S INCARNATION ESTABLISHES THE EVANGELICAL PRINCIPLE 371
EVANGELICAL DISPENSATIONALISM ON A HOLISTIC THEOLOGY 374
ALL TRUTH IS GOD'S TRUTH & IS USEFUL IN EVANGELICAL MODELS OF THEOLOGY: AVOIDING THE SACRED & SECULAR IDEOLOGY 376

Not All Truth is as Equally as Important; Some Truths Rank Higher than Other Truths in Evangelicalism 379
A Theological Triage: A Biblical Methodology of Wisdom 385
Dispensationalist Dr. Charles C. Ryrie on a Theological Triage 388
Summary: Evangelicalism Embraces an Incarnational & Holistic Integrated Theology within a Theological Triage Methodology.. 391

BIBLIOGRAPHY **393**

About the Author.. 418

Endorsements

While it is true that some branches of Arminianism have adopted a dispensational approach to Scripture, in North American history of Dispensationalism it has largely been promoted by both individuals and schools that were Calvinistic. Yet attack after attack they still accuse Dispensationalists as being Arminian, quoting only them or those Dispensationalists who were more guilty of using sensational approaches, especially in the realm of biblical prophecy, and ignoring the works of scholarly dispensational writers.

It is in this context that this new work by Keith Sherlin is a welcome contribution. Correctly entitled as *The Calvinism of Dispensationalism*, it is a work that intends to clarify all such misconceptions. He includes a number of anti-dispensationalists and shows how they have misunderstood the Calvinism of dispensational theology. He also deals with thirty seven past and present Dispensationalists showing how they clearly come from a Calvinistic perspective and there is nothing germane in dispensational theology that would automatically render it as non-Calvinistic.

Dr. Arnold G. Fruchtenbaum
Director of Ariel Ministries

Dispensationalism often gets mischaracterized by those even within its own camp as being non-Reformed or non-Calvinistic. This could not be further from the truth. As Dr. Sherlin demonstrates throughout this work, Dispensationalism's brightest thinkers were vocal advocates of a soteriology linked directly to Calvinism. Far from teaching different modes of salvation—a false charge often leveled by non-dispensationalists—Dispensationalism has its roots in the historic solas of the Reformation and affirms a Calvinistic soteriology. Further, because Dispensationalism consistently maintains a proper hermeneutical methodology, it naturally lends itself to the doctrines of grace promoted in Reformed theology without adopting a forced covenantal paradigm. While not every dispensationalist will agree with all of Keith's results, he has nonetheless provided a solid and much needed work that critics will find hard to dismiss.

Dr. Cory M. Marsh, MA, MDiv, ThM; PhD
Assistant Professor of Biblical Studies, Southern California Seminary

Many have a wrong impression about the origin of Dispensationalism; they think that it was developed through Arminian theology, but this is a miscarriage of information about history. It was the Plymouth Brethren of England who first discovered the Dispensational nature of the Bible, and they were Calvinistic in their doctrine.

In the great dispensational institutions where I taught we gave students the doctrines of total depravity, the absolute providence and sovereignty of God, divine election, and eternal security. These great truths are defensible scripturally and cannot be repudiated.

Keith Sherlin has done us a great theological favor by writing about Calvinistic Dispensationalism. Maybe this will inspire many to return to strong Bible study and the teaching
of the full counsel of God!

Dr. Mal Couch
Founder of Tyndale Theological Seminary

People often pit Calvinism and dispensationalism against each other. Here is a book that examines their relationship to each other, showing the possibility of a compatibility in many areas and including an examination of a history of this association over several centuries. Its distinction of Covenant Calvinists from Dispensational Calvinists is also quite helpful. There is much to gain theologically from reading *The Calvinism of Dispensationalism*.
Dr. Darrell L. Bock
Senior Research Professor of New Testament Studies,
Dallas Theological Seminary

This will be a helpful and needed resource to help answer the criticisms against Dispensationalism's view of salvation.
Dr. Robert P. Lightner
Professor Emeritus, Dallas Theological Seminary

The Calvinism of Dispensationalism traces the historical Reformed Calvinistic roots of biblical Dispensationalism in a stimulating read providing insights into Satanism's core philosophical views and its effect on the subjective epistemology promoted by progressive humanistic materialism and postmodernism. Through pseudo-philosophy and pseudo-science Satan, the "god of this world," actively seeks to blind men to truth of God and to exalt man as the Supreme Being. The negative impact of historical abandonment of sound hermeneutical methodology is considered and biblical resolutions to key soteriological barriers that have historically divided Calvinistic and Dispensational brethren are offered. Dr. Sherlin entreats Calvinist and Dispensational brethren to combine their significant resources in an effort to turn back the tide of philosophical satanic assault and advance the "faith once for all delivered to the saints." Read this book, grow in wisdom, learn from one of the best!
Terry Zeyen

Dr. Sherlin has taken on the unenviable task of reconciling two great theological traditions, Covenant/Reformed and Dispensational. The reconciliation is necessary because of our common adversary and the fallen world system. In this work he recognizes that soteriology is likely the greatest divide between the two, so he effectively shows that many leading dispensationalists were Calvinistic in their soteriology and this continues today. He offers several helps regarding the Dispensationalist's simultaneous recognition of progressive revelation and the unchanging plan of salvation. This work should be read by any who want to better understand the differences that divide these two great traditions and better work together to the glory of God.

Dr. Jeff Heslop
Professor of Theology, Tyndale Theological Seminary

Keith Sherlin has produced a masterful case for the compatibility of reformed theology and dispensationalism. This is no small feat considering the sea of ink that has been spilled on this subject over the past few decades. I gladly recommend it. The debate regarding dispensationalism and reformed theology is fierce in the 21st century. The lack of clarity in these theological waters, even among scholars, is astounding. As the debate rages on, Sherlin's clarity is a welcome addition.

Keith Sherlin has an ability to explain complex theological issues in an understandable way. Rarely has that gift been more helpful than with regard to these tough issues. If you want to understand the relationship of dispensationalism and reformed theology, look no further.

Dr. Braxton Hunter
President & Professor of Theology & Apologetics,
Trinity College of the Bible & Theological Seminary

I am pleased to commend this work by Dr. Sherlin for your edification. I have been a Dispensationalist for nearly the entirety of my Christian life and even became more firmly entrenched in my dispensational views following a conversion from the Arminian system to the Calvinistic one, especially after learning from Dr. Ryrie that most, if not all of the early dispensational theologians were Calvinists. There is a frequent charge leveled against those of us who hold to Dispensational Theology that we teach two ways of salvation, one of works in the Old Testament and one of grace in the New Testament, which charge is specious, at best, and slanderous at worst. A true Dispensational Theologian will **always** teach that, in all 7 Dispensations, salvation from sin and redemption to Christ is always and only a gift of sovereign grace from the gracious hand of a loving God. With a skill not often seen in Dispensationalism today, Dr. Sherlin addresses the age old charge of teaching two ways of salvation as well as the misguided notion, from Drs.

Sproul and Gerstner, that Calvinist Theology and Covenantal Theology are synonymous.

In laying these claims to rest, Dr. Sherlin weaves a tapestry of truth in the manner of a master storyteller, historian, and theologian all rolled into one. I would compare Keith's work, here, to a skilled surgeon carefully working to excise the cancer of ignorant presuppositional bias from the family of God. Dr. Sherlin points out, though not saying directly, that Christians, like many other families, have our squabbles and in this case the squabble comes from a misunderstanding and poor communication rather than any actual slight. I would consider this work to be complementary to Dr. Sproul's excellent work, *What Is Reformed Theology*? in that it guides us through the process of seeing that Dispensational Theology is a natural outgrowth of the Calvinistic understanding of Holy Writ. It is my hope that in reading this text, you will come to a better understanding of your faith and even if you do not come to embrace dispensationalism, that you would have a better appreciation of your dispensational brethren.

Rev. Matthew Sherro
Founding Pastor Abounding Grace Baptist Church
Teacher at Exploring the Truth

Can one be a dispensationalist and reformed? Many theologians have often wrongly advanced the notion that one cannot be a consistent dispensationalist and hold reformed views, particularly when it comes to the doctrines of grace. Dispensationalism is inherently linked to Arminian theology. However, Dr. Sherlin's latest book shatters this false perception. In an irenic tone, the author examines the writings of several covenant Calvinists and then presents informed arguments, both historically and exegetically, for the case that one can be a dispensationalist and a Calvinist, and still remain theologically consistent. He does this by examining some of the writings of very prominent dispensational scholars to show that they were both dispensational and reformed, and that what they advanced is biblically substantiated.

Dr. Sherlin's book has done a great service in highlighting the main points of this classic discussion because very few works have examined the conversation at this level. As such, readers are sure to walk away from this book with a greater appreciation of Dispensationalism's roots, and the reformed, non-covenantal, contributors who taught it. While

there may be some mild disagreement, I firmly believe that those who engage this book and ponder its implications will find their time and their money to have been well spent.
James R. Brooks, MAR, MDiv, DMin
Expositors Bible Teacher, Houston's Second Baptist Church

    This book, *The Calvinism of Dispensationalism*, by Dr. Keith Sherlin is a much needed work. He has dealt with misleading and inaccurate claims by Covenant theologians such as the late Dr. John Gerstner, the late Dr. R.C. Sproul and others who have tried to paint the entire dispensational movement as being Arminian in its soteriology. He has shown a pattern of Covenant theologians misrepresenting the position of those who were Calvinistic in their soteriology. Dr. Sherlin has selected 22 great leading dispensationalists who would rightly be classified as being Calvinists. While there has been a strain of Dispensationalism that has been Arminian oriented or Arminian leaning, that was not the case with early dispensationalists who made up the Calvinistic strain that continues on in today's times. This book answers the false claims that are made about dispensationalism on soteriology. I strongly recommend this work.
Bryan Cruz

    Dr. Sherlin presents a succinct analysis of the enemy's influence reflected in a pattern of disregard for the inherent dignity of God's image bearers followed by a historical survey of the challenges to unity for proponents of dispensational and covenant theologies. He then offers a clarification of the dispensationalist position and proposes a helpful path forward between the two camps which is no less than a clarion call to unite on common ground to counter the destruction of a disintegrating culture. While our enemy seeks to divide and conquer, it is the responsibility of believers to unite and remain salt and light in an ever-increasing darkness. The *Calvinism of Dispensationalism* lays the tracks for a way forward for both groups and offers great hope of victories yet to be won.
Josh Bailey
Pastor at Nooksack Valley Christ Community Church
BA, The Master's University
ThM (c), Southern Evangelical Seminary

Dispensationalism has become something of a theological pariah to many in American Christianity. I have experienced this firsthand in my years teaching in a relatively conservative evangelical seminary. Upon a single mention of the movement, eyes roll and students sigh. The cultural connotation of the term has frequently become associated with phenomena such as the Left Behind series, aggressive Zionism, and a general theological anemia. But perhaps this should not be, because the actual history and definition of dispensationalism is far more complicated, sophisticated, and biblically rooted than is commonly believed. Moreover, the dispensationalist tent is a large one, making it simply irresponsible to point our fingers at dispensationalism in general when trying to diagnose problems within the American church.

Keith Sherlin is well aware of these public relations problems, but he also sees value in certain streams of this misunderstood theological system. Moreover, he persuasively sets forth a novel case for harmonizing the theological system with other systems that are typically typecast as rivals, such as Calvinism and the related covenant theology. In this important and comprehensive work, Sherlin winsomely and capably takes on the task of unmasking dispensationalism, and through responsible systematic, biblical, and historical scholarship, works to reclaim dispensationalism for a new generation of theologians. Not everyone will agree with this book, but everyone can certainly learn much from it.

Sarah C. Geis
M.A., Denver Seminary, and Ph.D. Candidate at the University of Birmingham, U.K., Associated Faculty at Denver Seminary
Director of the Gordon Lewis Center for Christian Thought and Culture

Dr. Sherlin's meticulous, in-depth arguments and plentiful proofs demonstrate beyond the doubt of any honest Christian that Dispensationalism is not a rogue theology, still less a heresy. He gives plenty of evidence, by quoting many Reformed and Dispensational theologians, to show that Dispensational theology remains true to the same Calvinistic roots as Reformed theology.

James D. Quiggle
Theologian & Author of 72 books
MA & MTS from Bethany Divinity College & Theological Seminary

Dispensationalism was systematized as a consequence of the Protestant Reformation. Certainly there are dispensationalists who are Arminian, yet the truth is that the large majority of early North American dispensationalists were Calvinists, emerging from Anglican, Calvinist Baptist, Congregationalist, and Presbyterian denominations. They remained for some time in traditional denominations such as Baptist churches, Congregationalism, and Presbyterianism. If one is to rightly understand dispensationalism systematically, it is only logical to do so with an understanding of the doctrines of grace and the sovereignty of God that is distinctive of Calvinism. Dr. Sherlin's work demonstrates how dispensationalism emerged from those who were almost exclusively Calvinistic in their doctrine. The "soul" of Dr. Sherlin's research is to correct misunderstandings regarding dispensationalism that have given false accusations against it. Sherlin has given a positive representation of the Calvinism of dispensationalism.
Dr. Ron Bigalke
Professor, University of Pretoria

Over a period of 20 years of study I have moved from being a Dispensational Arminian Pentecostal to become a Baptist. Within that time, I also wrestled with the matter of Dispensational and Covenant Theology. One thing that I learned as I made that journey to my home as Reformed Baptist, is that in order to understand each other, we must do the basic task of listening to what the other person is saying. Dr. Sherlin has called attention to the tendency of those in the Covenant Theology camp to make assertions about Dispensational theologians without actually reading them. Others, who did read them, seemed to miss their Calvinistic soteriology which was hidden in plain sight. In hopes of seeing Reformed and Dispensational Calvinist theologians and pastors work together, Dr. Sherlin has catalogued both the misrepresentations of Dispensational theologians, as well as the actual views of prominent theologians of the Dispensational tradition. Read this work if you want to understand the history of the debate amongst bothers. More importantly, read the book if you want to understand what our brothers in the dispensational tradition actually believe and teach. You will find that while you may disagree with their dispensational approach to understanding the sweep of biblical history, you agree with them on key doctrines including the Doctrines of Grace. There has been and always

will be doctrinal issues that make it necessary to divide over biblical truth. Dr. Sherlin argues convincingly that Dispensational and Covenantal Calvinists have far more in common than they disagree over and should therefore be able to work together to advance the gospel. Being able to do that requires us to listen to and understand each other. Brother Keith's work provides a necessary step in pursuit of that unity, for the glory of God, and the good of the church. I cannot recommend this book more highly.
Dr. Dan Kitinoja
Pastor of Calvary Baptist Church

While I am not a Calvinist nor an Arminian, I firmly believe that one can be a Calvinist and Dispensationalist. Dr. Sherlin clears the air of the false charge that Dispensationalism is Arminian in nature with this work. He answers with an irenic tone the false charges from past Covenant theologians that Dispensationalism cannot be Calvinistic because Calvinism equals Covenant theology. Not only does Dr. Sherlin answer these false claims, but he deftly defeats the age-old false charge that Dispensationalism teaches two ways of salvation. While these are only a snippet of this wonderful work, these few would make the book worth the time and cost regardless of what it is. I strongly recommend this work.
Luke Morrison
Pastor Western Trail Cowboy Church
B.S. Moody Bible Institute
MDiv Liberty University
PhD student Liberty University

Foreword by Dr. Arnold G. Fruchtenbaum

Years ago, I was reading an article published by a Reformed ministry in England but written by a Messianic Jew in Israel. In the article he claimed that while modern day Dispensationalists deny that the Mosaic Law was a means of salvation, that was definitely the view of older Dispensationalists and he named Lewis Sperry Chafer, the founder of Dallas Theological Seminary (DTS) as evidence. By that point of time, I had recently completed my dissertation for New York University, what later was published as *Israelology,* and so I knew this was not true. My response was to send him a copy of a page from Chafer's book, *Grace,* first published in the 1930's where he states categorically that the Law was never given as a means of salvation but it served as a rule of life for those already saved.

My first three years of Bible college was at a school committed to Covenant Theology and that was where I heard many attacks on Dispensationalism, which I could recognize were simply not true. In my reading of so many Covenantalists for my dissertation and even subsequent to that, I was surprised to find that the critics of Dispensationalism never seem to have read what dispensational scholars have written, or if they have, simply choose to ignore what they have published. In fact, DTS from its very beginning was a Calvinistic school and never in its history did any faculty member teach what critics accuse them of teaching.

While it is true that some branches of Arminianism have adopted a dispensational approach to Scripture, in North American history of Dispensationalism it has largely been promoted by both individuals and schools that were Calvinistic. Yet attack after attack they still accuse Dispensationalists as being Arminian, quoting only them or those Dispensationalists who were more guilty of using sensational approaches, especially in the realm of biblical prophecy, and ignoring the works of scholarly dispensational writers.

It is in this context that this new work by Keith Sherlin is a welcome contribution. Correctly entitled as *The Calvinism of Dispensationalism*, it is a work that intends to clarify all such misconceptions. He includes a number of anti-dispensationalists and shows how they have misunderstood the Calvinism of dispensational theology. He also deals with thirty-seven past and present

Dispensationalists showing how they clearly come from a Calvinistic perspective and there is nothing germane in dispensational theology that would automatically render it as non-Calvinistic.

This whole work is written in an irenic style and thus concludes with a plea for Reformed theologians to engage in an honest evaluation and to realize the possibility of a union of the two branches insofar as soteriology is concerned.

Will they now be willing to "come and let us reason together"?

Arnold G. Fruchtenbaum,
Th.M; Ph.D
Ariel Ministries

Preface by Dr. Mal Couch[1]

Many have a wrong impression about the origin of Dispensationalism; they think that it was developed through Arminian theology, but this is a miscarriage of information about history. It was the Plymouth Brethren of England who first discovered the Dispensational nature of the Bible, and they were Calvinistic in their doctrine. In my younger years I taught at some of the most respected seminaries and Bible colleges in America and they were all Calvinistic in their thinking and teaching.

This brings me to another important point: Dispensationalism is not imposed upon the Bible, but the Bible *is dispensational* in its very nature and theological development. Many do not realize it but the great covenant theologian, Charles Hodge, held to all of the dispensations except the last one, and that is the millennial kingdom! Most dispensational advocates however do not hold to limited atonement, mainly because this view is not biblical. Dr. Robert Lightner points out that there are two passages of Scripture that strongly repudiate that view: 2 Peter 2:1. "False teachers will introduce destructive heresies, even denying the Master who bought them ..." And 1 John 2:2. "He Himself is the propitiation for our sins; and not for ours only, but also for those of the whole world."

In the great dispensational institutions where I taught we gave students the doctrines of total depravity, the absolute providence and sovereignty of God, divine election, and eternal security. These great truths are defensible scripturally and cannot be repudiated. Most evangelical schools have been in the past dispensational and Calvinistic in their doctrinal framework. No other view was taught.

Unfortunately, many of these great schools are now shifting to the left. Hard core doctrine is fading out and disappearing from the classes in

---

[1] Mal Couch wrote this for me prior to his death in 2013 from the initial brief manuscript, ideas, and outline of this manuscript where I had shown that it appeared most of the mainline and most famous Dispensationalists of the 19th through 21st century had embraced a Calvinistic soteriology. He encouraged me to consider this as a potential topic for later PhD work. I took that to heart and later did develop that outline into my PhD dissertation work which is the work you have presently before you (though modified some for publication).

theology. The schools are becoming Arminian in tone, and even liberal. Exegesis is no longer important, and the literalness of the Word of God is being set aside. Students are coming out confused and accepting Covenant theology. They are denying Dispensationalism. They no longer are able to discern and teach the Bible with sharp edges that confirm the doctrinal nature of the Bible. Most are into secular psychology and teach devotionals rather than verse by verse exegesis. It was Dispensationalism that supported careful observation as to what the text was saying. But this is no longer important among our young people and in our churches.

Keith Sherlin has done us a great theological favor by writing about Calvinistic Dispensationalism. Maybe this will inspire many to return to strong Bible study and the teaching of the full counsel of God!

Dr. Mal Couch, PhD, ThD
Scofield Ministries, Clifton, TX
Founder, 1st President of Tyndale Theological Seminary

Introduction by Dr. Ron Bigalke

The glory of God has implications for the entire person. For instance, a mind focused upon the Lord will be enlightened by the truth of his Word, the Holy Bible. The glory of God should be the highest thought for every Christian. Every aspect of life should be saturated with the profound apprehension of the majesty of God. Understanding the glory of God as revealed in Scripture ought to result in a realization of one's unworthiness to approach the presence of God as a creature, and much more as a sinner, and yet with adoring wonder to recognize that it is God who – by his grace – receives those who respond to Him in faith and repentance. Believing in God without reservation is reflected in a determined attitude that will have God's sovereignty affect every aspect of one's actions, emotions, and thoughts. The defining characteristic of a Christian is one who is saved by God's grace and then lives for God's glory.

A biblical perception of God's sovereign majesty will always involve a painful awareness of one's absolute depravity. The more one comprehends God's glory, the more that person will recognize the need for divine grace. True believers are made when God reveals his glory and majesty, in addition to a commensurate revealing of a person's sin in comparison to the Lord's holiness and sovereignty. In his *Institutes of the Christian Religion*, Calvin wrote, "we must infer that man is never sufficiently touched and affected by the awareness of his lowly state until he has compared himself with God's majesty" (1.I.3).

Calvinism, or the doctrines of grace, teach that God accomplishes in salvation what a sinner cannot do for himself or herself, which is true from the moment of justification throughout one's sanctification and ultimately to the glorification of the body. At a time infinitely prior to anyone "choosing" God, the Father elected certain people unconditionally in Christ Jesus. When those individuals were unable to remove their guilt (absolute, total depravity), the Son was the Lamb slain from the foundation of the world, laying down his life for his sheep. When those chosen in Christ would not respond in faith and repentance (for they were unable), the Father drew ("dragged") them through the Holy Spirit by his efficacious grace and He will be certain that none are snatched from his hand because the Lord God will be certain his elect remain faithful (persevere) to the very end. The doctrines of grace necessitate that a repentant sinner accept the sovereignty of God in salvation.

Swiss evangelist and hymn writer César Malan always enjoyed sharing his faith in God with others. Malan asked a young woman, who was seated at his table, whether she was a Christian. The woman, Charlotte Elliott, became rigid with irritation, responding that she would rather not answer that question. Malan apologized if he had given offense. Nevertheless, the witness of Malan became a decisive moment in her life for Charlotte could not remove the inquiry from her mind. Three weeks later, she met Malan and told him that ever since he had spoken to her, she was wrestling with the thought of receiving God's acceptance.

She wondered how she could gain God's favor. Malan replied, "You have nothing of merit to bring to God. You must come just as you are." Charlotte rejoiced at those words, and placed her faith in Christ. Although feeble and weak in body, Charlotte possessed a wonderful imagination, in addition to being cultured and thoughtful. She loved music and poetry, which is evident in her writing approximately 150 hymns. One of the finest and most commonly known of her hymns recalls the Christian witness of Malan; the hymn is entitled, "Just As I Am."

The classic hymn says, "just as I am, without one plea" which means the new believer has years of sinful habits and patterns to overcome. The subheading for the hymn was "him that cometh unto me I will in no wise cast out" (John 6:37). How wonderful to know that God receives all those who come to Him by grace through faith, and thereafter "He always lives to make intercession" for his people (Heb 7:25). The one who trusts in God has the promise of God's favor and peace, and with those blessings is God's enablement to live by his grace and for his glory. Calvinism, of course, has historically emphasized the doctrines of God's grace in salvation, and how those divine decrees manifest the glory of God.

The doctrines of grace are what both Covenant theologians and what many dispensational theologians celebrate. In my pastoral/missionary outreach to elected officials, I am entirely dependent upon the financial support and prayers of God's people; therefore, since I receive no government funding, I am always encouraging and enabling local churches to participate in the process. One of these churches embraces covenant theology and in my first meeting with the pastor, I identified myself as a premillennial dispensationalist, yet our bond was our commitment to the centrality of Scripture and the doctrines of grace. Indeed, this pastor was thrilled in knowing that someone committed to the doctrines of grace had a ministry in the statehouse. Recognizing that our eschatological differences are incidental to reaching capitol communities for Christ, the pastors and members of this local church have been and continue to be a great blessing and encouragement to the ministry of Capitol Commission. This is but one church among others that have become strategic prayer and financial partners, yet sadly, as Dr. Sherlin stated, one of God's people embracing dispensationalism often polarizes covenant churches from any ministry partnership. Such isolation among covenant Calvinists and dispensational Calvinists hinders the mutual evangelistic commission to make disciples of the Lord Jesus Christ.

Although the Protestant Reformation began officially on 31 October 1517 with Martin Luther nailing his 95 Theses on the church door at Wittenberg, John Calvin was the systematic theologian of the Reformation. As a theological system of thought, Calvinism obviously developed from the works of Calvin. The reforms of Protestantism eventually culminated in the development of dispensationalism. Dispensationalism was systematized as a consequence of the Protestant Reformation. Certainly there are dispensationalists who are Arminian, yet the truth is that the large majority of early North American dispensationalists were Calvinists, emerging from Anglican, Calvinist Baptist, Congregationalist, and Presbyterian denominations. They remained for some time in traditional denominations such as Baptist churches, Congregationalism, and Presbyterianism. If one is to rightly understand dispensationalism systematically, it is only logical to do so with an understanding of the doctrines of grace and the sovereignty of God that is distinctive of Calvinism. Dr. Sherlin's work demonstrates how dispensationalism emerged from those who were almost exclusively Calvinistic in their doctrine.

One thing is evident when reading the majority of dispensational critics and that is they ignore dispensational scholars, and focus instead upon those who are sensational in their approach to Scripture, especially with regard to Bible prophecy. One could rightly question if those sensationalists could even be rightly called dispensationalists, as they are inconsistent in their hermeneutic, particularly in employing a historicist perspective in regards to Bible prophecy. False accusations are plentiful among those who disagree with what they understand to be dispensationalism, which is one reason for Dr. Sherlin's work.

If you find yourself unable to respond effectively to unsubstantiated claims that dispensationalism is inherently Arminian (or even worse, semi-Pelagian), then Sherlin's work is going to benefit you by first explaining antithetical worldviews, divided theologies, and their relation to cultural consequences. The criticism of unorthodoxy from covenant Calvinists toward dispensationalism hinders a coalescent union, which should not be in terms of the doctrines of grace and the sovereignty of God. Sherlin, therefore, provided a summary of thirty-seven dispensationalists who affirmed a Calvinist soteriology, and then explained why diversity exists among covenant theologians and dispensationalists concerning the atonement of Christ, whether limited or unlimited (though this author believes a focus upon particular redemption would be more effective in resolving this issue, and demonstrating that belief in a "limited atonement" is not antithetical to dispensationalism).

A common untruth against dispensationalism is that it teaches a works based salvation for Old Testament believers. Sherlin demonstrates that salvation is by grace through faith *alone* in every dispensation. Moreover, God's foreknowledge means to love in advance, that is, a predetermined covenant relationship (such as God has with his chosen people, Israel), which is contrary to the perspective of open theism and the teaching of prescience in Arminianism. Sherlin's work concludes with a final plea as to the evidence overwhelmingly proving that dispensationalism offers a Calvinistic and practical soteriology. The "soul" of Dr. Sherlin's research is to correct misunderstandings regarding dispensationalism that have given false accusations against it. Sherlin has given a positive representation of the Calvinism of dispensationalism. One would hope that dispensationalists would find this work helpful in clarifying their own thinking. Christians are going to disagree with each other concerning all aspects of theology, yet respect and truthfulness should be characteristic of all believers, even toward those brothers and sisters with whom there is disagreement. The practical benefit of such is a more harmonious relationship in fulfilling the Great Commission.

Ron J. Bigalke, Ph.D.
Eternal Ministries, Inc.
Research Associate, New Testament department, University of Pretoria

Brief Book Summary by Keith Sherlin

Dispensationalism, or discontinuity theology, and Covenantalism, or continuity theology,[2] developed more systematically in the wake of the reformation era of church history. As these systematic theological paradigms developed side-by-side from the 17th through 19th century the advocates remained largely in association with one another under the umbrella of a theological triage.[3] Through those three centuries the

---

[2] I will define these two terms of continuity and discontinuity theology. The term discontinuity describes Dispensationalism. In this theology the interpreter sees God working through various historical ages as he incrementally unfolds his revelation from one administrative age (dispensation) to another. Some laws from one dispensation occur in the next while some laws are no longer directly applicable. Every theologian, as Dr. Lewis Sperry Chafer stated, that accepts Christ's sacrifice on the cross instead of making animal sacrifices, and who worships on Sunday instead of Friday at sundown till Saturday at sundown recognizes dispensational changes in Scripture. Furthermore, if a person sees an OT period, NT period, and a millennial kingdom and/or New Heavens and New Earth era then that person affirms at least two or three dispensations in Scripture. For Dispensationalists a plain or natural reading and interpretation of Scripture leads to these distinct administrative ages where God in his sovereign providence rules over his creation as he unfolds his glory through progressive revelation in each successive and complementary dispensation. The term continuity describes a theological system often classified as Covenantalism. In that theology the interpreter sees the providence of God working out the eternal covenants of Scripture through the various dispensations of time. Covenantalism generally sees the NT as the fullest expression and meaning of the OT revelation. As the revelation of God unfolds the single covenant of redemption stands out as the central theme of Scripture. Many OT promises, such as the promises made to Israel, become submerged, extend into, or transferred over to the body of Christ who in their system stands as the true Israel of God. Many in this system teach amillennial theology, i.e., we are now in the kingdom of God and there is no future earthly millennial rule of Christ to come on this earth. Those OT texts are generally allegorized or said to be symbolic. Some, however, do affirm a millennial kingdom to come, however they do so while still saying the true Israel is the body of Christ and in that kingdom to come there will be no distinction or different functional roles between ethnic Israel and the body of Christ in the kingdom age. Dispensationalism sees some discontinuity between ethnic Israel and the body of Christ (distinct and not the same, although saved the same way) while Covenantalism sees more continuity between Israel and the body of Christ.

[3] A theological triage, or graded doctrinal scale, recognizes that some doctrines in Scripture have greater weight and importance than other truths. Some use the term in a similar way as to how one uses the term emergency room triage. Some injuries and sicknesses require more immediate focus and attention than other injuries and medical

ideology and seeds of those two doctrinal systems matured together through the academy and the body of Christ at large with a particular emphasis in Europe and the United States of America. In particular, the United States academies for the most part housed both ideologies in the theology and philosophy departments. Unity amidst diversity reigned.

However, in the early to mid-twentieth century these two dominant schools of thought failed to remain in close harmony with one another. Though Dispensationalism had matured within the broad base of the reformation heritage, the new focus and emphases by some Dispensationalists on ethnic Israel and her promises within a more literal based eschatological position, created tension among the two schools of thought. This tension eventually erupted into a schism primarily over the doctrine of salvation. Covenant theologians, mainly of the Calvinist persuasion, launched a campaign against Dispensationalists and accused those in that persuasion of thought for embracing an unorthodox view of salvation. These criticisms have been constant and consistent in the last and present century.

Consequently, these two schools of thought have divided their resources and associations throughout the globe. Many academies, church bodies, mission organizations, and related evangelical bodies or organizations have suffered in a lack of organizational power because of

---

problems. If you walk into an emergency room with a sprained ankle you will receive attention in the triage later than someone who enters with a gunshot wound to the chest or someone who has just experienced a heart attack. Likewise, in theology some truths and some errors fall in different levels of urgency. While all truth is important, not every truth ranks as high as every other truth. A misunderstanding on numerous subjects such as the age of the earth, how best to interpret a particular parable, the most precise form of church government, how a particular spiritual gift is best used, the exact time of the rapture and more do not carry the same weight and importance as truths that pertain to the Trinity, the full inspiration of scripture, the deity and humanity of Christ, salvation from sin because of justification by grace through faith alone in Christ alone because of his vicarious substitutionary death, the physical resurrection of Christ, a physical future second coming, and a real heaven and hell would rank as higher on the scale of importance in Scripture. Jesus spoke of greater and lesser truths as well as greater sins (see Matt. 22:38-39; 23:29; John 19:11). Paul also spoke of some truths that took priority over others (see 1 Cor. 13:13; 15:3; 15:12-14; and Gal. 5:6). The Evangelical wing of Dispensationalism has historically embraced this theological triage in contrast to some theological versions that place every doctrine on the same scale. Evangelical Dispensationalists, those like Lewis Sperry Chafer, Charles C. Ryrie, and Norman Geisler have emphasized and recognized a graded scale of doctrines within the Scriptures.

these perceived differences in soteriology. That conflict has caused these two schools of thought to isolate from one another within the common evangelistic endeavor of making disciples under the lordship of Jesus Christ. Sadly, such a division has chilled the collective capability for the cause of Christ that has consequently allowed Satanic Humanistic Liberal Progressivism to fill the void in communities, states, nation, and to a degree globally.

Therefore, this work seeks to provide a thorough analysis of the problem as perceived by the Covenant Calvinist theologians with a response from direct sources within Dispensationalism t reveals a thoroughly Calvinistic Dispensationalist theological paradigm. In providing this response the research focuses on the most notable and well known Dispensational scholars of the twentieth and twenty-first century and their soteriology. It is not a book to prove that *all* Dispensationalists are Calvinists. It is a book that shows *some*, even some of the most respected leaders of the movement, have been within the basic or broad Reformed Calvinistic umbrella in regards to soteriology. Additionally, it seeks to provide a positive synthesis to any of the theological questions or criticisms that have been left unanswered by Dispensationalists, especially in the field of Old Testament soteriology. The conclusions of this study can, if properly applied, help reconcile two powerful ideologies for Great Commission organization.

Chapter 1. Antithetical Worldviews, Divided Theologies, and their Connection to Cultural Consequences

God's Providence in 1776 Births a Judeo-Christian Nation Upon Natural Law

On July 4th, 1776, when fifty-six people signed a document that a person may read in less than ten minutes because of its brevity in composition with only 1,458 words, world history, maybe even eternity, changed in a magnanimous manner. That year was the "most important day in American history,"[4] and in a larger context of world history the nations witnessed God's providence giving birth to what some believe has developed into the mightiest nation in all of world history.[5] In commenting on this effort for national independence, one of the most beloved forefathers of this nation, George Washington, stated that their "cause" was "noble" as it was the "cause of mankind."[6] Washington was not alone in his belief. Thomas Paine concurred by stating, "The cause of America is in great measure the cause of mankind."[7]

The thirteen "colonies of Great Britain on the North American continent were united in determination to be independent of British rule."[8] The rule they were under had become tyrannical, unresponsive to their needs, unjust towards their basic human rights, and hypocritical in the

---

[4] Gordon S. Wood, *One Day in History: July 4, 1776* (New York, NY: HarperCollins Publishers, 2006), vii.

[5] Ibid.

[6] George Washington, "*The Cause of American Independence*," in *Maxims of George Washington*, collected and arranged by John Frederick Schroeder (Mount Vernon, VA: The Mount Vernon Ladies' Association, 1989), 24.

[7] Thomas Paine, "*Common Sense*," in *Common Sense and Other Writings*, ed. George Stade (New York, NY: Barnes and Noble Books, 2005), 13.

[8] Mortimer J. Adler, *We Hold These Truths: Understanding the Ideas and Ideals of the Constitution* (New York, NY: MacMillan Publishing Company, 1987), 5.

consistent application of laws. Furthermore, many of the religious people were persecuted for their faith. That led to them desiring a new type of government where the people had religious and personal liberty.[9] Such atrocities led men and women from a vicissitude of societal sectors to seeing the need to build a new country where liberty prevailed under the rule of God as verified through natural law,[10] a law that calls for a "universal obligation."[11] Liberty became the watchword for the budding new nation. In fact "America's history and political ethos are all about liberty."[12] To such a cause, then General George Washington stated to his soldiers that he trusted "Providence" to guide their cause as "liberty, honor, and safety" were "all at stake" in their "efforts" to establish a "free and happy country."[13]

Because of those reasons, the Colonial Americans, who through representatives convened and wrote what some call the greatest political document in world history, the Declaration of Independence, fought to the death for their natural God given rights to life, liberty, and the pursuit of happiness. The signers of that Declaration were not only "enlightened men," "well educated," precise in "reason," and adherents to "science,"[14]

---

[9] Michael Farris, *The History of Religious Liberty* (Green Forest, AR: Master Books, 2015), 6, 460-467.

[10] Natural law is sometimes called the law of nature. This is not naturalism. Natural law means that within the universe some laws are universally binding on all people at all times in all places. These laws come from a higher entity, a Creator or some being or entity that legislates this above and over all people. Because of natural law people are born into a world with innate natural rights.

[11] John Eidsmoe, *Historical and Theological Foundations of Law Volume I: Ancient Wisdom* (Powder Springs, GA: American Vision Press and Tolle Lege Press, 2011), 404.

[12] Ron Paul, *Liberty Defined: 50 Essential Issues that Affect our Freedom* (New York, NY: Grand Central Publishing, 2011), XI.

[13] George Washington, *"Faith and Effort,"* in *Maxims of George Washington*, collected and arranged by John Frederick Schroeder (Mount Vernon, VA: The Mount Vernon Ladies' Association, 1989), 174.

[14] Mark R. Levin, *Liberty and Tyranny: A Conservative Manifesto* (New York, NY: Threshold Editions, 2009), 25.

but they were also all believers in God, his providential rule, and natural law.[15] In short, they held overall to a theistic Judeo-Christian worldview (even if with some cultural baggage left over from their European lineage). Those American forefathers and leaders understood the importance of uniting together on the major issues at hand to form a cohesive government. Unlike a significant portion of leaders today in the diverse theological and philosophical traditions, who refuse to unite and work towards common cultural civil and Christ centered goals under a common theological umbrella of core doctrine, those founders were from a variety of denominations and yet even so they were still "united" in their overall cause while also sharing an "emphatic" faith "that the Creator was the origin of their existence and the source of their reason."[16]

These signers and citizenry became a "new people, who through the Declaration, sought to justify in the eyes of the world their separation from the King of Great Britain and their 'right to assume, among the powers of the earth, the separate and equal station to which the laws of nature and of nature's God entitle them.'"[17] Take notice of the key words, "laws of nature." By natural law it is meant that because humanity is "endowed by [the] Creator with certain unalienable rights," these people have these rights "no matter" the person's religion or whether the person "has allegiance to any religion. It is Natural Law, divined by God and discoverable by reason, that prescribes the inalienability of the most

---

[15] John Eidsmoe, *Christianity and the Constitution: The Faith of our Founding Fathers* (Grand Rapids MI: Baker Books, 1987), 43. Eidsmoe is a constitutional law professor at the Thomas Goode Jones School of Law. He holds five advanced degrees in law, theology, and political science. In his list he shows that 38 to 40 of the 55 signers of the Declaration of Independence (about 69%) were *Calvinistic in their faith* (28 Anglicans, 8 Presbyterians, 2 Dutch Reformed, and 2 Lutherans, who were often classified as within the Reformed/Calvinistic tradition), 7 Congregationalists, 2 Methodists, 2 Roman Catholics, and 3 Deists. In fact, Eidsmoe highlights that the first Declaration of Independence was drafted by the Presbyterian Calvinists in Charlotte NC on May 20, 1775. That document was known as the Mecklenburg Declaration and was adapted in part into the 1776 Declaration (p. 25).

[16] Mark R. Levin, *Liberty and Tyranny: A Conservative Manifesto* (New York, NY: Threshold Editions, 2009), 26.

[17] John Eidsmoe, *Christianity and the Constitution: The Faith of our Founding Fathers* (Grand Rapids, MI: Baker Books, 1987), 43.

fundamental and eternal human rights—rights that are not conferred on man by man, and therefore, cannot legitimately be denied to man by man."[18] Natural law is a "philosophical system of legal and moral principles" that arise from a "universalized conception of human nature or divine justice."[19] The natural law ideology is the antithesis to "legal positivism" which rejects "the idea that law is recognized or created by morality or justice."[20] The bedrock ideology of a natural law permeated the hearts and minds of the new nation, even giving justification for their declared independence and right to a new government. As constitutional legal scholar Jenna Ellis says, "Divine Law" provided the "cornerstone" and "foundational level of authority" that made the Declaration of Independence legitimate in "announcing the new political sovereignty of the United States."[21]

Those Colonies, united by human will and by divine providence, made their case for their rightful revolt upon the principles of natural law. Because natural law is a concept that is at the heart of the very essence of the United States of America, it was and remains today a non-negotiable concept essential to a proper worldview (integral to a Judeo-Christian worldview), proper theology, and proper social legal structure based upon a covenant or contract of the people giving consent to form a government. Natural law (sometimes known as Divine Law) promotes the "concept" that a "higher law" exists over that of any individual or collective set of individuals.[22] This concept extends from its roots in the ancient Jewish

---

[18] Mark R. Levin, *Liberty and Tyranny: A Conservative Manifesto* (New York, NY: Threshold Editions, 2009), 27.

[19] *"Natural Law,"* in *Black's Law Dictionary*, ed. Bryan A. Garner (St. Paul, MN: West Publishing, 2009), 1127.

[20] *"Legal Positivism,"* in *The Wolters Kluwer Bouvier Law Dictionary*, ed. Stephen Michael Sheppard (Fredrick, MD: Wolters Kluwer Law & Business Publishers, 2011), 591.

[21] Jenna Ellis, *The Legal Basis for a Moral Constitution: A Guide for Christians to Understand America's Constitutional Crisis* (Bloomington, IN: Westbow Press, 2015), 61.

[22] David Boaz, *The Libertarian Mind: A Manifesto for Freedom* (New York, NY: Simon & Schuster, 2015), 41.

people who recognized that a "king was subordinate to a higher law" because every person is "judged by God's law."[23]

Ultimately that law and ideology led the Colonial Americans to cast aside the ungodly rule they were under, and, as "American revolutionaries" they sacrificed their fortunes, reputation, and ultimately even their own lives fight for "freedom, dignity, and individual rights."[24] In the Declaration of Independence our finite yet astoundingly astute, calmly courageous, and faithful forefathers recognized their right to such an endeavor came from "the laws of nature and of nature's God" who as the "Creator" "endowed" humans with "certain unalienable rights," rights they were willing to fight for by appealing to the "Supreme Judge of the world," beseeching his "Divine Providence" for "their protection."[25] Those forefathers and supporting citizenry were knowledgeable in facts, resolute in rationale, determined in devotion, and convicted to the core in their mission, quality traits that abound when a holy worldview permeates the mind. They in that age understood that the abandonment "of Natural Law is the adoption of tyranny in one form or another, because there is no humane or benevolent alternative to Natural Law."[26]

Only two forms of government exist: (1) systems based upon natural law, and (2) systems based upon fiat law or positive law. Legal systems that build upon natural law honor God and promote liberty. Legal systems that build upon positivism while denying natural law dishonor God and promote slavery, tyranny, and authoritarianism. Theologians and citizens ought to make sure they grasp these concepts as these truths comprise something non-negotiable for any theist, as it was for the founders of the United States of America. To deny or distort natural law is an effort to exalt man to God's throne, deifying him to a place of centricity that does not belong to man.

---

[23] Ibid.

[24] Ibid., 1.

[25] *Declaration of Independence* (US 1776).

[26] Mark R. Levin, *Liberty and Tyranny: A Conservative Manifesto* (New York, NY: Threshold Editions, 2009), 26.

Satan's Sinister Subversions of God's Goodness

Yet the ideology and practices that naturally arise from a Judeo-Christian worldview has opposition from an alternative worldview authored by a nemesis of God. Satan, the archenemy of God,[27] has from the beginning has been self-focused. He desired to be worshipped like God and sought power for himself (see Isa. 14:12-14). Though created by God, at some point in his history he "filled with pride because of his power and attainments" and "entertained the thought in his heart he could govern independently of God."[28] Ever since that moment, Satan's evil desire has never been relinquished. He has in the past and will in the future work tirelessly within every area that God has allowed him freedom to build a world that runs independently of God. He seeks to build a global world order under his power and rule to oppose his most hated enemy, Yahweh. Though he promises liberty he does so deceptively as his ideas cause slavery of the masses by a tyrannical rule.

Revelation gives some prophetic previews of this Satanic world order that shall one day come to fruition. In the future a "beast" (either a metaphor for a part of the Satanic order or some type of actual person leading a corrupt system) will "control the world economy."[29] As the Bible so plainly says of that season, "no one could buy or sell unless he had the mark, which is the name of the beast or the number of his name" (Rev. 13:17, NIV). Furthermore, in Revelation 17 through 18 we see the final order of this antichrist system. This Satanic system merges the economy, religions, and state together and that "united world order" will be known as the "religious Babylon," also known as the "great harlot," a giant "commercial Babylon"[30] that produces a naturalistic or materialistic

---

[27] M.F. Unger, "*Satan*," in the *Evangelical Dictionary of Theology*, ed. Walter A. Elwell (Grand Rapids, MI: Baker Book House, 2001), 1054.

[28] Donald Grey Barnhouse, *The Invisible War: The Panorama of the Continuing Conflict Between Good & Evil* (Grand Rapids, MI: Zondervan, 1965), 22.

[29] Tim Lahaye and Ed Hindson, *Global Warning* (Eugene, OR: Harvest House Publishers, 2007), 148.

[30] John Ankerberg and John Weldon, *One World: Bible Prophecy and the New World Order* (Chicago, IL: Moody Press, 1991), 17.

driven "culture without God."³¹ It will be a truly secular society that attempts to rely on self and not God for all facets of life. Preliminary aspects of that even exist now as Satan continually seeks to set the stage for these events of global control.

Satanism: A Sinister Seed for Other Worldviews such as Humanistic Liberalism

A brief overview of Satanism and Humanism is appropriate here. Yet before the reader progresses any further, it is important to qualify the following sections with this preliminary reminder. Though many people have embraced (consciously or unconsciously) in some sense or another Satanic ideology in the forms of humanistic liberalism, as will be elaborated in subsequent sections, it remains vital to keep a proper distinction between opposing the sinful ideas of people and the people themselves. Scripture is clear that we wrestle not against flesh and blood, but with principalities and powers of the spirit domain (Eph. 6:11-12). Many of the ideas noted herein are terribly sinister in nature. Sadly, many people embrace forms of Satanic Humanistic Liberalism, though often doing so without the realization they do so.

Therefore, in such cases, I am reminded of what the late Supreme Court Justice Antonin Scalia (1936-2016) said when dealing with people serving with him on the Court who had very wrong and harmful ideas. He said, "I attack ideas. I don't attack people. And some very good people have some very bad ideas. And if you can't separate the two, you" must "get another day job."³² This is true in these matters. Dispensationalists and Covenantalists, two types of theologians from the two dominating theological systems within a Judeo-Christian worldview, must gain a healthier perspective on lost culture and the larger cultural problem and attack those ideas, not the people who are in the image of God. Instead of being short-sighted and too focused on the supposed flaws of one another

---

³¹ Ibid., 66.

³² Charlie Spiering, *31 of Supreme Court Justice Antonin Scalia's Greatest Quotes*, [online]. Accessed 19 March 2016. Available from http://www.breitbart.com/big-government/2016/02/13/supereme-court-justice-antonin-scalias-greatest-quotes/; Internet.

they must grasp the serious threat to this nation, and consequently the world, from the competing Satanic worldview.

To understand the official worldview and ideology of Humanism, it first requires a brief analysis of the official religion of Satanism. Humanistic Liberalism is merely a subtle form of Satanism without the name or metaphysical view of anything supernatural, such as a real being known as Satan.[33] If Marxism is the daughter of Humanism,[34] which it is, then the mother of Humanism is Satanism. All false systems have someone as the originator of the movement or ideology. Satanism is the mother of Humanism, which has birthed many false philosophies, such as Marxism.

For Judeo-Christians, who will naturally affirm the full truthfulness of the entire Bible (verbal, plenary inspiration) because of its own verification and the inward witness of the Holy Spirit pointing them to such belief, there is no option but to believe Satan is a real being who "masquerades as an angel of light" (2 Cor. 11:14). Jesus, while walking on this earth, spoke of the reality of this being, and he explicitly taught that he worked through acts of aggression (such as murder)[35] and through deception (such as lies).[36] Satan's methodology is through violence and deception. Satan has been a murderer and liar from the beginning. Jesus taught that Satan "was a murderer from the beginning, not holding to the truth, for there is no truth in him. When he lies, he speaks his native

---

[33] Interestingly, Satanism as a religion generally does not believe in either God or a real being known as Satan. Most versions of Satanism, at least those originating from Anton LaVey's foundation, believe Satan is a metaphor that describes a world that revolves around each individual.

[34] David Noebel, *Understanding The Times* (Manitou Springs, CO: Summit Press, 1991), 25.

[35] Conservative Islam would be an example of Satan's ideology of aggression manifesting itself through a religion. Conservative Muslims who take the Koran in its plain words, i.e., through a plain or historical grammatical hermeneutic, will arrive at positions that promote violence towards those who are classified as infidels. Liberal Muslims, those who do not take the Koran in its original sense or are connected to the worship style but not its epistemology, often ignore the violent tones of the Koran.

[36] Secular Humanism, which will be thoroughly examined in subsequent sections, would be an example of Satan's deceptive ideology manifesting itself through a modern and postmodern lifestyle and worldview.

language, for he is a liar and the father of lies" (John 8:44, ESV). Those who deny Satan's reality and work are not followers of Christ but rather are participants (even if some are so unwittingly) with Satan and his global assault against God and his people.

"On April 8th of 1966, TIME magazine emblazoned" on its cover a "stark question, 'Is God Dead?'" On April 30th, Anton Szandor LaVey delivered the answer by proclaiming the birth of the age of Satan with the founding of the Church of Satan.[37] Since a Christ follower, what I often refer to as a Christicrat, realizes Satan has existed prior to human history, any form of a true Satanic religion has to have in some sense its roots beyond mere human history. LaVey merely organized the millennia of ideas into a more centralized system of thought with official writings conveying the worldview, establishing a written epistemology, and displaying its methodology for ideological discovery and implementation. LaVey even admits this. He says, "the basics of Satanism have always existed. The only thing that is new is the formal organization of a religion based on the universal traits of man."[38]

The Metaphysics, Epistemology, and Methodology of Satanism

Satanism has no metaphysical worldview per se. In their religion nothing exists beyond this world. They embrace an atheistic worldview and urge people to live for the here and now. As the Satanic High Priest Gilmore says, "we do not believe in the supernatural. To the Satanist, he is his own God. Satan is a symbol of Man living as his prideful, carnal nature dictates."[39] In fact, Satanists describe their essential worldview as the "philosophy" of "Epicurean atheism."[40] "All religions of a spiritual nature

---

[37] Peter H. Gilmore, *The Satanic Scriptures* (Baltimore, MD: ScapeGoat Publishing, 2007), xv.

[38] Anton Szandor LaVey, *The Satanic Bible* (HarperCollins Publishers, 1969), 53.

[39] Peter H. Gilmore, *The Satanic Scriptures* (Baltimore, MD: ScapeGoat Publishing, 2007), 31.

[40] Ibid., 186.

are inventions of man."⁴¹ They explicitly accept the "axiomatic premise that no gods exist as independent supernatural entities," leading each Satanist to recognition that their philosophy is "self-centered" because "each Satanist sees himself as the most important person in his life."⁴² Someone following the Satanic ideology, consciously or unconsciously, affirms that "life is the great indulgence" so "make the most of life" in the "here and now."⁴³

Though Satanism does not specifically confess a metaphysical worldview, it does have an epistemology. It naturally follows from their metaphysical view of reality (even though they do not confess a world beyond this physical world), which is basically naturalism. Though not seen as divine, the founder, or more accurately the organizer of the Satanic religion, LaVey, provided a book known as the Satanic Bible. That book has been a key guide to all subsequent ministers of the religion. The High Priest Gilmore accredits LaVey as a "great genius" who was able to "weave together seemingly disparate threads from many cultures and times, as he recognized them as emanating from a single, caliginous source."⁴⁴

Their key writings form in part their epistemology along with a hybrid of other aspects such as "natural instincts,"⁴⁵ personal "indulgence,"⁴⁶ and a chief focus on "individualism as one of its primary values."⁴⁷ This self-centered individualism means "each individual generates his own hierarchy of values and judges everything based on his own standards" because Satanists "appoint" themselves as "Gods in" their

---

[41] Anton Szandor LaVey, *The Satanic Bible* (HarperCollins Publishers, 1969), 44.

[42] Peter H. Gilmore, *The Satanic Scriptures* (Baltimore, MD: ScapeGoat Publishing, 2007), 208-209.

[43] Ibid., 33.

[44] Peter H. Gilmore, *The Satanic Scriptures* (Baltimore MD: ScapeGoat Publishing, 2007), 147.

[45] Ibid., 55.

[46] Ibid., 81.

[47] Ibid., 110.

"subjective universes."[48] The core written epistemology revolves around the "Nine Satanic Statements,"[49] the "Eleven Satanic Rules of the Earth,"[50] and the "Nine Satanic Sins."[51] These codes form the "rudiments of Satanic philosophy" as it is "based on human nature" that "comes naturally to most carnal people who have not been deeply indoctrinated in the anti-life and anti-rational belief systems."[52]

As to methodology, Satanism has two key modes for spreading its worldview and distinct ideas. Satanism "unflinchingly embraces Man as just another animal"[53] (a naturalistic macro-evolutionary anthropology) within the "Social Darwinism" scheme.[54] Satanism does not wish to be its own religion. Instead, Satanism has sought to permeate other religions and spread into those realms for *cultural permeation*. Satanic priest Gilmore has stated, "Satanism will permeate the societies of the globe as a *secular lifestyle*."[55] As they admit, their faith seeks to "influence the larger cultural movement without being recognized as such."[56] At this juncture in the history of the United States of America, their goal seems to have had a

---

[48] Ibid., 208-209.

[49] Anton Szandor LaVey, *The Satanic Bible* (HarperCollins Publishers, 1969), 25.

[50] Peter H. Gilmore, *The Satanic Scriptures* (Baltimore, MD: ScapeGoat Publishing, 2007), 27-28.

[51] Ibid., 28-31.

[52] Ibid., 31.

[53] Ibid., 108. How ironic is it that many Christians openly identify with Satanism by their denial of God creating Adam from the ground and embrace he evolved naturally from animals? A natural macro-evolutionary model of anthropology is not only weak scientifically but philosophically rooted in the express philosophy of Satanism. It cannot be justified either biblically or scientifically. Various theistic models of creationism exist, even gradual or incremental theistic evolutionary models. Even the theistic or gradual creation models deny naturalism and embrace creation ex-nihilo.

[54] Ibid., 26.

[55] Ibid., 56. Italics mine.

[56] Ibid.

significant amount of success. In fact, the advocates of secularism under the label of Humanism seem to believe the secularization of the world is indeed increasing. Humanist Paul Kurtz has explicitly stated, "the modern world has witnessed the widespread secularization of life."[57]

Additionally, those following Satanism's philosophy embrace "pragmatism" as their "guiding factor"[58] for living and extending their views. Their pragmatism is often another term for ethical relativism. Whatever a person's conscience believes is to be honored, promoted, and allowed. Conscience is king in a satanic worldview whereas in a Judeo-Christian worldview the conscience submits to natural law (general revelation) and supernatural law (special revelation, Scripture). An example of their distorted and evil pragmatism reveals itself very starkly in their sexual ethics. They embrace and promote the perverted ideology of a "live and let live" sexual ethic worldview. And in that worldview, they strongly promote the perversions of homosexuality and lifestyles opposed to heterosexuality.[59] The antichristian version of sex is all forms

---

[57] Paul Kurtz, *What is Secular Humanism* (Amherst NY: Prometheus Books, 2007), 15.

[58] Peter H. Gilmore, *The Satanic Scriptures* (Baltimore, MD: ScapeGoat Publishing, 2007), 82.

[59] Evangelicals need to distinguish between homosexual acts and homosexual temptations and desires. In a fallen world where all people have a sin nature a person's nature may lean or have dispositions towards sexual perversions. Just as some people are prone towards other types of sins so too some are prone towards that sin. But temptations and orientations do not require or necessitate actions upon those desires. All people are prone to lie by the sin nature (the "I" in the person is corrupted by sin) but we still hold people accountable for lying. Likewise, even if a person has homosexual desires they will be held accountable by God for agreeing with those desires. The body of Christ must also hold people accountable to biblical sexual ethics (the standard is listed in Leviticus 18 and reaffirmed in the NT). A homosexual who has no heterosexual desires must remain celibate if such desires are not altered. Wesley Hill's book, *Washed and Waiting* provides this model. He admits he has homosexual desires and has had such desires for as long as he can remember. Yet even so he still affirms that homosexuals may not act upon those desires if they truly desire to honor Christ with their lives. However, one concern that remains occurs when believers who struggle with this identify themselves as "gay Christians." Why would any saint identify themselves with any particular sinful trait? Should a saint who struggles with gluttony introduce himself as a "gluttonous Christian?" Should someone who struggles with envy identify themselves as an "envious Christian?" Those markers when used do not reflect the proper ideology for what it means to be in Christ Jesus. If you are in Christ you are a new creation, the old has gone (2 Cor. 5:17).

of sex that violate healthy heterosexual forms of sex.[60] Christ created heterosexual sex. Satan has authored its counter, an antichristian form of sexuality, homosexual sex and other perversions that promote unhealthy sexual acts.

Since Satanists affirm situational ethics, pragmatism or relativism, a life based upon indulgence where the people determine what truth is according to their own desires, a live and let live ideology permeates the entire religion of Satanism.[61] When examining that motif in the particular

---

Though all will struggle with sin until death or the Lord's return, introducing oneself with a primary marker rooted in some type of sin ignores the literal interpretation of numerous texts that speak of our status as saints in Christ. In short it glorifies the sin more than the glory of Christ's grace. The Bible teaches us where sin abounded grace did much more abound. To say or introduce oneself as a "gay Christian," reverses the order and says where grace abounded sin still much more abounded.

[60] The sexual sins listed in Scripture can be found explicitly listed in Leviticus 18. The N.T. does not alter the O.T. sexual ethic code once established from the Mosaic era onward. Jesus Christ affirmed this list (Matt. 5:17-20 & 15:19) as well as the Apostles with the Church at the Jerusalem Council (Acts 15:20). The English term "sexual immorality" used throughout the entire N.T. covers all of the sins listed in Leviticus 18. The one adjustment, an addition to the code given to Adam and Eve, came with the Mosaic Law era that added sibling relations to the list of prohibitions. Additionally, divorce and remarriage is not per se a violation of the sexual ethic code of Scripture (unless adulterous). Even an unjustified divorce can be forgiven and if not reconcilable to the degree of restoration, the offending party may still remarry. The toughest justice code in history, the Mosaic Law, allowed for divorce and remarriage (Deut. 24:1-4). The N.T. did not alter that permission either. Though never God's desired goal for a divorce to occur (Matt. 19:1-12), he does allow it and does forgive it. Also, at times God himself called on people to actually divorce or put away a covenant partner (Ezra 10). If a divorce is always sinful then how could God command it in Ezra's day? Furthermore, God himself describes himself as having divorced Israel. And lastly, for those who argue 1 Timothy 3:2 and Titus 1:6 forbids a divorce for ministerial leaders, such a position holds many flaws. The text is a positive statement not a negative statement. In other words, it is not saying what a man cannot be. Rather, it is stating what he, the male bishop, must be right now, i.e. a joined man. Also, if the literal hermeneutic is applied it yields a problem for those who claim it meant "not divorced." Paul could have easily used the term for divorce. However, he did not use that term. Also, to say a shepherd cannot properly shepherd because of a divorce fails to again take into account God is a shepherd yet he rightly divorced Israel for her sins. How can someone require more of a human than of God?

[61] Peter H. Gilmore, *The Satanic Scriptures* (Baltimore, MD: ScapeGoat Publishing, 2007), 155.

area of sexual ethics they, without any hint of proper shame, or due recognition of its medical dangers[62] or sociological deficiencies for a healthy family structure,[63] audaciously and with braggadocios boast that the official Church of Satan was the "first organized religious group to fully accept members regardless of their sexual orientation."[64] That is well suited for their pagan, perverted, and antichrist worldview. It makes logical sense that the Satanic church would be the first organized religion to embrace the antichrist model of sexuality. Some so-called Christian denominations once permeated with the antichrist secularization followed suit.

The permeation of ethical relativism as well as the subtle and even overt denials of logic, absolute truth, and even natural law led many towards embracing or accepting this perverted sexual ethic. It naturally follows that homosexuality is accepted as a legitimate lifestyle once the Satanic premise of pragmatism and relativism is embraced. If truth is determined by what someone desires or feels then just a mere desire or feeling to engage in consensual homosexual relations (or any other unhealthy sexual lifestyle) must be and is accepted within their religion. They have applied their master's theory and lived it out logically in regard to sexual ethics.

---

[62] Rajan Bhonsle, *"Homosexuality: A Doctor's Perspective,"* at *Body Mind and Beyond Complete Wellbeing* [online], accessed 11 January 2016, available from http://completewellbeing.com/article/homosexuality-is-it-worth-the-risk/; Internet. See also https://www.medinstitute.org/2012/06/anal-sex-a-dangerous-trend-3-2/.

[63] Christine Kim and Jennifer Marshall, *"New Research on Children of Same-Sex Parents Suggests Differences Matter"* at *The Daily Signal*, [online], accessed 11 January 2016, available from http://dailysignal.com/2012/06/11/new-research-on-children-of-same-sex-parents-suggests-differences-matter/ ; Internet. See also Judd Legum, *"Major New Study Finds Kids Raised by Same-Sex Couples are 'Healthier and Happier'"* at *Think Progress*, [online], accessed 11 January 2016, available from http://thinkprogress.org/lgbt/2014/07/05/3456717/kids-raised-by-same-sex-couples-are-healthier-and-happier/ .; Internet. Jamie Bryan Hall, *"The Research on Same Sex Parenting: 'No Differences No More'"* at *The Heritage Foundation*, [online], accessed 11 January 2016, available from http://www.heritage.org/research/reports/2015/04/the-research-on-same-sex-parenting-no-differences-no-more; Internet.

[64] Peter H. Gilmore, *The Satanic Scriptures* (Baltimore. MD: ScapeGoat Publishing, 2007), 98.

Satanism's amoral and situational ethic teaches that "each person must decide for himself what form of sexual activity best suits his individual needs."[65] This view of Satan, codified in the Satanic Bible, exists in a plethora of religions, philosophies, and ideologies. In the official Satanic religion they officially "condone any type of sexual activity which properly satisfies your individual desires," including "homosexual" and "bisexual" sex acts along with any "fetish" that will "enhance your sex life."[66] They shun "moral judgment based upon sexual behavior"[67] (we often hear the slogan "Do not judge me for my sexual lifestyle") and actively seek to promote "homosexuality and bisexuality to mainstream status."[68]

Those words about their goals to make their sexual ethic mainstream reveal their methodological philosophy. At this juncture, such an effort seems to have momentum, strength, and prominence in this century, especially now in Western culture within the United States.[69]

---

[65] Anton Szandor Lavey, *The Satanic Bible* (New York, NY: HarperCollins Publishers, 1969), 66.

[66] Ibid., 67.

[67] George A. Hart, *The Satanic Bible 2012* (No place of publication, 1999), 49. How often do we hear that philosophy today, the ideology that we ought not to speak against someone's *personal sexual lifestyle*. First, that mentality is at its core rooted in Satanic ideology. Satanism clearly promotes a situational sexual ethic where the person is his or her own god in his or her sexual relations. But secondly, if I know about the sexual lifestyle you are living then it is no longer *only personal* is it? Consequently, if a person shares or reveals his or her sexual lifestyle they ought to be properly exposed to the light of Christ which highlights honorable sexual actions in contrast to antichrist sexual actions (for the detailed list of sexual sins see Leviticus 18). That is the issue noted by Chief Justice John Roberts at the U.S. Supreme Court. He noted in the *Obergefell v. Hodges* case that the petitioners for the right for homosexual marriages "do not seek privacy. Quite the opposite, they seek public recognition of their relationships. . . ." (*The U.S. Supreme Court Decision on Marriage Equality*, by the Supreme Court of the United States {Brooklyn, NY: Melville House Printing, 2015}, 77).

[68] Ibid., 85.

[69] *The U.S. Supreme Court Decision on Marriage Equality*, by the Supreme Court of the United States (Brooklyn NY: Melville House Printing, 2015), 17-45. People, especially Christians, sometimes get confused on the difference between the natural law violation of homosexuality and the natural law principle of free association even for those in

Indeed, those efforts to make these perversions mainstream have been underway with heavy infiltration into the academy, especially elementary and high school curriculums.[70]

Satanism and its advocates (consciously or unconsciously) actively desire to see homosexuality, bisexuality, and any other perverted, biologically unnatural, or ungodly sexual desire promoted while they create a culture that shuns those who advocate for biologically normal, natural, godly, and Christ honoring sexual standards, a standard that has existed in all societies and cultures until 2001.[71]

---

unnatural relationships. Christians who believe Jesus and the Bible cannot in any way support homosexuality or the pagan idea of a so-called homosexual marriage. Those who join as homosexuals, or celebrate the union of homosexuals, yoke together with unrighteousness (2 Cor. 6:14-18). Those who try and support homosexuality from the Bible show their extreme ignorance of Scripture, or worse their deliberate dilution of plain prohibitions of Scripture. Additionally they show a reckless disregard of natural biology. A basic understanding of biology reveals the complementary nature of a penis and vagina. A natural penis to rectum symmetry does not exist. Nor can two vaginas naturally join in symmetry. Marriage, or the God joining act in the physical realm, is in one aspect a natural biological idea that has to do with complementary anatomy joining one another. Two persons, a male and female with proper anatomical parts, join (marry) together in marriage and create a physical union. People of the same gender cannot biologically and naturally join each other. They lack the proper anatomical parts. But two people of the same gender (as well as opposite genders) can assemble together peaceably. A peaceable assembly is a natural law right for all regardless of gender. Marriage (a biological idea {that also has mind & life commitments} and institution) is not the same as a peaceable assembly (a civil associational right). All marriages are (or at least should be when free from violence and coercion) peaceable assemblies, but not all peaceable assemblies are natural marriages. The failure to understand this has led to enormous confusion, chaos, and conflict in Christendom as well as among the citizenry. If this nation and individual states would all adopt the idea of the government only recognizing peaceable assemblies then all adults could peaceably assemble while leaving private citizens and religious organizations free to have their own ideas of what is or is not a true marriage.

[70] John A. Stormer, *None Dare Call It Education* (Florissant, MO: Liberty Bell Press, 1998), 41-53.

[71] *The U.S. Supreme Court Decision on Marriage Equality*, by the Supreme Court of the United States (Brooklyn, NY: Melville House Printing, 2015), 62. Those who promoted the idea of a right to so-called homosexual marriage admitted that "they were not aware of any society that permitted same-sex marriage before 2001." To say same-sex marriage is like saying a square circle. Such a concept does not exist. Peaceable assemblies do

Lastly, within their methodology not only do they embrace pragmatism (a form of ethical relativism) but they also embrace the positive law theory as a chief means unto their ends of cultural permeation.[72] This too makes sense. When a person embraces an atheistic metaphysic and an anthropologically centered epistemology, the methodology of pragmatism fits properly into their ethical theory, even political ethics. If there is no Creator external to this universe (a denial of metaphysics for only this physical realm), and if truth is only determined inside this physical world according to each person's determination of what is true for themselves (naturalism; an anthropocentric epistemology rooted in relativism), then it naturally and logically follows that when those people who think they create truth for themselves collectively join together in a governmental system they will determine what rights to create for people and what rights to take away from people (progressivism enacted through positive law).

Satanic High Priest Gilmore admits to this ideology. He says, "Satanists know there are *no natural rights* as the concept of rights requires someone or something to be doling them out, and in the past this was usually considered to be some God."[73] But as an atheistic religion they cannot allow for there to exist any natural rights or inalienable rights as the Declaration of Independence says. They instead believe, "the only rights one has are those given by the laws of the governmental structure

---

exist among all types of various unions. But the reason homosexual marriages have not existed in any culture until 2001 has been because for all of history marriage has been a biological complementary unit. No natural law right exists for this concept. It has to be created through a philosophy of legal positivism, the methodology found in Satanism and Humanistic Liberal Progressivism.

[72] *The U.S. Supreme Court Decision on Marriage Equality*, by the Supreme Court of the United States (Brooklyn, NY: Melville House Printing, 2015), 104. This was Supreme Court Justice Thomas' point in his dissent. He noted that the majority decision created a right (positive law) instead of recognizing a natural right. He specifically said the majority's decision rejects the "idea—captured in our Declaration of Independence—that human dignity is innate and suggests instead that it comes from Government. This distortion of our Constitution not only ignores the text, it inverts the relationship between the individual and the state in our Republic."

[73] Peter H. Gilmore, *The Satanic Scriptures* (Baltimore, MD: ScapeGoat Publishing, 2007), 88. Italics mine for emphasis.

under which you live, and ultimately, even these devolve into what you may attain for yourself using whatever personal power you might have."[74]

A satanic philosophy has three elements in their worldview that highlight how subjectivity permeates the entire religion. Its metaphysical worldview denies any external, universal, and objective truth. They instead adopt a naturalistic worldview. They then root their ideas as to what is good or evil, right or wrong, moral or immoral, and loving or unloving in the subjective realm of each person. Each person is his own god. How ironic it is that the Genesis account of humanity's first encounter with Satan reveals that very ideology in Satan's discussion with our first parents! This anthropocentric epistemology leaves Satanism and its advocates with an unstable, subjective, and situational source for the method of determining reality or truth.

Lastly, the methodology of Satanism is pragmatism magnified through positivism. They seek to permeate the culture with their ideology through attempting to persuade people to do what is most practical, of course as determined by those people and their own situational desires, and then collectively to promote that practical goal or goals through a positive law theory within the structure of government. The entire religion spreads the subjective and shallow worldview where man himself rules according to his or her experiences.

In short, it is a liberal worldview where man seeks to make everything conform around him in contrast to God and/or natural law. God desires for the world to revolve around him and his glory. Man, when ensnared by Satan's ideologies, wants the world to revolve around him and his own glory. The noted danger of this liberal ideology has been summarized well by Dr. R.V. Pierard from the University of Iowa. Concerning liberalism he says, "The major distinctive" of liberal ideology "is the desire to adapt religious ideas to modern culture and modes of thinking" while rejecting "religious belief based upon authority alone. All beliefs must pass the tests of *reason* and *experience*."[75] Man has a

---

[74] Ibid.

[75] R.V. Pierard, "*Theological Liberalism*," in *Evangelical Dictionary of Theology*, 2nd edition, ed. Walter A. Elwell (Grand Rapids, MI: 2001), 682-683. Italics mine. It is not that reason and experience are wrong or to be always avoided. Reason and experience have a place in a worldview and in ethics. However, reason must be connected to some form of authoritative revelation from God and one's experience must coincide with, or at

tendency to exalt his mind and experiences above God's thoughts as revealed in authoritative revelation.

Thus, Satanism or a satanic philosophy is a seedbed that sprouts Humanistic Liberalism because it places man at the center to determine what truth is. Liberals often despise or dilute authoritative truth that is external to them. External, objective, logical, verifiable truth calls people to account. The liberal religious mind does not want to be accountable to authority other than self. A religious liberal wants to be his or her own god, which is verified by his or her devotion to relativism and situational ethics instead of objective, logical, and universal obligatory ethics where the person is bound by duty to some specific belief and/or action. Liberals instead want to establish their subjective reasoning as the final and ultimate determiner of what is true, often guised under the rubric of their conscience.

Satanism Masquerades in Humanistic Liberal Progressivism and Positivism

The ideology of Satan is to make people seek independence from God. The Satanic religion or the widespread satanic philosophy seeks to (1) secularize the culture through exalting humanity to the center of reality, (2) liberalize the minds of people so they reject the authority of logic, authoritative revelation (Scripture and natural revelation), and objectivity for a primarily subjective metaphysic, epistemology, and methodology that is magnified and spread by (3) efforts to remove absolutist ethics and replace with pragmatism and relativism. In those three areas Satanism has significantly influenced and merged itself into one of the most dominant worldviews in the United States of America under the guise of Humanism or Progressivism,[76] especially in the "secular colleges and universities."[77] In fact, jurist and author James

---

least not contradict, that revelation. Reason and experience submit to revelation. God and his revelation do not submit to a person's reason and experience. In other words, objective truth does not conform to humans. Humans are to conform to objective truth.

[76] David Noebel, *Understanding The Times* (Manitou Springs, CO: Summit Press, 1991), 849.

[77] Ibid., 21.

Ostrowski believes that "progressivism" (one aspect of a secular Humanist worldview) "has been the dominant ideology in America for so long that it has been absorbed into the subconsciousness."[78] As the ideology of Judeo-Christian advocates seem to be splintering more and more, the ideology of Satan in contrast seems to be uniting together in many fronts, especially the front of secularism. It is this wave of secular thought that seems to be making major headway in this culture.

Satanism has masked itself, of course, yet its fundamental essence has been magnified through one ideology that currently dominates the field. Humanistic Liberal Progressivism is the fruit of Satanic ideology. Satanism, humanism, and progressivism, often triplets of intertwined ideology due to their disdain for authority,[79] especially God's authority, seek to build their metaphysical and epistemological foundational structures from diametrically opposite positions than those within Evangelicalism (which embraces a Judeo-Christian worldview).

The main difference between the specific religions of Satanism, Humanism as advanced through Liberal Progressivism is not so much in *ideology* as it is with *ceremonial practice*. As the Satanist Anton LaVey admitted of the two, "Satanism has both ceremony and dogma," whereas Humanism is "simply a way of life."[80] Yet Satanism's core philosophy aligns with the core philosophy of the official confession of Humanism, or as titled herein for more precision, Satanic Humanistic Liberal Progressivism.

All of those major aspects of the Satanic faith noted in the prior section exist also in the official Humanist confession of faith. Humanistic Liberalism is a more subtle silhouette of the ideology of Satanism, just without the name and ceremonial rituals. The Humanist religion, faith, or merely way of thinking and life affirms the same substantive views as does Satanism. Such should be no surprise. The real being Satan is the god

---

[78] James Ostrowski, *Progressivism: A Primer on the Idea Destroying America* (Buffalo, NY: Cazenovia Books, 2014), 21.

[79] Paul Kurtz, *Humanist Manifesto I and II*, ed. Paul Kurtz (Amherst, NY: Prometheus Books, 1973), 15-16.

[80] Anton Szandor Lavey, *The Satanic Bible* (New York, NY: HarperCollins Publishers, 1969), 50.

of this non-redeemed world (2 Cor. 4:4), and to be the god of this world he seeks to make people believe they are their own gods. When Satan can make people believe they can create, define, and implement their own ideology into the world and it be received as truth he has become those people's god.

In their metaphysical view Humanistic Liberal Progressivism rejects an external, objective, and universal truth. They deny anything beyond this physical world. Like Satanists who reject the idea of God, the Humanists believe "traditional theism" is an "outmoded faith" because there is "insufficient evidence" for anything "supernatural."[81]

Furthermore, in concert with Satanists, Humanists believe humans are a product of macro "*natural* evolutionary forces."[82] Again, their ideology is consistent. When a person rejects a world beyond this world, or a truth that exists apart from the physical world of the here and now, the philosophy, if consistent, promotes the idea of a naturalistic macroevolution, a theory severely lacking credibility from both biblical accounts and natural science studies that reveals no "scientific evidence" for "any real" *natural macro* "evolution."[83]

---

[81] Paul Kurtz, *Humanist Manifestos I and II*, ed. Paul Kurtz (Amherst, NY: Prometheus Books, 1973), 13, 16.

[82] Ibid., 17. Note the emphasis on "natural." Random selections/mutations upward and a denial of any supernatural influence or causation comprise the nature of atheistic naturalism. Some theists, of course, embrace a form of supernaturalism working in and through nature to order, create, or cause proper selections for upward mutations. Though not a thoroughly consistent view when working with a concordian view of revelation (concordian worldview means scripture and science harmonize) as seen by this theologian, such a position has merit and deserves recognition as a type of Christian perspective.

[83] Henry M. Morris and John D. Morris, *The Modern Creation Trilogy: Science and Creation*, Vol. 2 (Green Forest AR: Master Books, 1996), 13. The Morris scientists boldly state, "it is not too much to say there is literally no scientific evidence whatever—past, present, or future—for any real evolution. Belief in evolution is strictly a matter of faith" (p. 13). The entire volume covers a wide range of reasons why science actually disproves natural macro-evolution as a viable possibility. They do make a distinction between natural macro-evolution, which they say science does not support, and that of micro-evolution, or what they prefer to term "horizontal variation" or "recombination" (p. 30). As to age of the earth, the Morris' work shows a variety of ranges from 187,000 years to 500 million years. Another excellent work on the scientific support of Creation and the unsubstantiated theory of natural macro-evolution is, *In Six Days: Why Fifty*

In contrast, however, the Bible and Jesus Christ emphatically declare God as Creator. Various types of naturalistic explanations have been offered among the scientific and philosophical communities. One version of naturalism that has been popular has been the position that from nothing developed something. That position counters the non-theist naturalism science, which has yet to provide any rational explanation as to how nothing can produce or evolve into something. How can nothing evolve? Nothing lacks power or property to evolve from and into something else. How can nothing produce? To produce something requires power and effort. Indeed those claiming nothing produced something reveal the height of their insane ideas. Such an idea as that violates every fundamental law of science on cause and effect, the rules of philosophy, as well as theology. Such a concept violates the very essence of logic and rational thinking. Those who have tried to develop some explanation have offered propositions bordering upon or actually demonstrating sheer

---

Scientists Choose to Believe in Creation, edited by Dr. John F. Ashton (PhD CChem FRACI is Adjunct Professor of Biomedical Sciences at Victoria University, Melbourne, and Adjunct Professor of Applied Sciences at the Royal Melbourne Institute of Technology (RMIT) University, the largest Australian tertiary institution.) In this work scientists ranging from biologists, biochemists, physical chemists, geneticists, organic chemists, mathematicians, geophysicists, astronomers, zoologists, meteorologists, and more explain why the best science supports an intelligent design model instead of a macro-evolution model. Also, even for those who embrace some type of theistic evolution model (sometimes known as progressive creationism), the best scientific studies from that persuasion still rule out the idea of random, natural macro-evolution. Dr. Keith Miller edited a volume, *Perspectives on an Evolving Creation,* and in it he too brought together a host of science scholars, astronomers, geologists, paleontologists, anthropologists, biochemists, geneticists, philosophers, and theologians to explain why God has to be behind the meticulous design to the universe as he governs it through providence within an evolutionary model. Their models estimate that the age of the earth could be anywhere from 5 to 13 billion years old. In my opinion, the age of the earth is a mystery. No text of Scripture specifically tells us and therefore we ought not to elevate that matter to a first order issue. Furthermore, if the creation, destruction, reconstruction view is held it offers a unique model that could harmonize all of the various age models with one set of data arising from the angelic world and another set of data from the present human world. Yet, even so, whatever model is adopted among these options, all of the models that truly honor Jesus Christ deny natural macro-evolution and affirm a supernatural ex-nihilo. God brought matter into existence from nothing. Satanism and Humanism deny ex-nihilo creation. A Judeo-Christian worldview supports creation ex-nihilo.

lunacy. An example of that severe irrational thinking, maybe even delusional thinking, occurs in ancient Egyptian poetry such as the Leiden Hymns where a god did not exist and yet he "uttered himself into visible form" as he was "self-created."[84] It highlights the truth that this movement "has no rational basis in fact or logic."[85] A Creator that created the cosmos remains the most rational option of the main views for the origin of the cosmos because the "concept of self-creation is logically impossible."[86]

As to epistemology, Humanists show their identity within Satanism as they confess their Epicurean hedonism worldview. How does a Humanist know what is good or evil, moral or immoral, right or wrong, loving or unloving? They, like Satanists, look to themselves within the subjective realm. They affirm "ethics is autonomous and situational," that "life has meaning because we create and develop our futures," and that our goal in life is to find and/or strive for the "good life, here and now."[87] In their own words, they confess they are committed to "scientific naturalism" as they reject worldviews that are "spiritual" or "theological in character."[88] They believe the best way to discover truth is not by understanding it from any universal moral code, such as from a divine revelation codified in Scripture, or even from any natural law analysis, but merely by the "use" of "reason in framing" their own "ethical judgments."[89]

Likewise, their situational ethic, rooted in a subjective epistemology, comes to prominence clearly when also examining their

---

[84] Maynard Mack, "*The Leiden Hymns*," in *The Norton Anthology of World Masterpieces,* gen ed. Maynard Mack (New York, NY: W.W. Norton & Company, Inc., 1997), 45.

[85] James Ostrowski, *Progressivism: A Primer on the Idea Destroying America* (Buffalo, NY: Cazenovia Books, 2014), 49.

[86] R.C. Sproul, *Not a Chance: The Myth of Chance in Modern Science & Cosmology* (Grand Rapids, MI: Baker Books, 1994), 157.

[87] Paul Kurtz, *Humanist Manifestos I and II*, ed. Paul Kurtz (Amherst, NY: Prometheus Books, 1973), 17.

[88] Paul Kurtz, *Humanist Manifesto 2000: A Call for a New Planetary Humanism* (Amherst, NY: Prometheus Books, 2000), 24.

[89] Ibid., 33.

sexual ethics. They believe orthodox religious teaching that does not tolerate the full expression of "sexual proclivities" unduly represses "sexual conduct."[90] Because "reason and intelligence are the most effective instruments that humankind possesses,"[91] more so than any external universal truth standard that reason must be subject unto, they "reject all religious, ideological, or moral codes that denigrate the individual" or "suppress freedom," including sexual freedoms, where people "should be permitted to express their sexual proclivities and pursue their life-styles as they desire."[92]

Lastly, in their epistemology, they root their idea for the betterment of mankind ultimately within humanity itself. No God or Savior exists in their worldview, so again this view that mankind must save mankind highlights the consistent outworking of their ideology. What is the most disheartening as well as destructive part of the Humanist confession? They, as do the Satanists, teach that "no deity will save" humanity; people "must save" themselves.[93] The progress and hope of humanity rests not upon the Supreme Judge and Provident one over the universe (as our Declaration of Independence affirmed) but upon humanity alone.

What is the methodology for mankind to save mankind? Their methodology shares the same goal as the Satanic religion: cultural permeation and eradication of the Judeo-Christian worldview. As with Satanism's situational ethic (pragmatism guided by conscience centricity) the Humanists embrace that methodology along with the positive law theory for government. They claim to promote tolerance, but that claim rings hollow as they do not want to allow for any cultural, religious, or theological view that is deemed by them, collectively, as being "intolerant or repressive."[94] That Humanist perspective would rule out any tolerance

---

[90] Paul Kurtz, *Humanist Manifestos I and II*, ed. Paul Kurtz (Amherst, NY: Prometheus Books, 1973), 18.

[91] Ibid., 17.

[92] Ibid., 18.

[93] Ibid., 16.

[94] Paul Kurtz, *Humanist Manifesto 2000: A Call for a New Planetary Humanism* (Amherst, NY: Prometheus Books, 2000), 36.

for Christianity because Christian theology and teaching without a doubt does instruct people to repress their sinful urges (greed, anger, deceit, and malice towards others, lies, sinful sexual impulses, etc.).

In this so-called quest to make society more tolerant, though not tolerant for Christianity, the Humanists seek to implement their quasi-tolerant situational freedom upon all by legal mandate through the development of a legal system, even an "international law" system.[95] Humanists "deplore the division of humankind on nationalist grounds," and they advocate for transcending past the "limits of national sovereignty" so all can "move toward the building of a world community."[96] They desire to create a "transnational federal government" where the "global community" would function underneath a "system of international law that transcends the laws of the separate nations."[97]

Those transnational federal laws would, of course, be formulated and discovered from their consciences or through their reasoning alone disconnected from any universal moral code, universal laws of logic, or foundation from a universal natural law. What the collective masses agree on is that federal government would determine what rights people do have or do not have. No higher government or authority, such as God's law (natural law), would be recognized or honored.

Interestingly, this goal or method to implement the Humanist ideal seems to be a similar, if not identical, type of government that exists in the last days according to the book of Revelation. As noted earlier, in the Bible Revelation chapters 13, 17, and 18 present a scenario where the world is united under some type of antichrist ideological system. The Humanistic Liberal Progressivism worldview reveals its allegiance to seeing that one world government prophetic prediction come to reality, though without due realization of its true spiritual nature.

So what can, if anything through solidified power and presence, permeate society as a counter to this worldview that seeks to exalt man to the unifying central motif to all of life? Is there any hope for Christ-

---

[95] Ibid., 53.

[96] Paul Kurtz, *Humanist Manifestos I and II*, ed. Paul Kurtz (Amherst, NY: Prometheus Books, 1973), 21.

[97] Paul Kurtz, *Humanist Manifesto 2000: A Call for a New Planetary Humanism* (Amherst, NY: Prometheus Books, 2000), 53.

followers in the twenty-first-century and beyond? What ought we do today in order to try and leave for our children, grandchildren, and great grandchildren a honorable society that reflects the light, logic, and love of the Lord for all of the world to see? If a one world order is being planned, and if such an order might be on the horizon, what can the body of Christ do to either delay that manifestation, or if not delay it, work within existing systems with such great power that they may implement a God honoring government? Is there a plan and a pathway? There seems to be an avenue that at the minimum could help or at best possibly even thwart Satan (a means unto the end in God's decree), at least for a significant season, while missionaries extend the gospel through the Great Commission to draw in the last remaining people for the body of Christ (Rom. 11:25-32). But for such to come pass a problem that has divided two strong and powerful theological traditions needs to be resolved.

Statement of Problem: Covenantalism & Dispensationalism's Twentieth Century Division over the Doctrine of Soteriology

Though some may read the prior section and believe that Satanism and/or the satanic ideology with its permeation is the most significant problem, it is not the ultimate problem. I have often said in ministerial contexts, whether counseling or leading people through various personal or organizational crises, that the problem is never the biggest problem. How we handle the problem is the more important matter at hand when trouble arises. Successful people "confront well"[98] and successful movements or organizations see conflict as an opportunity for growth and advancement.[99] That seems to apply in this matter since Covenantalism and Dispensationalism experienced a major rift with one another in the twentieth century. These two schools have yet to properly recover from that, and the theological world, even the natural world at large, such as within the academies, suffers the consequences of the loss of organizational power in cohesiveness.

---

[98] Henry Cloud and John Townsend, *Boundaries Face to Face: How to Have that Difficult Conversation You've Been Avoiding* (Grand Rapids, MI: Zondervan, 2003), 10.

[99] Harold Myra and Marshall Shelley, *The Leadership Secrets of Billy Graham* (Grand Rapids, MI: Zondervan, 2005), 85.

Dispensationalism was birthed from within the womb of the Reformation heritage.[100] The literal hermeneutic (also known as the plain, normal, originalism, or historical grammatical hermeneutic)[101] that Luther, Calvin, and other Reformers applied to the doctrine of soteriology, which recovered the doctrines of salvation by grace alone, was then applied to other portions of the Bible by the Dispensationalists. The plain or historical grammatical hermeneutic method, when applied to other portions of the Bible (such as ecclesiology, Israelology, and eschatology), began to produce teachers of the word in the 1600's through 1800s that taught key components of Dispensationalism. Many of those teachers taught a premillennial view of Christ's coming, a rapture prior to the wrath of God, and that God had a sovereign plan with both Israel (earthly promises) as well as the eternal family of God, especially the body of Christ.[102] Throughout the seventeenth, eighteenth, and nineteenth century Dispensationalism was largely a growing movement within the context of its mother, Covenant Calvinism.

However, in the early to mid-part of the twentieth century the cordial, collaborative, and common bonds of mother and daughter were severed. The mother system seems to have thought the daughter had apostatized on the gospel concerning a singular plan of salvation. On the other hand, after the conflict arose, the daughter seemingly thought she had no need of her mother anymore. She would withdraw from the mainline denominations and historic academies in order to blaze her new trail.

But in retrospect it seems that both needed each other. Covenantalism needed Dispensationalism to help them see the diversity in the progress of revelation and God's plan with ethnic Israel. Furthermore,

---

[100] Thomas Ice, *The Calvinistic Heritage of Dispensationalism*, [online]. Accessed 13 November 2015, available from http://www.pre-trib.org/data/pdf/Ice-TheCalvinisticHeritag.pdf; Internet.

[101] Many people misunderstand what is meant by the term "literal." That term is a summary term for the proper scientific method of language analysis. It does *not* deny the reality of metaphors, euphemisms, similes, analogies, or other similar constructions that exist in Scripture.

[102] William C. Watson, *Dispensationalism Before Darby: Seventeenth-Century and Eighteenth-Century English Apocalypticism* (Silverton, OR: Lampion Press, 2015), 103-225.

the Dispensationalists' allegiance to a literal hermeneutic (otherwise known as the natural, plain, or historical-grammatical method) created an impenetrable fortress against liberalism and concurrently created among the Dispensationalists an allegiance to and affirmation of an inspired text that also guarded against rationalism by retaining their roots in God's revelation.

Sadly, many of the Covenant-led universities and seminaries abandoned that non-negotiable essential in the twentieth century. Liberalism and rationalism grew to dominate the scene. Dispensationalists did not give one inch in that area. The Covenantalists could have been greatly aided by the Dispensationalists in that area as liberalism crept into their academies and undermined the great historic academies such as Princeton, Harvard, Yale, Brown, and many more that capitulated to higher criticism and the new epistemology of subjective modernism, a worldview that even led to postmodernism.[103]

However, the Dispensationalists needed Covenantalism to help them keep the single eternal covenant of redemption in focus through all of the diverse dispensations. They needed a unifying principle to help them keep in proper perspective the one redeemed family of God. The unifying principles from Covenant theology were also helpful in the Covenant theologians remaining devoted to the unity of all the disciplines of thought. The "harmony of all knowledge" perspective was a necessary view that helped guard against segmenting the faith into a sacred and secular dichotomy that is often seen in some versions of fundamentalism, something some versions of Dispensationalism were prone towards.[104]

In essence the two needed one another to help each other find the unity amidst diversity in God's household universe, a universe that included in it within this nation many seminaries and universities. Yet that balancing model was not to be. A conflict brewed through the 1930s to the 1940s.[105] The divisive spirit of Satan, which manifests itself in

---

[103] See Millard J. Erickson, *Postmodernism* (Wheaton, IL: Crossway Books, 2002).

[104] John Hannah, *An Uncommon Union: Dallas Theological Seminary and American Evangelicalism* (Grand Rapids, MI: Zondervan, 2009), 156-161.

[105] R. Todd Mangum, *The Dispensational-Covenantal Rift: The Fissuring of an American Evangelical Theology from 1936 to 1944* (Eugene, OR: Wipf Stock and Publishers, 2007), 175.

schism and division among Yahweh's people, led great men and women of faith to break apart personally and organizationally. The Covenant theologians believed the Dispensational model, such as with a "Scofield-Chafer soteriology," meant people were saved in two ways, "one way in the Old Testament, another in the New Testament."[106]

The Covenant theologians' mistake on that was apparently in identifying all Dispensationalists with Scofield and Chafer. Unclear, or poorly worded statements, or infantile Dispensational systematic nuances in an early stage of systematic development should never have become the chief focus of critical analysis. Covenantalism seemingly overreacted to a few statements from some Dispensationalists and failed to use other clear Reformed Dispensational authors, like the Calvinist Baptist Dispensationalist Dr. J.R. Graves (1820-1893),[107] the Presbyterian Calvinist Dispensationalist Dr. James H. Brookes (1837-1897),[108] President and founder of Columbia University Dr. Robert McQuilkin,[109] Reformed Episcopal Dispensationalist James Martin Gray (1851-1935),[110] Anglican Bishop and a moderate Dispensationalist John Charles Ryle (1816-1900),[111] and probably Dr. J. Oliver Buswell (1895-1977).[112]

---

[106] Ibid.

[107] Ibid., 7-8.

[108] Timothy Demy, "*James Hall Brookes*," in the *Dictionary of Premillennial Theology*, ed. Mal Couch (Grand Rapids, MI: Kregel Publications, 1996), 64-65.

[109] R. Todd Mangum, *The Dispensational-Covenantal Rift: The Fissuring of an American Evangelical Theology from 1936 to 1944* (Eugene, OR: Wipf Stock and Publishers, 2007), 154-155.

[110] Steven L. McAvoy, "*James Martin Gray*," in the *Dictionary of Premillennial Theology*, ed. Mal Couch (Grand Rapids, MI: Kregel Publications, 1996),128-130.

[111] Steven L. McAvoy, "*John Charles Ryle*," in the *Dictionary of Premillennial Theology*, ed. Mal Couch (Grand Rapids, MI: Kregel Publications, 1996), 383-385.

[112] R. Todd Mangum, *The Dispensational-Covenantal Rift: The Fissuring of an American Evangelical Theology from 1936 to 1944* (Eugene, OR: Wipf Stock and Publishers, 2007), 82-93.

Instead of focusing on specific elements of *some* Dispensational teachers, the Covenant theologians went on the attack with overly broad generalizations of all Dispensationalists. These broad generalizations produced an environment full of animosity between the two theological traditions. These "all-or-nothing"[113] generalizations forced a "showdown" where Covenant theologians "provoked a controversy between movements" that may have been otherwise avoided "had they merely critiqued the views found objectionable in Scofield's and Chafer's theology as a set of incorrect, but isolated, viewpoints."[114]

Sadly, that generalization eventually led to the Presbyterian leadership boards denouncing Dispensationalism. That denouncement is largely seen to have come through a denominational report that was "adopted and distributed by the [General Assembly]," which effectively from 1944 onward produced a "definitive verdict against" Dispensationalism.[115] This action caused Dispensationalism to be separated "from its moorings in the Reformed tradition," and consequently produced an environment where some within Dispensationalism morphed into "becoming less Reformed, sometimes even anti-Reformed."[116]

A Failure to Apply a Theological Triage Organization Model

In the body of Christ, Dispensationalism and Covenantalism (or hybrid models of the two) have been the primary models that have opposed the sinful and antichristian ideologies of Satanic Humanistic Liberalism and its methodology of progressivism. Though the emphases among both traditions experience some conflict at times with each another, no other primary models of theology have developed within the body of Christ. Theologians invariably find themselves somewhere within the continuity and discontinuity continuum.

---

[113] Ibid., 199.

[114] Ibid., 197.

[115] Ibid., 163, 165.

[116] Ibid., 165.

Just as within the hard science field of medicine, two distinct medical degrees exist (M.D. and D.O. degrees). Both arise from a belief in the scientific method. So too, two major distinct models of theology exist in Christendom that arise from a belief in the sacred text of Scripture. The sacred texts of Scripture and their harmonious synthesis are to theology what the periodic table is to science, the foundational essence. Methodologically speaking, as allopathic medical programs (M.D.) and osteopathic medical programs (D.O.) dominate the medical profession as the standard medical degree programs, so too Covenant (continuity) and Dispensational (discontinuity) systems of theology constitute the standard biblical and theological approaches.

Interestingly in correlation, "allopathic and osteopathic schools both teach the same basic science curricula necessary to becoming a fully qualified doctor, but they have two very different approaches."[117] Likewise Covenant theologians and Dispensational theologians learn the same fundamentals of the faith under the authority of Scripture and how to apply those in ministry with theological quality and credibility to people while each system still retains a unique and different approach to *some portions* of Scripture.

Stress is laid upon some portions because both systems agree on many of the most essential portions of Scripture. The historical difference in approach is seemingly most often noted as a difference in the application of one's hermeneutic (consistency of use) and the relationship of God's eternal program to the historical progress of revelation in the space time continuum. That difference often comes into focus when dealing with issues concerning Israel, future prophetic portions of Scripture, and how the two testaments synthesize together with Israel and the church. Outside of those areas the two systems largely agree on the doctrinal fundamentals.

Yet some of the animosity between these two schools has been due to secondary and third order issues. If the one perceived issue of continuity in salvation could be resolved (the goal of this dissertation), which is a first order truth, then greater unity could occur at organizational

---

[117] Ibrahim Busnaina, "*How to Decide between an M.D. and D.O*" at *U.S. News and World Report* [on-line], accessed 1 May 2015; available from http://www.usnews.com/education/blogs/medical-school-admissions-doctor/2012/04/23/how-to-decide-between-an-md-and-a-do; Internet.

levels. I use the term perceived because it does not seem in reality to be a difference among some Dispensationalists and Covenantalists.

Nonetheless, because Jesus Christ teaches with absolute clarity that there is only one way for salvation (John 14:6) this is a first order issue of highest importance. This issue must be resolved for organizational unity to occur. No two people, collective body of people, or ministerial organization that claims the name of Christ can cooperate together if they do not agree that a person can *only* be saved by grace through faith in the Lord's atoning provision. Salvation is found in no other name (Acts 4:12).

Our common message that we must now and till the end of time must preach and teach is that anyone who dies without trusting Jesus Christ as their Lord and Savior, no matter how religious, no matter what other religion they belong to, and no matter how friendly, nice, educated, or any other accolade that can be applied to such persons, if they do not come to Jesus Christ as their Lord and Savior they shall die and suffer in the eternal judgment of hell. This is basic Christianity 101, and those who do not affirm this are neither following Jesus Christ nor Christianity as taught by Jesus and his apostles. Instead, they are imposters if they claim the name of Christ and yet deny this absolute non-negotiable fundamental of the Christian faith.

Any person, or any organization, or any so-called Christian association that denies that basic and fundamental perspective cannot be rightly classified as a Christian. Followers of Christ must, if they have integrity to live by the teachings of Christ, separate from those who deny the singular avenue unto salvation as it is a non-negotiable, fundamental, cornerstone doctrine for those who love Jesus as Lord. Those who teach otherwise teach something other than Christianity. They are building their lives and organizations upon the sand instead of the rock Jesus Christ. So it is understandable that if Dispensationalism were to teach some way to salvation other than only through Jesus Christ then Covenantalists must, if honorable to Jesus Christ and his Word, break fellowship from the Dispensationalists. The words of Jesus give a proper reminder of the two foundations of life.

> Everyone then who hears these words of mine and does them is like a wise man who built his house on rock. The rain fell, the flood came, and the winds beat against that house, but it did not collapse because its foundation had had been laid on

rock. Everyone who hears these words of mine and does not do them is like a foolish man who built his house on sand. The rain fell, the flood came, and the winds beat against that house, and it collapsed—it was utterly destroyed (Matt. 7:24-27, NET).

But that is the question at hand. Is it true that Dispensationalism and Covenantalism does and/or must differ with one another in the singular doctrine of redemption found only in Jesus Christ? This issue poses a problem,[118] one that does not seem to have (1) been thoroughly answered through historical research[119] and (2) through establishing an "arranged" positive synthetic system of "order and interpretation"[120] with Dispensational teachings within the twentieth and twenty-first century.

If such a synthesis does show similarity in the doctrine of redemption then the people from both systems of theology could do more collectively for the cause of Christ. A major dividing point could be resolved. That could help those in each system to unite with power, passion, and pleasure for purification of Christendom and beyond. The resources that have been split to build separate academies and ministries, and the energy spent in vilifying or vying against one another in debate and discourse, could be channeled and streamlined into more collective opposition at all levels where Satanism has infiltrated society through Humanistic Liberalism.

Seven Areas Where Satanic Humanism has Undermined Human Progress

Contextualizing the spread of Satanic Humanism may help believers realize how serious is the need for the body of Christ to unify in all sectors of society to counter the spread of a false ideology. Once the Dispensationalists and Covenantalists resolve the perceived differences on soteriology, they have an avenue to reconcile and work in more harmony

---

[118] Sharan B. Merriam and Edwin L. Simpson, *A Guide to Research for Educators and Trainers of Adults* (Malabar, FL: Krieger Publishing Company, 2000), 9.

[119] Ibid., 75-82.

[120] Ibid., 82.

with one another while they work out their other differences as partners in the faith, much like a family works out their differences while remaining a family unit and carrying out their primary tasks. So too Dispensationalists and Covenantalists, once soteriology is no longer a dividing line, could join together more collectively in the body of Christ, in the academies, and in social sectors to better combat Satanic Humanism through better utilization of their resources.

Where those resources would be applied is a matter of examining the cultural problems within the era one lives. Though Satanic Humanism has made many inroads throughout the nations of the world, and in particular the United States of America, seven specific areas deserve attention. Though some of these errors have been corrected, some have not. Examining these problem helps to highlight how in every era Satanic Humanism seeks to undermine liberty, love, logic, and law. These problems help to serve as a reminder to the advocates of the main systems of theology that a failure to work together leaves the culture susceptible to the spread of these irrational ideas largely rooted in Humanistic Liberal Progressivism and its methodology of positivism.

Irrational Ideology of Our Origins: A Denial of Logic Needed for Liberty

First, Satanic Humanism has invaded the academy. It has for many years been a place that "indoctrinates students into a false view of American history,"[121] even world history as a whole when the subject of origins has been explored. A large percentage of the state governed academies at all levels in the United States have science and philosophy departments devoted to really absurd and irrational ideas both cosmological and anthropological origins. That is *not* a reference about the debate between instantaneous creation advocates and those who affirm a type of incremental theistic creation (sometimes called theistic evolution). Those two models of the faith still agree that God created all original matter from nothing. They still affirm a rational basis to the faith (though with other differences among themselves). Instead this is referring to the lunacy where many promote the idea that nothing eventually produced something. This ideology denies the logic needed to preserve the law of

---

[121] James Ostrowski, *Progressivism: A Primer on the Idea Destroying America* (Buffalo, NY: Cazenovia Books, 2014), 176.

liberty in this land. It is irrationalism at its height and often promoted today by the power of the government.

Dispensationalism and Covenantalism oppose those illogical, irrational, and insidious ideologies. These ideologies must be opposed because if nothing produced something then no natural rights or natural law can exist. This insane ideology opens the door up for government to embrace the idea that the only rights people have are those that the government creates for people, i.e., *positivism*. The United States of America was founded upon the idea of natural law, yet a significant portion of state governed academies at all levels now use the taxed money of the citizens of the United States to indoctrinate students at all sectors in a worldview that is both humanistic as well as anti-American.

Liberty cannot be long preserved when the underlying logic that promotes liberty is nullified through irrational indoctrination. Even President Jimmy Carter, who is often weak theologically and philosophically, was certainly right when he noted that at the **heart** of the American way of life is both "spirituality and human liberty."[122] To deny the Creator of the creation motif (as recognized in our Declaration of Independence) is to deny our spiritual heritage. In the end that departure of our foundational ideology spells disaster for the liberty of the citizenry.

To such dangerous views that oppose natural law (which includes a theistic idea and some type of supra natural causation or influence over our origins) Thomas Paine, who might be properly classified as an early liberal or libertarian type founding father,[123] wrote in his work *Common Sense* that it is the duty of people everywhere to be on guard against those who declare war against the "natural rights of all mankind."[124] The natural law or inalienable rights idea cannot be diminished, diluted, or dethroned if a righteous democratic republic is to exist. For Paine, and any right-

---

[122] Bill Halamandaris, Quoting Jimmy Carter in *The Heart of America: Ten Core Values that Make Our Country Great* (Dearfield Beach, FL: Health Publications, 2004), 150.

[123] Philip, Mark, "Thomas Paine," *The Stanford Encyclopedia of Philosophy*, Winter 2013 Edition, Edward N. Zalta ed., [online]. Accessed 25 August 2015. Available from http://plato.stanford.edu/archives/win2013/entries/paine/>; Internet.

[124] Thomas Paine, *Common Sense and Other Writings*, ed. George Stade (New York, NY: Barnes and Noble Books, 2005), 13.

minded American, "natural rights are the foundation" to the people's "civil rights."[125]

Those who oppose this idea of inalienable rights that come from our Creator align themselves ideologically with a great ideological enemy against the good of the people in general and in particular against the fountain, heart, and soul of America, even the heart of God. Paine spoke clearly about the rational basis to the idea of a First Cause, a Creator to all that we see.

> The only idea man can affix to the name of God, is that of a first cause, the cause of all things. And, incomprehensibly difficult as it is for a man to conceive what a first cause is, he arrives at the belief of it, from the tenfold greater difficulty of disbelieving it. It is difficult beyond description to conceive that space can have no end; but it is more difficult to conceive an end. It is difficult beyond the power of man to conceive an eternal duration of what we call time; but it is more impossible to conceive a time when there shall be no time. In like manner of reasoning, everything we behold carries in itself the internal evidence that it did not make itself. Every man is an evidence to himself, that he did not make himself; neither could his father make himself, nor his grandfather, nor any of his race; neither could any tree, plant, or animal make itself; and it is the conviction arising from this evidence, that carries us on, as it were, by necessity, to the belief of a first cause eternally existing, of a nature totally different to any material existence we know of, and by the power of which all things exist; and this first cause, man calls God.[126]

That idea of a First Cause, a Creator God, establishes the basis to the foundation of America. Even the liberal Paine understood this because he advocated for the use of reason. Rational thought, instead of subjectivism, leads to the logical conclusion that a Creator created a

---

[125] Thomas Paine, "*The Rights of Man*," in *Common Sense and Other Writings*, ed. George Stade (New York, NY: Barnes and Noble Books, 2005), 129.

[126] Thomas Paine, "*The Age of Reason*," in *Common Sense and Other Writings*, ed. George Stade (New York, NY: Barnes and Noble Books, 2005), 280-281.

people who magnify their Creator by their existence. And in their existence they have natural rights that universally exist because of the one solitary source they owe their existence unto. That foundation, affirmed by the chief fathers and mothers of this country, is commonly rejected in many sectors where subjectivism in irrational thought has replaced objective rational thought. Such is the case in the areas where students are taught there is no Creator, no intelligent design to this universe or to humanity.

Involuntary Slavery: A Denial of Personal Liberty

Second, Satanic Humanism was the reason for the many years of involuntary slavery in the United States of America. Natural law reveals that all mankind is created with an inalienable right to liberty. Yet when Satanic Humanism is affirmed no Creator exists to establish those universal rights for all humans. It leads to positivism where those in power hold the authority to determine what rights people do have or do not have by the whim of their personal and collective interests. In the area of slavery, those in power often desired to keep black people enslaved so as to further their own economic interests. Slavery can best be condemned when a Judeo-Christian worldview is applied to the theory of law and rights. Thomas Paine said of slavery,

> That some desperate wretches should be willing to steal and enslave men by violence and murder for gain, is rather lamentable than strange . . . the savage practice . . . has been so often proved contrary to the light of nature, to every principle of Justice and Humanity, and even good policy, by a succession of eminent men.[127]

Both Dispensationalism and Covenantalism have the proper worldview to counter positivism and the ideology that seeks to rob people of personal liberty. Both embrace the view of a natural law for all people because all people come from a common Creator. And though some forms

---

[127] Thomas Paine, *Common Sense and Other Writings*, ed. George Stade (New York, NY: Barnes and Noble Books, 2005), 280-281.

of slavery have been abolished in the United States of America, some types still exist. Furthermore, since America was founded upon the cause for all of humanity, it highlights the point that this nation needs leaders devoted to working throughout the world to help end this evil practice in other regions where people's natural right to liberty is abridged.

Unjustified Expulsion of Native American Indians: A Denial of Natural Personal Property Rights

Third, Satanic Humanism is possibly a reason behind some cases of unjustified ousting of the Native Americans from their lands. When the United States developed, some of the leaders at times failed to apply the Judeo-Christian worldview to the situation they faced with the Native American Indians. In some of those cases it led to the government denying natural personal property rights. Unless a tribe or set of Indians acted with unjust aggression to forfeit their natural rights to a certain set of land, expulsion without just cause violates natural law.

In some cases, due to what were likely "economic" forces at work among the people, where they desired the Native American lands for themselves,[128] the Native Americans were forcefully uprooted and dispersed from their homeland. President Andrew Jackson, a strong advocate for "expansion," led the way in "ordering the brutal relocation of thousands of Native Americans from their homelands in the Southeast to clear the land for white settlers."[129] These actions probably did not align with the confession and underlying principles of the Declaration of Independence. In cases where the Indians may have forfeited their rights through unjust actions, expulsion may have been justified. But without such forfeiture, such actions conflicted with a Judeo-Christian worldview.

As Garrison noted, "in a society so recently grounded upon the rule of law and natural rights," such a position as was embraced was "brazenly

---

[128] Tim Alan Garrison, *The Legal Ideology of Removal: The Southern Judiciary and the Sovereignty of American Nations* (Athens, GA: University of Georgia Press, 2002), 7.

[129] Carter Smith, *Presidents: Every Question Answered* (Heatherton Victoria, Australia: Hinkler Books, 2014), 52.

unjust."[130] Dispensationalism and Covenantalism, however, recognize natural law and consequently natural property rights.[131] Their worldview conflicts with these types of actions as done to some of the Native Americans who were apparently in some cases uprooted without just cause.

Women Denied Equal Rights to Vote and to Economic Equality: A Denial of Political Liberty

Fourth, because of Satanic Humanism and its positivism ideology, women in this nation were for many years denied the right to have political liberty. Until the 19th Amendment to the United States Constitution was ratified in 1920, women could not vote.[132] Yet a Judeo-Christian worldview believes both men and women are created in the image of God and the Declaration of Independence affirmed this with its affirmation that all people were created equal. In Numbers 30 single women and widows could make vows that stood. These truths (and other texts as well) reveal that women could exercise their God-given rights. Men and women both have the natural right to look out for their own interests (natural, spiritual, & political interests) and in a democratic republic that means the right to vote as a means to preserve and protect their God-given image.

A Satanic Humanist worldview, because of its methodology of positivism, cannot logically and rationally support the underlying reason as to why all women should be able to vote. Affirming patriarchy where a grown woman voluntarily places herself under the headship of her husband (see Numbers 30:1-8; 1 Cor. 11:1-3; Eph 5:22-24; Col. 3:18; 1

---

[130] Tim Alan Garrison, *The Legal Ideology of Removal: The Southern Judiciary and the Sovereignty of American Nations* (Athens, GA: University of Georgia Press, 2002), 7.

[131] It is interesting that many today in government still do not believe in natural property rights. This is evident by the ideology that a person must pay property taxes forever on land that they own. If taxes are not paid on the land then the government may use force to remove you from the land that a person owns and seize it for their own use or to auction it off for economic benefit.

[132] Catherine E. Rymph, "*Equal Rights Amendment*," in *The Oxford Companion to American Law*, ed. Kermit L. Hall (New York, NY: Oxford University Press, 2002), 268.

Peter 3:6) does not equate to the idea that a woman with no husband or no headship has no natural God-given right to vote. In a humanistic worldview, if the majority of political leaders, which is still in this nation males, were to decide that women should not be allowed to vote, then the government could (theoretically) keep women from voting (or any other class of citizens the collective masses chose to deny such rights to). That is so because progressive positivism asserts that the *only* rights people have are those that the government, not God, grant to the people. The people do not have natural rights under a government run by legal positivism.

Another example, one that is a more modern issue, is a woman's equality in pay. Some progress has been made in this area in the legal system when mothers who are stay-at-home caretakers experience divorce. Courts for the most part today recognize their services at home through an economic lens, i.e., placing a monetary value on their homemaking services. But for many years that probably was not recognized due to an out of balance coverture legal doctrine.[133]

---

[133] *West's Encyclopedia of American Law*, edition 2. S.v. "coverture." Retrieved June 22, 2016 from http://legal-dictionary.thefreedictionary.com/coverture. Coverture is a legal doctrine whereby, upon marriage, a woman's legal rights and obligations were subsumed by those of her husband. Though Scripture affirms patriarchy, it also affirms that the two people who are one also remain two people when they become one in marriage. Both are true. Just as the Lord is one and three, so too a joined man and woman, who are in a permanent covenant union, remain one while also two. A legal coverture doctrine is something that if it exists would need to be agreed upon by the parties who enter into that type of covenant/contract through voluntary consent to the stipulations.

Dr. William Luck has stated, "Abraham considered Hagar to be Sarah's servant, though the Lord also calls her his. A dowry came with the bride but the husband was considered the manger of it. It was usually land. Land was owned in patriarchal system, but if a man had no male heirs the woman owned it, but could not sell it outside the tribe. When a woman was divorced, she generally took nothing out with her except the bride price and dowry (assuming she was not guilty of adultery). Laben's daughters considered the bride price Jacob paid for them by his years of work for them to be managed by their father. I'm not sure about individual pieces of property, such as jewelry. Children were generally considered to be the husbands, but Hagar took Ishmael with her, to the desire of Sarah. The concubines of King Ahasuerus seemed to have their own cosmetics, etc. I would guess that most substantial property was considered the husbands. But I see no reason why the husband couldn't have granted rights to women having their own property." If Dr. Luck's analysis is correct, and he has specialized in this field, it seems to me a coverture doctrine (spoken of specifically in Numbers 30) in biblical law and in a civil state law context should occur by way of mutual agreement prior to the entrance to that covenant.

Additionally, some studies still suggest that women who do the same work as men do not receive the same pay as the men.[134] Though the best way to accurately determine this by a sound methodology is disputed,[135] it can be emphatically said that if there is truth to the studies that argue women do not receive the same pay for doing the same work as men with the same amount of experience in the particular field, then the natural law of equality of all people has been denied again. The problem in these studies, however, occur when the analysis does not take into account that sometimes a male and female doing the same job have different years of experience or different experiential qualifications (educations, years in the field, etc.).

Additionally, some women leave the workforce to have children and be a homemaker. Consequently, if studies do not take this into consideration the results can be skewed. Nonetheless, if or when analysis is done correctly and thoroughly, the same type of pay should exist if the

---

No man or woman has to marry, and if they do, they could by mutual agreement agree to such a system. In that model the hierarchical model would remain while also establishing mutual boundaries and parameters by their discussion and agreement upon the terms to their relationship they would make vows to honor. In a way this would be something like a prenuptial agreement in which the two people establish what will be common property, what is subsumed into the head of the family, and what property of both remains to each person. Certainly we see in Proverbs 31:16 a woman with her own property and resources: "She considers a field and buys it; from her own income she plants a vineyard" (NET). An unbalanced coverture doctrine would, therefore, seem to be one that unilaterally forbids a woman from any and all rights to owning anything. A balanced coverture doctrine could exist when the parties, prior to entering the union, agree upon what terms will exist in the conjugal/marital relationship in regards to property, income, and resources from each and collectively accumulated. Of course, this would require the real freedom for two people to make real and substantial contracts with one another upon their terms without the government having a monolithic standard that everyone must accept as their own.

[134] Editorial Board, *Women Still Earn a Lot Less Than Men,* New York Times, [online]. Accessed 14 June 2015, available from http://www.nytimes.com/2015/04/14/opinion/women-still-earn-a-lot-less-than-men.html?_r=0; Internet.

[135] Infographic, Do Men Really Earn More Than Women?, *Payscale*, [online]. Accessed 28 June 2016, http://www.payscale.com/gender-lifetime-earnings-gap; Internet.

same number of years of service exists with the same educational and professional qualifications by the male and female.

However, Dr. Catherine Hill highlights that numerous studies seem to suggest a disparity still exists.[136] In such cases as these, it would be wise to remember the words of Thomas Hobbes, whose influence greatly shaped the founding leaders of the United States of America in regard to unalienable rights, a social compact for government, and the value of a limited government.[137] He correctly asserted that "whatsoever right any man requireth to retain, he allow every other man [person] to retain the same . . . . this . . . is properly termed equity."[138] A failure in this area violates the natural rights of women and violates the principle of equality magnified through equity of resources justly distributed to those who earn through just labor services.

If this is so, then Dispensationalists and Covenantalists ought to work together in order to reverse this modern problem for the working women of our society. Both theological traditions could collectively educate the society on the precious value that the feminine gender brings to the table in all sectors of society. That could begin by, at the minimum, ensuring equal pay and benefits to match the economic value their work brings to the economy when there are truly equal qualifications, education, and services.

---

[136] Catherine Hill, *The Simple Truth About the Gender Pay Gap*, [online]. Accessed 20 July 2015. Available from http://www.aauw.org/research/the-simple-truth-about-the-gender-pay-gap/; Internet.

[137] Michael Warren, *Thomas Hobbs,* [online]. Accessed 20 July 2015, available fromhttp://www.americassurvivalguide.com/thomas_hobbes.php; Internet.

[138] Thomas Hobbes, *Human Nature and De Corpore Politico*, ed. J.C.A. Gaskin (Oxford, NY: Oxford University Press, 1994), 94.

Abortion for Convenience: A Denial of Natural Life

Fifth, Satanic Humanism is at the root of the pro-abortion ideology that has plagued this nation since the infamous *Roe v. Wade* Supreme Court case. The Court lacked a proper understanding of science concerning the conception and gestation of the child in the womb. They did not understand the science we do today. *In fact, they even agreed that if it is true that the fetus in the womb is a person then the government must (not may) protect that life because that is the fundamental purpose of government.* As they said,

> if the fetus is a "person" within the language and meaning of the Fourteenth Amendment . . . . [and] if this suggestion of personhood is established, the appellant's case, of course, collapses, for the fetus' *right to life would then be guaranteed* specifically by the Amendment. The appellant conceded as much on reargument. On the other hand, the appellee conceded on reargument that no case could be cited that holds that a fetus is a person within the meaning of the Fourteenth Amendment.[139]

Both sides that argued in the Roe case realized that if it is true that the material in a woman's womb was really a human being (a person) then an honest and just government must (not may) protect that human being if that government is honest to its own confession of purpose. To do otherwise is to be an unjust and dishonest government. The Supreme Court Justices and both appellant and appellee agreed that such would be required if the material in the womb is a person. But the appellee argued from a flawed unscientific position asserting the idea the material in the womb was not a person.

However, as new models of technology grew in the nation, such as fetoscopy and ultrasound, the realization became clearer than ever that the fetus in the mother's womb indeed was a person, a human being. In fact it was those developments that helped medical doctor Bernard Nathanson, a once ardent advocate for abortion, to repent of his satanic inspired ideas in

---

[139] *Roe V. Wade*, 410 US 113 (Supreme Court 1973).

favor of medical assisted murder and to embrace an emphatic and ardent pro-woman and God honoring pro-life ethic.[140]

Yet when the methodology of Satanic Humanism is adopted (positivism), those in power can deny all matters of logic and science and merely contradict the laws of logic to promote their satanic lifestyle of personal indulgence and pragmatism, the key theme in Satanism. Their ethic is rooted not in "philosophy" or "logic," but instead is grounded upon "emotion."[141] In this area of abortion, such a pro-choice for murder ethic damages women and undermines their uniqueness and nobility by degrading them through the horrors of abusing them emotionally through the destruction of their own flesh and blood.

It is obvious that when people reject natural law and the moral absolutes of God for subjective ethical relativism (the self-indulgence ethic of Satanism), the sanctity of life is undermined. Like the Satanic religion, the secular Humanist worldview with its progressivism and positivism methodology embraces pragmatism. As jurist Ostrowski says, "pragmatism, with its denial of objective truth, is the ideal epistemology for progressivism, an ideology that has no rational basis in fact or logic."[142] This sinful ideology undermines the reason why any and all life must be defended.

An example on how logic is denied within the pro-abortion ideology will help highlight the error within that worldview. Some questions will help highlight the logic that is often denied in this issue of abortion. If a mother is not obligated to care for her child in the womb, why is she obligated to care for her child outside the womb? How does a mere *location change* her obligation to protect life? The same question

---

[140] Robert P. George, *Bernard Nathanson: A Life Transformed by Truth*, [online]. Accessed 28 July 2015. Available from http://www.thepublicdiscourse.com/2011/02/2806/; Internet.

[141] James Ostrowski, *Progressivism: A Primer on the Idea Destroying America* (Buffalo, NY: Cazenovia Books, 2014), 23.

[142] Ibid, 49. I would not classify pragmatism as an epistemology per se. It can be technically defined that way if by that it means a person's authority is whatever he believes works for him. However, it would be more proper to say that the person is one's own authority (an anthropocentric epistemology) and its method of discovery from that epistemology is the application of pragmatic means.

applies to government. If the government's role is to protect the rights of people to life, then does not government have an obligation to sustain and protect life?

Some leaders of the pro-death abortion ideology realize their inconsistent logic and they are now actually applying their ideology consistently by promoting the idea that children outside the womb should not be protected by law.[143] Of course, instead of repenting of their sinful views on abortion they go deeper into sin and extend their sinful ideas to children outside the womb. They advocate that a child does not become really a human with rights until he or she can take care of oneself.

Many within that pro-abortion movement disguise their sin under the vernacular of freedom of choice. It seems by doing so they think their ideology is a pro-liberty ideology. But as Harvard University professor of Government, Dr. Michael J. Sandel, says, "if it's true that the developing fetus is morally equivalent to a child, then abortion is morally equivalent to infanticide. And few would maintain that government should let parents decide for themselves whether to kill their children."[144] Stop and read that sentence again. If the fetus is a human being, which science and Scripture both affirm, then to support abortion is to support *infanticide*.

The answer is that location does not change the rights of any innocent human being. That is why even the pro-life feminist movement says abortion is a violation of basic historic feminist principles such as "nonviolence, nondiscrimination and justice for all. Abortion violates all three."[145] Historically feminism, which has over two hundred years of pro-life history with it, asserts that "abortion is discrimination based on age, size," and "location."[146]

---

[143] Mairead McArdle, "*Trending: More College Students Supporting Post Birth Abortion*," at *The College Fix* [online]. Accessed 11 January 2016, available from http://www.thecollegefix.com/post/19896/; Internet.

[144] Michael J. Sandel, *Justice: What's The Right Thing to Do* (New York: USA Farrar, Straus and Giroux, 2009), 251.

[145] "Feminists For Life | Women Deserve Better® Than Abortion," *Feministsforlife.Org*, last modified 2016, accessed June 22, 2016, http://feministsforlife.org/-taf/2005/PWA2005.pdf.

[146] Ibid.

All of this shows why it is extremely illogical and dangerous to shift to pragmatism and subjective ethical relativism as a theory for ethics, especially in regard to a human being's right to life. Even the original historical feminist movement, which is radically different than the gender-feminism that is, by their own admission, a form of witchcraft,[147] understood that abortion of a child was murder. Historical feminist Susan B. Anthony called abortion "child murder."[148] Historical feminist Elizabeth Cady Stanton stated that abortion was "infanticide."[149] And the historical feminist Alice Paul, who authored the 1923 Equal Rights Amendment to the United States Constitution, even stated that "abortion is the ultimate exploitation of women."[150] The first female to receive a medical doctor degree in America, feminist Elizabeth Blackwell (1821-1910), said this: "The gross perversion and destruction of motherhood by the abortionist filled me with indignation, and awakened active

---

[147] Naomi Goldenberg, *Changing of the Gods: Feminism and the End of Traditional Religions* (Boston MA: Beacon Press, 1979), 86-114. Many people fail to see the difference between basic historic feminism and gender feminism. Gender feminism (or new feminism), as properly defined by philosophy professor Dr. Christina Hoff Sommers, is an ideology and movement "preoccupied with their own sense of hurt and their own feelings of embattlement and siege" (*Who Stole Feminism: How Women Have Betrayed Women*, p. 24-25). Gender feminists "believe that all our institutions, from the state to the family to the grade schools, perpetuate male dominance. Believing that women are virtually under siege, gender feminists naturally seek recruits to their side of the gender war. They seek support. They seek vindication. They seek ammunition" (Sommers, p. 16). Goldenberg, a gender feminist, explicitly states that they as "witches believe that by selling women a male god, Judaism and Christianity have denied women the experience of seeing themselves as divine beings" (Goldenberg, p. 90). This ideology differs from basic historic feminism. Old feminism simply desired to see women have the same equal treatment under law as men (Sommers, p. 24). New feminism, or gender feminism, is an angry movement that hates the idea of women being under a God-Man, Jesus Christ, and instead it opts for a worldview where they believe as a "feminist movement" they are "engaged in the slow execution of Christ and Yahweh" (Goldenberg, p. 4).

[148] "Feminists For Life | Women Deserve Better® Than Abortion," *Feministsforlife.Org*, last modified 2016, accessed June 22, 2016, http://feministsforlife.org/-taf/2005/PWA2005.pdf.

[149] Ibid.

[150] Ibid.

antagonism. That the honorable term 'female physician' should be exclusively applied to those women who carried on this shocking trade seemed to me a horror. It was an utter degradation of what might and should become a noble position for women."[151]

Dispensationalism and Covenantalism could collectively work together in this field to reverse the pro-death culture that has swept through this nation. Both systems of theology could educate the populace on the value of life and the natural law that opposes abortions for convenience. Collectively these two systems of theology could combine resources at all academy levels and by doing so make an impact on one of the most tragic cultural issues of the twentieth and twenty-first century.

Laws Interfering with Parental Authority: A Denial of Natural Parental Liberty

Sixth, the positivism, or so-called progressive movement, has also worked to infiltrate the world and this nation with an idea to nullify the right of natural parental liberty with their children. This is a movement led by the United Nations' Convention on the Rights of the Child.[152] As some understand this treaty, it could undermine at least ten areas of parental rights over their child by transferring those decisions to either the federal or transnational governmental authorities.[153] Matters pertaining to religious instruction and discipleship, sexual ethics, corporeal punishment,

---

[151] Ibid.

[152] United Nations of Human Rights, *Convention On The Rights Of The Child*, Ohchr.Org [online]. Accessed 22 June 2016, available from http://www.ohchr.org/en/professionalinterest/pages/crc.aspx; Internet. It appears that in some cases this ideology already exists in the United States where parents have at times been denied the right to make reasonable decisions for their children. Some have labeled this matter "medical kidnapping." See this link: http://medicalkidnap.com/2016/03/02/medical-kidnapping-a-threat-to-every-child-in-america-today/

[153] Parental Rights, *20 Things You Need to Know About the UN Convention on the Rights of the Child,* 20 *Parentalrights.Org*, [online]. Accessed 22 June 2016, available from http://www.parentalrights.org/index.asp?Type=B_BASIC&SEC=%7BB56D7393-E583-4658-85E6-C1974B1A57F8%7D; Internet.

and even criminal proceedings against children close to the age of majority would be governed by this treaty and removed from the parents and local governmental authorities and placed with either the national government or with the United Nations.

Both Dispensationalism and Covenantalism, due to their common Judeo-Christian worldview, would find many areas in this troubling. Dispensationalists would be extremely concerned as they tend to interpret Revelation as teaching a future secular one world government. Yet Covenantalists who do not share that futuristic view of Revelation still have many reasons to be concerned. The rejection or removal of parental authority to discipline, disciple, and determine many aspects of care for their own children violates almost all of the reformed confessions of faith that place that duty with the parents and not with the government. Therefore, Dispensationalists and Covenantalists have enough common ground that they could work together collectively in order to oppose the larger cultural problem of Satanic Humanistic Liberal Progressivism.

So-Called Homosexual Marriages: A Denial of Natural Biological Law

Seventh, Satanic Humanism as advanced through positivism denies natural biological law. This positivism effort has come to fruition most prominently in the recent U.S. Supreme Court decision where it redefined a natural biological term, marriage (the joining of two opposite yet complementary genders), and affirmed the right for homosexuals to marry. Biology clearly teaches that men cannot join other men sexually in a *natural way*. Anal intercourse is not biologically natural nor medically a healthy lifestyle practice. A woman does not have a penis in order to naturally penetrate the vagina of another woman for the sex act. The biological laws of nature govern what is a true marriage. Marriage has always been a biologically defined institution. As Dr. Ryan T. Anderson stated, "marriage is a comprehensive union of sexually complementary spouses."[154] Because the term marriage is defined by biology the subsequent institution of marriage is a "natural institution."[155]

---

[154] Ryan T. Anderson, *Truth Overruled: The Future of Marriage and Religious Freedom* (Washington, DC: Regnery Publishing, 2015), 17.

[155] Ibid., 187.

Yet with the recent *Obergefell v. Hodges* case of 2015, the biological institution was altered for a pragmatic model that allows for personal indulgence to be the controlling factor as to what is determined to be legal or not. Natural law in this decision was ignored. *Though homosexuals do have a right to peaceable assembly*, as guaranteed by both natural law and the U.S. Constitution's first amendment, that terminology was ignored and instead the Court used a biological term to describe a new status of homosexuals before law. A government can justly support a peaceable assembly of any set of persons without redefining natural laws of biology.

In concert with the ethos of Satanic Humanism's personal indulgence ethic where each person defines his or her own destiny, the Court's decision followed suit with that ethos by asserting that this ruling is rooted in each person's right for "self-definition" because they have a right for this "autonomy to make such profound choices."[156] That Court seems to have made an effort to give or place a value on the homosexual lifestyle. As Jenna Ellis says, "the highest Court in the United States told the LGBT community that their homosexual lifestyle was not just legal privately, but morally validated openly through government recognition and social celebration and therefore equally as valued as heterosexual unions."[157]

However, the natural law definition affirmed for millennia was overturned for this radical pragmatism that supposedly allows people to define the institution through autonomy and self-definition, as if personal perspectives may in reality alter natural biological law. Homosexuals do have a natural law right to peaceably assemble, but they do not have a natural law right to marry, i.e., join one another naturally through biologically complementary anatomy. As noted in his dissent, Supreme Court Justice Clarence Thomas criticized the decision as a rejection of the idea that "human dignity is *innate*," something the advocates of positivism

---

[156] Anthony Kennedy, *The U.S. Supreme Court Decision on Marriage Equality* (Brooklyn, NY: First Melville House Printing, 2015), 29.

[157] Jenna Ellis, *The Legal Basis for a Moral Constitution: A Guide for Christians to understand America's Constitutional Crisis* (Bloomington, IN: Westbow Publishing, 2015), xxvii.

deny because they believe rights come from "Government."[158] In this case, the government created a right that conflicts with natural biological law, i.e., they ruled within the positivism methodology through redefining a natural biological term. A solution existed by using peaceable assembly language.

Justice Thomas also added, "When the Framers proclaimed in the Declaration of Independence that 'all men are created equal' and 'endowed by their Creator with certain unalienable Rights,' they referred to a vision of mankind in which all humans are created in the image of God and therefore of inherent worth. That *vision is the foundation upon which this Nation was built.*"[159] Yet the natural law associational right of peaceable assembly was not what the Court granted or recognized.[160] They created a new right that conflicts with natural law. Supreme Court Justice Alito recognized this radical departure of definitions and stated that this ruling mirrored a "postmodern meaning."[161] In the spirit of positivism they

---

[158] Clarence Thomas, *The U.S. Supreme Court Decision on Marriage Equality* (Brooklyn, NY: First Melville House Printing, 2015), 104. Italics mine.

[159] Ibid., 119. Italics mine.

[160] The ideal way to resolve this debate and division among the citizenry is to remove the term marriage from all constitutions and statutes and to replace those with the terms peaceable assembly. Governments give or grant business licenses to acknowledge the reality of the organization (note that acknowledgment of it and creation of it are not the same). It would be the same principle at work with personal private associations. Marriage is in one sense a biological term. It cannot be altered in truth as long as biology remains as it has from the beginning of human history. Therefore, governments could give benefits to businesses and personal private peaceable assemblies without disrupting the natural perspective of marriage. Natural law does allow for homosexuals, or for any set of adults, to freely and consensually join together to form an association for whatever personal reasons they so desire. That could be honored and supported by all people no matter what religion they affirm. The problem in this matter has arisen due to the term "marriage" that has been used. Christians, orthodox Jews, and even Muslims do not endorse the idea of homosexual marriage because the idea is like an oxymoron. It is like saying a square circle. The concept or reality does not exist. The word homosexual or a same gender association by default negates the idea of marriage because marriage is at a base level a biological term meaning complementary external sexual anatomy (penis to vagina) and inner neurological complementary designs joining one another.

[161] Samuel Alito, *The U.S. Supreme Court Decision on Marriage Equality* (Brooklyn, NY: First Melville House Printing, 2015), 124.

invented a "new right" and then by that decision the government will "impose that right on the rest of the country."[162]

This invention of a new right is positivism in action. The same spirit and ideology that gave the power of the majority to oust Native Americans from their lands, to enslave black Americans, to deny women the right to vote and have equal pay, and to murder human beings merely because they are located in a womb, is the same power at work in this decision. It is a decision that means "those with political power and cultural influence" determine what is "right" for the "rest of the country."[163]

Again, a Judeo-Christian worldview, as espoused by both Dispensationalists and Covenantalists, rejects this positivism ideology that is the methodology of Satanic Humanism. Genuine or mature Christ following and Bible believing Christians, if consistent to their allegiance to Christ, will not support homosexual marriages because the Bible plainly supports from Genesis to Revelation only heterosexual marriages. Not a single example exists anywhere in the entire Word of God of any homosexual marriage.[164] It is fictitious imagination at hallucinogenic levels to assert otherwise. Those who claim otherwise and attempt to

---

[162] Ibid., 130.

[163] Ibid.

[164] Leviticus 18 in Scripture provides a list of what God sees as sexual sins. Like the term kingdom in the NT, which carries the idea from the OT, the term sexual immorality in the NT carries the idea over from the OT. The list as given in Leviticus 18 has been summarized by the NT term porneia (in English that is sexual immorality). In Acts 15 we see that the Apostles applied to the body of Christ this OT concept by this summary term. Therefore, this law remains in both the OT and NT. Sometimes you will see people exhibit their ignorance and confusion by asserting that since some laws in the OT are not followed none of the OT laws are to be followed. They will pick out various laws. For example, some will cite the dietary laws, or the clothing laws, or the sacrificial laws and then claim that since we are no longer under those the laws against homosexuality no longer apply. They then will often redefine the term homosexual in the NT to mean something other than male to male sexual relations. It is true that *some* laws of the OT are not restated in the NT. But the laws of sexual immorality remain consistent from the Leviticus 18 text throughout the rest of Scripture and history. Maybe one of the best books to show the error of that has been by Dr. Robert Gagnon who wrote *The Bible and Homosexual Practice*. Gagnon, however, seems to hold to some form of the JEDP theory and in some places seems to think Jesus corrected so-called loop holes in Moses' law.

promote the Bible supports their position reveal not only their obvious bias, but even worse their moral dishonest nature. To affirm "homosexual marriage" or "same gender marriage" is not only a violation of a Judeo-Christian worldview, but it is fundamentally a violation of natural reality. It is like saying a square circle. The concept does not exist. Neither can such a marriage exist because without the anatomy of a penis and vagina (and inner corresponding complementary nature of the brain) a natural biological joining cannot take place. They may have a peaceable assembly under the right of natural law as well as Constitutional Law, but the term marriage as historically and biologically defined does not comport with two persons of the same gender.

Dispensationalism and Covenantalism could effectively together make a major impact for the good on helping the culture recognize natural truth in this area. Academies at all levels could promote this matter both from a scientific perspective (natural revelation) as well as from a biblical perspective (special revelation). Both social science and the hard sciences highlight how damaging homosexual families are for children and for the individual health of the persons engaged in homosexual activity, especially male homosexual activity. And since Dispensationalists and Covenantalists affirm divine inspiration of Scripture, both recognize the text itself unequivocally denounces non-heterosexual forms of sexuality as sinful and weights to be cast aside. These two traditions working together could help educate the citizenry on the natural law of biology and why it is important to preserve.

Importance of the Subject: The Two Main Theologies Need to Cooperate in a Theological Triage to More Effectively Counter a Crumbling Culture

Those seven issues noted in the prior section highlight how the seditious Satanic Humanistic Liberalism has in the past spread through the culture and even how it is currently spreading throughout the land. As a summary, the seven cultural manifestations of antichristian ideology noted were:

1. Irrational Ideology of Our Origins
2. Involuntary Slavery
3. Unjustified Expulsion of Native American Indians

4. Women Denied Equal Rights
5. Abortion for Convenience
6. Laws Interfering with Parental Authority
7. Unnatural Marriages

The culture has in the past and still in the present suffers from some ideologies that undermine world progress towards truth, liberty, and justice under the Lordship of Christ Jesus. And contributing to the spread of its ideology has been the fault of an unnecessary division among the main theological traditions in evangelicalism. Since the two main systems of theology parted from one another organizationally in the early to mid 1900s, they have failed to impact the culture throughout the United States as they could have, had they remained in cordial cooperation with one another.

The continuity and discontinuity systems needed each other to help provide the academies throughout the nation with a holistic, integrated, evangelical model of theology that incorporated into it all the disciplines of knowledge, in contrast to some fundamentalist versions of theology that bifurcated the disciplines of knowledge into the sacred secular dichotomy.[165] These two theologies and the teachers of each model needed each other to help produce a fully integrative or more holistic theology, which is a science in itself. Dr. Gordon R. Lewis and Dr. Bruce A. Demarest have described what an integrated theology means,

> Integrative theology utilizes a distinctive verificational method of decision making as it defines a major topic, surveys influential alternative answers in the church, amasses relevant biblical data in their chronological development, formulates a comprehensive conclusion, defends it against competing alternatives, and exhibits its relevance for life and ministry. Integrative theology is a *science*. On the basis of the entirety of special and general revelation, it

---

[165] R.C. Sproul, *The Consequences of Ideas: Understanding the Concepts that Shaped Our World* (Wheaton IL: Crossway Books, 2000), 203. See also the following: George M. Marsden, *Fundamentalism and American Culture* (Oxford NY: Oxford University Press, 2006), 124-135, 199-221. George M. Marsden, *The Soul of the American University: Form Protestant Establishment to Established Nonbelief* (Oxford NY: Oxford University Press, 1994), 317-331.

develops a comprehensive, noncontradictory set of convictions on topics significant for Christian life and service. As a comprehensive science, integrative theology, like synthetic philosophy, tries to draw upon relevant lines of evidence from God's external world as reasonably interpreted by the empirical sciences, and from internal experience as responsibly interpreted by psychology, axiology, ethics, epistemology, and ontology.[166]

That type of integrative ideology seems to be what the Dispensationalist Dr. Lewis Sperry Chafer had in mind when he defined systematic theology.[167] He seemed to have desired to see systematic theologies build a holistic worldview and theology that intertwined all of the special revelation of God with the general revelation of God. Dispensationalist Dr. Paige Patterson certainly has taken that view as well. As he has well stated,

> All truth is God's truth. The discovery of truth, whether scientific, mathematical, philosophical, historical, or theological, is the discovery of the ways and orderings of an omnipotent, omniscient, and benevolent God. To love or even tolerate ignorance within oneself is inconsistent with the recognition and love of God.[168]

But Covenantalism would or could affirm that as well. Both theologies could help pull all of the various disciplines of knowledge into a workable whole. The Covenant tradition (with its unifying principle emphasis) and Dispensational tradition (with its diversity principle emphasis) seems to be, to use a colloquialism, a hand in glove combination. But the vacuum created by their split has left many sections

---

[166] Gordon R. Lewis and Bruce A. Demarest, *Integrative Theology* (Grand Rapids, MI: Zondervan, 1996), 25.

[167] Lewis Sperry Chafer, *Systematic Theology*, vol. 1 (Grand Rapids, MI: Kregel Publications, 1993), 5.

[168] Paige Patterson, *Johnny's Teacher—The Problem and the Solution* (Wake Forest, NC: Magnolia Hill Papers II, 1997), 9.

of the academy and nation void of the combined ideology, resources, and supporters from these two traditions.[169]

The work of the reformation began in Europe in the 1500s, and it then spread to America by the colonial Americans. The universities established here were products of the reformed heritage being transplanted from Europe to this new country. But with the split in the Covenant and Dispensational segments the reformed ideology that collectively dominated the academy up until the early 1900s suffered a great loss. Progress was consequently lost. The universities founded upon the principles of the reformation, and the nation founded upon a Judeo-Christian worldview and natural law, began to lose their anchor to truth as the roots of Satanic Humanistic Liberal Progressivism began to infiltrate the nation and universities in early twentieth century.[170]

One example of a major university discarding their heritage has been Princeton University. Under Dr. Woodrow Wilson's Presidency from 1902-1910,[171] the University began to discard their heritage for a new modernism ideology that contrasted a Judeo-Christian worldview. Dr. Wilson's shift to modernism and progressivism can be seen in his rejection of the ideology of inalienable rights from God as so stated in the Declaration of Independence.[172] Some even believe his political ideology

---

[169] I recall my mentor Dr. Mal Couch once talking to me about how some Dispensationalists had in some ways minimized the emphasis on the sovereignty of God. Couch was, to the contrary, an ardent advocate for an emphasis of Scripture that acknowledged God's sovereignty and overarching providence. In my ThD dissertation under Dr. Couch he embraced with great enthusiasm my integration of Reformed/Calvinistic theology within a Dispensational model. In conversations about that work, he thought I had developed a much needed model for an evangelical theology from those two traditions. Though he did not per se like my terminology of a covenant of works and a covenant of grace, he did affirm the eternal covenant of redemption. Too, he thought that my integrative model was much needed for a holistic model of theology that avoided the pitfalls of fundamentalism.

[170] James Ostrowski, *Progressivism: A Primer on the Idea Destroying America* (Buffalo, NY: Cazenovia Books, 2014), 18.

[171] Trustees of Princeton University, *The Presidents of Princeton University: Woodrow Wilson*, [online]. Accessed 3 April 2016. Available from https://www.princeton.edu/pub/presidents/wilson; Internet.

[172] "Woodrow Wilson – Conservapedia," *Conservapedia.Com*, last modified 2016, accessed June 22, 2016, http://www.conservapedia.com/Woodrow_Wilson.

established the vision that led to the "creation of the United Nations,"[173] which as an entity tends to undermine this nation's founding ideology of national sovereignty as it aligns with the secular Humanist worldview of a transnational world government.

This shift towards modernism (which includes within it the secular Humanism worldview) began to take root throughout the many major historic universities and seminaries in the nation. As those universities and seminaries began to embrace modernism and progressivism (the fruits of Satanic Humanistic Liberalism) those academies became difficult places for Christ following evangelical teachers to remain in leadership roles.[174] As time progressed, some Covenant theologians morphed into the encroaching modernism and altered their theology.[175] Those Covenant

---

[173] Carter Smith, *Presidents: Every Question Answered* (Heatherton Victoria, Australia: Hinkler Books, 2014), 170.

[174] Mal Couch, *The Fall of Evangelical Seminaries: A Lesson From The Past* [online]. Accessed 15 January 2016. Available from http://www.galaxie.com/article/ctj04-12-07; Internet.

[175] E.Y. Mullins at The Southern Baptist Theological Seminary would be an example of a conservative evangelical who allowed a more modernistic theological ideology to enter the seminary (a humanistic secularized worldview and ideology). Though Mullins was probably one of the best and most balanced low Calvinistic theologians in SBC history (he seems to have embraced sublapsarian views), he seems to have allowed for some infiltration of liberal ideas into the seminary. In a few areas, his own theological method may have paved an avenue or allowed for a seed to form for that infiltration. Even the greatest of men this side of heaven have some flaws that we can see upon historical reflection. This is not to discredit him in the many areas he did have right. George Marsden has noted that Mullins tried to argue "religion should be held separate from both philosophy and science" (*Fundamentalism and American Culture*, p. 216).

He possibly took that road because he did not understand or embrace a concordian view of Scripture, i.e., scripture and science must harmonize since both are revelations of the same God. Though trained under a staunch evangelical conservative, Dr. James P. Boyce (the seminary's founder), Mullins seemingly began to loosen his affiliation with that conservative theological paradigm just enough that it allowed ideologies (primarily experienced based) antithetical to the school's founding principles to gain at least some ground inside the seminary. His shift seems to have been enough that it left room for the subsequent students to drift further which then created a safe haven for an ideology that would later sprout enough to gain momentum that haunted the entire Southern Baptist denomination throughout most of the 1900s until the counter efforts of the conservative resurgence began to stem the tide in the 1980s.

theologians who did retain an evangelical witness were eventually pressured to leave or even at times ousted from the mainline universities and denominations. Dr. J. Gresham Machen, a leader of the old Judeo-Christian worldview and evangelical position, left Princeton to help establish Westminster Theological Seminary.

Dispensationalism, largely due to its hermeneutic, retained its overall conservative roots in the early 1900s and rejected the encroaching modernism and progressivism models of theology and worldviews. Yet due to the Dispensationalists' thorough and relentless opposition towards encroaching modernism and progressivism ideology, along with their conflict with the Covenant theologians, they eventually had to also depart those mainline universities and seminaries to start their own independent academies at all levels. One of those, Dallas Theological Seminary, became the flagship academy for the new independent evangelicals who were no longer welcomed in the historic universities and seminaries.[176]

That fracture, though freeing many evangelicals and fundamentalists from the conflict and from the encroaching modernism, left them with fewer resources to influence or help the mainline academies throughout the states towards any conservative or evangelical ideology. Additionally, left to themselves, some Dispensationalists did fail to see the need of a holistic and integrated theology. That consequently led to a much stronger independent spirit that allowed for less organization, unity,

---

It probably was not Mullins' ideas in and of themselves, but the students that later took some of his weaker spots further and those students birthed the fruit of liberalism. Most all students trained in the S.B.C context from around the late 1950s and early 1960s (the years of ministry of Mullins' students) until the 1990s were heavily trained in secular Humanism (theological liberalism, a form of Humanism with just a religious bent to it). Almost all of the major fundamental doctrines of the Christian faith were diluted or discarded by the seminary professors in all six of the S.B.C. seminaries and many of the colleges and universities were immersed in theological liberalism. Many of those universities eventually left the Southern Baptist denomination in order to pursue their atheistic and humanist endeavors. See Al Mohler's article "*A Tale of Two 'Baptist' Colleges*," http://www.christianpost.com/news/a-tale-of-two-baptist-colleges-60978/. Also see James C. Hefley's "*Truth in Crisis*" volumes and Paige Patterson's "*An Anatomy of a Reformation*."

[176] John Hannah, *An Uncommon Union: Dallas Theological Seminary and American Evangelicalism* (Grand Rapids, MI: Zondervan, 2009), 124-125.

and cohesiveness, all necessary components for massive movement influence on a broad national scale.

That longstanding breach of unity in the body of Christ has left these two schools of thought fighting "old battles . . . instead of funneling the trillions of dollars" they receive from their supporters and having it flow "through their systems toward the one goal of making a significant difference in our world"[177] by countering and combating the Satanic Humanism that dominates the national ethos. This split in Protestantism, the evangelical movement, that stemmed from the Reformation created this vacuum that Satan has filled throughout the twentieth and twenty-first century.

No doubt, Dispensationalism is still a dominant religious perspective in the body of Christ, even though as a movement it did not remain within the historic universities and seminaries. The body of believers that have either been influenced by or identify as some type of Dispensationalist is massive around the nation and globe. Dr. Craig Blaising has stated that Dispensationalism is "one of the most widespread and influential traditions in evangelical theology today."[178] Additionally, he says, "if you are an evangelical Christian, it is most likely that you know of some who call themselves dispensationalists. And it is just as likely that you have certain beliefs and interpretations of Scripture that have been shaped in some way by dispensationalism."[179]

No one can deny that Dispensational theology has made a clear mark on the history of the church from its early seed forms, to its rise of prominence in the 1800s, and down to the current day.[180] It has made invaluable contributions to Christianity at large in various denominations

---

[177] Bob Roberts Jr. *Transformation: How Glocal Churches Transform Lives and the World* (Grand Rapids, MI: Zondervan, 2006), 14. Glocal is not misspelled. That is the term used by the author.

[178] Craig A. Blaising, *Progressive Dispensationalism* (Grand Rapids, MI: Baker Books, 1993), 9.

[179] Ibid.

[180] Doros Zachariades, "*Dispensation*," in the *Holman Illustrated Bible Dictionary*, eds. Chad Brand, Charlie Draper, and Archie England (Nashville, TN: Broadman and Holman Publishers, 2003), 432.

and local churches.[181] Gary Demar, a non-dispensationalist writing in 2001 (who has as of 2023 apostatized into the heresy of full preterism), has noted that the eschatological views of Dispensationalism through the writings of popular author Tim LaHaye have surpassed in sales the greatest pieces of literature in history. Demar noted that the *Pilgrim's Progress* (1678), authored by John Bunyan, *Ben-Hur: A Tale of the Christ* (1880) authored by General Lew Wallace, and the modern Charles M. Sheldon's work *In His Steps*, which sold approximately two million copies in America and four million abroad, have all been surpassed by LaHaye's *Left Behind* series, which sold "more than forty million copies."[182]

David Brog, writing in 2003, revealed that LaHaye's works have at that time sold "more than fifty-five million copies."[183] When LaHaye died in 2016, his works had sold around eighty million copies. This means that the Dispensationalist ideology has permeated and spread to more people than the ideas of the most popular books ever sold in literature's previous history.

But even so, that widespread influence in the early 1900s did not help the historic seminaries or universities retain their evangelical witness. Furthermore, throughout the twentieth century they as a movement did not gain traction in any way to help those mainline academies that turned liberal in the middle part of the twentieth century to return to their roots. Covenantalists who attempted to remain in the mainline academies were either marginalized or diluted to such a degree they made little to no difference in the organizations for the cause of Christ. Dispensationalists, once ruled against within their reformed organizations, were forced out causing them to lose an organizational connection to the mainline academies and related organizations in the nation.

---

[181] Elmer Towns and Thomas Ice, "*Dispensationalism*," in *The Popular Encyclopedia of Bible Prophecy*, eds. Tim Lahaye and Ed Hindson (Eugene, OR: Harvest House Publishers, 2004), 81.

[182] Gary Demar, *End Times Fiction: A Biblical Consideration of the Left Behind Theology* (Nashville, TN: Thomas Nelson Publishers, 2001), xii. Sadly, as of this date, Demar has fallen into heretical apostasy as a full preterist.

[183] David Brog, *Standing With Israel: Why Christians Support the Jewish State* (Lake Mary, FL: Frontline Publishing, 2003), 59.

Nonetheless, Dispensationalists did continue to permeate the many different denominations and other Christian organizations throughout the nation. Though Dispensationalists did not make many inroads into the mainline historic academies, especially after those academies turned liberal, the Dispensationalist's permeation into other sectors of the overall body of Christ does seem to reveal that the movement's intent was not to destroy the unity of the God's people in history (as sometimes accused) but to provide a sure basis for unity. The movement seems to promote something that the overall singular body of Christ desires or identifies with doctrinally. Dr. Blaising again has well stated:

> Interdenominational schools and ministries have attempted to carry on that vision to varying degrees, a vision which has helped contribute to the sense of evangelical identity in some quarters of evangelicalism. Dispensationalists, of course, were not the only evangelicals to emphasize the authority of the Bible. But their transdenominational vision and their practical orientation to expositional ministry made *an emphasis on Scripture* a hallmark of the movement, one that continues today as well.[184]

This spirit has been made known through the movement's ability to interact with so many persuasions of theology, even with and within different denominations.[185] Observing Dispensationalism's permeation into various portions of Christ's body seems to show it has the motive and ability to work with many when there may be significant disagreement in certain secondary order and third order doctrinal areas, so long as the Bible is the chief focus of all matters of interpretations. This transdenominational element makes the Dispensational movement more of

---

[184] Ibid.

[185] It appears that a double stream exists within Dispensationalism. Chafer and subsequent adherents in his tradition were of the Evangelical persuasion. These Dispensationalists seem to have more ability to merge, assimilate, and permeate various denominations and segments of Christ's body. However, another stream exists. These are the fundamentalist Dispensationalists. They would be more of the separatist and pilgrim like tradition of Dispensationalism. Chafer's heritage, the Evangelical wing of Dispensationalism, seems to be more of the non-conformist puritan strand, or something closely related to that.

a grace centered, encouraging, optimistic movement in that it seeks to first and foremost make Scripture, not creed, tradition, personal conscience, nor denominations the ultimate authority in all matters of faith and practice.[186]

So the ethos within Dispensationalism gives the system the necessary core structure needed to help rectify the dilemma that has existed since the division from their reformed mother roots in the 1940s. Dispensationalism can make inroads to all sectors of the academy and body of Christ because they place Scripture as first priority, not creeds.

That "Scripture first" priority model helps Dispensationalists to develop and grow easier in truth discovery than those bound by extra-biblical human documents such as creeds or elaborate confessions that go beyond the first order essentials. So long as the Bible is adopted as the sole or supreme standard for truth, then Dispensationalists normally seek to work with others for higher causes than against those with whom there are minor variations in doctrine, at least the Evangelical stream of Dispensationalists would. This offers a glimpse of hope.

The Dispensationalists, not bound to creedal formulations, could, if organized properly, lead the way back into the academies at all levels to help reignite a reforming flame like that of the Protestant Reformation. Yet to do so they would need to emphasize their ability to harness a holistic theology that values the positive contributions from the Covenant tradition. It would require the Dispensationalists and Covenantalists to cooperate within mainline academies and organizations so as to promote the essentials, while they have their own intramural discussions on differences without animus and division. Though a longer than normal quote, the words of Dispensationalist Dr. Ryrie seem appropriate here:

> Unfortunately, the representation of the dispensational viewpoint has not always been with integrity . . . . Neither the older nor the

---

[186] In some denominations or religious traditions Creeds take such a prominent place that it makes it practically difficult to correct course due to the binding nature of their Creed over the teachers, even the collective body of teachers. For example, Edmund Schlink, a Lutheran theologian, says, "the Confessions are incomparably and uniquely binding beyond all pronouncements which the church's teachers may otherwise make, and references to the Confessions have more weight in dogmatics than patristic quotations." From *Theology of the Lutheran Confessions*, translated by Paul F. Koehneke and Herbert J.A. Bouman (Philadelphia PA: Fortress Press, 1961), 30-31.

newer dispensationalists teach two ways of salvation, and it is not fair to attempt to make them appear so to teach. After all, a man has to be taken at his word or all means of communication breakdown. It is certainly fair to attempt to prove a position illogical, but it is never fair to attempt to misrepresent that position either by misquoting or selective quoting. Straw men are easy to create, but the huff and puff it takes to demolish them are only huff and puff . . . . A sense of priority is also important. The temptation for any Christian preacher or writer to get off on a tangent or to ride a hobby horse is a very great one. That is true in doctrine, and it is true in matters of living . . . . Knowing and proclaiming this whole counsel of God is our desire, yet we all need priorities in our proclamation of doctrine. Some doctrines in the Bible are more central than others. Paul placed a high priority on the right understanding of the gospel (Gal. 1:8-9). He placed a low priority on the doctrine of the observance of particular days (Col. 2:16-17). Some doctrines should be given priority over others. We who are dispensationalists would do well to remember this. "Dispensational truth" is not necessarily the most important thing in the Bible. Even prophecy, though a major theme, should not constitute the whole of one's preaching. The spiritual life, which is without question a high priority doctrine, can be overdone . . . . It may [also] help to be reminded of some of the important doctrines to which dispensationalists subscribe wholeheartedly. After all, dispensationalists are conservatives and affirm complete allegiance to the doctrines of verbal, plenary inspiration, the virgin birth and deity of Christ, the substitutionary atonement, eternal salvation by grace through faith, the importance of godly living and the ministry of the Holy Spirit, the future coming of Christ, and the eternal damnation of the lost. Those who are divided from us in the matter of dispensationalism or premillennialism may remember the areas in which they [Covenant theologians] are united with us. As already noted, some doctrines are more important than others, so it particularly behooves us not to cut off our fellowship from those who share similar views about these important doctrines. There are few enough these days who believe in the fundamentals of the faith, and to ignore those who have declared themselves on the side of the truth of God is unwise. Something is wrong with our circles of fellowship, sense of priority, or doctrine of unity when conservatives view fellow conservatives as the opposition party and then find their theological friends among those who are teaching and promoting error.[187]

Such efforts exist because the Dispensationalist takes a literal (normal, standard, or plain) reading of Scripture and thus understands that in God's household-universe, just like any rightly governed home, some truths take precedence over others and some truths are the most important for the particular moment in time and history. If ever there is a time for that need it is today in this nation. The nation needs discipleship and they need it not only from the pulpits but also from the educational academies across the land. For this to occur the Dispensationalists must learn to work with those who do not share all the details of their eschatological paradigm. Of course, it is a two way-street, Covenantalists must recognize the Dispensationalists as their true family in Christ so long as the gospel and first order doctrines are embraced.

Dispensationalist Dr. Norman Geisler has properly highlighted the fact that some truths take priority over truths. This principle is vital for the two main theological traditions to learn how to work together again for the greater cause of Christ through all sectors of the nation as they oppose the larger pagan worldview that is infiltrating many sectors. Geisler has stated, "Not all moral laws are of equal weight. Jesus spoke of the 'weightier' matters of the law (Matt. 23:23) and of the 'least' (Matt. 5:19) and the 'greatest' commandment (Matt. 22:36)."[188] The Dispensationalist, if following his or her allegiance to historical grammatical hermeneutics, takes this teaching from Scripture literally, and it leads him or her to realize not all truths are so essential that it requires separation from other believers if they do not have identical doctrinal convictions. Dispensationalists, if true to their evangelical heritage, make the grace, love, logic, cross of Christ, and direct first order doctrinal truths the preeminent theme and essentials in his or her ministry, even a ministry contextualized in the academies in partnership with those who are not

---

[187] Charles C. Ryrie, *Dispensationalism* (Chicago, IL: Moody Press, 1995), 210, 212.

[188] Norman Geisler, *Christian Ethics: Options and Issues* (Grand Rapids, MI: Baker Book House, 1989), 116.

Dispensationalists. Such themes naturally flow from one's soteriological perspective. A proper soteriology can help produce those characteristics in the heart of the believer.

Also, a proper understanding of a Dispensational soteriology by the Covenant Calvinist theologian could create much more harmony in the body of Christ. As briefly noted and nuanced through prior sections of this introduction, Dispensationalism and Covenantalism, if harmonized in the major areas of agreement (while retaining their non-essential distinctive features), could work collectively more to ward off the spread and permeation of a Satanic Humanistic Liberalism worldview and its spread through progressivism and positivism. Organizationally these two traditions could constitute a massive wave of counter intelligentsia towards the proliferation of paganism that progressivism has proffered. Such an effort would not per se be limited to just religious circles either. A truthful, honorable, and biblically justified merging of these two giants of the theological world in organizational sectors could possibly produce organizational missions dedicated to reforming, revitalizing, and if necessary reconstituting social sectors such as the academies as well as including governments at both local and national levels.

That is so because Dispensationalism and Covenantalism both affirm natural law in contrast to progressivism's positive law theory.[189] A coalescing of these two theological systems in a theological triage[190] would allow them to produce holistic theology systems that aid those called not only to ministerial roles in the sphere of grace, but also those who are called into the ministerial roles in the sphere of justice.

Covenantalists and Dispensationalists should neither see each other as the enemy nor divide themselves from one another in local ministry contexts. The differences that remain between the two systems, once the issue of soteriology is resolved, are mostly secondary and third order

---

[189] Stephen Michael Sheppard, "*Jurisprudence, Legal Positivism,*" in *The Wolter's Bouvier Law Dictionary*, ed. Stephen Michael Sheppard (New York USA: Wolters Kluwer Law and Business Publishing, 2011), 591. Legal positivism is a theory of law that asserts that a law is only a real law if it is recognized or established by officials. It does not affirm natural law or common law.

[190] R. Albert Mohler Jr., "*The Pastor as Theologian,*" in *A Theology for the Church*, ed. Daniel L. Akin (Nashville TN: B&H Publishing, 2007), 930-932.

doctrinal matters. In those areas there needs to remain internal discussions and debates while they do ministry together in a shared and unified worldview that exposes the diabolical, destructive, and damnable evils from the pagan worldviews that dominate the culture around us.

As just prior noted, Ryrie offers a healthy insight when he says, "some doctrines are more important than others, so it particularly behooves us not to cut off our fellowship from those who share similar views about these important doctrines. There are *few enough these days* who believe in the fundamentals of the faith, and to ignore those who have declared themselves on the side of the truth of God is unwise."[191] Local geographical church bodies, ministry organizations, and academies ought to be able to have mature leaders who can lead their organizations in a collective missional organization that combats not one another but instead counters a crumbling culture that needs Christ Jesus as Lord and Savior. Since he is the one and only hope for all humanity, surely Dispensationalists and Covenantalists can unite organizationally around that first order, non-negotiable, divine truth and those truths closely associated with that essential.

A Question to Explore: Is There a Continuity Calvinistic Dispensational Soteriology?

In order for that proposed solution for the two main theological traditions to cooperate more in organized settings, they must come to terms with the gospel and overcome the historical issue that caused the split between them. In reviewing the literature from the Covenant/Reformed persuasion of theology, many from that tradition accuse Dispensationalism, and by default Dispensationalists (in some cases all by default),[192] as being unorthodox in their understanding and

---

[191] Charles C. Ryrie, *Dispensationalism* (Chicago, IL: Moody Press, 1995), 212. Italics mine.

[192] Professors Chad Brand and Tom Pratt along with others assert that Dispensationalism as a whole requires (not just may) multiple avenues of salvation. Sometimes this is because of the view of two types of elect people in the Bible, Israel the elect ethnic nation and the spiritual elected ones unto eternal salvation. It appears the failure of non-dispensationalists to understand Dispensationalism's dual types of election has led to

teaching of the gospel. Such a stern and sharp ideological divide in this matter led to the Covenant theologians excommunicating Dispensationalists from their circles in the early part of the twentieth century. The culture has suffered from the years of an apparently misplaced battle among what could be and ought to have been friendly theological cousins.

It continues today with the unnecessary separation among churches, academies, and ministerial organizations. Consequently, a proper question for this subject is as follows: *Is there a Continuity Calvinistic soteriology among the nineteenth through twenty-first-century Dispensationalists and, if so, what does that type of Dispensational soteriology present?* The two-part question provides a basis for both *historical inquiry* as well as *an interpretation of that historical data.* As for historical inquiry it allows for the assertions against Dispensationalism to be answered precisely from primary sources, i.e., from the pens of Dispensational teachers in the twentieth and twenty-first century.

Furthermore, the question requires that if the assertions from the Covenant Reformed/Calvinistic persuasion do not stand true then a positive, holistic interpretation of Dispensational and Calvinistic soteriology can be arranged and presented as a viable interpretation of that historical theological stream. Or if it is true, that Dispensationalism precludes a Covenant Continuity Reformed/Calvinistic soteriology paradigm, then that data needs to be arranged and presented as well through an interpretation that reveals such a conclusion.

In reviewing the literature from the Covenant/Reformed persuasion of theology many from that tradition accuse Dispensationalism, and by ipso facto Dispensationalists, as being unorthodox in their understanding and teaching of the gospel. Some Covenant Calvinist theologians seemingly assert three main issues against Dispensationalism: (1) Dispensationalism does not and/or cannot have a single continuity plan

---

confusion. All of the spiritually elected people in the LORD constitute the single one spiritual family of God.

Yet in this one family there are different historical members. Some are in the bride of Christ and others are not. Just as a physical earthly family can have various members in it, so too it seems the dispensationalists (at least those more Calvinistic forms) see one family of God with various members in it. Too, the Trinity could serve as a basis for this. The Godhead is one yet with three distinct members in it.

of redemption and instead teaches multiple plans of salvation; (2) Dispensationalism is Arminian/Semi-Pelagian in its soteriology instead of Calvinistic; and (3) Dispensationalism is weak on the overall sovereignty of God in both history and redemption. Sometimes these three concepts are expressed in a singular sentence. At other times the critics separate out these ideas into these three distinguishable categories.

The Methodology to Answering the Question

First, a review of the primary leaders of the Covenant Calvinist tradition will show the arguments that this tradition has been making against the Dispensational tradition. This position held by the Covenant Calvinist tradition seems to have existed for well over fifty years in the body of Christ. Therefore, a review and survey of those particular key accusations or assertions will set the stage for the specific areas that need examination from the teachers of the Dispensational tradition.

Second, in the quest to be as objective as possible, this research will evaluate and highlight the primary writings of some of the most well known and most highly trained, respected, and published Evangelical Dispensationalists[193] of the twentieth and twenty-first centuries. By examining first hand material with a focus on their articulation of the doctrine of God's sovereignty overall and soteriology in particular, that effort should bring forth some clarity on what a significant portion, though of course not all, Dispensationalists have taught on the doctrine of God's sovereignty and application of that sovereignty to a holistic soteriology.

Third, the methodology too will only evaluate those who claim or show evidence of affirming a Calvinistic and Dispensational view of Scripture. The Covenant Calvinists assert that the system of Dispensationalism, because of its Israel and Church distinction, cannot as a system affirm a singular, continuity, Calvinistic model of soteriology. Therefore, it does not require that a thesis show *all* Dispensationalists

---

[193] I classify all Dispensationalists as Evangelicals though some Dispensationalists quoted may be more aligned with the ecclesiastical structures of Fundamentalism. In such cases it is proper to keep in mind that all Fundamentalists are at least Evangelical on the core doctrines of the faith. However, not all Evangelicals are Fundamentalists as to be a Fundamentalist one usually has to embrace some type of non-hierarchical doctrinal scale and/or a type of spatial separatism (see Ernest Pickering's work, *Biblical Separation*).

embrace a singular, continuity, Calvinistic soteriology, and overall sovereignty of God emphasis. All that is needed is to show that *some* Dispensationalists indeed have and do affirm a view that aligns with a Reformed/Calvinist perspective on soteriology and overall sovereignty.

Additionally, it is only required to show that not only do some affirm such a Calvinistic continuity model of soteriology but that the system of Dispensationalism itself may do so without violating its core principles. Nothing within Dispensationalism precludes it from being able to easily embrace a Calvinistic continuity model of soteriology. In fact, the evidence seems to show that if the historical grammatical hermeneutic is applied consistently by the Dispensationalist he or she will arrive at a theological position fairly Calvinistic as well as unified in a Christological soteriology through all dispensations of history.

Fourth, once a historical analysis has been completed, this work will seek to synthesize from an Evangelical, Calvinistic, and Dispensational perspective the texts pertaining to the doctrines of God's sovereignty, grace, and man's responsibility. From that synthesis it will seek to defend the position that a normal historical grammatical hermeneutic, something essential to Dispensationalism, applied to Scripture yields a basic position more in line with God's sovereignty in salvation. Dispensationalism has historically recognized the emphasis in Scripture as God-centered in the doctrine of redemption rather than man-centered.

This seems to be something that has not been recognized by many from within the Reformed/Covenant theological tradition when evaluating Dispensational theology's soteriology. Dispensationalism is, or can easily be, generally speaking harmonious to an Augustinian/Reformed paradigm of thought because of its allegiance to historical grammatical interpretive methodologies. Both systems can use the same hermeneutic to soteriology texts.

Consequently, people within those two traditions ought to be able to come closer to one another in fellowship and mission when this first, and in some aspects second order, doctrine has common agreement among the two systems. In fact, to honor the teaching (Matt. 5:9) and prayer (John 17:23) of Christ for peace and unity in the body of Christ, as well as to meet the urgent need of the hour because of global advancement of Satanic Humanistic Liberalism, such a move should occur with due diligence when neither side has to discard first order doctrines or undermine the gospel.

An effort for more harmonization of Dispensationalism and Covenantalism around the gospel and first order truths could create a stronger missions method to stem the tide of Satanic Humanistic Liberalism. Colleges, universities, seminaries, geographical bodies of Christ, and missional organizations could partner together more effectively to combat the tide of Satanic Humanistic Liberal Progressivism that is undermining world progress.

This Book's Primary Point

The *position* of the work is that research reveals solid evidence that throughout the nineteenth through the twenty-first-century there have been some Dispensationalists, even primary leaders of the movement, that have indeed embraced a singular, continuity, Calvinistic model of soteriology while also affirming distinct members within the singular redeemed family of God. The *purpose* of this dissertation is narrow in focus with a distinct threefold objective: (1) to discern and delineate a soteriology of specific Dispensationalists who claim to affirm a Calvinistic soteriology; (2) to establish from those historical theologians a positive, holistic, and synthetic Reformed and Dispensational model of soteriology that honors a singular family of God ideology while also retaining the key distinctive markers of Dispensationalism with the various peoples of God in that one redeemed family; and (3) by that evidence and synthesis chart an honorable course where Dispensationalists and Covenantalists may overcome the historic division over a wrongly perceived first order doctrinal difference and consequently by that resolution freeing their consciences so they may peacefully and passionately cooperate with one another in a theological triage Great Commission ministry model.

Therefore, the overarching goal of this book is to reveal the specific and direct evidence, both historically and through current synthesis of biblical as well as historical data, that seems to refute the sweeping and broad generalizations by the Covenant Calvinist theologians that a Dispensationalist does not and cannot logically or consistently embrace a continuity and Calvinistic model of soteriology while also retaining a dispensational model of theology for the family of God in history. Evidence from past Dispensationalists and from this current writer, who identifies himself as a type of Dispensationalist, reveal that someone may embrace a thoroughgoing model of Dispensationalism while also retaining a some form of a Reformed model of soteriology in particular and theology in general.

Layout of the Book

This book consists of seven chapters including this introductory chapter. Chapter two elaborates on the two main types of evangelical theologies, Dispensational (Discontinuity) theology and Covenant (Continuity) theology along with the specific criticisms from that latter persuasion and tradition of thought. A litany of critical assertions has been made by the Covenant tradition against the Dispensational tradition for many decades and those criticisms have not yet abated.

Chapter three will specifically focus on thirty-seven Dispensationalists who affirm a Calvinistic/Reformed view of soteriology. Specific teachings from these Dispensationalists will be used to counter the specific criticisms of the ten Covenant Calvinists referenced in chapter two. In particular the doctrines of depravity, election, and efficacious grace will receive the priority of focus.

Chapter four will present the diversity among the Covenant Calvinists and Dispensationalists in general on the doctrine of the atonement, a subject that is often glossed over and/or apparently ignored by the Covenant critics of Dispensationalism. The debate over the extent of Christ's atonement is not an anomaly only within Dispensationalism. Even within the history of Covenant Calvinism a person will find a severe struggle to find consensus on that particular tenet of the faith. Additionally, within this doctrinal diversity there seems to be an avenue the Dispensationalist may travel to resolve such a tension by the application of a literal hermeneutic within a Trinitarian systematic grid to accomplish a balanced perspective on the extent of the atonement.

Chapter five presents a solitary dispensational model of soteriology from the Old Testament to the New Testament. That model will show that evidence exists that Dispensationalism can and has set forth a view of redemption where all believers form a single family of God even though there remain historical distinctions in the overall family of God. Yet this chapter also highlights some of the confusion created by some Dispensationalists due to the vernacular used in describing N.T. saints as "in Christ" while not designating that language for O.T. saints. A resolution to that dilemma is also proposed.

In chapter six this work will from a Dispensational perspective examine and exegete a few key biblical texts on God's foreknowledge, God's eternal decree, and explain Dispensationalism's stance against Open Theism and mere prescient/foresight models of election. It will cover the relationship between God's omniscience and man's responsibility and propose a balanced synthetic model that harnesses the strengths of both emphases found within Scripture while not minimizing either perspective.

Chapter seven offers a summary and conclusion to the book by proposing that the system of Dispensationalism and the Reformed system of theology can practically harmonize and coalesce together in a complementary theological and philosophical union. By way of summary it will show that the narrow primary soteriological points of Calvinism that are popular in Reformation theology align well with traditional Dispensationalism. Certainly some within Dispensationalism concur with that Reformation paradigm that includes the traditional points of a soteriological Calvinist construct, and a soteriological continuity rooted in the eternal covenant of redemption. Such consensus ought to, consequently, end the classic division in the body of Christ and help these two traditions of thought merge their hearts and minds, and naturally by way of practicality too their resources, into a more harmonious relationship for the cause of the gospel within the Great Commission.

Chapter 2. The Covenant Calvinists' Criticisms of Dispensationalism that Hinder a Coalescent Union

Personal Familiarity and Interest with this Interfaith Debate of the Decades

This historical and theological problem is one that I have followed for many years throughout my academic journey. Accordingly, because this division among the body of Christ has intrigued me for years, the topic sustains my interest and stimulates my imagination[194] in numerous avenues. The topic captivates my interest as this subject extends back to my first semester of undergraduate studies at North Greenville University. Within the first week of college, I discovered that among our student body, and even among some of the professors of theology, there stood a difference in the understanding of how God saved sinners. The issue of how God redeemed sinners caused some conflict among not only the student body but also within the theology faculty as well as surrounding ministers of the community.

At that time, I knew very little concerning the weightier and underlying theological themes relating to the gospel. I knew the basic facts about salvation. Yet as I studied Scripture with more discipline and depth, issues such as God's sovereignty, election, Covenant theology, and Dispensational theology became important topics sparking curiosity in me for quests of spiritual and academic study. Along that journey notable differences were highlighted and evaluated among the body of Christ.

I recall in particular my first tension with the idea of God's sovereignty over the reprobate in my New Testament survey class. Dr. Hal Freeman answered a question of mine concerning a passage in the book of Romans concerning election and reprobation (Romans 9). Needless to say, at that juncture I was not ready to award him with any praise for his answers. Rather, as with many who first encounter the doctrine of God's

---

[194] David Madsen, *Successful Dissertations and Theses: A Guide to Graduate Student Research from Proposal to Completion* (San Francisco, CA: Jossey-Bass Inc., Publishers, 1992), 34.

sovereignty in salvation, I would probably have been more inclined to hope for some ominous omen towards any who taught such ideas. Nonetheless, despite the unpopularity of this position with God's sovereignty, the professor affirmed that he believed in the doctrine of reprobation in some form. At this time in my theological journey, I had not yet studied much of anything on the various ideas on how reprobation worked in various theology models.

For the entire first year of college, I labored over these doctrines that many then and today classify as the "sovereign grace of God"[195] or the "doctrines of grace known as Calvinism."[196] Teachers would at times in lecture refer to the sovereignty of God, and the students daily debated the issues. The subject arose as often as did people's forks at the dinner table.

At the end of the spring semester, I promised myself that I would dive into the subject that summer while I had time to study that issue alone. However, one summer did not satisfy my heart. I purchased every book I could find on the topic. By the summer's end, I had developed an extensive library of over one hundred or so volumes related to this topic from the pens of the most notable intelligentsia among Christendom. Some of the works promoted Covenant Theology (and also more often than not Calvinism) while others countered that position under the umbrella of the theological system known as Dispensationalism (which seemed to have a mixture of Calvinists, modified Calvinists, and some Arminians too).

As I learned of the heated debate between these two broader theological perspectives, Covenant Theology and Dispensational Theology, I quickly realized that Covenant theologians were those that almost unanimously promoted the Calvinistic view of salvation. I also learned that the Covenant theologians strongly criticized not only the broad system of Dispensationalism but also the view of salvation from Dispensationalism that the Covenant theologians viewed as a serious error.

---

[195] Edwin H. Palmer, *The Five Points of Calvinism* (Grand Rapids, MI: Baker Books, 1972), 6.

[196] David N. Steele, Curtis C. Thomas, and S. Lance Quinn, *The Five Points of Calvinism: Defined, Defended, and Documented* (Phillipsburg, NJ: P&R Publishing Company, 2004), xviii.

This difference deeply intrigued me then as it presently does today. Many Covenant theologians wrote extensively that Dispensationalism caused great havoc in churches and that the system destroyed the gospel of grace. For example, one work in particular I read branded Dispensationalism and categorically labeled Dispensationalists for their supposedly Arminian soteriological position. The work *Lord and Christ* by Ernest Reisinger discussed the inherit dangers of Dispensationalism.

Reisinger, a Calvinist Covenant theologian, made a strong assertion that Dispensationalism stood for a weak Arminian theology. At that time in my academic journey I had not read a credible rebuttal of God's sovereignty in salvation and I was looking for one to effectively refute the Calvinist thought. In Reisinger's book I found these words against Dispensationalism:

> The nonlordship position is just the tip of a theological iceberg, a product of a faulty philosophical system and the literal hermeneutic of dispensationalism. I have noted that nonlordship is a child whose father is Arminianism and whose mother is dispensationalism. . . . the larger dispensational system of theology is diametrically opposed to that theology found in the pages of the Westminster Confession, the old Baptist Confession of 1689, and the Heidelberg Catechism. Dispensationalism would have been declared erroneous by the Synod of Dort, as was her husband Arminianism. Dispensational theology is nothing less than a frontal attack on Covenantal and Reformed theology.[197]

Those harsh and condemnatory words prompted my heart to study more about this system called Dispensationalism. At the time I figured maybe the Dispensational model of theology had an answer for the Covenant Calvinist theologian. In my thinking, maybe the Dispensationalist could reveal a position concerning God's saving work that would not present God's unconditional elective love of some solely by his ultimate choice. I hoped that the Dispensationalist could present

---

[197] Ernest C. Reisinger, *Lord and Christ: The Implications of Lordship for Faith and Life* (Phillipsburg, New Jersey, P&R Publishing, 1994), 17.

from Scripture and sound reasoning an alternative view than that which I found among the more Calvinistic tradition. My heart desired to find a reputable scholar or set of scholars to help me escape the weight I felt from the writings of the more Calvinistic theologians within Covenant theology.

With those hopes in mind, I endeavored to accumulate various Dispensational works in order to study their view on soteriology. For me then, as well as today, it only made sense to examine the various options and to examine those options as presented by the theologians who embraced the positions. From my perspective, too many today speak for a position or against a position without due diligence to really know the underlying ideas of each position. A mark of educational depth and mental maturity manifests itself in thorough research of contrasting ideas, even to the point of being able to argue for a perspective one does not really even personally affirm.

As I read the Dispensational theologies then, I had a hope that they might provide a solid and full refutation of God's sovereignty in salvation (the more Calvinistic expressions of it) and bring to me some relief in that gruesome issue that vexed my mind and heart. Though I did not realize it at that time, I at that season of my spiritual journey desired for my will to be more primary and center stage in the doctrinal discussion of salvation. My soteriology was more "me" centered instead of Christ centered.

Little did I know that such studies would offer me in fact a third alternative view, a view that retained not only the basic elements of God's sovereignty in salvation but extended that sovereignty to even other areas such as Israel's election and unconditional promises. The Dispensationalists I read too were most often a unique type of Calvinist.[198]

---

[198] It seems to me that there could be a case made that some Dispensational Calvinists, at least like some of those within the Baptist environment, are more in line with the Sandy Creek style of Calvinism than the Charlestonian Calvinist tradition. Or, outside of the Baptist ecclesiastical circles, it might be safely argued that some Covenant Calvinists are of the higher Calvinist traditions (much like the modern Reformed Protestant denomination; often supralapsarian models) whereas the Dispensational Calvinists align more with the low Calvinist tradition in the vein of maybe someone like Andrew Fuller, William Carey, E.Y. Mullins, W.A. Criswell, or even a Lutheran persuasion that honors the ideology of Martin Luther (much like the modern Missouri Synod Lutheran denomination; often infralapsarian or sublapsarian models). The various types of Calvinism are listed here at this link:

They generally did not embrace double predestination nor did they attempt to squeeze the all-inclusive texts of Christ's death into some grid that explained away the wideness of Christ's atonement for a view that his death benefited just the elect. They seemed, at least to my way of thinking, to strive for a very precise or careful balance between God's sovereignty on one hand and man's responsibility on the other hand.

Yet these Dispensationalists generally affirmed without reservation God's sovereign omnipotence and his unconditional elective love. That mixture was somewhat odd after being inundated with many monographs promoting the standard five point classical Calvinist scheme of soteriology, some that even affirmed a double predestination theory. Consequently, Dispensationalism in general seemed to avoid the common pitfalls of pressing a sovereignty or Calvinistic system so far that it implicated God for sin in the world.

Though many Calvinists would demur otherwise, it is ominously troubling to comprehend a confession that God does not author sin yet simultaneously hear within those of that confession an affirmation that God actively damns a soul by working unbelief into them for the purpose of damnation. John Calvin seems to have been conflicted himself in how to explain these matters. Sometimes he seems to have adopted an active decree that caused sin and damnation. In some places, however, he seems to have adopted views that recognized a passive decree where God allowed people to damn themselves by their own choice to destroy themselves. Thankfully, as he aged and wrote commentaries, he seems to have obtained more balance. Sadly, some fail to recognize his revisions.

Dispensationalists have often expressed concerns about ideologies or doctrinal teachings that promote God as the agent causing sin and damnation (high Calvinism models, often supralapsarian decree models). For example, Dispensationalist Dr. Paige Patterson opined how "troubling" it is to realize some forms of Calvinism lead to the "inevitable conclusion that a thoroughly consistent" Calvinistic "message made God in some way or another the author of evil," which creates a severe problem

---

https://reformedforhisglory.wordpress.com/2013/08/09/types-of-calvinism-a-comprehensive-list/

for his holiness as well as calls "into question both the justice and the universal love of God."[199]

Dispensationalists, at least from my observations and historical affiliations within Dispensationalism, have generally steered clear of such problems. Though that is not to say Dispensationalism does not have its own share of inadequacies and theological banana peels on which many have slipped in their theological pilgrimage. Yet it is to say that at least in this area their allegiance to historical grammatical hermeneutics, the original or plain interpretive methodology, seems to have governed them well in those areas and protected them from slipping into what may appear logical to their humanly devised system, but in reality may not display very well God's more pure form of logic upon such matters as verified by the specific words of the sacred text.

Nonetheless, the twentieth and twenty-first-century has contained an ongoing series of criticisms against Dispensationalism's soteriology. The charge made against Dispensationalism, which it is unorthodox, did not come only from Dr. Earnest Reisinger. Over the years in following this debate I accumulated numerous works from both the Dispensational tradition and the Covenant tradition. Those from the Covenant tradition regularly questioned Dispensationalism's orthodoxy in the doctrine of redemption.

Yet in accumulating these diverse resources it highlighted that those systematic models are really the only two options for those who affirm the full authority of Scripture. For now, even with about 2000 years of reflection and rhetoric from the least to greatest in intelligentsia, no theologian or movement of theologians who honor the authority of Scripture has really created any new model outside of these two systems. Even my own model, which I describe as a sublapsarian sequenced soteriology (Dynamic/Sequenced Sovereign Salvation), still has much alignment with the various aspects from the main models.[200] This is so

---

[199] Paige Patterson, "*Foreword*," in *Salvation and Sovereignty* by Kenneth Keathley (Nashville TN: B&H Publishing, 2010), viii.

[200] I would describe my model in the way that I heard Paige Patterson once describe the doctrine of election to me at an evangelism conference in South Carolina. Election is unconditional on what lost man does (he or she contributes nothing to it), yet it is conditioned on what God does. Too, E.Y. Mullins (who also seemed to be a sublapsarian style of Calvinist as I am) articulated a sequenced election in what some of us call

because the categories that we work with as theologians have been established by God himself in the holy text.

Though a continuum exists as to how much continuity and discontinuity one adheres to in his or her particular enunciation of the models, the fact remains even so that these are the models the person must work with if serious about biblical studies. Every theologian who embraces the eternal divinity and historical humanity of Christ along with the reliability and truthfulness of Scripture will find themselves somewhere within one of these models, if not maybe even in a synthesized hybrid of the two.[201]

Through gathering the many volumes pertaining to Covenant (continuity) and Dispensational (discontinuity) systems I grew tremendously in my theology overall. In particular I have strengthened my understanding concerning these two theological systems and how they have developed over history and how they have interacted with each other.

However, it occurred to me in reading through the writings of many Dispensational theologians that many of these theologians have historically presented a picture of a sovereign God that seems to contrast the picture I should have found according to the Covenant Calvinist theologians' criticisms. Behind many, though certainly not all, of my

---

aeviternity (a period of reality in between eternity and earthly time). Mullins spoke of this in his work *A Christian Religion in its Doctrinal Expression* (p. 347). When God chose or chooses to elect person "A" he also takes into the account the good works that person will do as he considers to elect person "B" in the sequence. In such a model the means unto the end remains holistic and intertwined. It would explain why in Scripture that even though God alone elects we still read that the blood of souls can still rest on the hands of those who fail to witness (see Ezekiel 3; 33; & Acts 20). High supralapsarian models of election and predestination seem to exclude any means or sequence in how God elects. Though God does not elect based upon man's faith response (as in Arminianism), he does seem to determine in accordance with the witness of the previously elected and converted ones that he uses (see Eph. 2:10) for the progression of election and conversion. As the Calvinist Spurgeon prayed, "God save the elect and elect some more." The eternal of election of sinners has within it the means God established for the salvation of these people. Yet these means do not include the actions of the lost for one's own election and conversion. Lost man contributes nothing to his own election and conversion.

[201] Walter Kaiser seems to be a good example of someone who steers a mediating position between the standard Covenantal schemes and the standard Dispensational schemes. His promise theology seems to have a mixture of both systems.

varied sources of Dispensational writers I have found teachers who stood as renowned scholars in their field of study and who also embraced what appears to be overall a thorough Calvinistic continuity soteriology model.

The writings from some of the prominent Dispensationalists of the twentieth and twenty-first-century, like that of Dr. Lewis Sperry Chafer,[202] Dr. John Walvoord,[203] Dr. Charles Ryrie,[204] Dr. Dwight Pentecost,[205] Dr. Robert Lightner,[206] Dr. John MacArthur,[207] the Doctors of the Feinberg family,[208] Dr. Arnold G. Fruchtenbaum,[209] and more, seem to show Dispensationalism does have a strong root to the Calvinistic continuity soteriology of the Reformation era. It seems severely inaccurate, maybe even dishonest, to suggest that Dispensationalism either cannot or does not have a significant portion of that tradition which accepts an Augustinian[210]

---

[202] Lewis Sperry Chafer, *The Ephesian Letter: Doctrinally Considered* (New York, New York, Loizeaux Brothers, 1935), 34-37. See also Lewis Sperry Chafer, *Systematic Theology*, vol. 1 (Grand Rapids, MI: Kregel Publications, 1993), 222.

[203] John Walvoord, *The Holy Spirit* (Grand Rapids, MI: Zondervan Publishing, 1958), 119.

[204] Charles C. Ryrie, *Basic Theology: A Popular Systematic Guide To Understanding Biblical Truth*, (Colorado Springs, Colorado: Chariot Victor Publishing, 1996), 312.

[205] J. Dwight Pentecost, *Things Which Become Sound Doctrine* (Grand Rapids, MI: Zondervan Publishing, 1969), 140.

[206] Robert P. Lightner, *Sin, the Savior, and Salvation: The Theology of Everlasting Life* (Grand Rapids, MI: Kregel Publications, 1991), 148.

[207] John MacArthur, *The MacArthur New Testament Commentary: Acts 13-28* (Chicago, Ill: Moody Press, 1996), 94.

[208] John S. Feinberg, *Continuity and Discontinuity: Perspectives on the Relationship Between the Old and New Testaments*, ed. John S. Feinberg (Wheaton, Ill: Crossway Books, 1988), 70, 71.

[209] Arnold G. Fruchtenbaum, *God's Will & Man's Will: Predestination, Election, & Free Will* (San Antonio, TX: Ariel Ministries, 2013), 31-95.

[210] Alan Cairns, "*Augustinianism*," in *Dictionary of Theological Terms* (Greenville, SC: Ambassador Emerald International Publishing, 2002), 47-48.

and Protestant Reformation soteriology in the tradition of Luther[211] and Calvin.[212]

A Goal from this Work: A Hopeful Reconciliation within a Theological Triage

In monograph after monograph, many Dispensational theologians seem to offer substantive answers to their Covenant Calvinist critics. In doing so they seem to present a picture that exalts God's glory and sovereignty in the doctrine of soteriology. Covenant theologians appear to have strong disdain, which they have time and again expressed, against Dispensational theologians. What I *should* have found, according to Covenant theologians, has differed from what I have found over the years in accumulating materials on this topic.

Consequently, could a thorough response from the historical teachers of the Dispensational system to the Covenant Reformed accusations, along with an arranged order presenting a Dispensational soteriology, help resolve much of the unnecessary division in the body of Christ between these two theological traditions? More unity within the body of Christ would occur if these two traditions could recognize how much unity does exist with each other within the doctrine of redemption. If the other fundamentals of the faith are embraced, and the gospel itself agreed upon, then these two traditions could organizationally combine resources for the global efforts of the Great Commission. Instead of splitting and splintering from one another and in that diluting organizational resources, greater unity could help bring with it greater organizational resources for advancing the gospel of Christ.

Additionally, as a byproduct of realizing there is unity among these two traditions on the doctrine of soteriology, this could greatly help these two branches of Christendom learn how to cooperate together in a

---

[211] Timothy George, "*Martin Luther*," in *Biographical Dictionary of Evangelicals*, ed. Timothy Larsen (Downers Grove, IL: Inter-Varsity Press, 2003), 375-379.

[212] D.F. Wright, "*John Calvin*," *Biographical Dictionary of Evangelicals*, ed. Timothy Larsen (Downers Grove, IL: Inter-Varsity Press, 2003), 109-112.

theological triage[213] paradigm of ministry for the Great Commission of making disciples. Just as allopathic and osteopathic medical doctors work together for a person's overall health and healing (often in the same medical practice), though with different methodologies, so too both Dispensational and Covenant theologians should be able to positively work together for the cause of the gospel, especially when they agree on the fundamentals of the faith, including most importantly the gospel. This unity should be strengthened more when the nuanced versions of God's sovereignty align between the two traditions.

Maybe there needs to be a radical reformation today through a breed of theologians who are courageous enough to avoid being schismatic and sectarian over non-essential doctrines. As Dr. Hugh T. Kerr says, Protestantism has a major problem of falling prey to "sheer negativism" when it as a movement understands itself "as no more than a protest movement in reaction to what it regards as falsehood and error."[214] A Covenant theologian and Dispensational theologian ought to be able to lead the way in a positive presentation of Christianity when they are allies in the cause of the gospel. The danger of "scholasticism and superstition, all the denominational bickering and sectarianism have obscured the essence of the Christian gospel," and because of that these two systems of theology, if properly balanced with a proper understanding of the essentials, could lead the way "out of the confusion and ambiguity which preclude the possibility of affirming a positive message."[215]

As the conclusions of this research will show, Dispensationalists generally are not only in agreement with the Covenant Calvinists on the fundamentals, but *some* are also in line with the Covenant Calvinists in their soteriology. That alignment produces an even stronger bond that ought to be recognized by both traditions. Dr. Charles C. Ryrie has wisely said to this matter:

---

[213] R. Albert Mohler Jr., "*The Pastor as Theologian*," in *A Theology for the Church*, ed. Daniel L. Akin (Nashville, TN: B&H Publishing, 2007), 930-932.

[214] Hugh T. Kerr, *Positive Protestantism: A Return to First Principles* (Englewood Cliff, NJ: Prentice Hall Publishers, 1963), 4.

[215] Ibid., 17.

Some doctrines are more important than others, so it particularly behooves us not to cut off our fellowship from those who share similar views . . . . There are few enough these days who believe in the fundamentals of the faith, and to ignore those who have declared themselves on the side of truth of God is unwise. Something is wrong with our circles of fellowship, sense of priority, or doctrine of unity when conservatives view fellow conservatives as the opposition party and then find their theological friends among those who are teaching and promoting error. . . . There are . . . large areas of agreement between dispensationalists and nondispensationalists.[216]

A Plethora of Historical Criticisms

Although Ernest Reisinger's view concerning Dispensational theology has been stated above, this one statement does not suffice. The numerous statements to follow in this literature review may astound any reader that has even a little theological perspicacity. The assertions made by some Covenant Calvinist theologians show how gravely concerned they are over the gospel. Such concern itself is commendable. Yet their accusations imply that Dispensational theology falls outside of any legitimate interpretive options for a Christian theology. In some places the assertions make Dispensationalism sound more like a false world religion rather than a legitimate interpretive option within the umbrella of conservative orthodox Christianity.

It would not have been unusual for one or two less than noble ministers to speak sanctimoniously against a particular theological tradition. In this social media-driven world critics abound at every angle. Even more so, it would not have caused undue shock for a professional theologian here and there to make unsound and unfair remarks toward a particular theological tradition. Libraries with historical works from all ages of time contain thousands of volumes that successfully prove that writers, teachers, preachers, and the like at times make unsound and unfounded remarks against theological persuasions they do not affirm.

---

[216] Charles C. Ryrie, *Dispensationalism* (Chicago, IL: Moody Press, 1995), 212.

However, if any representative of Christianity embarks to expose some theological position as flawed, erroneous, heretical, or devilishly deceptive it only goes without saying that the individual should present the view with honesty. Furthermore, the research to which the conclusions are drawn ought to be wide enough and comprehensive enough to offer credibility to the conclusions. In the case of the research herein, it shows that the assertions from the Covenant Calvinist critics are not presenting a full and balanced picture of Dispensationalism in regards to soteriology. With that being said, it appears that *Dispensationalism has suffered more harm from dishonest representations than it has from its own tensions and discrepancies, especially when concerning the doctrine of soteriology.*

Some may think this statement is an exaggeration. Therefore, I will present some of the charges of error laid against Dispensationalists from several literature sources. Later in this work I believe the historical data from many Dispensationalists will offer a counter to those unjustified assertions from our Covenant Calvinist friends. I think any honest or objective reader will be able to discern then the difference between what the Covenant theologian *says* the Dispensationalist believes and what many Dispensationalists *actually* believe and specifically teach.

Over Fifty Years of Criticisms from the Covenant Calvinist Tradition

There have been numerous theologians in the past 50 or so years from the date of this writing that have accused Dispensationalism as an inherently Arminian or Semi-Pelagian system of theology. Two constant accusations appear throughout various monographs. Some accuse Dispensationalists of teaching multiple plans of salvation, i.e., one plan of redemption for Israel and another plan for the body of Christ. Additionally, some accuse Dispensationalists as being Arminian and/or unorthodox on the sovereignty of God in the application of grace to sinners.

However, such accusations do not seem to hold true when evaluating the mainline Dispensationalists that have been the primary leaders of the movement. Sure, there have been *some* Dispensationalists that have embraced Arminian or Semi-Pelagian views. For example, Finis Jennings Dake adopted a Dispensational view of Scripture within an

Arminian non-Calvinistic model.[217] His popularity spread an Arminian view of Dispensationalism.

Furthermore, some of this occurred too as the Charismatic and Pentecostal movements embraced the Dispensational view of Ecclesiology (the Church), Israelology (Israel's role), and Eschatology (End Times; Prophecy) while rejecting the foundational principles of historical grammatical interpretation in the areas of soteriology (salvation). In the early twentieth century this Charismatic movement developed and overall embraced the increasingly popular system of Dispensationalism. Charismatic Pentecostalism latched onto Dispensationalism, though without its consistent application of the normal or original intent hermeneutic in the doctrines of man's sin and God's sovereignty in history and grace. Shortly after that movement was born or emphasized in the early 1900s, this movement incorporated into its theology many aspects of Dispensationalism in the areas of eschatology.[218]

But all that is needed to counter the Covenant Calvinist/Reformed persuasion of thought is to show that *some* Dispensationalists do not teach an Arminian or Semi-Pelagian view of salvation. If some (or certainly if many, as will be shown) within Dispensationalism are thoroughly within the Continuity Calvinist or Reformed stream of thought in soteriology that alone disproves the sweeping thesis that Dispensationalism itself automatically by default leads to an unorthodox view of salvation.

Additionally, if a majority or even a significant portion of the primary Dispensational leaders teach not only a solitary continuity in the plan of redemption with Israel and the Church, but also embrace a Calvinistic view of sovereignty in the application of grace, that adds even more weight to the view that Dispensationalism is neither inherently Arminian nor unorthodox in the doctrine of soteriology. I use the term unorthodox to refer to the view that multiple plans of salvation exist in scripture. Such a view, held by any teacher of any tradition, violates a fundamental of the faith and constitutes an unorthodox view. An Arminian or faith based view of election would not make one unorthodox so long as

---

[217] Finis Jennings Dake, *God's Plan for Man* (Lawrenceville, GA: Dake Bible Sales, 1977), 876.

[218] Robert G. Clouse, "*Pentecostal Churches*," in *The New International Dictionary of the Christian Church* (Grand Rapids, MI: Zondervan, 1978), 763-764.

justification by faith alone has been embraced. But for those in the more Calvinistic persuasion, they would see that prescient view of election as an error. If the evidence yields the position that Dispensationalism has a strong history of affirming a single plan of salvation as well as a significant dedication to salvation by the Lord's sovereign providence of electing sinners unto redemption, which I believe such evidence does exist and that will be shown in subsequent chapters, then that evidence speaks strongly against the criticisms from the Covenant theology tradition.

Nonetheless, it seems wise to note why a gap may exist in Dispensational literature concerning the doctrine of salvation. Due to the massive amount of effort put into defending and promoting the doctrines of end times, the distinction between Israel and the church, and other related doctrines within those areas, it remains plausible that many Dispensationalists may have failed to precisely articulate, write enough, and/or defend the doctrines of sovereignty in salvation. If so, that lack of precision, stress, and emphasis in this area may have left the movement (as a whole) with a void concerning God's sovereignty in salvation and/or the unity among the family of God in the plan of redemption. This void may have opened the doors for many to come forth in the Covenant Calvinist tradition to challenge the Dispensational system in this area.

Many from the Covenant Calvinist camp have openly charged Dispensationalists as being heretical. Leading scholars in that movement, who certainly have the ability and skill to make solid evaluations evidenced by the credentials they hold, have apparently erred and presented a skewed and flawed picture of what Dispensationalists believe. Even worse, there is to date no movement to openly correct and alter this by admitting this error among their tradition.

Specific Literature with Assertions Against Dispensationalism from the Covenant Reformed Theologian

Numerous authors have launched complete works against Dispensationalism. As noted earlier, the charges set forth against Dispensationalism revolve around the doctrine of soteriology. The criticisms examined in this section range from pastors and professors. They all generally present the same theme in one sense or another. The criticisms have been fairly constant from the middle of the twentieth century until the present.

1. A.W. Pink (1886-1952)

As a student in Moody Bible Institute, though only for a short time, A.W. Pink initially embraced a Dispensational view of theology. Throughout his life he served as a pastor to numerous churches ranging from Colorado, California, Kentucky, and South Carolina.[219] "Biographer Iain Murray observes of Pink, 'the widespread circulation of his writings after his death made him one of the most influential evangelical authors in the second half of the twentieth century."[220]

As he developed in his theological understanding he eventually rejected Dispensational theology.[221] He then offered some stern criticisms against the tradition. He speaks of Dispensationalism as teaching a view of Old Testament salvation that took place without grace. In his words, Dispensationalism taught salvation of Old Testament saints by works.[222]

He argued in contrast to this perception that "The Old Testament saints were subjects of the same everlasting covenant, had the same blessed Gospel, were begotten unto the same ecclesiastical heritage as the New Testament saints. From Abel onwards, God has dealt with sinners in sovereign grace, and according to the merits of Christ's redemptive work—which was retroactive in its value and efficacy."[223] According to Pink, Dispensationalism was a "pernicious error."[224]

---

[219] A.W. Pink, *A Study on Dispensationalism*, Editor's *Biography of A.W. Pink* (No place of publication, Gideon House Books, 2015), 5.

[220] Ibid., 6.

[221] James Quiggle has noted that the reason Pink departed from Dispensationalism pertains to the Hyper-Dispensationalism teachings some introduced to him. As Quiggle stated, "he left because someone introduced him to hyper-dispensationalism: a complete separation of the OT from the NT. His neo-Puritan sensibilities would not accept that error, and he unfortunately condemned the entire dispensational system because of it." Furthermore, it appears he moved into more of a supralapsarian form of Calvinism, an extreme version (aka: High/Hyper Calvinism or Bezanism).

[222] A.W. Pink, *A Study on Dispensationalism*, Editor's *Biography of A.W. Pink* (No place of publication, Gideon House Books, 2015), 24.

[223] Ibid., 25.

[224] Ibid., 8.

His words leave little room for doubt as to what he thought of Dispensationalism. His criticisms against Dispensationalism make it appear that Dispensationalism rejects the gospel of grace, embraces a works view of salvation, and robs the Old Testament saints from the same heritage or destination as the saints of the New Testament. His views could hardly be any more demeaning to a theological system.

2. C. Norman Kraus (1924-2018)

As a Mennonite theologian, professor of theology at Goshen College, and graduate of Princeton Theological Seminary, Mr. Kraus joins the plethora of twentieth century theologians in asserting that Dispensationalism has a serious flaw in the doctrine of soteriology. Though more cordial and conciliatory in tone and presentation than some, Kraus still took issue with Dispensationalism as a whole system. While acknowledging his appreciation for the Dispensational tradition in its effort to "preserve historic Christian concepts at a time when they were being sacrificed on the alters of liberalism and higher criticism," Kraus still accused the Dispensational interpretation of Scripture as being a position that employs "a different approach to salvation in each dispensation."[225] Kraus recognized that at the time of his writing Dispensationalists had tried to "vigorously" answer "the charge that dispensations were ways of salvation," but even so his conclusion was that it was "difficult to see" how their defense to such accusations of more than "one way of salvation" could be "taken seriously."[226]

3. Clarence Bass (1922-2021)

In similar fashion to A.W. Pink, Dr. Bass in his earlier years embraced Dispensationalism. Bass says of himself, "I was reared in the dispensational system, and the formative years of my spiritual development occurred under the ministry of a godly pastor who taught

---

[225] C. Norman Kraus, *Dispensationalism in America: Its Rise and Development* (Richmond, VA: John Knox Press, 1958), 19, 118.

[226] Ibid., 117, 120.

it."[227] Bass seems to have maintained this perspective of theology until sometime into his doctoral program where his studies on J.N. Darby began to lead him towards a different view of theology. At that point he claims he saw Dispensationalism's "basic hermeneutical pattern of interpretation" as a position "broadly divergent from that of the historic faith."[228]

Dr. Bass concluded that the distinction of Law and Grace in Dispensational theology requires those within that persuasion of thought to embrace multiple plans of redemption in contrast to a unified view of redemption. In his mind the logically consistent Dispensationalist must believe Israel, who lived under the law, and the Church, who lives under grace, must therefore come to God through different avenues. As he says,

> The presupposition of the difference between law and grace, between Israel and the church, between the different relations of God to men in the different dispensations, when carried to its logical conclusion will inevitably result in a multiple form of salvation—that men are not saved the same way in all ages . . . . This distinction implies that there are two principles under which man has been saved—law and grace.[229]

Dr. Bass' views show that he thought the Dispensational system inherently leads to multiple plans of redemption. In fact, he states that after leaving Dispensationalism he realized that the "unity of the divine redemptive plan" became "meaningful" to him.[230] This unity of redemption he found meaningful supposedly cannot or will not exist in a logically coherent Dispensational system. Multiple plans of redemption for Israel, the Church, and even in the future for other believers in other

---

[227] Clarence B. Bass, *Backgrounds to Dispensationalism: Its Historical Genesis and Ecclesiastical Implications* (Grand Rapids, MI: Baker Book House, 1960), 9.

[228] Ibid.

[229] Ibid., 36.

[230] Ibid., 9.

ages must occur, according to Bass' understanding, in a Dispensational system.²³¹

Yet Bass realized there were strong protests by Dispensationalists to those types of assertions. Even so, in spite of such vehement protests where "Dispensationalists do insist that there is no multiple basis of salvation in their system," Bass concludes that the Dispensational system itself makes a "protest against them" because "if one were to take seriously the dichotomies involved here—Israel-church, church-kingdom, gospel of the kingdom — gospel of grace, etc. — would one not conclude, in spite of protest to the contrary, that multiple basis is inevitable for one who orients his theology in this system?"²³²

4. Curtis Crenshaw (b. 1945) & 5. Grover Gunn (b. 1949)

Covenant Calvinist theologians such as Curtis Crenshaw and Grover Gunn have also made strong criticisms against Dispensationalism. Their thoughts continue to define Dispensationalism as a system implying multiple plans of redemption as well as an Arminian soteriology. They have said:

> When students of the Bible come into the doctrines of grace (TULIP), they nearly always leave Dispensationalism . . . . The inherit weaknesses in dispensationalism have not really been changed, such as the assertion that Israel and the church are distinct (with all the implications for two ways of salvation) . . . . Perhaps the reason is that they are so taken up with eschatology that they have no consensus in soteriology. I have seen untold dozens of books by dispensationalists on eschatology but none by a compendium of dispensational scholars on soteriology. In the new book, *Dispensationalism, Israel and the Church*, the same Arminianism prevails. We repeatedly read of God's grace being "provided," that saints "can" have God's grace, and that

---

[231] Ibid., 36.

[232] Ibid., 36.

redemption is "made possible." Potential words are all they can muster since they do not believe in effectual grace.[233]

In particular, certain key points from that deserve attention. Their charges against Dispensationalism are as follows: (1) embracing the doctrines of grace produces a theological environment that naturally leads away from Dispensationalism; (2) inherent weaknesses exist in the Dispensational system itself, which is defined as the two tier structure of promises in God's plan for Israel and the Church; (3) God having a plan for Israel and a plan for the Church implies two ways of salvation; (4) eschatology has been the main focus of Dispensationalism and not soteriology;[234] and (5) Arminianism continues to be the main mantra of modern Dispensationalists.

Some may believe that the accusation made by Crenshaw and Gunn does not exist in this present century. But that is not the case. Others join that twentieth century chorus in this century and continue to assert that Dispensationalism does not or cannot affirm an orthodox continuity view of soteriology, much less affirm a Calvinistic continuity model.

6. *Chad Brand (b. 1954-2023) & 7. Tom Pratt (b. 1945)*

Dr. Chad Brand was my former systematic theology professor when he taught at North Greenville University. He has made similar claims as what Crenshaw and Gunn made. Dr. Brand, who most recently taught theology at The Southern Baptist Theological Seminary, a seminary

---

[233] Curtis Crenshaw and Grover E. Gunn III, *Dispensationalism Today, Yesterday, and Tomorrow* (Memphis, TN: Footstool Publications, 1985, reprinted ed. 86, 87, 89, 94, 95), xi, xii, 77.

[234] Of the stated criticisms I would concur that the first 200 years of the movement known as Dispensationalism did indeed spend an enormous amount of time on the doctrines of ecclesiology and eschatology, which naturally meant other doctrines like soteriology would receive less focus. Such attention likely did leave a vacuum within the area of soteriology. The prominent voices of the movement, who wrote full treatises of theology, did write and teach on salvation. But by popular demand the Dispensationalists were apparently largely in demand for their emphasis on eschatological themes.

where scholarship has always been promoted as a central priority,[235] has, along with Tom Pratt, recently stated that Dispensationalism "requires multiple pathways to . . . salvation."[236] Note that they said *requires*.

Dr. Brand and Tom Pratt assert even more specifically this: "We believe that a careful reading of the literature of both traditional (more explicitly) and, in some case, progressive dispensationalism (more implicitly and ambiguously) will verify this conclusion, if only in the failure to state unequivocally that personal salvation has always been achieved by grace through faith."[237] They do mention, however that "perhaps more clarity will be forthcoming as the debate continues."[238]

Maybe this work will provide that "unequivocal" assertion and "clarity" that Pratt and Brand would like to see. If it does, will they (or other Covenant Calvinists) yield and admit such a clear position exists? Only time will tell. Certainly it seems as if others have countered those assertions already and yet still such criticisms have not died.

8. Russell Moore (b. 1971)

Likewise, Dr. Russell Moore, former professor at Southern Baptist Theological Seminary, who earned his Ph.D from The Southern Baptist Theological Seminary, wrote in a similar vein as did Brand and Pratt. He asserted that the older forms of Dispensationalism had "difficulty" in

---

[235] Gregory A. Wills, *Southern Baptist Theological Seminary 1859-2009* (Oxford, NY: Oxford University Press, 2009), 311.

[236] Chad O. Brand and Tom Pratt Jr., "*The Progressive Covenantal View*," in *Perspectives on Israel and the Church: 4 Views*, ed. Chad Brand (Nashville, TN: B&H Publishing Group, 2015), 236. Dr. Brand was and is one of the most instrumental teachers in my life. Though we differ in this area, I have the utmost respect for him. Through his teachings I embraced some of the most important doctrinal truths for an Evangelical faith. He is a great teacher, father, and husband and I praise God for his life, love, and leadership.

[237] Ibid., footnote 12.

[238] Ibid.

articulating a unified view of soteriology.²³⁹ He, however, does offer some praises of the newer Progressive Dispensationalism models for their now "one unified plan of redemption."²⁴⁰ But as noted above, Brand and Pratt, still apparently believe that even some progressive Dispensationalists affirm multiple avenues to salvation.²⁴¹ So Moore and Brand agree in their view that historic Dispensationalism had two plans of redemption while differing to a degree on the newer Progressive Dispensationalism model. It would be interesting to know their stand on modern Dispensationalists who might be classified as a revised form of Dispensationalism but not per se Progressive Dispensationalists. Would they still be classified as teaching two plans of redemption?

9. *Reginald Kimbro (b. 1962)*

Reginald Kimbro wrote an entire work attempting to show that "Calvinism and Dispensationalism remain mutually exclusive."²⁴² In chapter five, "Dispensationalism and the Doctrine of Salvation," the author wrote to show an inherent heresy permeates the Dispensationalists' view of salvation. Again he laid out the often repeated charge that Dispensationalists believe in multiple plans of salvation. In chapter six, "Current Dispensational Unrest Over the Nature of Salvation," the author pursued the doctrines of grace in particular. He examined the acronym TULIP²⁴³ in light of the statements from many of the prominent Dispensational teachers. It appears, however, the author selectively cited statements to make an unaware reader believe the Dispensationalist

---

[239] Russell D. Moore, *The Kingdom of Christ: The New Evangelical Perspective* (Wheaton, IL: Crossway Books, 2004), 91.

[240] Ibid.

[241] Chad O. Brand and Tom Pratt Jr., "*The Progressive Covenantal View*," in *Perspectives on Israel and the Church: 4 Views*, ed. Chad Brand (Nashville, TN: B&H Publishing Group, 2015), footnote 12, 236.

[242] Reginald C. Kimbro, *The Gospel According to Dispensationalism: A doctrinal survey of the system that permeated Fundamentalism* (Toronto Canada, Wittenburg Publications, 1995), 4.

adheres to Arminian theology. In one of his most pointed statements he says,

> The history of the twentieth century provides many examples of influential leaders embracing Dispensationalism while forsaking the consistent Calvinism of their heritage in the process. Except for retaining the misstated doctrine of eternal security, Dispensationalism embraced a thoroughly Arminian theology, though few of its adherents did so consciously.[244]

10. Donald G. Bloesch (1928-2010)

Even modern systematic theologies have accused Dispensationalists of presenting a skewed gospel. One particular systematic revisited one old charge that seems to have been answered by Dispensationalists for years. Dr. Donald G. Bloesch, a Covenant theologian, stated, "Contrary to what some dispensationalists allege, the theme of salvation by grace alone (sola gratia) is very much evident in the Old Testament as well as the New."[245] This accusation refers to the idea that supposedly Dispensationalism teaches the entire O.T. was a period of Law and the N.T. is a period of grace. This division, according to their perspective, means Israelites were saved by obedience to the Law and believers after the time of Christ are saved by grace.

11. Robert L. Reymond (1932-2013)

Another systematic work stresses that same point, yet with more vigor. Professor Robert L. Reymond wrote along the same line as Donald Bloesch. Dr. Reymond asserted that Dispensationalism teaches

---

[243] TULIP is an acronym that stands for Total Depravity, Unconditional Election, Limited Atonement, Irresistible Grace, and Perseverance or Preservation of the Saints.

[244] Ibid., 153.

[245] Donald G. Bloesch, *Essentials of Evangelical Theology*, vol. 1, *God, Authority, and Salvation* (Peabody, MA: Prince Press, 1998), 181.

discontinuity in the plan of redemption. Note clearly what Reymond thought of the two systems of theology in their perspectives on soteriology.

> It is difficult to conceive of two evangelical perspectives on the Old Testament faith differing more radically. The Covenantal perspective stresses the unity and continuity of redemptive history; the dispensational perspective stresses the discontinuity of redemptive history. The former insists that the Old Testament saints were saved through conscious faith in the future, anticipated sacrificial work of the promised Messiah in their behalf. The latter insists, since the Old Testament saints *did not know* about his future sacrificial work because God had not revealed it to them, that they were saved through a general "faith toward God . . . manifested in other ways." In these regards these two theological systems are mutually exclusive. One may be pardoned if he were to conclude then that these two views advocate *different* Old Testament plans of salvation, the *former* insisting upon the necessity of faith in the person and sacrificial work of the coming Messiah for salvation, the *latter* insisting upon the necessity of faith in God for salvation that was actually devoid of any conscious awareness that "without the shedding of [Messiah's] blood there is no forgiveness" (Heb. 9:22). But this means, since the dispensational scholars happily affirm that the New Testament saint believes unto a salvation with a faith which has precisely Messiah's death work as its saving object, that, from the perspective of the saints before and the saints after the cross, there are *at least two* different plans of salvation in Scripture. I say "at least two . . . plans . . ." because dispensational scholars actually insist that Old Testament saving faith in God was manifested in "different *ways,*" depending on the dispensation, and to prove the point they refer to the "long record in Hebrews 11:1-40."[246]

---

[246] Robert L. Reymond, *A New Systematic Theology of the Christian Faith* (Nashville, TN: Thomas Nelson Inc., 1998), 509-510.

Such thoughts seem to ignore, as will be shown, the mainstream of Dispensationalism that does not appear to have taught a discontinuity view of salvation between the testaments. Ambiguous statements, which may exist, should never serve as the guide to interpreting the clearer statements. Much of the teaching from Dispensationalism seems to have been thoroughly sound in the doctrine of a solitary continuity of salvation in both the O.T. and N.T. by God's grace alone through faith in that grace alone. The Calvinistic portion of Dispensationalism does not seem to have denied the idea of God's one elect family through all ages.

12. John Gerstner (1914-1996) & 13. R.C. Sproul (1939-2017)

Two other famous and modern theologians of the twentieth and twenty-first-century deserve our attention. Dr. John Gerstner and Dr. R.C. Sproul both have sharply criticized Dispensationalism and its doctrine of salvation. Gerstner mentored Sproul so it makes sense to examine the assertions of both theologians together. Sproul seems to have adopted his mentor's views in this area, and he continues to present similar views in the twenty-first-century concerning Dispensationalism that Gerstner did in the twentieth century.

Gerstner had some of the most impeccable credentials. "He earned both a Master of Divinity degree and a Master of Theology degree from Westminster Theological Seminary. He earned his Doctor of Philosophy degree from Harvard University in 1945," and after serving as a pastor in several places he accepted "a professorship at Pittsburgh-Xenia Theological Seminary, where he taught church history for over 30 years. He was a visiting professor at Trinity Evangelical Divinity School in Deerfield, Ill., and adjunct professor at Knox Theological Seminary in Fort Lauderdale", Florida.[247]

In regard to Dispensationalism Dr. Gerstner has denounced the system as a "dubious form of evangelicalism."[248] If we take his word "dubious" seriously, and in a normal manner, does that mean he thought it

---

[247] "John Gerstner | Theopedia," *Theopedia.Com*, last modified 2016, accessed June 22, 2016, http://www.theopedia.com/John_Gerstner.

[248] John Gerstner, *Wrongly Dividing the Word of Truth: A Critique of Dispensationalism* (Morgan, PA: Soli Deo Gloria Publications, 2000), 113.

was questionable to even call Dispensationalism an Evangelical faith? If so could his words be much harsher? He asserted that Dispensationalism belonged to the "Arminian" tradition of theology and is a "spurious form of Calvinism."[249]

Additionally, Gerstner taught that Dispensationalism's positions on "the creation of man, the fall, the atonement, soteriology, and eschatology" were a "variation of the Arminian system."[250] Dispensationalism is supposedly a "thoroughgoing departure from Calvinism."[251] In his review of the basic five points of Calvinism, as popularly labeled in the subject of soteriology,[252] Gerstner stated that Dispensationalism failed to embrace total depravity[253] while embracing conditional love and election.[254] He focused in particular upon Lewis Sperry Chafer, H.A. Ironside, and Norman Geisler.[255]

In regard to the third point of the five points of Calvinism, the doctrine of limited atonement, Gerstner links the Dispensationalist doctrine to the other two prior points. He says, "With regard to the atonement, Dispensationalists believe that, since man is not totally depraved and is conditionally elected, Christ died to save all men."[256] In this section he critiques again Lewis Chafer and Charles Ryrie. He also includes a lengthy critique of Robert Lightner's view of the atonement.

---

[249] Ibid.

[250] Ibid., 115.

[251] Ibid., 115-116.

[252] Often people use the common acronym TULIP to delineate the main five points of the doctrine of salvation. T = total depravity; U = unconditional elective love; L = limited atonement; I = irresistible grace; and P = preservation and/or perseverance of the saints.

[253] John Gerstner, *Wrongly Dividing the Word of Truth: A Critique of Dispensationalism* (Morgan, PA: Soli Deo Gloria Publications, 2000), 117-122.

[254] Ibid., 122-128.

[255] Ibid.

[256] Ibid., 131.

When Gerstner discusses Dispensationalism on the doctrine of irresistible grace, sometimes called effectual grace, he continues his diatribe against the tradition by saying that the system "does not teach this cardinal Reformed doctrine."[257] He taught that "in some ways 'irresistible grace' is the most telltale evidence of the presence or absence of Calvinism."[258] Throughout this chapter Gerstner critiqued again Dispensationalists like Lewis Chafer and John Walvoord but then added to the mix the Dispensationalist Dr. Billy Graham.[259] He qualified his critique of Dr. Graham with a merciful tone by saying that he realized Graham was "not a professional theologian."[260]

Yet in his summary of Dispensationalism overall on this point he asserted that "both dispensationalism and Arminianism are synergistic soteriologies. God and man work together and contribute their share."[261] This assertion by Gerstner would place Dispensationalism in the same ideology of Roman Catholicism as they teach salvation is accomplished by God and man cooperating together.[262] According to Gerstner, "if there is any difference between Dispensationalism and Arminianism at this point, it is merely that Dispensationalism *thinks* it is Calvinistic,—a case of mistaken identity."[263]

Lastly, if the prior statements were not pointed enough, Gerstner stated in chapter eight that "Dispensationalism is five point Arminianism"

---

[257] Ibid., 148.

[258] Ibid.

[259] Ibid., 155.

[260] Ibid., 156. A case can be made, however, that Dr. Graham affirmed the doctrines of election and predestination. Lewis Drummond's Work, *A Canvas Cathedral* seems to reveal Graham affirmed that only those elected in eternity past would be drawn to the crusades and to respond to the invitation he offered after preaching.

[261] Ibid., 160.

[262] Council of Trent, January 13, 1547, Article 4 and 5.

[263] John Gerstner, *Wrongly Dividing the Word of Truth: A Critique of Dispensationalism* (Morgan, PA: Soli Deo Gloria Publications, 2000), 160.

as well as "dubious Christianity."[264] Again, does that word dubious attached to Christianity mean Gerstner doubted that Dispensationalism or Dispensationalists were even within the family of God? Earlier he doubted or questioned if they were Evangelical. Then in this section he doubts if they are even Christian or within the sphere of Christianity. Is there any doubt that Gerstner believed Dispensationalism was heresy? His next section answers that for us.

For the next twenty-five pages Gerstner argued that Dispensationalism teaches multiple avenues of salvation. In conclusion he wrote, "Dispensationalism teaches more than one way of possible salvation" and because of this they are in "heresy."[265] That statement seems to imply he believed a true or thoroughgoing Dispensationalist could not truly be a part of the family of God. He even asserted that "recent dispensational attempts to correct their theological system at this point are only another pathetic instance of putting on a band-aid to heal a fatal internal wound."[266] His language could hardly be any harsher.

In a similar vein as Gerstner, Dr. R.C. Sproul has written along the same lines on this topic. It appears Sproul carries the same disdain towards Dispensationalism as did his mentor Gerstner. His views, though often more irenic, retain the same basic premise as did Gerstner's views. For example, Sproul seems on the one hand to admit there are legitimate "four point Calvinists" who "object" to the "concept of limited atonement,"[267] but on the other hand he seems to deny that possibility saying that "holding to the L in TULIP [Limited Atonement] is the litmus test of whether one really believes what the other letters represent. . . . we cannot believe one and not believe the other."[268] Such a stance would mean his logic denies any four point Calvinistic Dispensationalist the right to claim

---

[264] Ibid., 168.

[265] Ibid., 193.

[266] Ibid.

[267] R.C. Sproul, *Everyone's a Theologian: An Introduction to Systematic Theology* (Sanford, FL: Reformation Trust Publishing, 2014), 166.

[268] Ibid.

the title Calvinistic. That type of thinking runs parallel to how his mentor Gerstner thought on these matters.

Nonetheless, a brief preliminary note of gratitude is proper here. Though Sproul seemed to err here in his analysis of Dispensationalism, I still have deep admiration and respect for his life and legacy.[269] I have more in common with him than I do in differences. He was overall a solid Evangelical with an effervescent heart and mind for the Lord Jesus Christ. His literature, love, and legacy for the major truths of the Christian faith remain a bright ray of light for the cause of Christ. And to be honest I may never be the man in Christ that he was or do as much for Christ as he has done in his life. I am grateful for him and I appreciate him from the depths of my heart. Many of his works have touched my life and matured me in my walk with Christ.

However, people should realize that even the greats like Graham, Moody, Wesley, Calvin, Luther, and Augustine and the like had their theological errors and biases that they never relinquished. All theologians have some bias. Some of these are known publicly, while on the other hand some are never known publicly. With Sproul, though a devout scholar and a staunch evangelical theologian, his bias against Dispensationalism seems to be revealed by comparing what he said Dispensationalists of the twentieth and twenty-first-century believe versus what many really have taught.

Of course, Dispensationalists must never close their hearts and minds to good brothers like Sproul. All good Christ following brethren should view Sproul in a positive light whenever and wherever possible, despite our differences in this area, and work together for the cause of spreading the gospel in Jesus Christ. Nonetheless, my discoveries about Sproul's remarks are as follows.

Two works in particular have revealed Sproul's disdain against Dispensationalism. Like his mentor Gerstner, Sproul has attempted to establish an irreconcilable dichotomy between Dispensationalism and Reformed/Calvinist Covenant theology. Sproul uses the term Reformed as

---

[269] It is interesting that he had a Dispensationalist, Dr. John MacArthur, speak at his funeral. He and John developed what appears to have been a close friendship over the years.

a synonym for Covenant theology in the work *Grace Unknown: The Heart of Reformed Theology*. In that work he wrote:

> Reformed theology has been nicknamed "Covenant theology," which distinguishes it from Dispensationalism. Dispensational theology originally believed that the key to biblical interpretation is "rightly dividing" the Bible into seven dispensations, defined in the original Scofield Reference Bible as specific testing periods in redemptive history.[270]

If someone possessed little understanding about Dispensationalism he/she could easily conclude from such a statement that a Dispensationalist could not embrace a Reformed or Calvinistic theological system. Yet if one reads Sproul's entire book he would find major themes that many Dispensationalists would wholeheartedly embrace. In Part one, *Foundations of Reformed Theology*,[271] Sproul divided his book into these sections: "(1) Centered on God, (2) Based on God's Word Alone, (3) Committed to Faith Alone, (4) Devoted to Prophet, Priest, and King, (5) Nicknamed Covenant Theology."[272]

Can a Dispensationalist affirm all or most of those? It appears historically they can, have, and do. It appears from my research that a Dispensationalist could read the first four sections of part one and agree with almost every statement written in the pages. Additionally, some Dispensationalists have embraced a form of Covenant theology by their belief in the theological covenants.[273]

In section two of the work Sproul simply expounded the doctrines of grace, i.e., the five points of Calvinism. Likewise, it appears from my research that many Dispensationalists have embraced the doctrines of

---

[270] R.C. Sproul, *Grace Unknown: The Heart of Reformed Theology* (Grand Rapids, MI: Baker Book House, 1997), 99.

[271] Ibid., 7.

[272] Ibid.

[273] Robert P. Lightner, *Evangelical Theology: A Survey and Review* (Grand Rapids, MI: Baker Books, 1986), 270.

grace. So, what is the only major point with which a Dispensationalist would disagree? Many Dispensationalists disagree that a Reformed soteriological position stands in natural opposition to the theological system of Dispensationalism.

For example, some Dispensationalists have argued for "their logical and theological compatibility."[274] As the Dallas Seminary professor Dr. Stephen Spencer said, "Reformed theology and dispensationalism are not mutually exclusive terms, but are (or can be) mutually compatible . . . . an individual could be consistently aligned with both Reformed theology and dispensationalism."[275] Therefore, it seems a case may be made that a Dispensationalist could agree basically with every major section of Sproul's work. However, Sproul presented the exact opposite.

Sproul has also written to present Dispensationalism under the umbrella of Arminianism. To accomplish this, Sproul primarily focused upon the founder of Dallas Seminary, Dr. Lewis Sperry Chafer. Sproul isolated statements of Chafer's writings and then attempted to prove that Chafer embraced a modified Arminian theology.

First, Sproul presented Dr. Chafer as unclear on his doctrine of total depravity, the fountain head of a Calvinistic soteriology. Sproul, in *Willing to Believe: The Controversy over Free Will*, wrote this in conclusion concerning Chafer's view of the will of man,

> There is a degree of vagueness in . . . Chafer's view of freedom . . . . On the surface [he] seem[s] to adopt Edwards's view. But Chafer's treatment of the question is brief and fails to analyze closely the work of the will. We must withhold judgment until we see how Chafer understands the work of the will in regeneration.[276]

---

[274] Stephen R. Spencer, "*Reformed Theology, Covenant Theology, and Dispensationalism,*" in *Integrity of Heart, Skillfulness of Hands: Biblical and Leadership Studies in Honor of Donald K. Campbell*, eds. Charles Dyer and Roy B. Zuck (Grand Rapids, MI: Baker Books, 1994), 239.

[275] Ibid., 247.

[276] R.C. Sproul, *Willing to Believe: The Controversy over Free Will* (Grand Rapids, MI: Baker Books, 1997), 193.

Sproul also alleged that Chafer believed regeneration is dependent upon man's *work* of faith, thus labeling his view as "conditional regeneration."[277] If this be true then he has discredited Dr. Chafer's view of total depravity. How can a totally depraved will that is bound to sin contribute or move to regeneration without a supernatural cause leading to that effect? Dr. Sproul understands this theology as well as the molecular scientific principle of cause and effect and works to present Chafer as weak in this doctrine of man's depravity.

Naturally of course, Sproul then proceeded to present Chafer as denying the irresistible or effectual grace of God. If man's will is not enslaved to sin, as Sproul suggests is the view of Chafer, then lost unregenerate man may assist God in his or her own new birth process (as Roman Catholicism asserts). Therefore, the doctrine of efficacious grace is distorted along with the view of man's depravity. Such a position is supposedly by implication a works oriented view of salvation instead of a grace based view of salvation. Sproul in his ardent attempt to make this Chafer's view stated,

> Chafer appears to be saying that the call God gives only to the elect is efficacious, but not inherently irresistible. It is always effective because the persuasion is so strong. But its efficacy still rests on the unconstrained human will, and this without the benefit of regeneration . . . . Reformed theology agrees that our response to the inner call of God is a free one, in that the subject exercises his choice freely. But Reformed theology also affirms that the work of regeneration so changes the disposition of the soul that the soul is truly made willing, and this is foreign to Chafer's view. So Chafer is not in harmony with the I of TULIP, irresistible grace.[278]

Next, when Sproul evaluated Chafer's view of election, he noted what he considered several red flags. Interestingly though, Sproul struggled to disprove Chafer's adherence to unconditional election. So how did Sproul handle this? First, he made statements like this, "Chafer

---

[277] Ibid., 194.

[278] Ibid., 200.

seems to take a strong stand in favor of unconditional election."[279] Secondly, since he could not with certitude disprove Chafer's allegiance to unconditional election/love, he steered the discussion away from election and back to the issue of what comes first, faith or regeneration.

Nowhere did Sproul admit that Chafer did indeed teach unconditional election even after quoting statements from Chafer that ran parallel to a Covenant Calvinist soteriological view. Sproul's final analysis apparently came out in this statement, "John Gerstner laments that the Dispensational sound on unconditional election is uncertain at best."[280] Sproul could only muster up words such as Chafer "seeks to distance himself" from Arminian views of election,[281] or that he "seems" to agree with unconditional election.[282]

Such language from Sproul might carry some weight if there were not clear, consistent, definitive, and counter statements from the pen of Dr. Chafer to prove otherwise. Such statements from the writings of Chafer, and other Dispensationalists as well, show that Sproul along with a coterie of other Covenant theologians have not accurately presented what many of the Dispensationalist teachers endorse concerning God's sovereign grace. It appears a deep bias clouded Sproul's analysis. It looks as if he just could admit the plain obvious fact that Dr. Chafer taught with clarity the doctrine of eternal election. It makes it appear as if Sproul did not want to accept and take Chafer at his own words.

14. Keith A. Mathison (b. 1967)

Dr. Keith Mathison, a close associate to Dr. R.C. Sproul, teaches at the Reformed Bible College where he "is professor of systematic theology. He earned his Ph.D. from Whitefield Theological Seminary" and he "is an associate editor of Tabletalk magazine, associate editor of The Reformation Study Bible, and author of several books, including *From*

---

[279] Ibid., 201, italics mine.

[280] Ibid., 202.

[281] Ibid.

[282] Ibid., 201.

114

Age to Age: The Unfolding of Biblical Eschatology and *Given for You: Reclaiming Calvin's Doctrine of the Lord's Supper.*"[283] Like Sproul and Gerstner he takes a very hard stance against Dispensationalism and categorizes the entire system as flawed in the doctrine of soteriology.

First, Mathison argues that Dispensationalism denies that there is one family of God, all believers of all the ages.[284] His Covenant Calvinism sees all people being placed into Israel. In other words, there is natural Israel (all who are Jews) and the spiritual Israel (all believers). His exegesis of Romans 11 asserts that the olive tree is natural Israel and that when Gentiles in this age come into a relationship with Christ they are "grafted into the good olive tree."[285] By default, because he sees the olive tree as Israel, instead of the tree being the eternal covenant or Christ, when grafted into the tree the Gentiles by default are then Israel, the "true Israel of God."[286] He believes that Dispensationalism denies the unity of all believers. In his conclusion of his chapter on the unity of God's people he says this:

> No one is saved who is not a part of the body of Christ. The dispensational doctrine of two separate bodies of believers is biblically indefensible. Nowhere does the bible support the view that some are saved apart from the body of Christ. Jesus Christ is the head of one body of believers, which includes every believer since Adam.[287]

Second, Mathison in his work moves from the implications above on Dispensationalism teaching there are people who are saved apart from Christ to his specific analysis of the Dispensational doctrine of salvation.

---

[283] "Reformation Bible College | Academics," *Reformation Bible College*, last modified 2016, accessed June 30, 2016, http://reformationbiblecollege.org/academics/.

[284] Keith A. Mathison, *Dispensationalism: Rightly Dividing the People of God* (Phillipsburg, NJ: Presbyterian and Reformed Publishing Company, 1995), 32-37.

[285] Ibid., 33.

[286] Ibid.

[287] Ibid., 37.

In the following six chapters he takes issue with Dispensationalism's modified Calvinism position.[288] In his analysis of Dispensationalism's view on Total Depravity he asserts that teachers like Dr. Charles C. Ryrie promote an idea that "man's faith becomes the basis for regeneration," which he calls "Arminianism."[289]

He places also in this camp two of Ryrie's teachers, Dr. Lewis Sperry Chafer and Dr. John Walvoord.[290] In his conclusion on the Dispensational doctrine of depravity he asserts, "Dispensationalism has adopted a semi-Pelagian, Arminian doctrine not based on Scripture and has rejected the Calvinistic doctrine of total depravity rooted deeply in Scripture."[291] In chapter eight Mathison asserts that "dispensationalists have a confused doctrine of election—an unstable mixture of conditional and unconditional election. As a result, the biblical doctrine is corrupted."[292]

In chapter nine he asserts that Dispensationalism "openly espouses the Arminian doctrine of unlimited atonement."[293] In chapter ten Mathison asserts that the "dispensational doctrine of unlimited atonement destroys the notion of irresistible grace."[294] Does Mathison think this way of the many great unlimited atonement Reformed teachers of his own heritage (Luther, Baxter, Matthew Henry, all the unlimited atonement signers at the Synod of Dort)?

Too, Mathison says that because Dispensationalism often says faith precedes or occurs together with regeneration that this makes the Dispensational soteriology an Arminian view. He says, "the dispensational doctrine of regeneration conflicts with irresistible grace. If the Holy

---

[288] Ibid., 45.

[289] Ibid., 49.

[290] Ibid.

[291] Ibid., 50-51.

[292] Ibid., 54.

[293] Ibid., 59.

[294] Ibid., 71.

Spirit's work of regeneration depends upon man's faith, as dispensationalists maintain, then man limits the sovereign work of the Spirit. This essentially Arminian view—that regeneration is based upon and follows faith—replaces irresistible grace with a cooperative effort between man and the Holy Spirit."[295]

Mathison, who has been a close associate, if not a disciple, of R.C. Sproul for many years, continues to accuse Dispensationalism as a whole, not just some but the movement in totality, of affirming an unorthodox and/or semi-Pelagian doctrine of soteriology that contradicts the soteriological position of the Reformed tradition. His analysis leaves the reader with the view that a person cannot embrace Dispensationalism as well as a Reformed soteriology. His views, like others before him, paint a picture that the two theologies are mutually exclusive and incompatible.

Summary of the Literature's Assertions

Each charge laid against Dispensationalism relates to the issue of soteriology. Several different charges have been set forth in the above discussion. However, each charge somehow revolved around Dispensationalism's supposed rejection of the Reformed or Calvinistic continuity view of salvation. Reisinger argued that Arminianism is married to Dispensationalism, and thus we now have the non-Lordship view of salvation. Pink, Kraus, Bass, Kimbro, Moore, Brand, Pratt, Crenshaw and Gunn argued that Dispensationalism teaches two plans of salvation and/or that the system has thoroughly embraced Arminianism. In Bloesch's systematic work he claimed that Dispensationalists have not accepted that grace operated in the Old Testament. This thought, expanded further in Reymond's systematic work, accuses Dispensationalism of not only two plans of salvation but several more than two plans.

Next, the renowned scholars Gerstner and Sproul stated that a theologian cannot embrace Dispensationalism and Reformed or Calvinistic theology at the same time. And in conclusion to Sproul's critique of Dispensationalism was the individual analysis of one of the most prominent Dispensationalists of all time, Dr. Lewis Sperry Chafer. Sproul attempted to show that Chafer, a godfather to the Dispensational

---

[295] Ibid.

movement, did not embrace the Calvinist Protestant doctrine of soteriology.

Lastly, Mathison, a longtime colleague with Sproul, continued the same assertions about Dispensationalism as did Sproul. According to Mathison, Dispensationalism is weak on the doctrine of man's depravity, God's sovereignty in grace, and because of that the system is mostly Arminian in orientation. He, therefore, continues to assert the same accusations against Dispensationalism today in the twenty-first-century that were expressed in the twentieth century.

In this book, such accusations will be evaluated thoroughly to test and see if the actual teachings of Dispensationalism do in some cases support a Reformed or Calvinistic-Covenant continuity soteriology. This research reveals that many Dispensationalists, even the main ones of the movement, did or do embrace some form of a Reformed or Calvinistic soteriology. I propose historically a case may exist to classify it more so as a Clementian-Calvinistic model (Clement lived from 35 to 99; Calvin lived from 1509 to 1564) in contrast to a Bezanite form of Calvinism (Beza lived from 1509 to 1605 and altered basic or historic Calvinistic doctrine, producing extreme or high Calvinism), but that case is for another historical work beyond this one. Furthermore, the primary leaders of the Dispensational movement in the twentieth and twenty-first-century reveals that major Dispensational leaders within Dispensationalism have taught a unified and solitary doctrine of redemption. In short, clear evidence exists that Dispensationalism neither historically nor presently teaches two or more avenues for redemption.

Chapter 3. Calvinistic Dispensationalists on God's Decree, Man's Depravity, Election, and/or Efficacious Grace

As shown from the previous chapter, there have been numerous theologians in the past fifty years from the date of this writing that have charged Dispensationalism as an inherently Arminian or Semi-Pelagian system of theology. Such accusations do not seem to be true when evaluating the mainline Dispensationalists that have been the leaders of the movement. Sure, as already noted, there have been *some* Dispensationalists that have embraced Arminian or Semi-Pelagian views. Too, there may be some who erroneously have believed the O.T. saints were personally saved by the keeping of the law (some who might believe that may not even be Dispensationalists).

However, even some of those who might make or have made statements supporting some type of works oriented plan for O.T. saints could be interpreted differently so as to show it meant "saved" or "just" in the sense of one being delivered or protected from the penalty of the divine state law (God's civil penalty for breaking a theocratic law). Law abiding citizens in the theocratic kingdom were right or in good standing with the divine state law (theocratic civil code of the OT). These comments do not have to be interpreted as implying or teaching that a person was right in the eternal righteousness sense of the term that comes only through grace and faith in the Lord to redeem.[296]

---

[296] For example, Dr. Lewis Sperry Chafer has stated: "According to the Old Testament, men were just because they were true and faithful in keeping the Mosaic law . . . . Men were therefore just because of their own works for God, whereas the New Testament justification is God's work for man in answer to faith (Systematic Theology, volume 7, p. 219). Additionally, he said, "Turning to the Law of Moses, we discover that it presents no other relation to God for the individual than this same covenant of works" (Ibid, 4:211). Statements like these, and others from Chafer and other Dispensationalists have been used by critics to say Dispensationalists like these, or even Dispensationalism as a whole, believes in two plans of salvation. However, the idea behind the Mosaic Law, and the covenant of works as administered in the Dispensation of the Law through Moses, has to do with external civil righteousness. It would be like me in my role as a criminal court judge in my state saying to someone: "If you obey this legal code we have in the state of SC you will be righteous (rightly related to the state authorities) and saved from the penalty of the consequences of breaking these law codes." In this sense there is a civil or

More likely it seems too that some Arminian or Semi-Pelagian infiltration may have occurred as the Charismatic and Pentecostal movement embraced the Dispensational view of Ecclesiology (the Church), Israelology (Israel's Role), and Eschatology (End Times; Prophecy) while rejecting the foundational principles of literal interpretation in the area of soteriology (salvation). Both Dispensationalism and Pentecostalism gained prominence in the early twentieth century and so a merging of the two streams of thought does not stretch beyond the realm of reasonableness.

Additionally, due to the massive amount of effort put into defending and promoting the doctrines of end times, the distinction

---

legal code that if obeyed by external action that person is considered to be just or living rightly related to the state. It seems many fail to recognize that the Law of Moses and the Dispensation of the Law dealt with a divine state theocracy. To be saved as a nation the nation as a whole had to obey the Mosaic code, which they did not do and thus they were divinely disciplined through dispersion as predicted by Deuteronomy 28:15-68. To be saved or delivered from those curses the Jews had to obey the Law of Moses and if so Deuteronomy 28:1-14 would be applicable. Divine blessings were bestowed upon the Jews as a national ethnic people for obedience to the divine state law just as blessings flow to people who obey the civil/criminal law codes of their respective state and/or country today. Of course, believers obeyed from a heart of faith. Two realms existed in the Old Covenant code. The external divine state law code (the Covenant of Works or Mosaic Law Code in the Law Dispensation) as well as the internal promise and/or covenant of grace that was progressively building and unfolding from Genesis 3:15 onward that culminates into the eternal new covenant of Jeremiah and Ezekiel that is inaugurated at Christ's death and resurrection and sending of the Holy Spirit in Acts 2. The seeds of eternal grace were in the Old Testament and Old Testament saints experienced God's grace. But the formal and fully blossomed eternal covenant of grace does not take priority and apply until the death and resurrection of Christ, and sending of the Holy Spirit for indwelling in the New Covenant Dispensation. OT saints were in Christ and eternally regenerated by grace through faith in the Lord. But these OT saints did not experience the same level of grace and indwelling presence of the Spirit as the NT saints. NT saints experience the fuller revelation and experience of life in the New Covenant. The Covenant of Redemption/Grace is not formally structured and established until Acts 2, not before. The Old Testament structure was one of legal and external priority (yet with some grace) whereas the New Covenant is a structure of internal grace priority with also a Law Code with it, the Law of Christ. This stark contrast is discussed by Paul in 2 Corinthians 3. The Old Testament Law Code was a "ministry of death, carved in stone" whereas the New Covenant dispensation is a "ministry of righteousness" that exceeds the glory of the old. Clearly God promised blessing for obedience. He specifically said this in Deuteronomy 28 as well as many other places.

between Israel and the church, and other related doctrines within those areas, many Dispensationalists apparently failed to write enough to defend the doctrines of grace. Due to the lack of stress and emphasis in this area it left the movement as a whole with a void concerning God's sovereignty in salvation.

This void opened the doors for many to come forth in the Covenant Calvinist tradition to challenge the Dispensational system in this area. Many from the Covenant Calvinist camp have openly charged Dispensationalists as being heretical. Leading scholars in that movement, who certainly have the ability and skill to make more solid evaluations than they have done, based upon the credentials they hold, have erred and presented a skewed and flawed picture of what Dispensationalists believe. Even worse, there is to date no prominent movement to openly correct and alter this by admitting this error among their tradition.[297]

Dispensationalism, like its counter system Covenant theology, indeed has its variances. I doubt if anyone would argue that all Dispensationalists agree on every doctrine. Dispensationalism basically has agreement in the particular doctrines of ecclesiology, Israelology, and eschatology. These three areas historically have remained the primary focus for Dispensationalists. However, Dispensationalists have developed views of soteriology since they examine all of Scripture.

Furthermore, since the fundamental basis for the Dispensationalist position rests upon the goal to interpret scripture in a normal manner through the application of a historical grammatical hermeneutic, the probability of a Dispensationalist also affirming the doctrines of grace seems to be high because that interpretive methodology leads to

---

[297] A few Covenant theologians have admitted that this charge of a works salvation gospel or a multiple plan of redemption ought to be dropped. For example, Dr. Fred H. Klooster, a Covenant Reformed theologian from Calvin Theological Seminary, has readily acknowledged these old charges against Dispensationalism need to be dropped. He specifically says, "the old charge should be dropped. One must proceed from the acknowledgement that Dispensationalism recognizes a single way of salvation throughout Scripture. . . . This agreement is a cause for joy; its acknowledgment should not be made grudgingly" (*"The Biblical Method of Salvation: A Case for Continuity,"* in *Continuity and Discontinuity: Perspectives on the Relationship Between the Old and New Testaments*, edited by John Feinberg, p. 133). That was 1988. However, the charges against Dispensationalism continue well beyond 1988. For twenty plus years the inaccurate allegations continue into the present.

conclusions of a sovereignty emphasis. A casual perusal of texts like Ephesians 1 reveals that the first person pronoun "I" is not used a single time. If nothing else that alone reveals the weight of emphasis that God desired to stamp on the pages of Scripture.

Consequently, if a Dispensationalist is true to his or her literal hermeneutic confession, then he or she will likely arrive at conclusions within the general domain of recognizing God's sovereign work in redemption. The question then remains: Does Dispensationalism or a significant portion of teachers within Dispensationalism teach a Protestant, Calvinistic, and continuity view of soteriology? The answer you receive largely depends on whom you ask. If you ask the theologians quoted in the previous section, they would respond emphatically no.

However, there appears to be sufficient proof to the contrary. Many Dispensationalists embrace whole-heartedly the doctrines of grace. Technically, if a Dispensationalist honors his/her allegiance to historical grammatical interpretation when interpreting soteriological passages, he must adopt some type of a view of salvation that emphasizes God's sovereignty administered in and through his providential governing in his house-hold universe. An Evangelical who applies the longtime tested standard of a historical grammatical hermeneutic arrives at interpretive conclusions that recognize the sovereignty emphases of Scripture. Yet, even so, it must be properly noted that when a person says, "Dispensationalism as a system is equivalent to Arminianism," as many have done, that type of ideology misses a focal point of Dispensationalism. The system of Dispensationalism historically has placed its emphasis elsewhere in theology.

Nonetheless, despite its focal points being elsewhere, as a historical movement Dispensationalism was birthed within the Reformed heritage. Dr. Thomas Ice has noted that it "may be surprising, to some, to learn that Dispensationalism was developed and spread during its first 100 years by those within a Reformed, Calvinistic tradition."[298] In light of that context, it makes sense to understand why Dispensationalism did not write much in the field of soteriology. The movement, already immersed in a

---

[298] Thomas Ice, "*The Calvinistic Heritage of Dispensationalism*," [online]. Accessed 10 November 2015. Available from http://www.pre-trib.org/articles/view/calvinistic-heritage-of-dispensationalism; Internet.

Reformed context, made its focus in the areas that their contemporaries had not focused upon. Dispensationalism therefore began to focus on extending the principle of the reformation further into other doctrinal areas that had not received as much attention in their own heritage. The doctrines of ecclesiology, Israelology, and eschatology were highlighted more than in previous generations. Extensive writings in those areas dominated the Dispensational literature in the late nineteenth and twentieth century. Dispensationalist Dr. John Feinberg has well stated the issue.

> . . . neither Calvinism nor Arminianism is at the essence of Dispensationalism. Some Calvinists are nondispensationalists, and others like myself, are dispensationalists. The same is true for Arminians. This matter is not at the essence of Dispensationalism, because Calvinism and Arminianism are very important in regard to concepts of God, man, sin, and salvation. Dispensationalism becomes very important in regard to ecclesiology and eschatology, but really is not about those other areas. Some think salvation is at the heart of Dispensationalism, because they erroneously think Dispensationalism teaches multiple methods of salvation. Those who properly understand the position realize its emphasis lies elsewhere.[299]

Within the above statement, John Feinberg classified himself as a Calvinist. All Calvinists do not belong in the Covenant theology camp. The book containing that quote was devoted to the Dispensational Calvinist S. Lewis Johnson. Apparently Johnson loved and taught Calvinism. Theologian C. Samuel Storms stated this concerning Johnson's love for the doctrines of pure grace.

> S. Lewis Johnson is a Calvinist, quintessentially. And given the opportunity to do so, he'll be glad to tell about it. I am sure when

---

[299] John S. Feinberg, *Continuity and Discontinuity: Perspectives on the Relationship Between the Old and New Testaments*, ed. John S. Feinberg (Wheaton, Ill: Crossway Books, 1988), 70, 71.

others think of Dr. Johnson they are reminded of his unswerving loyalty to the inerrancy and authority of Holy Scripture, or his emphasis on the primacy of the local church, or perhaps his insistence on excellency in all aspects of life and ministry. But I think principally of his zeal for the doctrines of grace, doctrines which he loves, lives, and passionately proclaims to all who will listen. As far as Lewis Johnson is concerned, Calvinism is just another name for the biblical gospel, and it is to that gospel and its sovereign Lord that he is and ever will be committed.[300]

It will serve the reader well to also realize that not all Covenant theologians have misrepresented Dispensationalism or individual Dispensationalists. Some rightly have recognized that many from outside the Covenant camp still maintain firm orthodoxy. If one reads the antagonistic works listed earlier and does not balance those by reading actual writings from Dispensationalists, then the reader could easily conclude that Dispensationalism stands outside of the orthodox faith.

However, O. Palmer Robertson, a Calvinist Covenant theologian, aptly wrote that Dispensationalists often have stood on the side of orthodoxy, not against it as some of the above writers have attempted to present. He stated,

> As the dispensational perspective is being evaluated, it should not be forgotten that covenant theologians and dispensationalists stand side by side in affirming the essentials of the Christian faith. Very often these two groups within Christendom stand alone in opposition to the inroads of modernism, neo-evangelicalism, and emotionalism. Covenant theologians and dispensationalists should hold in highest regard the scholarly and evangelical productivity of one another.[301]

Many of the theologians from the covenant camp have ignored this advice and appraisal. Of course, this author realizes it is a two way street

---

[300] Ibid., 322, 323.

[301] O. Palmer Robertson, *The Christ of the Covenants* (Phillipsburg, New Jersey: Presbyterians and Reformed Publishing, 1980), 201-202.

and that certainly some Dispensationalists may not very well appreciate some of the Calvinist Covenant scholars. I personally am very fond of many Reformed Covenantal Calvinist writings from theologians like Dr. John Calvin, Dr. John Gill, Dr. Jonathan Edwards, the famous Princeton scholars Dr. B.B. Warfield, Dr. Charles Hodge, Dr. A.A. Hodge, Dr. William G.T. Shedd, Dr. Louis Berkhoff, Dr. Robert Reymond, Dr. D. James Kennedy, Dr. R.C. Sproul, Dr. Wayne Grudem, and more.

Robertson openly recognized that many Dispensationalists have maintained scholarly, evangelical, and conservative positions. Some of these scholars, and all that I will mention in subsequent sections, have also tenaciously taught the Reformed or Calvinistic perspective of salvation while avoiding Arminian notions. A historical survey of twentieth and twenty-first-century Dispensationalism reveals a very different picture than what has commonly been taught by a significant set of voices among the Covenant Calvinist tradition.

In the remaining portion of this chapter I will present a voluminous amount of evidence from the pens of twentieth and twenty-first-century dispensationalists who have affirmed a Calvinistic soteriological position. I will focus primarily on their statements pertaining to God's sovereignty, man's depravity, the doctrine of election unto grace and/or predestination, and the application of that by the Spirit in what is often termed efficacious, effectual, or irresistible grace. In fact, the doctrine of election alone has been stated by the Covenant Calvinists as the one main or central element to distinguish it from other forms of soteriology. Covenant theologian Dr. Keith Mathison has stated, "the doctrine of election is considered by many to be the heart of Calvinism."[302]

Therefore, I will for the remainder of this chapter address mainly those doctrines pertaining to God's sovereignty (verified through his general decree and particular acts of election and the application of grace) which are required due to man's depravity. As for the atonement of Christ, I will devote a full chapter to that one doctrine due to the historical diversity by both systems of theology. Dispensationalism has had within it both five point Calvinists and four point Calvinists.[303]

---

[302] Keith Mathison, *Dispensationalism: Rightly Dividing the People of God* (Philipsburg, NJ: Presbyterian and Reformed Publishing, 1995), 52.

[303] Within the Reformed Calvinistic model there are three main models of how God conceives or plans his decree within his house-hold universe. Supralapsarian,

infralapsarian, and sublapsarian models. Dispensationalists have normally remained more so in the infralapsarian and sublapsarian models because the supralapsarian models seem to undermine God's holiness as magnified through justice. How can God effect or cause or implant original or fresh sin into someone and then hold that person accountable for something that he alone supernaturally caused to happen? That issue seems to be why the Reformed Calvinist theologian Dr. William G.T. Shedd stated it remains important to retain and emphasize both the active decrees of God and permissive decrees of God. Throughout history when those distinctions and doctrines of God's active and passive will have been lost it has led to schism and revolts among the disciples in that model. Jacob Arminius and his followers from him developed from a revolt against Theodore Beza's double predestinarian (all active decrees) model. It seems today in this century the reaction by the Southern Baptist Traditionalists against those who claim to align with the Calvinist founders of their denomination might be because of a reaction against those high forms of Calvinism. If one reads Dr. Leighton Flowers' writings, it seems he largely speaks against Calvinistic models that would more generally align with the supralapsarian models. He and I discussed this in a friendly conversation online for about three hours. He more often than not wrongly equates high Calvinism (Bezanism) as merely Calvinism. His book, *The Potter's Promise*, on numerous occasions addresses a type of Calvinism that views God as the author of sin. As he stated: "When I was a Calvinist, I believed that God's glory was best made manifest through his meticulous control over everything all vessels do" (p. 15). The key words, "control over everything all vessels do," highlights what type of model he had embraced. Infralapsarians and especially sublapsarians, understand the point made by Dr. William G.T. Shedd on the permissive decree of God. God allows within his decree a permission of sin and evil. Flowers seems to have revolted against a model that made everything in all of history intertwined with God's active decree of causation. In his mind, it seems he thinks that Calvinism means the same decree that brought about creation from nothing is the same decree that purposed and brought about sin into the universe. That may indeed represent some models of Calvinism, such as supralapsarian models, but it certainly is not the more nuanced and balanced models. Dispensationalism has almost always rejected any formulation that makes God appear to have authored sin because of our devotion to literal hermeneutics above and prior to any systematic override of particular texts. Flowers admits that he was a five point Calvinist (p. 3) prior to leaving that model of faith. Flowers does rightly state that "not all Calvinists are the same" (p. 5), but he tends to still focus mainly throughout his work on the model that presents God as ordaining everything in the universe, even election and damnation, in the same way. Yet throughout his book, Flowers highlights points about judicial hardening where God allows people through ongoing sin to destroy themselves (pp. 50-52; 130-131). Those points he makes fit well within a sublapsarian model of Calvinistic thought. But by his own admission he cannot grasp how one can affirm unconditional election and conditional damnation. He admits this in his footnote 114 on page 120. He noted here that he thinks a standard Calvinistic reading of Romans 9 results in this double predestination view. In his words, if mankind's natural condition of total inability {note he used a high Calvinistic term, inability instead of depravity} is brought to pass by sovereign decree, which no Calvinist

Yet Covenant theology has also had the same hybrid within it. For any Covenant Calvinist theologian to assert that because some Dispensationalists do not embrace the limited atonement doctrine as formulated by those after the Synod of Dort—that such proves they are weak or Arminian—is not only to criticize Dispensationalism but even their own heritage, even Martin Luther and John Calvin, as well as the people who composed the Synod of Dort. Some at the Synod of Dort affirmed a limited view, and others affirmed an unlimited view, and some a hybrid of the two.

Therefore, in that section, I will show the diversity of the atonement view even within Covenant theology's heritage. Even the Reformed Covenant theologians do not agree among themselves on some specifics of the atonement such as its extent. Much literature has been produced arguing that even Calvin himself did not affirm a limited atonement as so articulated by today's Reformed theologians. Because a solid amount of evidence exists concerning the extent of the atonement question, that evidence created a significant stir of controversy and debate even at the strongest Calvinist convention in church history, the Synod of Dort. Therefore, I will focus primarily upon the main portions of the doctrines of grace that all Calvinistic theologians affirm, which are historically the doctrine of man's depravity, God's unconditional love in election and predestination, and the efficacious application of that love through grace that wins the heart of the lost.

---

could consistently deny, then how can the charge of equal ultimacy be denied with anything more than a distinction without a difference" (p. 120)? It seems he clearly shows his hand of theological cards. He has built his model from a view that works against models of theology that teach God caused one to be born in a condition of sin. But this fails to take into account that many models of Calvinistic thought (infralapsarians and especially subalapsarians) that see Adam as having original liberty in Eden (as did Lucifer) and he, as well as all others in history, willingly and freely choose sin and depravity. Sin occurs because of God's *permission* of it in the world. God allows this through his decree of permission. Flowers seems to be, therefore, in a reaction mode to the high Calvinism model that he was either taught and/or embraced himself. It seems he did not grasp a more balanced and mature model of thought as expressed more in infralapsarians and especially sublapsarian models. Until Flowers and company rightly and regularly define which form of Calvinism is being analyzed in their critiques (extreme-supra; strong-infra; moderate-sublapsarian), misrepresentation and inaccuracies will abound.

As to the doctrine of the preservation or perseverance of the saints I will not devote much time to that subject. Even Gerstner admitted that Dispensationalists usually affirmed the doctrine of preservation of the saints. Granted, some Reformed or Calvinistic theologians prefer to define it along the lines of preservation of the elect whereas others tend to define it along the lines of perseverance of the saints. Generally speaking this is often an issue of semantics. This subtle difference even among the Reformed also exists among the Dispensationalists. The differences among Dispensationalism and Covenant Calvinism do not seem, therefore, as pronounced in that area as with the other three principle areas. In some cases that difference amounts merely to semantics or a preferred term. In fact, if someone affirms man's depravity, God's sovereign election, and God's efficacious grace that person will almost invariably affirm some type of Reformed view of eternal salvation for the elect, however that may be delineated or termed

Thirty-Seven Dispensationalists of the Nineteenth to Twenty-First-Century who Affirmed a Calvinistic Soteriology

1. John Nelson Darby (1800-1882)

Though some think Darby founded the movement of Dispensationalism, the best historical scholarship shows otherwise. Dispensationalism has seeds and formulations in the early church era just after the apostolic age ended.[304] Of course, it remains true that Darby functioned as a key forefather and a major figure to systematize those concepts that have existed throughout church history.[305] Also, though not the founder, he remained one of the most gifted teachers to the Plymouth

---

[304] William C. Watson, *Dispensationalism Before Darby: Seventeenth-Century and Eighteenth-Century English Apocalypticism* (Silverton, OR: Lampion Press, 2015), 3-11. See also, *Discovering Dispensationalism: Tracing the Development of Dispensational Thought from the First to the Twenty-First Century*, eds., Cory M. Marsh & James I. Fazio.

[305] Larry V. Crutchfield, *The Origins of Dispensationalism: The Darby Factor* (Lanham, MD: University Press of America, 1992), 1.

Brethren movement of Christianity.[306] Throughout his ministerial life he translated the Bible into three languages (German, French, and English) and he served the poor and children in need through compassionate generosity.[307] He left a literary legacy of more than fifty volumes.[308] He taught for Trinity College in Dublin, and while in his homeland he served with intense passion his local church body.[309]

One of the chief aspects of Darby's theology hinged upon his view that God's counsel cannot fail. According to Darby, nothing in all of creation can thwart, nullify, or defeat God's counsel and purpose.[310] This overriding theme in Darby's writings and ministry remained so strong and evident that the historian Dr. George Marsden stated Darby remained an "unrelenting Calvinist."[311]

In regards to man's sin nature, Darby taught that man had died in his spirit towards God though he remained alive in the flesh. As he stated, "his flesh is alive and active as regards to evil; it is utterly dead as regards to God—not one movement of soul in the natural man towards him."[312] This concept aligns with the standard Calvinistic view that man has no inward orientation that he or she will use to move or grasp Christ and the gospel in faith. Man will not obey God's command to repent and trust in Christ for salvation because mankind in a natural condition has no

---

[306] G.C.D Howley, "John Nelson Darby," in *The New International Dictionary of the Christian Church*, edited by J.D. Douglas (Grand Rapids, MI: Zondervan, 1978), 283.

[307] Ibid.

[308] Larry V. Crutchfield, *The Origins of Dispensationalism: The Darby Factor* (Lanham, MD: University Press of America, 1992), 7.

[309] G.C.D Howley, "John Nelson Darby," in *The New International Dictionary of the Christian Church*, edited by J.D. Douglas (Grand Rapids, MI: Zondervan, 1978), 283.

[310] Larry V. Crutchfield, *The Origins of Dispensationalism: The Darby Factor* (Lanham, MD: University Press of America, 1992), 60.

[311] George M. Marsden, *Fundamentalism and American Culture* (Oxford, NY: Oxford University Press, 2006), 46.

[312] J.N. Darby, *The Collected Writings of J.N. Darby*, edited by William Kelly, Doctrinal Number 3, Volume 10 (Winschoten, Netherlands: H.L. Heijkoop, 1972), 195.

movement towards God. According to Darby mankind in a natural state is "alive to sin and lust" yet because of that attachment the person is "dead towards God."[313] The same resurrection power that raised Christ from the dead also works to make man come alive to God in grace.[314] That resurrection power view of Darby highlights his view of what many term as efficacious or effectual grace.

In addressing the matter of God choosing us in Christ before time began Darby referenced 2 Timothy 1:9. In Darby's thought God chose us in Christ before the foundation of the world.[315] God has "predestined unto the adoption of children" as we have been placed "in Him" (Christ Jesus).[316] From that spot of election the elect are "called according to God's purpose" so that we the elected ones will be "conformed to the image of his Son."[317] This sovereignty extended to us in God's love that displayed "the will of his grace" upon "poor wretched, vile sinners."[318]

Too, we know from history that D.L. Moody, who was not a five point Calvinist, and J.N. Darby, who was a five point Calvinist, experienced some conflict over this doctrine.[319] Their conflict or tension in this area existed because Darby could not convince Moody that God chose, atoned for, and drew only the elect to faith.[320] This noted tension between them verifies too that one of the most prominent figures in the

---

[313] Ibid., Expository Number 5, Volume 26 (Winschoten, Netherlands: H.L. Heijkoop, 1971), 120.

[314] Ibid.

[315] Ibid., 257.

[316] Ibid., Expository Number 6, Volume 27 (Winschoten, Netherlands: H.L. Heijkoop, 1971), 128.

[317] Ibid.

[318] Ibid.

[319] Lyle W. Dorsett, *A Passion for Souls: The Life of D. L. Moody* (Chicago, IL: Moody Publishers, 1997) 136-137.

[320] Ibid.

2. Dr. James Robinson Graves (1820-1893)

Few will deny the significance that Dr. J.R. Graves had on American fundamentalism and Baptist life. Someone might describe him as polarizing yet powerful, cantankerous yet courageous, and sometimes as vociferous as valiant when preaching and teaching.[321] Not only was his oratory ministry a recognizable ministry, but also his written ministry flourished as well with many papers and books.[322] He has been mostly remembered, however, for his contributions in promoting the landmark movement of theology. Certainly none with any ounce of historical lucidity would deny or fail to recognize that he polarized many through his assertions that the only true faith of Christianity existed inside the line of Baptists extending all the way back to John the Baptist in some type of unbroken succession.[323] Some have gone so far as to say that Landmarkism created the greatest internal crisis in Southern Baptist life in the nineteenth century.[324]

With that much controversy surrounding a man and a movement he led, who by his personality sometimes seemed to love conflict and "where none existed he tried to create it,"[325] it seems obvious that many could easily overlook, miss, or forget what he embraced in his views on Dispensationalism and Calvinism. But one particular book that he wrote covered both themes and revealed his unified synthesis of both Calvinism and Dispensationalism.

In his work, *The Work of Christ in the Covenant of Redemption; Developed (Consummated) in Seven Dispensations,* Dr. Graves clearly

---

[321] H. Leon McBeth, *The Baptist Heritage: Four Centuries of Baptist Witness* (Nashville, TN: Broadman Press, 1987), 448.

[322] Ibid.

[323] Ibid., 447.

[324] Ibid.

[325] Ibid., 448.

established his Calvinist soteriology. His doctrine materialized in God's sovereign providence that unfolded or revealed the eternal covenant of redemption progressively through seven dispensations. This progressive revelation ended in the earthly millennial kingdom (the 7th dispensation) with a restored ethnic Israel where Christ rules over the world as the King over the earth. In speaking of that sovereign providence Dr. Graves stated, "God's determinate counsel underlies all his acts."[326] Graves placed the eternal covenant of redemption in that determinate counsel of God. God, as Father, Son, and Spirit, determined or ordained in this eternal covenant man's salvation. Each member participated in the "determinations, elections, and decrees."[327] God alone planned and executed this eternal covenant without unregenerate man's involvement or assistance.

When Dr. Graves wrote of the errors of Arminianism, per his usual robust style, he did not speak softly. He stated,

> All men are by nature Arminians; and the absolute sovereignty of God is a doctrine hateful to the natural and depraved heart. False teachers have taken advantage of this natural feeling, and have for ages inflamed the prejudices of Christian men and women against any exercise of sovereignty on the part of God in this Covenant, either as to his 'determinate counsel,' his electing love, or his distinguishing grace.[328]

In Graves' theology he taught that the eternal covenant of redemption unfolded throughout history in distinct dispensations. God in these distinct dispensations progressively applied his sovereign grace through providence. God purposed, purchased, and providentially secured the salvation of only the elect. As he stated, Jesus Christ's sheep are those his Father gave to him in the Covenant of Redemption."[329] For those who

---

[326] J.R. Graves, *The Work of Christ in the Covenant of Redemption; Developed in Seven Dispensations* (Texarkana, TX: Bogard Press, 1883), 53.

[327] Ibid., 80.

[328] Ibid., 96.

[329] Ibid., 98.

do not come to Christ, the nonelect, they discover that they are "not his sheep."[330]

Graves' theology promoted a solid Calvinistic soteriology. As a Dispensationalist he affirmed that Christ would come for his saints to resurrect them and then after the tribulation come for his foes to conquer them.[331] For him the sovereignty of God revealed itself in God judging the nations through the horrible tribulation, his return as sovereign King to overthrow evil, and his sovereign fulfillment of the promises made to all of his creation, which certainly included his covenant promises made to ethnic Israel that he through sovereign election brings to faith in the Messiah.[332]

It is because Graves affirmed God's sovereign providence that he held to the view that when Christ returns he shall fulfill his promise in the Abrahamic Covenant. In the final eras of earthly history Christ Jesus becomes the "yes" or "fulfillment" to the nation of Israel who has long waited for her promises to come to actualization. As Graves noted, "Up to this time we are now noting only one promise of it {the Abrahamic Covenant} has been fulfilled, viz., Christ, the promised seed, has appeared and from Abraham's posterity; but all the land promised has never yet been possessed by his descendants, nor have they become as the stars in multitude, nor has all the nations of earth, in his seed—Christ—been blessed.[333] For Graves, to see the eternal covenant of redemption as it unfolds historically, you must accept God is both sovereign over Israel and the Church, and that he will fulfill his exact promises to save and bless his people without fail, because nothing can thwart the sovereign providential decree of almighty God.

---

[330] Ibid.

[331] Ibid., 391-405.

[332] Ibid., 475-530.

[333] Ibid., 504.

3. Dr. Lewis Sperry Chafer (1871-1952)

The leading founder and organizer of Dallas Theological Seminary, Dr. Chafer, established himself as a chief forefather in the field of Dispensationalism.[334] His eight volume set of systematic theology became the classic representation of a full systematic theology within that tradition of thought. The legacy of his seminary has also been a bulwark for the spread of Dispensationalism throughout the globe. Some have recognized Dallas Seminary as the flagship seminary for Dispensationalism in America.

Yet Chafer received an unjust critique from Dr. R.C. Sproul. This early Dispensationalist believed and taught salvation by sovereign grace alone through faith alone. In his individual writings and in his major treatise of systematics, Chafer taught what many know as Calvinism. Theologians, such as Sproul, Reymond, Reisinger, Clarence Bass, and more have either intentionally or unintentionally misrepresented Chafer. These individuals have labeled him as an Arminian theologian. Those mistakes should not occur from any skilled theologian.

Dr. Chafer's writings clearly present a Calvinistic view not only to salvation but also to every event that happens in the universe. Any competent reader can conclude this by spending time reading the works of Chafer. Though a lengthy quote, the whole section reveals the clear conviction that Dr. Chafer had concerning the doctrine of God's sovereign grace. For instance, concerning election to salvation in Ephesians 1:4-6 Chafer wrote,

> What could be more orderly than that the contemplation of the divine dealing with man should begin with a declaration of God's sovereignty in election? Whatever God bestows upon His creatures must of necessity, be absolute in its nature. He discovers nothing in fallen man other than an object of His super-abounding grace. The first man, Adam, stood before God on the ground of a natural perfection, being the true representative of God's creative purpose; but Adam fell from the estate of natural perfection and from that

---

[334] I have categorized these Dispensationalists by the date of their births. The oldest date of birth and then subsequently by date for the following Dispensationalists.

time, both for Adam and his posterity, only regenerative grace could commend any human being to God. No obligation rests upon God in the exercise of His grace. He may, and does, choose whom He will. He neither sees, nor foresees, any good in man which might form a basis of His blessings. Whatever good is found in redeemed man is wrought in him by divine grace. God does design for those whom He chooses that they shall be 'holy and without blame before Him;' but this is the result which is wrought by God in grace, and is never wrought by man. Certainly man has not chosen God. Christ emphasized this when he said, 'Ye have not chosen me, but I have chosen you.' Even the first man when unfallen and wholly free to choose did not choose God; how much more is it certain that fallen man will not of himself choose God! Therefore the provision of the ground of redemption is not enough in itself; the perverted will of man must be divinely moved. The unregenerate heart must be rendered willing as well as transformed in its essential character. All of this God undertakes and accomplishes in sovereign grace. He elects, He calls, He inclines the heart, He redeems, He regenerates, He preserves, and He presents faultless before His glory those who are the objects of His sovereign grace.[335]

Notice the words that Chafer used to describe how God redeems a person. He said that God "neither sees, nor foresees, any good in man which might form a basis of His blessings." Such a statement alone suffices to show that Chafer does not endorse any prescient view of election. Furthermore, he said that God does choose whom he will to save. He then specifically says that God "chooses" and that for one to be holy, this must be "wrought by God in grace" when the "perverted will of man" is "divinely moved." Chafer polishes these words by adding that God does perform that salvific task through "sovereign grace." If that is not enough, then notice he says that it is God who "elects, calls, inclines the heart, redeems, and regenerates" the lost soul. The rest of Chafer's quote is as follows:

---

[335] Lewis Sperry Chafer, *The Ephesian Letter: Doctrinally Considered* (New York, NY: Loizeaux Brothers, 1935), 34-37.

On the other hand, He employs means to the accomplishment of His purpose. On the divine side, the awful demands of sin must be met by the sacrifice of His only begotten Son. It is not enough that sin shall be declared to be sinful; it is required that its curse shall be borne by the Lamb of God, the will of man must be moved, regeneration must be wrought by the Spirit, and every spiritual and heavenly blessing must be secured by the setting up of an actual union with Christ. On the human side, when man's opposition to God is divinely broken down, he then believes to the saving of His soul.... While there is very much in the doctrine of divine election which transcends the limitations of the finite understanding, it is true that man originates nothing—not even sin, since sin began with the angels of God. It is God who hath chosen His elect, and while this selection is both sovereign and final, nevertheless, not one human being who desires to be saved and who complies with the necessary terms of the gospel will ever be lost. Though the doctrine of divine election presents difficulties which are insolvable by the finite mind, the fact of divine selection is not limited to God's choice of some out of the many for eternal glory; it is observable anywhere in the universe. There is a variety in all God's creation. There are classifications among the angels. One star is said to differ from another star in glory. Men are not born of the same race with the same advantages, nor with the same native abilities. These variations in estates of men cannot be accounted for on the basis of the efficacy of the free will of man. Men do not choose their race, their life conditions (whether it be in civilization or in heathendom), nor do they choose their natural gifts. On the other hand, it is as clearly disclosed to those who will receive the revelation, that God's attitude toward the entire human family is one of infinite compassion and boundless sacrificial love. Though the two revealed facts—divine election and the universality of divine love—cannot be reconciled within the sphere of human understanding, here, as elsewhere, we may honor God by believing and by resting in Him. Therefore, to God be all the glory! And to Him be given the first consideration! Those systems of religious thought which require that the doctrine of God shall conform to the doctrine of the supremacy of man, which begin with man, defend man, and glorify man, are fundamentally wrong and therefore are productive of God-dishonoring error. . . . The true system of religious thought begins with God, defends God, and glorifies God; and the creature is conformed to the plan and purpose of the Creator. The fall of man alone can account for the wickedness of heart which resists the divine supremacy.[336]

The above quote reveals several important doctrines that Chafer commonly espoused. Chafer clearly believed in unconditional election. He specifically stated, "It is God who hath chosen His elect, and . . . this selection is both sovereign and final." He understood it was a difficult subject. But even so he saw God's sovereignty in selection throughout the world. He said, "Though the doctrine of divine election presents difficulties which are insolvable by the finite mind, the fact of divine selection is not limited to God's choice of some out of the many for eternal glory; it is observable anywhere in the universe." Some people are born in countries where there is no gospel. Some are born with a high IQ and some are born with a low IQ. People do not choose who their parents are, or where they shall be born. Many of life's circumstances are selected for us by God. That is the doctrine of election in the natural realm according to Chafer.

He added again that "Though the two revealed facts—divine election and the universality of divine love—cannot be reconciled within the sphere of human understanding, here, as elsewhere, we may honor God by believing and by resting in Him." In spite of the difficulty, Chafer took the position that this doctrine required a humility and trust in God as he is, God of the universe. For Chafer, man contributed nothing to his own election. As he said, "While there is very much in the doctrine of divine election which transcends the limitations of the finite understanding, it is true that man originates nothing." This truth seems to have stood as an essential to his understanding in the plan of salvation.

Also readers will find in the above quote that Chafer held to efficacious grace; he taught that God must "move" and "incline" the will to come to Christ. Salvation occurs when God breaks man's will through "divine" actions. Nowhere will a person find in his teaching any Arminian bents, any humanistic language, or any hint of anything less than God's

---

[336] Ibid.

sovereign grace bestowed upon elected and depraved sinners. His criticism against a man-focused religion could not be any sharper. He stated, "Those systems of religious thought which require that the doctrine of God shall conform to the doctrine of the supremacy of man, which begin with man, defend man, and glorify man, are fundamentally wrong and therefore are productive of God-dishonoring error." His words clearly position him as an advocate for the sovereignty of God and the opponent of any man centered theology, such as often produced or presented with Arminianism.

Even in Chafer's systematic work, which he published later in life, he echoed the same view. Chafer wrote on the *Decree of God* in his systematic theology works. His words there resonate with a true Calvinistic spirit. Within his systematic notes, a person will find a strong God, one who answers to no individual or created being; Chafer presented a sovereign, wise, and omniscient God. A few selected quotes will reveal that even in his late years he believed the sacred Scriptures concerning an orthodox salvation, and in this orthodox view he aligned himself with the Reformed stream of Christian history. If any theologian ignores or misses the precise statements from this systematic work, then that theologian more than likely went to the text with a biased opinion. Clearly these quotes will prove Chafer stood in line with historic Calvinism, or otherwise termed the Reformed Protestant position, in regard to salvation. In volume one Chafer wrote this concerning God's sovereignty:

> The sovereignty of God is discerned in the absolute manner in which all things have been assigned their respective places in creation, in appointing to men their day and generation as well as their bounds of their habitation, and in the exercise of saving grace.[337]

Chafer even criticized the Arminian view. In no sense did he recognize the system as honoring to the holy Scriptures. He said of the Arminian view,

---

[337] Lewis Sperry Chafer, *Systematic Theology* (Grand Rapids MI: Kregel Publications, 1993), 1:222.

> The Arminian notion that the will of man is sovereign in its power to resist the Almighty must be denied, since it is everywhere refuted in the history of God's dealing with men. God may, for good reasons, allow man's will to prevail; but He does not have to do so. He has power over every will to cause it to do His good pleasure.[338]

Chafer went on to quote the biblical texts Isa. 46:10 and Eph. 1:11 to back up his argument that God truly exercises omnipotence over the entire universe. He extended his criticism of Arminianism by adding that,

> Published systems of theology which either omit the doctrine of divine decree, or oppose the doctrine, are justly reprehensible. They remove the rudder from the ship and set it afloat subject to wind and tide. It is a dishonor even to a man to assert that he does not act with purposed, rational ends in view, or that he does not employ worthy means to realize those ends.[339]

Chafer's writings also reveal that he understood and embraced the doctrine of divine selection. According to Chafer, God would only save those whom he had set his heart upon eternally. The will of man, in orthodox theology, must be inferior and beneath the will of God. To reverse this creates havoc in the doctrine of God's omnipotence. Chafer said,

> The will of the creature is a creation of God and in relation to it God sustains no timidity or uncertainty. He made the creature's will as an instrument by which He might accomplish His sovereign purpose and it is inconceivable that it should ever thwart His purpose. As bearing upon the sovereignty of God over all creatures, the student should read with reverent attention Isaiah 40:10-31 and Job 38: 1-41.[340]

---

[338] Ibid., 1:229-230.

[339] Ibid., 1:231.

[340] Ibid., 1:241.

In the same section, *Divine Decree of God*, Chafer also argued that election stood apart from any worthiness from the creation; a depraved person could have no worth in God's sight that would cause God to love him/her enough to bestow his eternal elective love upon the person. Elective love comes only by God's sole decision to grant his everlasting grace. His elective love is more than a mere *plan* of salvation. On the contrary, God's elective love centers in upon a particular individual and enacts whatever means necessary to cause that one to come to saving faith. This particular work occurs only for a certain group. Chafer wrote,

> The term election should not be construed to mean only a general divine purpose to provide salvation for all men. It refers to an express divine purpose to confer salvation on some, but not all. Nor should it imply that God will bless those who believe. It rather specifies those who will believe. Some, but not all, are written in the Lamb's book of life. Evasion of the plain words of Scripture secures nothing in the understanding of this most solemn subject . . . . . As the ground of His election, He foresaw no difference in character of one over another. His choice is not based on anticipated worthiness. Election is an act of grace apart from works. Neither faith nor good works is the cause of divine election. They are rather the fruit of election. Men are not first holy and then chosen; but rather are first chosen and then holy. It was that they might be holy that they were chosen. The destiny of Isaac's sons was determined before they had done anything good or bad, that the fact of sovereign election might stand without complication (Rom. 9:11-13). The fact that a supposed conditional election is the belief of the majority is due, doubtless, to the reluctance on the part of man to admit that no merit resides in his natural self.[341]

In the next section Chafer took up the issue of retribution, or the teaching that God leaves the non-elect in their sins, allowing them to have their own way through refusing Christ and grace, and consequently to receive eternal damnation at death or at his coming. Concerning this issue,

---

[341] Ibid., 1:245.

Chafer taught clearly that some were elected while others were left to their own destruction.

> There is that in the purpose of God which is styled retribution. As an act of God, the term means that some are rejected whom He does not elect . . . . New and wholly undeserved blessings are extended to the elect, while the nonelect reap only the just recompense of their lost estate. God does for one class what He does not do for the other, but both aggregations pass before His mind and become objects of His determination. Exceedingly painful expressions are used in the Scriptures to describe the divine decision regarding the nonelect. They are "not written" in the book of life (Rev. 13:8); they are "vessels of wrath fitted to destruction" (Rom. 9:22); they were "before . . . ordained to this condemnation" (Jude 1:4); they "stumble at the word, being disobedient: whereunto also they were appointed" (1 Pet. 2:8). God is said to love some less than others (Mal. 1: 2, 3). Some are called the "election," and some are called "the rest" (Rom. 11:7). A dispassionate reading of Romans, chapters nine and eleven, will result in the assurance that, whatever men may believe or disbelieve regarding the matter, the Word of God is bold in declaring that some are appointed to blessing and others are to experience condemnation.[342]

If any person will evaluate Dr. Chafer's words and not approach this study with a biased opinion, then the analyzer should recognize that this chief forefather of twentieth-century Dispensationalism taught clearly the doctrines of grace, otherwise known as the Protestant Reformed doctrine of God's sovereignty in salvation. According to Chafer, God alone elected and saved sinners alone. But if the sections above are not enough, Chafer also expressed his view again with a clear stance in his systematic theology under the section specifically pertaining to soteriology.

When he defines the term election he says it means a "sovereign divine purpose so formulated as to be independent of human merit,

---

[342] Ibid., 1:247.

descent, or cooperation."³⁴³ This truth is something that Chafer later calls an essential truth. He recognized that this truth was a hard position for many to accept, which again reveals he took the less than popular route that is akin to an Arminian or unqualified free will position. He says,

> God has by election chosen some to salvation, but not all. This truth, too often resisted for want of understanding of the nature of God, or of the position He occupies in relation to His creatures, is reasonable; but it is distinctly a revelation. This, as before stated, cannot be doubted by those who are amenable to the Word of God. It is disclosed concerning individuals that they are chosen in the Lord (Rom. 16:13), chosen to salvation (2 Thess. 2:13), chosen in Him before the foundation of the world (Eph. 1:4), predestined to the adoption of sons (Eph. 1:5), elect according to the foreknowledge of (1 Peter 1:2), vessels of mercy which He hath before prepared unto glory (Rom. 9:23). There can be no question raised but that these passages contemplate an act of God by which some are chosen, but not all. The idea of election or selection, cannot be applied to an entire class as unrelated to any others. Hidden in the word election is the implied truth, which is unavoidably a part of it, that others are not chosen, or are passed by.³⁴⁴

Some embrace the doctrine of election with a view that has been labeled foresight or prescient election. By this they basically in some form or another believe that God looks into the corridor of time and history and sees who will embrace him by faith. Those he sees coming to him are then elected in eternity and predestined to adoption. Dr. Chafer clearly rejected this view and stated that

> election is unto faith and holiness. It is no slight error to confuse these issues and make faith and holiness the cause and election the effect . . . . it is revealed that men are not first holy and then elect;

---

[343] Lewis Sperry Chafer, *Systematic Theology* (Grand Rapids MI: Zondervan, 1993), 3:167.

[344] Ibid., 3:172.

but they are first elect and that election is unto holiness . . . . It may be added that acceptable works and qualities are not resident in any fallen human being, except these characteristics are wrought in the human heart by divine energy. It would therefore be folly to expect that God would foresee in men what could never exist. Doubtless, multitudes of people cling to conditional election lest they be forced to recognize the depravity of man.[345]

Chafer's view on election was so strong that he even went so far to state that "divine election is immutable."[346] In his words God is so powerful and so wise that he has "never created a human will as an instrument to defeat His own purpose. He creates them that they may serve His immutable will. Since God is the Creator of all things, it is absurd to suppose that He who creates cannot determine the choice and destiny of that which He has wrought."[347]

Such words can only mean that Chafer stood in line with the historical company of Calvinistic thought. No person reading those words or his works, unless with a deep presupposition and bias against either Chafer and/or some other doctrinal animus against him, could arrive at any other conclusion than Chafer affirmed the full sovereignty of God as historically expressed in the Reformed traditions. Only a dishonest manipulation of the facts could yield a position where one believes Chafer embraced an Arminian, free will centrality view of election and salvation.

As with Moody and Darby, we can also see that others viewed Chafer as a Calvinist. Just as Moody had an issue with Darby over his Calvinism so too did evangelist Dr. John R. Rice who had issues with Chafer over his Calvinism. Dr. Rice thought that both Darby and Chafer were Calvinists.[348] According to Rice he and Chafer dialogued over this through letters to one another. Rice's analysis of Chafer was that not only

---

[345] Ibid., 174.

[346] Ibid.

[347] Ibid.

[348] John R. Rice, *Predestined for Hell* (Murfreesboro, TN: Sword of the Lord Publishers, 1958), 98.

was a he a Calvinist but that he was a hyper-Calvinist.[349] Rice seems to have characterized Chafer as a hyper-Calvinist because of the way in which Chafer handled his gospel invitations in the service.[350]

Though Rice's analysis and identification of Chafer as a hyper-Calvinist does not align with the facts of history, his recognition that Chafer had a definite Calvinistic view of salvation that impacted the way he did evangelism remains accurate. Chafer himself spoke of how the invitational system should remain simple and distinguished from the act of believing in Christ. Chafer, as a Calvinist, taught that when God elected a person and drew him or her to faith in and through effectual grace, the person experienced conversion and regeneration at that moment even before walking down the aisle to pray or confess Christ. He tried to make sure people did not confuse the public confession or response with the actual moment of belief and confession in faith. Chafer taught that God through his sovereignty moved the person to faith. Chafer taught the person should then, after believing in Christ for salvation, declare or make public the miraculous conversion he or she had experienced so as to avoid thinking that the walking of the aisle or prayer merited or earned eternal grace.[351] This type of criticism from Rice and distinct concern by Chafer only makes sense if Chafer taught a Calvinistic soteriology.

4. Dr. Herbert Lockyer (1886-1984)

As a dispensationalist and prolific author, Lockyer produced over fifty books of theology. One of his most famous series was the *All of the Bible* series which totaled twenty-one volumes.[352] He attended "Glasgow Bible Institute and graduated at the top of his class. He subsequently earned doctoral degrees from Northwestern Evangelical Seminary and the

---

[349] Ibid., 98-99.

[350] Ibid., 99.

[351] Lewis Sperry Chafer, *True Evangelism: Winning Souls by Prayer* (Grand Rapids, MI: Zondervan, 1919), 17-20.

[352] "Top Christian Writers Authors - Christianbook.Com", *Christianbook.Com*, last modified 2016, accessed June 30, 2016, http://www.christianbook.com/html/authors/3221.html.

International Academy in London."³⁵³ Speaking of Lockyer, Dr. Billy Graham stated that he "was unquestionably one of the spiritual giants of our century, and his prolific writings will continue to make an impact on countless Christians for generations to come if our Lord tarries."³⁵⁴

Lockyer's writings reveal his alignment as well with a Reformed/Calvinist soteriology. First, in reference to man's depravity, Lockyer understood man as totally depraved. He says, "The fall resulted in the total depravity of man, which means that although he is not altogether bad, every part of his nature became tainted by sin."³⁵⁵ Sin in man's fall was "universal" and it caused a "loss of communion with God" as it produced "spiritual death" that ultimately results in "eternal punishment."³⁵⁶ Speaking to man's need for the rebirth he describes the radical nature of man before regeneration:

> Man is born in sin (Psalm 51:5) and needs to be born again. By reason of sin, the sinner is spiritually dead and cannot receive the impartation of new life (Romans 8:6; Ephesians 2:1; 1 Timothy 5:6; Revelation 3:1). Apart from God, he cannot perceive or understand the things of God (1 Cor. 2:14), and he must be reborn if he is to 'see' and 'enter' the presence of God (John 3:35). Being unregenerate he lacks eyes to see the kingdom and the power to enter. He also has no affinity with the Spirit and capacity for spiritual things. Without the Spirit, the sinner is 'a child of the devil' (John 8:44: 1 John 3:10).³⁵⁷

These statements reveal his affirmation of man's depravity, a depravity that cripples man and places him in a place of spiritual deadness. Man in

---

[353] Ibid.

[354] Ibid.

[355] Herbert Lockyer, *All the Doctrines of the Bible* (Grand Rapids, MI: Zondervan, 1964), 145.

[356] Ibid.

[357] Ibid., 178-179.

this condition has no spiritual life which he can use or build upon to earn and gain God's eternal grace.

Second, he defines three interrelated terms: foreknowledge, election, and predestination. Of foreknowledge he says that it means "to define and determine beforehand, to mark out boundaries in advance. All the details of our salvation were arranged in a past eternity before time commenced."[358] As to election he defined that biblical term in the individual sense as God's "sovereign and eternal choice of persons (Eph. 1:4)."[359] This election also means "those divinely chosen cannot perish, for they were chosen in Christ before sin entered or the course of human responsibility commenced. Thus elected, neither the state of the one elected nor his doing can destroy God's eternal purpose. All who are saved are the 'vessels of mercy, which he had afore prepared unto glory (Romans 9:23).'"[360]

He then defines predestination. For him this means "the effective exercise of the will of God by which things determined by him are brought to pass."[361] It is the "exercise of divine sovereignty in the accomplishment of God's ultimate purpose or decree."[362] How is this sovereignty determined? Does something external to God determine what he decrees or predestines? Lockyer answers in the negative. He says, "God purposes in himself. He is never influenced by any external consequences. The whole reason for our redemption sprang from within God."[363] The people of God "existed in God's mind, eternally, before" they "existed in time."[364]

---

[358] Ibid., 152.

[359] Ibid.

[360] Ibid.

[361] Ibid., 152-153.

[362] Ibid., 153.

[363] Ibid.

[364] Ibid.

In commenting on the drawing work of the Spirit that brings about regeneration Lockyer states that "three persons of the Godhead are bound together in the regeneration of the soul."[365] This divine transaction is the act of God penetrating "deeply into the spirit-part of man," which "can only be effected by God the Spirit."[366] This inward effect cannot "come by way of self-effort or self-determination. We were not born, physically, by any desire or decision on our part. Just as our earthly parents were responsible for our entrance into the world, so God, by his Spirit, is responsible for our new birth and entrance into a spiritual realm."[367]

The drawing power of the Spirit alone brings about the new birth. "No human influence or agency can produce a regenerated person."[368] When the human side operates with the divine side repentance and faith take place. But even the "repentance, then, is God's sovereign gift" as it is "produced by his goodness, and is unto life (Acts 11:18)."[369] Repentance unto salvation is "not of man. It is God-produced."[370] For Lockyer the ideas of regeneration and conversion were "distinct yet indissolubly connected."[371] The work of God in regeneration "is the inward expression of which conversion should be the outward expression."[372]

---

[365] Ibid., 180.

[366] Ibid.

[367] Ibid., 179-180.

[368] Ibid., 180.

[369] Ibid., 174.

[370] Ibid.

[371] Ibid., 177.

[372] Ibid.

5. Dr. Alva J. McClain (1888-1968)

Dr. McClain served in numerous roles within the conservative body of Christ. He taught as a professor at Philadelphia School of the Bible, the Bible Institute of Los Angeles, Ashland College, and Ashland Theological Seminary. Additionally, he was the founder and first president of Grace Theological Seminary and Grace College in Indiana. He served in that role until 1962.

McClain also served as a charter member of the Evangelical Theological Society. He also participated in the revision of the famous Scofield Reference Bible. He loved this project so much that he had someone drive him to the dedication of that new Scofield edition. Lester Pifer picked up McClain and his wheelchair and drove him to Chicago for the dedication ceremony. Shortly after this ceremony McClain died.

God used this man to defend the truths of the faith and to promote conservative Christianity. The Lord took a young football and baseball player, who while playing baseball experienced a bad injury, and redirected this man's steps into Christian ministry. After losing a battle with modernism in Ashland, and upon being terminated, God led him to establish a new school that he dedicated his life too.

McClain published a commentary on Romans. In this text he made it clear that he affirmed the doctrine of eternal election and the need for efficacious grace to move a depraved sinner to faith in Christ. His identification with a Calvinistic view of salvation stands out with clarity in this commentary.

As to depravity when commenting on Romans 3, McClain taught that man stands condemned in sin. All people have turned away from God and none seek after God. Depravity has debilitated mankind. He said, sin has caused people to have "derangement in mentality, spiritual incomprehension."[373] Sin impacts mankind so deeply that lost man will not understand God, or the spiritual things related to God and the gospel. McClain summarized this wretched condition saying: "In all that man is,

---

[373] Alva J. McClain, *Romans: The Gospel of God's Grace* (Chicago, Ill: Moody Bible Institute, 1973), 94.

in all that he says, in all that he does, there is the taint of depravity and sin. That is the meaning of total depravity."[374]

When commenting on Romans 8 and the golden chain of salvation idea, McClain articulated the idea God elected in eternity and then from this he foreknew these people that he would in time effectually call to faith and then subsequently bring those to glorification. He stated, "his eternal purpose comes first, then foreknowledge, then predestination."[375] This election by God from eternity means for McClain that the one elected unto salvation cannot lose that salvation.[376]

Next in Romans 9, McClain explains the doctrine of election as God's positive choice to save while also rejecting a positive decree of election unto damnation. In McClain's view this chapter discusses God's election of some which consequently causes some to question if God can be good if he exercises his sovereignty in that way.[377] McClain wrote that "God is . . . sovereign when it comes to bestowing his judgment."[378] While rejecting the warped supralapsarian view, McClain presented the view that God did not create man in sin. All men from Adam, who freely sinned, come forth as marred clay. From this lump of sinful humanity, God works to redeem by election. McClain articulated the view with these words:

> God makes no man a sinner. Remember this: God takes the clay as he finds it, and the 'clay' here is man who is already a sinner . . . . God created him good, holy, and righteous, but the clay that the apostle is talking about here is sinful clay. Out of that clay every man stands alike. Every man is a sinner, every man deserves judgment. God has a right to pick out one man from that mass and have mercy upon him, and let the other man go if he wants to. . . . Two different classes of vessels are referred to here—one class of

---

[374] Ibid., 97.

[375] Ibid., 168.

[376] Ibid., 169.

[377] Ibid., 175.

[378] Ibid., 181.

vessels is fitted for destruction, the other is fitted for glory. . . . the middle voice of the Greek verb means that man fits himself for destruction . . . . on the other hand, if any man ever reaches heaven it will not be because he fitted himself for heaven, but because God fitted him for heaven.[379]

McClain embraced a Calvinistic soteriology. He affirmed man suffered from a debilitating condition of sinful depravity. Yet God elected people unto salvation. This grace and mercy fitted and led the elect to believe in the Lord for salvation. Those not elected were allowed to refuse grace and fit themselves unto damnation. His views convictions as expressed in this commentary align with the Reformed-Calvinistic position.

6. Dr. Donald Grey Barnhouse (1895-1960)

In the middle of the twentieth century Barnhouse became one of the most well-known and popular Bible teachers of the United States. Dr. W.C. Ringenberg has stated that Barnhouse may have been the "most widely followed American Bible teacher during the early middle decades of" the twentieth century.[380] He served as pastor of the famous Tenth Presbyterian Church in Philadelphia from 1927 onward for his entire pastoral career. Over 455 radio stations broadcast his Bible teachings.[381]

In describing the theology of Barnhouse, Dr. Ringenberg stated that he affirmed Calvinism and fundamentalism. Among that mix he was also classified as an advocate of Dispensationalism.[382] His teachings on eschatology consisted of "elaborate eschatological schemes."[383] Of those

---

[379] Ibid., 183.

[380] W.C. Ringenberg, "*Donald Grey Barnhouse*," in the *Evangelical Dictionary of Theology*, ed. Walter A. Elwell (Grand Rapids, MI: Baker Books, 2001), 142.

[381] Ibid.

[382] Ibid.

[383] Ibid.

schemes Barnhouse affirmed the essential elements that constitute Dispensationalism (Israel/Church distinction, pre-tribulational rapture of the church, ethnic Israel's salvation, and the premillennial view of Christ's kingdom reign).

Without a doubt, when someone reads the sermons or writings of Barnhouse his Calvinistic soteriological themes surface with regularity and with clarity. First, he stands in unison with the Calvinistic doctrine of man's original, natural, and total depravity by birth. Of this doctrine he says, "Nowhere in the Bible is man presented as standing in right relationship to God. Everywhere he is revealed as a rebel against God, his nature of corruption and depravity hardening and deepening as times goes on . . . . men hate the doctrine of original sin and seek to deny its existence, but it still stands."[384] The sin of Adam caused his spiritual life with God to die.[385] This original corruption of Adam extends to all of mankind. "The effects of sin upon Adam were spiritually genetic. Just as the genes in germ plasm affect the transmission of physical characteristics to children, so there is transmission of the seeds of spiritual death to each and every descendant of Adam."[386] This corruption infiltrates man to such a degree that Barnhouse says the "natural man does not receive the things of the Spirit."[387] Man in an unregenerate condition cannot comprehend the things of God or even the deceitfulness of his or her sin.[388]

Consequently, and second, because of that depravity, Barnhouse taught that God had to elect some in Christ since no one would come unless this act had been done by God on behalf of some. As he says, "the mind of the unsaved man is in a state of hostility to God," and because of this hostility the mind "of the unsaved man will not submit to the law of

---

[384] Donald Grey Barnhouse, *Romans: God's Grace* (Grand Rapids, MI: Wm. B. Eerdmans Publishing Company, 1959), 3:28, 29.

[385] Ibid., 31.

[386] Ibid., 32.

[387] Ibid.

[388] Ibid.

God, and, much more important, it cannot thus be subject."[389] This depravity is so thorough that "if God does not intervene to do his work of grace, not one human being will come to God. If God had sent masses of angels to preach the gospel to the lost race and had not applied any supernatural power within the individual, not one member of the human race would ever have accepted Christ as Savior."[390] Man due to his depravity and position in Adam has lost free will. "Man's free will died in Adam"[391] according to Barnhouse. Clearly this type of presentation conforms to the doctrine of man's depravity and the need for efficacious grace.

Third, it even appears that Barnhouse embraced the idea that regeneration precedes or causes faith. In his thought it seems that efficacious grace produces regeneration and then that miraculously granted faith flows from the new life. Of this he says, "Salvation is not a reward for faith; grace provides the saving faith which the Holy Spirit implants in the hearts of those whom God has chosen, and this God-given faith becomes the first fruit of the new life bestowed."[392]

This type of calling and grace Barnhouse categorized as "irresistible."[393] As he describes his own conversion experience he highlights that he had new life before he even heard or believed. "Salvation begins with God. He must initiate the process of salvation by quickening those who are dead in sin. . . . I know for me the matter has been forever settled. I know that I was dead and was made alive by Christ. With that new life I believed in him. . . . in my own case that I was given

---

[389] Donald Grey Barnhouse, *Romans: God's Heirs* (Grand Rapids, MI: Wm. B. Eerdmans Publishing Company, 1959), 3:37.

[390] Ibid., 3:38.

[391] Donald Grey Barnhouse, *Romans: God's Grace* (Grand Rapids, MI: Wm. B. Eerdmans Publishing Company, 1959), 3:73.

[392] Ibid., 3:134.

[393] Ibid., 3:123.

life, eternal life, by God through Christ. I used that eternal life to hear his Word and to believe on the Father who sent the Son."[394]

Fourth, Barnhouse provides a specific time in which God determined to decree this grace upon some of the human race. He speaks of the doctrine of unconditional election before the foundation of the world. Of this subject he says, "Scripture tells us that we were chosen in Christ before the foundation of the world (Eph. 1:4) . . . . In his eternal decrees God determined that he should not be solitary forever, that out of the multitude of sons of Adam a vast host would become sons of God, partakers of the divine nature and conformed to the image of the Lord Jesus Christ."[395]

Fifth, Barnhouse makes it clear that this election before the foundation of the world, or as he sometimes translates it, before the "disruption, or ruin, of the world,"[396] did not occur because of mere prescient foreknowledge. Of those who make God's election contingent upon mere prescience (advance knowledge), Barnhouse accused those

---

[394] Donald Grey Barnhouse, *Romans*: *God's Heirs* (Grand Rapids, MI: Wm. B. Eerdmans Publishing Company, 1959), 3:162.

[395] Donald Grey Barnhouse, *Romans*: *God's Freedom* (Grand Rapids, MI: Wm. B. Eerdmans Publishing Company, 1959), 3:35.

[396] Donald Grey Barnhouse, *Revelation: An Expositional Commentary* (Grand Rapids MI: Zondervan, 1971), 239. Barnhouse taught the idea that the angelic world existed before the human world. Thus, he saw a time space between Genesis 1:1 and Genesis 1:2. In that time frame Satan fell into sin and the world of that age was judged and destroyed. Then the rest of Genesis speaks of God refashioning or recreating a world in which humanity would live upon. Numerous Dispensationalists of the past have taught this position (Eric Sauer; C.I., Scofield; Arno Gaebelein; Medical Doctor M.R. Dehaan; J. Vernon McGee; W.A.Criswell, and Clarence Larkin to name a few). A modern advocate of this in Dispensational circles is the Hebrew Christian theologian Dr. Arnold G. Fruchtenbaum. One strength of this view is that it recognizes Lucifer/Satan sinned first in the universe. Some wrongly say no death existed prior to Adam & Eve's sin. This cannot be true. Satan was tempting Adam and Eve and thus in sin prior to their sin. Whenever Lucifer sinned at that point a death happened in his relationship with God. Lucifer experienced a separation from God, a death, and that brought sin into the universe. Adam and Eve brought sin into the line of humanity and the world of humanity.

teachers of "dragging God down out of eternity and making him like his creatures of time."[397] He defined foreknowledge of God this way:

> God's foreknowledge is an advanced determination to carry through a plan which he has eternally purposed in the counsels of his own will, and which is to be carried through without variation because the Lord brings to pass all that he has thus determined and decreed. . . . That God's foreknowledge is not merely advance knowledge but a definite predetermination is shown by the fact that these two ideals are expressed by the same Greek word when applied by our Lord Jesus Christ himself. Peter writes, "you were redeemed . . . with the precious blood of Christ, as of a lamb without blemish and without spot; who verily was foreordained before the foundation of the world" (1 Peter 1:20). Thus we must conclude that the foreknowledge of him who is omnipotent, omniscient, and unchangeable, is nothing more or less than an eternal decree that began in the heart of God who would not be frustrated by the fact that men sinned . . . .[398]

Sixth, this efficacious or irresistible call differs from the external outward call. Often found in Reformed/Calvinist soteriology models is this concept of two types of callings of God. One calling is the external calling and the other is the inward or effectual calling.[399] A general or outward call may be done by the proclamation of the gospel. But the Holy Spirit must apply it inwardly to make it effectual according to a Calvinist soteriology model. Barnhouse clearly communicated his belief in a general outward call that did not guarantee the person experiencing the conversion unto faith. He says, "the outward call comes to all men. It is the proclamation of the gospel to the whole race."[400]

---

[397] Donald Grey Barnhouse, *Romans: God's Heirs* (Grand Rapids, MI: Wm. B. Eerdmans Publishing Company, 1959), 3:159.

[398] Ibid., 3:160,161.

[399] Michael Horton, *For Calvinism* (Grand Rapids, MI: Zondervan, 2011), 105-106.

[400] Donald Grey Barnhouse, *Romans: God's Heirs* (Grand Rapids, MI: Wm. B. Eerdmans Publishing Company, 1959), 3:168.

He adds further, "the two calls set forth in the Bible must be carefully distinguished one from another. The one is an outward call that is universal, and the other is an inward call that produces life in a believer. . . . The inward call of God is the effect of his eternal predestination and purpose to conform those whom he has chosen to the image of his Son."[401]

Seventh, it also appears that Barnhouse embraced the idea of limited atonement. Since I will devote an entire section to this subject from a Dispensational tradition I will refrain from too much elaboration here. It is true that it appears more Dispensationalists are modified or four point Calvinists. However, some, as it seems with Barnhouse, have embraced a five point Calvinist soteriology model. In describing the passages where the phrase "all men" is used he opts to interpret those within the standard five point Calvinist interpretive methodology[402] that such words "may not be interpreted to mean every member of the human race. . . . In many passages of the New Testament the words *any man, every man, all men,* most surely mean any *believing man, every believing man, and all believing men.* A believer is one who has believed God's verdict about his own sin, and God's verdict that on the cross the sin of the sinner is placed upon the Savior, and the righteousness of the Savior is placed to the account of the sinner."[403] These comments appear to show that Barnhouse limits the extent of the atonement of Christ to just those that come to faith.

7. Dr. Merrill F. Unger (1909-1980)

Merrill Unger earned his BA from Johns Hopkins University. Then he earned a Th.M. and Th.D. from Dallas Theological Seminary. He then returned to Johns Hopkins University to complete a Ph.D. in Hebrew and Semitic languages. He served for around twenty years in Dallas Theological Seminary teaching Old Testament and Semitics.

---

[401] Ibid.

[402] Duane Edward Spencer, *Tulip: The Five Points of Calvinism in the Light of Scripture* (Grand Rapids, MI: Baker Books, 1979), 35-43.

[403] Donald Grey Barnhouse, *Romans: God's Grace* (Grand Rapids, MI: Wm. B. Eerdmans Publishing Company, 1959), 89-90.

As a dispensationalist Dr. Unger produced many scholarly works on the Bible. His Old Testament Commentary, Commentary on the Gospels, his Bible Dictionary, and Handbook to the Bible were excellent sources for biblical and theological truth.

He articulated in his writings man's depravity, God's sovereign elective love, effectual grace, and the preservation of the saints in grace as they persevered in faith in the Lord Jesus. Unger would fall within the Calvinistic umbrella of theological persuasion. He also taught that salvation, as presented throughout the all dispensations, occurred by grace through faith. He believed in an eternal covenant made within the Trinity before time began that established and guaranteed the salvation of many, i.e., the elected ones.[404] He taught that Hebrews 13:20 affirmed a "redemptive covenant before time began, between the Father and the Son" existed, and that by that "covenant we have eternal redemption."[405] That single solitary covenant of redemption verifies his dedication to a single plan of redemption that transcends all dispensations.

In regards to man's depravity he affirmed the helpless condition of man. In a natural condition outside of eternal grace, people are "utterly lost, cut off, helpless," and fallen under demon control."[406] As to divine election, he stated God exercised his will in a "sovereign act" where he in "in grace" before time and in "eternity" chose a people "from the human race for himself."[407] He stated, "God the Father chose us in eternity past in him."[408] In describing the doctrine of election in his Old Testament Commentary Unger taught that Jeremiah had been called and set apart in the womb "before he was born."[409] This work of God in and for Jeremiah

---

[404] Merrill F. Unger, *Unger's Bible Handbook*, revised by Gary N. Larson (Chicago, IL: Moody Press, 2005), 613.

[405] Ibid.

[406] Ibid., 548.

[407] Ibid., 547.

[408] Ibid.

[409] Merrill F. Unger, *Unger's Commentary on the Old Testament* (Chattanooga, TN: AMG Publishers, 2002), 1347.

was "predestinated in God's eternal foreknowledge and secret counsel."[410] For Unger that act of God with Jeremiah displayed the teaching of Ephesians 1:4-5 in the Old Testament context.[411]

His view of election naturally flowed from his perspective on God's sovereignty and absolute providential rule. He stated of God, "the possession of the most complete sovereignty is a necessary part of the proper conception of God and is abundantly declared in the Scriptures (e.g., Pss. 55:1; 66:7; 93:1; Isa. 40:15, 17; 1 Tim. 6:15; Rev. 11:17)."[412] For Unger, God did not limit himself by creating a man with a will. God had the power, right, ability, and wisdom to rule in and through all of creation, including man's will. As he stated, "the sovereignty of God is absolute. He is under no external restraint whatsoever. He is the Supreme Dispenser of all events."[413] Though God has made mankind in his image with the power "of choice between good and evil," God has still in his sovereign providence worked in such a way that he "rules over them in justice and wisdom and grace."[414]

In regards to drawing grace and regeneration, Unger's theology articulates a position that man's will does not contribute anything to his calling, drawing, or regeneration. In speaking of John 6:37 Unger explained that the Father's "divine sovereignty" is "manifest in the efficacious drawing of them."[415] This efficacious grace or drawing work of the Lord works in such a way with their "free will" that they "voluntarily" receive or accept Christ.[416] In affirming his position of

---

[410] Ibid.

[411] Ibid.

[412] Merrill F. Unger, "*Sovereignty of God*," in *The New Unger's Bible Dictionary*, ed. R. K. Harrison (Chicago, IL: Moody Press, 1988), 1214.

[413] Ibid.

[414] Ibid.

[415] Merrill F. Unger, *Unger's Commentary on the Gospels* (Chattanooga, TN: AMG Publishers, 2014), 486.

[416] Ibid.

monergism, Unger spoke of regeneration from John 3 as something miraculous. He stated, "natural humans," by "their own intellectual acumen or effort, can never comprehend" regeneration nor can they "effect it" because it can be "effected only by God's Spirit and understood only through" the Holy Spirit's "teaching ministry in the soul."[417]

In a summation of the entire work of God in redemption, Unger described this work of God in a Calvinistic way by teaching that God did the electing and drawing of those elect to grace in Christ Jesus. Writing on John 17:2b he stated, "the giving of eternal life to the elect" pertains to the ones "chosen from eternity past in the plan and foreknowledge of God (Eph. 1:3)." These elect ones are the ones that the Father has given the Son" so that then God will "bestow eternal life upon them" as those elect ones would "believe and receive it."[418]

Unger had similar thoughts on Matthew 11:27. In that text, like those in John's gospel, Unger thought this text "emphasized divine sovereignty" in salvation.[419] Additionally, in Matthew 16, Unger highlighted how the divine work of election and illumination in the soul occurred with Peter when he confessed Christ. God had worked a "divine revelation" in Peter that did not occur through "natural perception or human teaching."[420]

In Romans 8, Unger understood the Bible to teach that our salvation rested in God's good will towards us that spanned from eternity. God "foreknew us," he "predestined us to Christ-likeness," he "called us," he justified us," and in his mind he has even already "glorified us."[421] These truths mean that once Christ's atonement has been applied to us, and we are placed in Christ's eternal graces, that the elect believer becomes "inseparable from Christ" as "nothing in time or eternity can

---

[417] Ibid., 461-462.

[418] Ibid., 570.

[419] Ibid., 88.

[420] Ibid., 120.

[421] Merrill F. Unger, *Unger's Bible Handbook*, revised by Gary N. Larson (Chicago, IL: Moody Press, 2005), 509.

separate" the elect "from God's love manifested in Christ."[422] For Unger, the Bible "strongly emphasized" the "safety and security of the believer."[423]

8. Dr. W.A. Criswell (1909-2002)

W.A. Criswell served as a senior pastor at First Baptist Dallas for fifty years and while there led the membership up to twenty-six thousand members.[424] "More than fifty books would come from his pen, and he would travel to the ends of the earth preaching."[425] Criswell classified himself as a Calvinist teacher.[426] His sermons and writings on Revelation reveal his allegiance to a dispensational hermeneutic and view of scripture. His teachings seem to show clearly that his confession of being a Calvinist is accurate. In speaking to God's overall sovereignty Criswell stated,

> The grand foundational truth of history, of all life and living, is that God is sovereign and that God has an immutable purpose for the world. Things that to us are adventitious, haphazard, and by chance are not so to God. He works in all things and has a purpose and a perfect plan . . . . A part of God's sovereignty is that he bring to pass his immutable decrees . . . . The purposes of God will not and cannot fail.[427]

---

[422] Ibid., 510.

[423] Ibid.

[424] Paige Patterson, "*W.A. Criswell*," in *Theologians of the Baptist Tradition*, edited by Timothy George and David S. Dockery (Nashville, TN: Broadman and Holman Publishers, 2001), 236.

[425] Ibid.

[426] Paige Patterson, "*An Interview with W.A. Criswell*," in *The Church at the Dawn of the 21st Century*, edited by Paige Patterson, John Pretlove and Luis Pantoja Jr. (Dallas, TX: Criswell Publications, 1989), 6.

[427] W.A. Criswell, *Great Doctrines of the Bible, Volume 5, Soteriology*, edited by Paige Patterson (Grand Rapids, MI: Zondervan Publishing, 1985), 126, 127, 128.

When speaking to the narrower subject concerning election of some to salvation Criswell embraced the standard Calvinist position. His view was that in eternity past God elected some to salvation and those elected ones would come to faith in Christ at some point in history. Of this doctrine he stated that Acts 13:48 means "those that were not appointed to eternal life did not believe. Those who were elected believed."[428] He even taught that it was due to God's elective sovereign will that Israel must come into possession of the land promised to the patriarchs in the Old Testament. Criswell believed that "no matter what anybody says, in politics, in headlines, in the courts of the nations, God promised the land of Israel to Abraham and to his seed, Isaac and Jacob. There is plenty of room in this earth for everybody else. That land belongs to them. It is in the elective purpose of God and cannot be disannulled."[429]

For Criswell, the doctrine of election guaranteed that Christ's death would not be in vain. The doctrine of election meant that with certainty some would come to faith in Christ. As he said,

> God promised Jesus before the creation of the world . . . that if he suffered and died for the sins of the fallen race, God would give him a people. He would not die in vain. Somebody would believe; somebody would accept; somebody would be saved. God would give to Christ a people after he suffered and died for the sins of the fallen race. That is election.[430]

Additionally, Criswell took a clear stance on the efficacious work of the Spirit to draw a person to faith. His views align well with the standard doctrine of a Reformed soteriology in the area of the drawing work of the Spirit upon the elect. Concerning Ephesians 2:1 and 2:5 Criswell taught,

> How can a dead corpse raise himself? How can he change himself? He is dead. He does not have eyes to see. He does not have ears to

---

[428] Ibid., 135.

[429] Ibid., 137.

[430] Ibid., 139.

hear. He does not have a heart to feel. He does not have a will to respond. How can a dead man change himself? All the human efforts at our command cannot regenerate the soul or change the life.... How can a man ever be saved? How can he ever present himself before the Lord if he is dead and without Christ and without hope and without God? Somehow God must lift him up. God must intervene. God must do a miraculous work. We have to be changed if we are ever able to stand in the presence of the Lord God Almighty. By nature we are shut out. Except a man be born again, he cannot see the kingdom of God. We have to be changed. Our nature, our souls, our hearts, our lives have to be changed, regenerated, born again.[431]

For Criswell this sovereign work of regeneration did not hinge upon a person's will. He believed that a miracle had to occur in order for the man to move towards Christ. As he says, "God's prerogative is to create. God's omnipotence regenerates.... the same omnipotent God who made us can remake us and regenerate us so that we are born again into the spiritual kingdom of the heavenly Father."[432]

9. Dr. John Walvoord (1910-2002)

Dr. Lewis Sperry Chafer's successor at Dallas Seminary also stood in the same line concerning the doctrines of grace. John F. Walvoord took the reins of Dallas Seminary from Chafer after his death in 1952[433] and led the next generation of Dispensationalists. Dr. John Hannah, a historian and Dispensationalist, stated in his analysis of Walvoord that the man "defended the Augustinian, Calvinist interpretation of sin, Christ, redemption, and grace..."[434] Such a statement readily proves itself when

---

[431] Ibid., 88, 89.

[432] Ibid., 92, 94.

[433] John Hannah, "*John Walvoord*," in *Dictionary of Premillennial Theology*, ed. Mal Couch (Grand Rapids, MI: Kregel Publications, 1996), 420.

[434] Ibid., 421.

The Calvinism of Dispensationalism

evaluating the evidence from the writings of Walvoord. One work in particular that proves his Calvinistic bent[435] is his work on the Holy Spirit.

Walvoord, in *The Holy Spirit,* expressed his understanding of efficacious grace in contrast to common grace which works within the entire world. Efficacious grace limits itself only to those who the Lord destines to come to him as his child. Walvoord wrote of efficacious grace this:

> Efficacious grace is a theological term having in view the work of the Holy Spirit in moving men to effective faith in Jesus Christ as Savior. After common grace which is antecedent, efficacious grace is the first aspect chronologically and logically in the work of the Spirit in man's salvation. It is a theme of Scripture greatly misunderstood and misrepresented, but few doctrines are more determinate in their bearing on theology as a whole. It involves the whole point of view of the sovereign and effective direction of God of all events to fulfill God's purposes. It affects the most important work of God in saving men . . .[436]

He added that this doctrine arises from the abundance of Scripture that speaks of the Spirit calling and securing salvation in God's people. "The Scriptures speak frequently of a divine call to salvation which results in certain salvation (Rom. 1:1, 6, 7; 8:28, 30; 9:11, 24; 11:29; 1 Cor. 1:1, 2, 9, 24, 26; 7:15, 17, 18, 20, 21, 22, 24 . . . Eph 1:18 . . . 1 Thess. 2:12 . . .

---

[435] I say his bent not because Walvoord failed to actually teach a particularist view of redemption, but because Calvinism and Reformed theology cover much more than simply soteriology. The Calvinism of the Reformation and the Reformed faith of today have expressed their systems in detailed fashions. These views normally present themselves under what has been generally labeled Covenant theology; Walvoord, then, naturally holds to an early church, Augustinian, and Calvinistic view of salvation but not necessarily a Calvinistic/Reformed view of the eschaton or ecclesiology, which is normally amillennial, postmillennial, or covenant premillennialism with a post-tribulation rapture view.

[436] John Walvoord, *The Holy Spirit* (Grand Rapids, MI: Zondervan Publishing, 1958), 119.

2 Peter 1:3, 10)."[437] These were a select few of the passages Walvoord thought presented the efficacious grace of God.

The issue of conditional or unconditional regeneration, otherwise known as synergism or monergism, determines whether one stands in line with the Reformation stream of thought on salvation (monergism) or on the Arminian/Pelagian stream of thought on salvation (synergism). Walvoord clearly presented salvation as monergistic. He said "efficacious grace . . . is an act of God dependent solely upon God for its execution. Reformed theologians are in substantial agreement upon this point, and the Scriptures bear a consistent testimony."[438] Walvoord added that any divine calling results not from human volition but rather from the almighty hand of God. He stated that "never in the Scriptures is divine calling attributed to human choice. It is rather an act of God proceeding from omnipotence and sovereignty."[439] Notice the word "never." Walvoord took a staunch and clear position with that type of emphasis.

Walvoord even went so far as to link this doctrine with man's sinfulness that naturally caused him to stand in a helpless and depraved state. Therefore, in Walvoord's eye, efficacious grace stems from man's inability to believe unless God's grace causes belief. He stated,

> In keeping with their [the Reformers' view of salvation] doctrine of total depravity and total inability, Reformed theologians have insisted that efficacious grace is an immediate act of God accomplished without human assistance. While they freely admit the necessity of the work of common grace as antecedent in which the individual hears and understands the gospel and sees his own need of salvation, efficacious grace is defined as the instantaneous work of God empowering the human will and inclining the human heart to faith in Christ. Efficacious grace immediately results in the salvation in all cases because it is accomplished by the omnipotence of God.[440]

---

[437] Ibid., 120.

[438] Ibid., 121.

[439] Ibid.

[440] Ibid., 121-122 (Brackets are mine).

To back this statement Walvoord quoted at length the Westminster Confession of Faith,[441] and then he added these words,

> . . . efficacious grace is an immediate act of God which by its nature cannot be resisted. As Charles Hodge writes: "According to the Augustinian doctrine the efficacy of divine grace in regeneration depends neither upon its congruity nor upon the active cooperation, nor upon the passive non-resistance of its subject, but upon its nature and the purpose of God. It is the exercise of 'the mighty power of God,' who speaks and it is done. This is admitted to be the doctrine of Augustine himself." Efficacious grace is irresistible not in the sense that it is resisted and all such resistance is overcome, but it is irresistible in the sense that it is never resisted. Its nature forbids it. It is irresistible in that it is certainly effectual. A.H. Strong, accordingly, prefers not to use the term irresistible: "We prefer to say that this special call is efficacious, that is, that it infallibly accomplished its purpose of leading the sinner to the acceptance of salvation. This implies two things: (a) That the operation of God is not an outward constraint upon the human will, but that it accords with the laws of our mental constitution. We reject the term 'irresistible,' as implying a coercion and a compulsion which is foreign to the nature of God's working in the soul. (b) That the operation of God is the originating cause of that new disposition of the affections, and that new activity of the will, by which the sinner accepts Christ. The cause is not in the response of the will to the presentations of motives by God, nor in any mere cooperation of the will of man with the will of God, but is an almighty act of God in the will of man, by which its freedom to choose God as its end is restored and rightly exercised (John 1:12-13)."[442]

How much clearer could Walvoord be when he asserted such grace "cannot be resisted"? Walvoord then listed his reasons why efficacious

---

[441] Ibid., 122.

[442] Ibid., 123. The quote from Charles Hodge is from Hodge's *Systematic Theology*, 2:680. The quote from A. H. Strong came from his *Systematic Theology*, pp. 792-93.

grace must of necessity occur before salvation can result. Three of his reasons included (1) "An act of God must be effectual," (2) "The doctrine of efficacious grace is vital to predestination," and (3) "Total depravity and spiritual death require efficacious grace."[443]

If doubt still remains concerning Walvoord's view of salvation then the next quotes should clear all doubt. No doubt whatsoever can arise from his discussion of regeneration. Walvoord did not see multiple avenues of salvation. He did not think some were saved by works and others saved by grace. Rather, for him all were saved by the divine act of regeneration. Regeneration alone saves any person who has ever been saved. He agreed with the classical Reformed view that man's will contributes nothing to his own regeneration and attainment of grace. He wrote,

> Reformed theology has definitely opposed the introduction of any means in accomplishing the divine act of regeneration. The question of whether means are used to effect regeneration is determined largely by the attitude taken toward efficacious grace. Pelagian and Arminian theologians, holding as they do to the cooperation of the human will and the partial ability of the will through common grace or natural powers, recognize to some extent the presence of means in the work of regeneration. If the total inability of man be recognized, and the doctrine of efficacious grace believed, it naturally follows that regeneration is accomplished apart from means . . . . In the act of regeneration, however, the human will is entirely passive. There is no cooperation possible. The nature of the work of regeneration forbids any possible human assistance. As a child in natural birth is conceived and born without any volition on his part, so the child of God receives the new birth apart from any volition on his part. In the new birth, of course, the human will is not opposed to regeneration and wills by divine grace to believe, but this act in itself does not produce the new birth. As in the resurrection of the human body from physical death, the body in no way assists the

---

[443] Ibid., 124-125.

work of resurrection, so in the work of regeneration, the human will is entirely passive.[444]

Thus, from the above statements, Walvoord makes his Calvinistic position clear. Any person should realize that Walvoord stood in the historic line of a Protestant Reformed/Calvinistic soteriology. He, as did many of the prominent Dispensationalists, stood within the orthodox faith that salvation rested in grace and not upon human effort; he taught that salvation solely rests within the hands of God. He thoroughly believed that "all grace stems from Christ's death on the cross for our sins."[445] Just like his predecessor and mentor, Lewis Sperry Chafer, Walvoord did not waver on the doctrines of grace. According to Walvoord, salvation has always been by grace alone from the beginning of history to the end of history. He also contributed to Dispensationalism's overall development as a system that followed Chafer's advice: a theology must center on God and not around man. To that end Walvoord worked and with that goal his doctrine of redemption, as applied by the Holy Spirit, presents to those who will read it a Dispensational/Calvinistic understanding.

10. Dr. J. Dwight Pentecost (1915-2014)

J. Dwight Pentecost, a long time professor of Dallas Seminary, and author of one of the most famous books on the Second Coming of Christ, *Things to Come: A Study in Biblical Eschatology,* taught a clear view to the doctrine of predestination. Salvation, for Pentecost, did not occur because of man's self-activity to gain God's favor; salvation did not occur because of any effort of man. For Pentecost, salvation belongs entirely to the Lord through his sovereign application of grace. The doctrine of predestination, even though it is broader than election, will exhibit the root of a person's view concerning the work of God in redemption and the extent of his view of mankind's depravity. If a person adheres to a Reformed view of predestination then the person will almost automatically have a logical and biblical view of man's depravity. Totally depraved

---

[444] Ibid., 133.

[445] John Walvoord, *End Times: Understanding Today's World Events in Biblical Prophecy*, ed. Charles Swindoll (Nashville, TN: Word Publishing, 1998), 94.

people must be elected and predestined unto salvation for there is no other means to receive salvation. J. Dwight Pentecost, had this to say concerning predestination.

> It [election] has to do with selection. It has to do with separation unto Himself. And election has to do with the choice of the individuals who comprise those through whom the divine purpose established by foreordination will be fulfilled. God was going to work through individuals whom He separated unto Himself. And election is the sovereign work of God, according to His own purpose and will, predetermined by His foreordination, in which he selects those through whom the divine purpose will be fulfilled. We refer you again to Ephesians 1:4: we were chosen, in Christ, before the foundation of the world, that we should be holy and without blame before Him.[446]

Pentecost went on to explain that those who were then elected to fulfill the role that God had decreed for them, salvation and forgiveness of sin, God then predestined them to that end purpose of receiving the inheritance God preplanned for the individual.[447] Pentecost wrote that predestination always points to the final end of the plan that God has designed. God "predestinated us-and what was the end, or the aim? The adoption of children."[448]

Not only did Pentecost show that election and predestination occur through God's own will, but he also clearly explained that this action of God did not come to pass because of any foreseen goodness in man. In other words, God did not choose after merely foreseeing a good act from an individual that possesses meritorious qualities. God elected simply because of His own goodness not because of man's goodness. To refute the foreseen faith view Pentecost stated,

---

[446] J. Dwight Pentecost, *Things Which Become Sound Doctrine* (Grand Rapids, MI: Zondervan Publishing, 1969), 140.

[447] Ibid., 141.

[448] Ibid., 141.

> A widely held interpretation is that God has elected those who He knows will accept Christ as personal Savior. This is an erroneous interpretation, for if God elected those who He knew beforehand would accept Him as Savior, then God has not foreordained, God has not decreed, God has not foreknown; but rather, God has exercised His omniscience, and has limited Himself by the will of man. God is no longer a sovereign God if He elects those who He knew would accept Him as Savior.... God is then subject to the whims of the human will, and God cannot act upon, nor go beyond, the limits of the human will.[449]

Even Pentecost's understanding of foreknowledge contributes to his identification with the more Calvinistic perspective on the doctrines of grace. Foreknowledge definitely means that God foreknows the event that will come to pass. When Pentecost said above, "God has not foreknown," he uses the term foreknowledge to mean more than mere prescience. God's foreknowledge, according to Pentecost, rests upon the fact that a decree has occurred. God knows because he decrees.[450] Pentecost did not embrace an idea that God knew by learning or by exercising some level of omni-observance to the world at large and thereby discovering what would occur in time and history. He distinctly taught the contrasting view that God knows because as a rational being he determined his own knowledge about history because history flows from his own eternal mind.

Again this esteemed and well-known Dispensationalist espoused the basic theme of Calvinism in regard to the doctrine of salvation. God's work of salvation rests within the power of God. Man does not contribute *anything* to his redemption. Again, here is another prominent Dispensationalist who does not support Arminianism.

---

[449] Ibid., 139.

[450] Ibid., 138.

11. William MacDonald (1917-2007)

Like many Dispensationalists, MacDonald did not have a formal seminary education. Yet his whole life was devoted to learning the English Bible. He knew very little Greek or Hebrew yet he "knew the Bible as well as any scholar."[451] He earned a Bachelor's degree from Tuft's College and a Master's degree in Business from Harvard University. He served in the United States Navy for four years and later went to Emmaus Bible School. He remained associated with this Bible School for eighteen years. Six of his years there he served as President.[452] He authored over eighty books during his lifetime and one of those was the famous *Believer's Bible Commentary*.

Writing on man's sin nature, MacDonald affirmed the Reformed/Calvinist view. He held to the representative nature of Adam over the entire human race. "Everybody sinned in Adam; when he sinned, he acted as the representative for his descendants."[453] People are classified as sinners in three distinct ways: (1) sinners by birth from sinful parents that runs back to the first parents Adam and Eve; (2) sinners are such by their own choice to sin in practice; and (3) sinners are so because of their ultimate rejection of Jesus Christ.[454] When commenting on Romans 8:8, which says, "those who are in the flesh cannot please God," he says this means the corruption of the person is so pervasive that "there is nothing an unsaved person can do to please God, no good works, no religious observances, no sacrificial services, absolutely nothing."[455]

---

[451] "William Macdonald | William-Macdonald.Org," *William-Macdonald.Org*, last modified 2016, accessed July 1, 2016, http://www.william-macdonald.org/index.php?page=211.

[452] "My Heart, My Life, My All | William-Macdonald.Org," *William-Macdonald.Org*, last modified 2016, accessed July 1, 2016, http://www.william-macdonald.org/index.php?page=212.

[453] William MacDonald, *Believer's Bible Commentary*, ed. Art Farstad (Nashville, TN: Thomas Nelson Publishing, 1990), 1687.

[454] Ibid., 1698.

[455] Ibid., 1709.

In speaking of Romans 8:7 he stated, "The sinner is a rebel against God and in active hostility to him."[456] The lost will of man "wants to be its own master," the sinful will of lost man does not "bow to" Christ's "rule. Its nature is such that it cannot be subject to God's law. It is not only the inclination that is missing but the power as well. The flesh is dead toward God."[457] This position speaks clearly of his affirmation of man's natural depravity that limits his willingness to obey Christ Jesus.

When speaking of God's elective love he embraced the idea that some people are objects of an eternal love that sets them apart for salvation. He affirms a single doctrine of election and a passive doctrine of reprobation.[458] In particular he says of Romans 9:15, "All people are condemned by their own sin and unbelief. If left to themselves, they would all perish," yet "God chooses some of these condemned people to be special objects of his grace."[459] MacDonald then concludes by Romans 9:16 that "ultimately destiny of men or of nations does not rest in the strength of their will or in the power of their exertions, but rather in the mercy of God."[460] This is so because as Romans 9:21 teaches, "God has the absolute power and authority to make a vessel for honor with some of the clay and another for dishonor with some."[461]

To clarify further, MacDonald explained in detail that these elected people were chosen not by prescience but by God's own divine decree. In examining 1 Peter 1:2 that pertains to God's foreknowledge he writes, "elect according to the foreknowledge of God the Father . . . means that in a past eternity, God chose them to belong to himself."[462] He realized that this "doctrine of divine election is not always popular, but it does have this

---

[456] Ibid.

[457] Ibid.

[458] Ibid., 1718-1719.

[459] Ibid., 1718.

[460] Ibid.

[461] Ibid., 1719.

[462] Ibid., 2250.

virtue—it allows God to be God. Attempts to make it palatable to man only succeed in detracting from the sovereignty of God."[463] He understood this issue may appear on the surface to be contradictory (a paradox), or that there is some mystery to this subject, as does other Reformed/Calvinist scholars,[464] for he says, "Any difficulty in reconciling God's election and human responsibility lies in man's mind, not in God's."[465]

When speaking of the "golden chain of salvation,"[466] which refers to five key interconnected concepts (foreknowledge-predestination-calling-justification-glorification), MacDonald affirmed the Calvinist perspective. He spoke of this when interpreting Romans 8:29-31. He described these verses, like Sproul does, as the "golden chain of redemption" and this chain makes the "conclusion inevitable."[467] God's foreknowledge, which is "not mere intellectual knowledge," is an active knowledge that "embraced only those whom he foreordained or predestined."[468]

And then those whom God foreknew, these were predestined "in eternity," and then those predestined were "also called in time. This means that he not only hears the gospel but that he responds to it as well. It is therefore an effectual call."[469] This effectual call is not the same as the general call.[470] The effectual call is "conversion-producing."[471] Those

---

[463] Ibid.

[464] R.C. Sproul, *Chosen By God* (Wheaton, IL: Tyndale House Publishers, 1986), 46-47.

[465] William MacDonald, *Believer's Bible Commentary*, ed. Art Farstad (Nashville, TN: Thomas Nelson Publishing, 1990), 2250.

[466] R.C. Sproul, *Grace Unknown: The Heart of Reformed Theology* (Grand Rapids, MI: Baker Books, 1997), 146.

[467] William MacDonald, *Believer's Bible Commentary*, ed. Art Farstad (Nashville, TN: Thomas Nelson Publishing, 1990), 1712.

[468] Ibid.

[469] Ibid., 1713.

[470] Ibid.

foreknown are predestined, those predestined are called, those called are then justified, and then those justified will for certain be glorified. He summarizes saying, "For every million people who are foreknown and predestined by God, every one of that million will be called, justified, and glorified. Not one will be missing!"[472]

It is clear where MacDonald stood on the doctrines of grace. He affirmed as a Dispensationalist the depravity of man, God's unconditional elective love, and the sovereign application of Christ's gracious atonement to a sinner who is efficaciously called and moved to faith in Christ as Lord and Savior. He affirmed both a Dispensational[473] and Calvinist view of scripture.

12. John A. Witmer (1920—2007)

Dr. Witmer was born in Lancaster Pennsylvania. After his education he became a seminary professor at Dallas Theological Seminary. He earned a Masters degree from Wheaton College. He then earned his ThM and Th.D degrees from Dallas Seminary and taught at Dallas Seminary for many years. He retired in 1987. During that time he also served as the Head Librarian. In examining his Romans commentaries in the The Bible Knowledge Commentary and in the Twenty-First Century Biblical Commentary Series readers can easily see where he stood on the doctrine of God's elective grace.

Witmer affiliated himself with the United Evangelical Brethren. He contributed articles regularly to Christianity Today, Gospel Herald, and Moody Magazine. He also wrote the Romans commentary in The Bible Knowledge Commentary produced by Dallas Seminary faculty. Additionally, with Mal Couch, he authored the Galatians and Ephesians commentary in the Twenty-First Biblical Commentary Series edited by Ed

---

[471] Ibid.

[472] Ibid., 1713.

[473] MacDonald's interpretation of key texts like Daniel 9; Acts 1:6-7; Romans 9, 10, 11; Ephesians 3:1-13; 1 Thessalonians 4-5; and Revelation 21-22 show his agreement with the basic truths of Dispensationalism. Additionally, he affiliated for years with Emmaus Bible College. That college remains by doctrinal confession a Dispensational school.

Hindson and Mal Couch. In these works, one can easily see that Witmer embraced a Calvinistic soteriology.

In Romans 3 Witmer described mankind as sinful and in depravity. Apart from the Holy Spirit, mankind has so much depravity that people cannot produce the fruit of the Spirit. As he said, "they have no inner spiritual capacity whereby they can" exercise righteousness towards others.[474] "Sin causes" people to "be selfish and self-centered."[475] With Adam "the entire human race was plunged into sin."[476] Mankind comes forth from the womb with a sinful Adamic nature. In his words, "humankind is totally depraved and deserving of only condemnation."[477]

However, God has acted to rescue some through a gracious eternal election. Witmer explained that this election did occur on the basis of mere foresight of who would believe. Instead, Witmer embraced eternal, unconditional election. He stated of Romans 8:28-30 that God's foreknowledge means God established a "meaningful relationship with a person based on God's choice (cf. Jer. 1:4-5; Amos 3:2) in eternity before Creation. 'He chose us in him before the Creation of the world' (Eph. 1:4)."[478]

In contrast to the critics who claim Dispensationalism equals an Arminian soteriology model, Witmer, like so many others in Dispensationalism, unequivocally asserted God's election has no basis in the effort of lost man. In other words, lost man contributes nothing to his own election. In Witmer's words:

> From eternity past he had a plan that included our redemption carried out in time. . . . He chose the believer before the world was

---

[474] John A. Witmer, "Romans," in *The Bible Knowledge Commentary*, eds. John Walvoord & Roy Zuck (USA: SP Publications, 1983), 449.

[475] Ibid.

[476] Ibid., 450.

[477] John Witmer & Mal Couch, *Galatians & Ephesians: By Grace Through Faith*, ed. Ed Hindson (Chattanooga, TN: AMG Publishers, 2009), 140.

[478] John A. Witmer, "Romans," in *The Bible Knowledge Commentary*, eds. John Walvoord & Roy Zuck (USA: SP Publications, 1983), 449.

put into place. . . . There is no indication in the New Testament of a 'double predestination.' In fact, just the opposite seems to be true. Paul, when speaking of the idea of election in Romans 9:14-24, indicates God is waiting patiently for the lost to come to him. But because of the power of sin and the rebellion of the human heart, none will come by their own accord. . . . God 'prepared beforehand for glory' the elect . . . but he never says that God 'prepared beforehand' the lost for perdition. . . . Scripture makes it clear that no human being ever seeks God and that all fall short of his glory (Rom. 3:10-11). God was under no compulsion to choose any. . . . The manner in which God chose was unconditional. . . . This is an unconditional act on his part for his greater glory.[479]

Furthermore, these elected ones experience the drawing graces of the Lord in history. That grace moves the elect to faith. Witmer commenting on Ephesians 2 noted that man's salvation does not occur from "any kind of human effort."[480] In Witmer's theology, "faith is never self-produced; faith is created in us. The faith that saves is created by the saving grace of God."[481] Again, these positions reveal that Witmer aligned with the Calvinistic perspective of soteriology.

13. Dr. Charles C. Ryrie (1925-2016)

Around the globe the ministry of Charles C. Ryrie has influenced the young and the old. It is not only Ryrie's work *Dispensationalism* that has enlightened the masses, but also he has blessed many students at the seminaries and colleges that he served. He served the majority of his time at Dallas Seminary in Texas. I studied under him through Tyndale Seminary, also in Texas. Two of his courses, Dispensationalism and the book of Corinthians, remain very vivid memories for me because of the time spent with him and the valuable lessons from those courses.

---

[479] John Witmer & Mal Couch, *Galatians & Ephesians: By Grace Through Faith*, ed. Ed Hindson (Chattanooga, TN: AMG Publishers, 2009), 116-119

[480] Ibid., 142.

[481] Ibid.

Through his lectures, systematic doctrinal notes, books, and personal ministry he guided many into an understanding of an Evangelical Dispensationalism. His teachings have not always been directed toward the well-educated and trained theological ears. Ryrie also spent his time training some children of the faith through writing object lessons for children. Either in the classroom, or in everyday spirituality, many agree that this man truly lived with a goal of *Balancing the Christian Life* (one of his many books) in all that he does.[482]

However, Ryrie's view of salvation must be examined. Did Charles C. Ryrie promote a Calvinistic soteriology or an Arminian, Semi-Pelagian, or Pelagian doctrine of redemption? Was Ryrie truly balanced in his presentation of the doctrines of grace? Did Ryrie, a staunch apologist for Dispensationalism, which is supposedly Arminian, wed himself to Arminianism?

Reading Charles Ryrie's works will in no way lead someone to an Arminian/Pelagian view of salvation. A humble reading of Ryrie's own words should seemingly convince someone of his own allegiance to a Reformed soteriology. It would be hard to imagine someone reading Ryrie carefully and from his writings being led to embrace something else. Ryrie agreed with the classic doctrines of man's total depravity, God's sovereign choice of many but not all to salvation, and the efficacious and eternal application of Christ's substitutionary death for those whom God alone draws to his son Christ Jesus. Ryrie believes salvation has always been by grace.

Ryrie's systematic work reveals his allegiance to the orthodox view of depravity and, it also denies the other false theories that attempt to alleviate man's total depravity or modify his depravity. Ryrie stated that,

> Depravity means that man fails the test of pleasing God. He denotes his unmeritoriousness in God's sight. This failure is total in that (a) it affects all aspects of man's being, and (b) it affects all people . . . . Positively, total depravity means (a) that corruption extends to every facet of man's nature and faculties;

---

[482] *Expressions of Thanks* in *Basic Theology Applied: A Practical Application of Basic Theology in Honor of Charles C. Ryrie and His Work*, eds., Wesley and Elaine Willis and John and Janet Master (USA: Victor Books/SP Publications, 1995), 313-330.

and (b) that there is nothing in anyone that can commend him to a righteous God.[483]

Ryrie added that the theories of Pelagianism, Semi-Pelagianism, Socinianism, Arminianism, and Neoorthodoxy[484] skew the true doctrine of inherited original sin. Ryrie aptly commented on the theory of Socinianism; for Ryrie that theory denied the "deity of Christ," as well as "predestination, original sin, total inability, and penal substitution."[485] Does that sound weak concerning the doctrines dear to a Calvinistic soteriology?

Again, it would seem that anyone reading that who understands a basic soteriology rooted in a Calvinistic model and who does not have a bias against Dispensationalism would not conclude he was weak in regard to the radical corruption of man. He clearly affirmed the foundational doctrine of man's depravity.

In the same work Ryrie defended the Biblical doctrine of election against those theories which oppose unconditional election. Ryrie expounded upon the three main views of election that have been taught in Christendom. He discussed the various views of election beginning with "Foresight election," which Henry C. Thiessen promoted; he discussed "Corporate Election," a view that Karl Barth and Robert Shank presented; and lastly he presented the "Individual Pretemporal" view of election, which is also known as the Reformed view.[486] So what did Ryrie espouse? Is Ryrie in the Arminian camp concerning election, or does he clearly promote the Calvinistic view of unconditional election? His words seem unmistakably clear:

> Election emphasizes God's free choice of individuals to salvation (the election of Christ, Israel, or angels are not under

---

[483] Charles C. Ryrie, *Basic Theology: A Popular Systematic Guide To Understanding Biblical Truth,* (Colorado Springs, Colorado: Chariot Victor Publishing, 1996), 218-219.

[484] Ibid., 220.

[485] Ibid.

[486] Ibid., 310, 311.

consideration here). When Paul uses the verb he uses it in the middle voice, indicating that God's choice was made freely and for His own purposes (1 Cor. 1:27-28; Eph. 1:4). Individual Thessalonians were chosen (2 Thess. 2:13); as many as were set (previous to their believing) in the group of those who would have eternal life did believe (Acts 13:48); Paul was a chosen instrument (for salvation and service, Acts 9:15; Gal. 1:15); and some individual's names were not written in the Book of Life from the foundation of the world (Rev. 13:8; 17:8), which must mean some were. Election is unconditional and individual.[487]

If the above does not display clarity upon the subject then it would appear that a person's bias overshadows his objectivity. However, Ryrie did not conclude the subject there; he said more. Ryrie added his thoughts concerning the opposite side of the doctrine election, which is retribution. He said,

Retribution means deserved punishment, while preterition is the passing over of those not elected to salvation. Both terms avoid the concept involved in double predestination or reprobation which means foreordination to damnation. None of these terms appear in the Scripture, though the idea is clearly taught in Romans 9:18, 21; 1 Peter 2:8; and Revelation 17:8. Therefore, the Scriptures do contain a doctrine of preterition though there is not a decree to condemn in the same sense that there is a decree to elect. Obviously the very idea of election has to include the idea of the greater number out of which they were chosen, and those who were not chosen were certainly passed by.[488]

The statement above runs extremely close and parallel to the words of the renowned Calvinist scholar, R.C. Sproul, who said,

---

[487] Ibid., 312.

[488] Ibid., 313, 314.

> To understand the Reformed view of the matter [the issue of the non-elect] we must pay close attention to the crucial distinction between *positive* and *negative* decrees of God. Positive has to do with God's active intervention in the hearts of the elect. Negative has to do with God's passing over the non-elect. The Reformed view teaches that God positively or actively intervenes in the lives of the elect to insure their salvation. The rest of mankind God leaves to themselves. He does not create unbelief in their hearts. That unbelief is already there. He does not coerce them to sin. They sin by their own choices. In the Calvinist view the decree of election is positive; the decree of reprobation is negative.[489]

Both Ryrie and Sproul addressed the issue the same way. Both agree that it is God who elects freely and solely by his own sovereignty. They also agree that God actively intervenes to secure the redemption of the elect. Lastly, they both agree that God does not actively cause the non-elect to remain in unbelief; God simply leaves them in their own sin, which naturally leads to destruction. Yet with this much agreement between the two theologians, Sproul still wrote that Ryrie has ideas that run contrary to the Reformed idea of unconditional election.[490]

Such a conclusion by Sproul seems to reveal a bias that he has against this Dispensationalist. That bias apparently has chilled his more often than not intelligent and reasonable investigative method. Therefore, he now uses his mind to fancifully create a false chasm that he has created between the Covenant and Dispensationalist's view of salvation. To express this false chasm, Sproul attacked the prominent leaders of Dispensationalism such as Chafer, Ryrie, and others. Whether one is a Covenant theologian or a Dispensational theologian, a person must not press biases so that separation occurs where natural unity actually exists. And it seems these texts by Ryrie reveal his allegiance to a Reformed stream of thought on soteriology.

---

[489] R.C. Sproul *Chosen By God: God's Perfect Plan for His Glory and His Children* (Wheaton, Ill: Tyndale House Publishers, 1986), 142-143.

[490] R.C. Sproul, *Willing To Believe* (Grand Rapids, MI: Baker Books, 1997).

14. Dr. Earl D. Radmacher (1931-2014)

As an educator Dr. Radmacher spent thirty four years within Western Conservative Baptist Seminary. In those years he served as a professor, Dean, President, and then Chancellor.[491] He earned a Bachelor of Arts degree and Masters of Religious Education degree from Bob Jones University. Later he earned his Master of Theology and Doctor of Theology from Dallas Theological Seminary.[492]

Radmacher contributed all the articles on the doctrine of soteriology in a work produced in 2003 by Dallas Theological Seminary, *Understanding Christian Theology*. His views on God's sovereignty, election, and efficacious grace align with a Reformed/Calvinist persuasion of thought in that work. Though some evidence exists that in the last few years of his life he distanced himself from a strong or even moderate Calvinistic viewpoint, most of his life and ministry he taught views that aligned with what some classify as four point Calvinism.

In the work *Understanding Christian Theology*, Radmacher builds off of the prior chapters dealing with man's sinful and depraved condition written by Dr. Robert Pyne, who presented a position of man's radical corruption. His perspective followed the same line of reasoning as that of Martin Luther and Jonathan Edwards. The "will is in bondage to sin, and it will not be released except through the outside intervention of the Spirit of God."[493] That outside intervention, redemption by the grace of God, occurs according to Radmacher by God alone because humanity is "spiritually dead."[494]

---

[491] Hersch Lange and Shawn Lazar, "A Tribute to Earl Radmacher," *Grace Evangelical Society*, last modified 2016, accessed July 1, 2016, http://www.faithalone.org/magazine/y2014/A-Tribute-to-Dr-Radmacher.pdf.

[492] Ibid.

[493] Robert Pyne, "*The Effect of Sin on Human Nature*," in *Understanding a Christian Theology*, eds. Charles R. Swindoll and Roy B. Zuck (Nashville, TN: Thomas Nelson Publishers, 2003), 749.

[494] Earl Radmacher, "*What Does Salvation Mean*," in *Understanding a Christian Theology*, eds. Charles R. Swindoll and Roy B. Zuck (Nashville, TN: Thomas Nelson Publishers, 2003), 808.

God's work in salvation begins in eternity by his act of electing some to receive a special blessing of grace. Though all are justly condemned in sin God elects some out of the condemned race to receive a blessing they otherwise would never have desired or chosen without God's sovereign decree of grace. As he says of Ephesians 1:4, "Election is God's sovereign, gracious plan before creation to save those who believe, not because of any foreseen merit in them, but only because of his good pleasure. This is a sovereign plan because God was under no obligation to elect anyone, and it is an act of grace because the recipients are totally undeserving."[495] If God had not elected some then "none would have believed."[496]

In regard to foreknowledge, Radmacher rejects the idea that God's foreknowledge as referenced in Romans 8:29 means mere foresight. As he says, "The problem with this [foresight] view is that the object of foreknowledge . . . is not a person's faith but is a person ('whom'). That is, God foreknew the person, not something he or she would do."[497]

These people who are foreknown and elected at some point in their lives are supernaturally called. Just as God called Christ from the grave, and a miracle occurred as Christ arose from the grave, so too for a lost person a miracle occurs as Christ calls him or her from spiritual death to spiritual life. Radmacher speaks of this supernatural miraculous call as "the effectual call of the Holy Spirit."[498] He examines several passages of Scripture that speaks to this calling. One of those he focuses on is Acts 16:14 where the Bible speaks of Lydia's conversion. He says:

> In Philippi, Paul, Silas, Timothy, and Luke preached the Word to women, including Lydia. That was the invitation, the general call. When Lydia responded, she was saved. That was what theologians call the effectual call. The general call presents the message that "Christ died for our sins." But the hearer needs to believe (John

---

[495] Ibid., 818.

[496] Ibid., 819.

[497] Ibid.

[498] Ibid., 862.

20:31). In the general call in Philippi God led Lydia to listen to what preachers said ("Lydia heard us," Acts 16:14). Then what happened? "The Lord opened her heart to heed the things spoken by Paul." She listened to all four speakers intently, but the Holy Spirit used Paul's message to open her heart. The word "opened" (*dianoigo*) stressing opening up wide, like double folding doors. In Lydia's case all the elements are present: the message of the human witnesses; the convicting of the Holy Spirit; the response of the listener; the opening of Lydia's heart, the place of deepest reflection; and the effectual calling (salvation).[499]

To further illustrate his point about this miraculous calling, Radmacher turned to the famous Calvinist pastor of London, C.H. Spurgeon. He used one of Spurgeon's natural world illustrations to describe this work of God.

The general call of the gospel is like the sheet lightening we sometimes see on a summer's evening—beautiful, grand—but who ever heard of anything being struck by it? But the special call is the forked flash from heaven; it strikes somewhere. It is the arrow shot between the joints of the harness.[500]

Radmacher then moves to the discussion of regeneration. Like other Reformed/Calvinist theologians he sees the Bible plainly teaching that the new birth is like the physical birth. Just as man does nothing to contribute to his own conception and birth physically so too he does not do anything to contribute to his spiritual birth. He says, "When God gives life to a spiritually dead person, we call it 'regeneration.'"[501]

What does Radmacher say as to how this occurs? Does man cooperate in this act of regeneration? He answers, "Childbirth illustrates several truths about regeneration. First, just as an unborn baby is totally helpless in the birthing process, so no one can contribute to his or her spiritual birth. Those who believe 'were born, not of blood, nor of the will

---

[499] Ibid.

[500] Ibid., 863.

[501] Ibid.

of the flesh, nor of the will of man, but of God' (John 1:13). Salvation is 'not by works' (Eph. 2:9; Titus 3:5). Just as an infant cannot contribute to his birth, so no human can save himself."[502]

These positions by Radmacher make it clear that he too affirmed (at least for most of his life and ministry) the doctrines of grace as articulated by the Reformed/Calvinist heritage. At the very end of his life he seems to have altered his views in these areas. But for most of his life, he taught, man does not earn his place in the grace and love of God. He clearly taught that God places his unconditional love upon the sinner and by amazing grace draws that person to a new life in Christ Jesus. Therefore, his views as expressed in the majority of his life and ministry agreed with the Calvinistic view of salvation.

15. Dr. Norman Geisler (1932-2019)

I recently discovered an error in my own thinking about Dr. Geisler's position on the doctrine of election and grace. In the initial draft of this book (a prior PhD dissertation), I left Geisler out of the list of Calvinistic Dispensationalists. However, in 2018 I was accepted into a 3rd PhD program and my research field related to Amyraldian soteriology. Dr. Geisler claimed to be within the Amyraldian field. My research proposal related to whether or not Geisler did affirm an actual Amyraldian-Calvinistic view of redemption.

Consequently, North-West University accepted my proposal to analyze his soteriology within my overall analysis of Amyraldian Calvinism. This is what I wrote in my initial hypothesis: "The hypothesis for this research is that Norman Geisler's confession of a modified Calvinistic soteriology does not retain sufficient continuity with the main truths and positions of any of the three major forms of a Reformed Calvinistic soteriology." My research and the evidence, however, proved that he did indeed affirm more of a Calvinistic soteriology than not. I was wrong in my initial thoughts on Geisler. I will share in the next set of seven paragraphs what my conclusions were in regard to Dr. Geisler's Calvinistic views. In the future, I will publish this dissertation from North West University as a book.

---

[502] Ibid.

Of the three Calvinistic streams (supralapsarians, infralapsarian, sublapsarians), Geisler did have more continuity with the sublapsarian stream. From some of the criticisms from R.C. Sproul and James R White, it seemed as if Geisler may not really have landed in a moderate Calvinist perspective. Their allegations against him made Geisler appear to have more continuity with Arminian/Wesleyan views than with the Amyraldian or moderate Calvinist perspective. However, with closer examination it seems that their criticisms were too strong and overly exaggerated.

Geisler cannot be categorized properly in the broad Arminian/Wesleyan view of soteriology. Geisler cannot be classified in particular with the Arminian/Wesleyan view of election. Since how one defines election is almost always determinative of one's identification within the Calvinistic stream or not, it seems reasonable to conclude that Geisler is within a type of Calvinistic stream.

Geisler agreed with the moderate Calvinists that mankind fell into sin by permission and not by divine causation. He also taught that human will retained a sacred status even while totally depraved. In his view depravity meant that mankind was thoroughly corrupted, not that his will was totally disabled or eradicated.

Additionally, Geisler, like other moderate Calvinists in the sublapsarian stream, placed atonement prior to election. This is fundamental to all sublapsarian models of theology. Geisler's operational order (no eternal logical order) makes his view unique and somewhat difficult to place because of that element. But even so, with Geisler also adopting unlimited atonement, another key mark of the Amyraldian or moderate Calvinist stream, this position bolsters his continuity with the sublapsarian Amyraldian stream.

Geisler, however, did not make strong associations with common grace and prevenient grace as elements of what Christ purchased on the cross. The seed forms of that idea exist in Geisler's thought, especially in relation to infant salvation, because of Christ's atonement curing the Adamic sin passed on to infants, but he failed to develop this idea. Sublapsarian Calvinists have commonly taught that all forms of grace stem from the death of Christ. In this element Geisler did not have as much continuity as one might expect, since Geisler held to an unlimited atonement view, as do all sublapsarians.

As to effectual grace, Geisler has continuity here with the moderate Calvinist view in the Amyraldian stream. Geisler defined this as effectual persuasion. He rejected the idea of coercion. He also rejected the idea of calling it irresistible grace. He also penned a unique phrase. He labeled it "irresistible on the willing." In this way he formed a hybrid model of monergism that led to a synergistic conversion. One might even be able to make the case that Geisler's model allows for a process type of conversion as articulated by Billy Graham and others who have recognized a sequence in conversion. It seems possible to see Geisler as explaining God having no sequence while mankind in time experiences grace in a sequence.

However, Geisler did not explain with extensive detail what factors made a person willing in order that the grace would be effectual. That undeveloped aspect of his soteriology has left him open to more severe criticisms from teachers in the more rigid and higher forms of Calvinism who question his continuity with any form of Calvinism. Nonetheless, his effectual persuasion model, that had some elements of monergism and synergism in it (a hybrid model), has some interesting connections to some other moderate Calvinists. Geisler seems to have affirmed some type of drawing grace process that has been articulated by other moderate Calvinists.

Additionally, as with the other two forms of Calvinism, Geisler agreed that people do not contribute to their own election. This again clearly means he cannot rightly be categorized as an Arminian/Wesleyan in his view of election. All moderate Calvinists agree with this point. Mankind does nothing to obtain election, or to lose it. God elects and people freely receive Christ. That emphasis on God's sovereign will and human responsibility points to twin truths in moderate Calvinism. Though not always explained in precision, moderate Calvinists have made a serious effort to preserve both truths. Geisler has made that effort as well. He has continuity here with moderate Calvinists and discontinuity with Arminian/Wesleyan views of election.

In a future date, I will publish that that North-West PhD dissertation that sets forth in extensive detail why Geisler does qualify as a sublapsarian (moderate) Calvinist. He did reject extreme (supralapsarian) and strong (infralapsarian) Calvinistic ideas. In doing so, he received some pointed critiques from those like James R. White and R.C. Sproul who wrongly painted him as Arminian. Sadly, to some Calvinists, anything short of their own version of Calvinism makes one an Arminian.

Sometimes theologians suffer from hardened categories whereby they fail to see a range or pendulum within a theological family. Instead, they narrow the category to such a fine degree that anything not exactly in that degree places the people outside of a particular theological stream. In this case, numerous voices have done that to Geisler. It had even convinced me, prior to 4 years of extensive research reading all of his works along with Amyraldian literature through history, that Geisler could not be rightly classified as any type of Calvinist. Though only a super small portion of quotes below, these will highlight the main point as to my conclusion offered above as to why Geisler was within the Calvinistic stream of Dispensationalism.

As to depravity, Geisler embraced the ideas common in Calvinistic streams on man's depravity. From Adam all people inherit a sin nature. People are born with a "propensity to sin" because the "effect of sin on God's image in fallen human beings is pervasive, extending to every dimension of his being—body and soul, mind and will."[503] He embraced the ideas as a moderate Calvinist that the person in sin can be classified as "totally depraved."[504] In explaining how serious and corrupted people are in sin Geisler stated:

> Sin does penetrate and permeate our whole being. Humans are born wholly, not partially, depraved; that is, every aspect of our being is affected by sin. No element of human nature is unaffected by inherited evil. . . . depravity brings spiritual darkness and blindness to unbelievers. . . . The result is that there are several actions the unaided human will *cannot* perform. For one thing, the human will cannot, unmoved by divine grace, seek God. Paul said, "There is no one who understands, no one who seeks God" (Rom. 3:11). Further, human will cannot initiate salvation. . . . the human will cannot attain his own salvation: "It does not, therefore, depend on man's desire or effort, but on God's mercy" (Rom. 9:16). . . . each individual is totally depraved, for sin has extended to every part of his being. He is a fallen person, including mind, emotions,

---

[503] Norman Geisler, *Systematic Theology in One Volume* (Minneapolis, MN: Bethany House Publishers, 2011), 786-787.

[504] Ibid., 787.

> will, and body. . . . Hence, God's grace is the only force in the universe that can overcome the natural irredeemability of human beings. Grace alone . . . is the only cure for humankind's total depravity. Grace, and only grace, can overcome the vast and devastating effects of sin (Titus 2:11-13).[505]

Geisler's view of depravity aligns with the Calvinistic view. As a moderate (sublapsarian) Calvinist he embraced total depravity with some qualifications that made it distinct from total inability as taught in all forms of supralapsarian Calvinism and often in infralapsarian models.

In evaluating the doctrine of election, Geisler's position without doubt contrasted the Arminian/Wesleyan foresight model. Geisler embraced eternal election, a choice made by God outside of earthly time and not based on man's faith. Most all Calvinists view election as the most decisive point that places one in either the Calvinistic stream of theology or in the non-Calvinistic stream of theology. For Geisler, he explicitly affirmed election took place in God's own mind and nature (he affirmed essentialism and rejected voluntarism). This eternal election consequently meant too that God effectually led these elected ones to faith. These quotes reveal the heart of Geisler's view.

> Election is not based on or dependent on foreknowledge.[506]

> God does not choose us based on his knowing we would choose him.[507]

> Election was from eternity. Salvation was not decided or gained in time, and it cannot be lost in time. 'God chose us in him before the creation of the world (Eph. 1:4). . . . Salvation was effected in eternity and for eternity.[508]

---

[505] Ibid.,787-789.

[506] Norman Geisler, *Chosen But Free: A Balanced View of Sovereignty and Free Will* (Minneapolis, MN: Bethany House Publishers, 2010), 67.

[507] Ibid., 182.

[508] Norman Geisler, *Systematic Theology, Volume 3*, p. 315.

Geisler rooted election in eternity and because of that he also affirmed this guaranteed the "eternal security" of those elected.[509] If election occurs from within time then salvation in his perspective could be lost in time. However, for him, God elected in eternity and not based on man or man's faith that occurs in time.

Furthermore, Geisler embraced a Thomistic view of God and his attributes. Therefore, election took place in the mind of God in accordance to his nature. Man could not move the unmoved mover. In a seminary class at Southern Evangelical Seminary, I watched Geisler act this out with chairs in the front of the class as he explained the unmoved mover idea. Geisler rejected the idea that God passive recognized the actions of free people and that moved God to elect. Geisler explained it this way.

> God was active, not passive in bringing about the event . . . God . . . is totally sovereign in the sense of actually determining what occurs. . . . God is 'Pure Actuality,' with no potentiality whatsoever in his being. As such, nothing can act upon him; he can only act on all other things since they alone have potentiality in their being. He is immutable, and nothing can change him. . . . we [argue] against this kind of 'Arminianism.' . . . So God sovereignly and actively *decrees* that our salvation would take place *through* the instrumentality of our free choice, along with whatever persuasive (but noncoercive) influence of his grace upon us He knows will be necessary to get us to make the decision to accept his totally gracious offer of salvation. In other words, God actively predetermines what will take place *through* his perfect knowledge of himself and all creatures, which flow from him.[510]

Hardly can that view espoused by Geisler qualify as foresight election or Arminianism. As Geisler rightly stated of his view, "it has more similarities with what is traditionally viewed as 'Calvinistic,'" and therefore, he preferred to call his view "moderate Calvinism" to

---

[509] Norman Geisler, *Chosen But Free: A Balanced View of Sovereignty and Free Will* (Minneapolis, MN: Bethany House Publishers, 2010), 186.

[510] Ibid., 183.

distinguish himself from "extreme Calvinism and extreme Arminianism."[511]

Lastly, not only did Geisler affirm total depravity and sovereign election from eternity, in contrast to earthly faith based election or foresight election, but Geisler also affirmed a type of effectual grace that moved the elect to believe. Geisler held a slightly different type of effectual grace than some other moderate Calvinists. For one, he, like Millard J. Erickson (a 4 point Amyraldian Calvinist), embraced the idea that drawing grace would move one to faith and then upon faith the person experienced regeneration. This was also a view held by several other Dispensational Calvinists (Criswell, Barackman, Fruchtenbaum, and others).

Some have wrongly asserted that to believe faith occurs prior to regeneration makes one Arminian. It does not. Whatever effects (causes) the movement of faith and the definition of election remains decisive for whether one aligns more within the Calvinistic stream or the non-Calvinistic stream. Geisler's view of election along with effectual grace that worked on man in such a way that it led the elect to freely believe places him on the Calvinistic side of the position. Geisler stated the following on effectual grace.

> God's saving grace is effectual, always accomplishing the salvation of those who receive it.[512]

> God's grace is not only before salvation, but it is also efficacious in producing salvation in the elect . . . . It accomplishes . . . the salvation God has foredetermined for them and by which he accomplishes what he has ordained.[513]

To summarize Geisler's view, he correctly noted that "Arminians" would not agree to classify his views as "Arminian or even moderate

---

[511] Ibid., 185.

[512] Ibid., 186.

[513] Norman Geisler, *Systematic Theology, Volume 3*: Sin, Salvation, p. 222.

Arminian" views.[514] He stated too his views were in line with teachers he taught with at Dallas Seminary who have been recognized too as Calvinist Dispensationalists. He said that his views were in the same line as that of John Walvoord and Charles Ryrie.[515] Geisler taught with those two during his tenure as a professor at Dallas Seminary. Furthermore, Geisler listed Lewis Sperry Chafer in that list as well. [516] Chafer, Walvoord, and Ryrie were all Dispensational Calvinists. Therefore, these summary words by Geisler rightly explain why he indeed ought to be classified as a Dispensational Calvinist. For 15 to 18 years I was wrong on Geisler's view and I had listed him in the non-Calvinistic stream of thought on election and grace. Geisler, however, stood on this view against Arminian views.

> [The] Arminian view faces several difficulties. . . . the biblical data seem to say more than God simply *knew* what was going to happen. It appears God actually *determined* what would happen and that he even assures its accomplishment by effectively working to bring it about. . . . God's sovereignty means he is in control of all that happens, even the free acts of human beings. . . . If God's choice to save was based on those whom he knew would choose him, then it would not be based on divine grace but on human decision. This flies in the face of the whole biblical teaching on grace (cf. Eph. 2:8-9; Titus 3:5-7; Rom. 11:6). It is contrary to the clear teaching that salvation does not spring from the will of man. Believers are 'children born not of natural descent, *nor of human decision* or of a husband's will, but born of God' (John 1:13). Paul adds that salvation does not 'depend on man's desire [will] or effort, but on God's mercy' (Rom. 9:16).

In my final analysis of my PhD dissertation related to Geisler, approved by internal and external faculty (one external scholar who

---

[514] Norman Geisler, *Chosen But Free: A Balanced View of Sovereignty and Free Will* (Minneapolis, MN: Bethany House Publishers, 2010), 186.

[515] Ibid., 147-148.

[516] Ibid., 148.

worked with Geisler for years), his writings qualify him as an Amyraldian Calvinist. If one uses the S.A.V.I.O.R. acronym,[517] instead of T.U.L.I.P., for how to properly analyze Amyraldian Calvinism, then Geisler easily fell within a 5 to 5.25 range of the 6 point S.A.V.I.O.R. Calvinism model. The problem, however, is that often the extreme or strong Calvinists speak and write as if there is only a monolithic model of Calvinism. Geisler recognized this problem too stating, "the problem with much of the [extreme sovereignty] is that it has only two categories: its understanding of Calvinism and the opposing view it calls Arminianism."[518]

Not all Calvinists, however, make that sloppy type of error. For example, the brilliant and solid Dr. B.B. Warfield rightly recognized various levels of Calvinistic thought and spoke of the ranges that exist in Calvinistic thought. More can be explored on this when I publish this dissertation related to Geisler. It is enough for now to show that Geisler was a Calvinistic Dispensationalist. When I wrote this dissertation (2013-2016) I left Geisler out of the list because I had misunderstood his views largely based upon the critique of some Calvinists against his position (White and Sproul).

16. Dr. Rolland McCune (1934-2019)

While preparing this original manuscript for my 2nd PhD dissertation under Dr. Elliot, I had never heard of Dr. McCune. I had studied under or with some very well known Dispensationalists of the 20th century too (Charles Ryrie, Robert Lightner, Arnold Fruchtenbaum, Mal Couch, Paige Patterson, Norman Geisler, William F. Luck, and more). Yet through all of my studies and interactions with many professors and their works I do not recall this name being mentioned or referenced in various lectures or written works.

However, his three volume Biblical Systematic set published in between 2009 and 2010 offers some wonderful insights into this northern Calvinistic Dispensationalist who was affiliated with Detroit Baptist Theological Seminary from 1981 to 2009 (10 years as president). For

---

[517] SAVIOR stands for Sacred Creation, Abandoned goodwill, Victorious Atonement, Intellectual Immutable election, Overcoming grace, & Regenerated forever.

[518] Norman Geisler, *Chosen But Free: A Balanced View of Sovereignty and Free Will* (Minneapolis, MN: Bethany House Publishers, 2010), 183.

fourteen years he was on the faculty of the Central Baptist Theological Seminary of Minneapolis, serving as a professor and in various administrative roles. He earned his Bachelor of Arts degree from Taylor University, Fort Wayne Campus (Indiana), and then earned his Bachelor of Divinity, Master of Theology, and Doctor of Theology degrees at Grace Theological Seminary in Winona Lake, Indiana. Grace Theological Seminary is well known as a school devoted to Dispensationalism.

In his writings he makes it unmistakably clear that God alone elects, calls, moves one to faith, and secures one in the atonement of Christ Jesus. In volume three of his systematic set he devotes twelve chapters to the doctrine of salvation. Those discussions on salvation, however, build from his understanding on the sovereign providence of God. In volume one of his systematic he discusses in specificity the idea of God's sovereign decree that governs the universe. Through this section he agrees with and pulls quotes from famous Reformed Calvinist theologians such as Dr. A.H. Strong, Dr. Charles Hodge, Dr. A.A. Hodge, and Dr. Wayne Grudem.

In speaking of God's decree he stated that God's decree is "one all-inclusive and comprehensive purpose, plan, and will."[519] This plan of God means according to McCune that "God does whatever he pleases (Pss. 115:3; 135:6)."[520] God's plan and purpose is so definite that McCune states that it is "changeless. God has no alternate plans in case something goes wrong with his original plan. Change in purpose arises because of ignorance, lack of wisdom or power, or unfaithfulness to an original purpose."[521] He uses numerous texts to support these assertions (Acts 2:23; James 1:7; Ps 33:11; Isa. 24:24-25 and Isa. 46:9-10).[522]

This absolute sovereign providence extends even to the free acts of mankind. "The good acts of believers are predestined by God; Paul notes that they are 'created in Christ Jesus for good works, which God prepared

---

[519] Rolland McCune, *A Systematic Theology of Biblical Christianity* (Allen Park, MI: Detroit Baptist Theological Seminary, 2009), 1:310.

[520] Ibid., 1:312.

[521] Ibid., 1:313.

[522] Ibid., 1:314.

beforehand (*protoimadzo*) that we would walk in them' (Eph. 2:10)."[523] He unequivocally rejects the idea that God's decrees of conditional in nature as often found in Arminian and Provisionism[524] theologies. As he stated, "God's decrees are not conditional in the sense that they are suspended on a pure contingency or some indecision somewhere else."[525] This decree materializes in earthly historical time in a certain and efficacious manner.[526]

That decree in eternity applies specifically to the doctrine of salvation. For McCune the Pelagian, Arminian, and Wesleyan views of man's will undermine the biblical witness concerning man's total depravity.[527] At the heart of Dr. McCune's view of depravity the doctrine of man's selfish nature comes to the forefront. As he says, "total depravity means that when the unsaved do right it is for selfish purposes and not for God's glory."[528] This depravity leads people to suppress truth, to pursue idols, and it incapacitates the person from properly understanding spiritual

---

[523] Ibid., 1:316.

[524] Dr. Leighton Flowers has termed the more Arminian based version of Southern Baptist soteriology that rejects unconditional election, yet affirms eternal security, as Provision theology (provisionism). This theology aligns with the other terms often used such as SBC Traditional soteriology. Flowers often wrongly calls Bezanism theology Calvinism and in doing so misrepresents the lower forms of Calvinistic thought. Bezanism is a view of omnicausality (all is actively decreed and providentially caused by God). That is high Calvinism, or more precisely called Bezanism (formulated by Theodore Beza). Flowers rarely interacts with the more moderate forms of Calvinistic thought. He has even in fact refused to debate moderate Calvinists. Dr. Flowers regularly fails to understand and correctly explain how the doctrine of God decreeing the permission for sin differs from actively decreeing sin. He diverts from dealing with the matter often by asserting the idea is a distinction without a difference, which is false. A substantial difference exists in saying God causes original sin and God allowing original sin.

[525] Rolland McCune, *A Systematic Theology of Biblical Christianity* (Allen Park, MI: Detroit Baptist Theological Seminary, 2009), 1:319-320.

[526] Ibid., 1:321.

[527] Rolland McCune, *A Systematic Theology of Biblical Christianity* (Allen Park, MI: Detroit Baptist Theological Seminary, 2009), 2:70.

[528] Ibid., 2:64

truths.[529] In his model of soteriology, the "only antidote for this condition is spiritual life."[530]

For McCune, that spiritual life that cures only occurs through God's sovereign decree to elect and draw that elected one to faith in Christ Jesus for salvation. In his model "salvation and all its attendant blessings and responsibilities begin with election."[531] In establishing his definition McCune turns to numerous Calvinistic confessions and theologians to define this term. He quotes approvingly from the London Baptist Confession, the New Hampshire Baptist Confession, John Gill, James Petigru Boyce, W.T. Conner, A.H. Strong, and Alva J. McClain.[532] He also narrows down his definition to distinguish between election and predestination. Election is the decree that pertains to "eternal life" issues whereas predestination "has reference to God's eternal, overall plan and purpose and includes or comprehends all things. Nothing is outside the predestination or decree of God in either its permissive or directive sense."[533]

Dr. McCune has argued that the personal pre-temporal doctrine of unconditional election runs through both the O.T. and N.T. Texts such as Genesis 18:19 and Psalm 65:4 highlight this doctrine in the O.T. In the N.T. texts such as John 6:37, Romans 8:28-30, 2 Timothy 1:8-9, and Revelation 13:8 speak of the elect and nonelect.[534] In McCune's teaching on personal election, God chooses first and history flows outward to manifest that decree. He rejected foresight or prescience election.[535] In agreeing with Dr. B.B. Warfield, he concurred with Warfield's view that

---

[529] Ibid., 2:64-66.

[530] Ibid., 2:65.

[531] Rolland McCune, *A Systematic Theology of Biblical Christianity* (Allen Park, MI: Detroit Baptist Theological Seminary, 2010), 3:3.

[532] Ibid., 3:4.

[533] Ibid., 3:4-5.

[534] Ibid., 3:10-13.

[535] Ibid., 3:20-21.

The Calvinism of Dispensationalism

"God's foreknowledge in the prescience sense is merely a transcript of his will."[536]

God's foreknowledge according to McCune means that "God knows persons not just the actions of persons. *Proginosko* is an expression of election or foreordination, and it connotes favor and love rather than abstract intellectual foresight."[537] In his teaching God's foreknowledge is more "pre-arrangement" and "forethought" than foresight or foreknowledge.[538] He used numerous scriptures that he thought taught this: Romans 8:29; Acts 2:23; Acts 4:27-28; 1 Peter 1:20; and Romans 11:2.[539]

In regards to the means to accomplish the salvation of the elect, Dr. McCune embraced the idea of efficacious grace. He affirms the standard classic Calvinist view that two types of calls to salvation exist in Scripture, (1) a general common call that is universal in scope and (2) a specific particular efficacious call to salvation.[540] The general common grace call to all may be "resisted" and that resistance brings "culpability."[541] However, the efficacious call of God always results in the salvation of the elect.[542] This powerful work of grace will "infallibly accomplish its final end of bringing the elect sinner to Christ and to the inevitable glory of eternal bliss without fail."[543]

Unless a reader has severe bias, or a dishonest heart, these statements by McCune prove without question what type of soteriology he embraced as a Dispensationalist. He affirmed the sovereign decree of God

---

[536] Ibid., 3:21.

[537] Ibid.

[538] Ibid.

[539] Ibid., 3:21-22.

[540] Ibid., 3:38-48.

[541] Ibid., 3:41-42.

[542] Ibid., 3:43-48.

[543] Ibid., 3:48.

that could not be thwarted and that did not hinge upon contingent choices of humanity or creation in order to come to pass in historical time. He without reservation affirmed man's total depravity that rendered him in a helpless and hopeless condition. He taught that God elected without conditions being met from lost man. He rejected that election hinged upon God's foresight. Lastly, he affirmed that God called the elect to faith through efficacious grace that always led the sinner coming to experience by faith the specific blessings of the atonement of Christ for their salvation. The limited aspect of the atonement meant that "certain benefits" of the atonement of Christ are "limited to those who receive them—i.e., believers or the elect."[544] The "death of Christ fully guarantees what it is designed to accomplish and, of course, fully accomplished what it guarantees."[545]

17. Dr. Paul Enns (b.1937)

Paul Enns is a graduate of Dallas Theological Seminary. He earned both his Th.M. and Th.D. degree from that seminary and has published a variety of works over the span of his ministerial career. In addition to a prolific pen he has also taught at numerous seminaries and colleges throughout the United States. He has taught at Winnipeg Bible College, Dallas Theological Seminary, Northwestern College, Luther Rice Seminary, Talbot Theological Seminary, and Southeastern Baptist

---

[544] Rolland McCune, *A Systematic Theology of Biblical Christianity* (Allen Park, MI: Detroit Baptist Theological Seminary, 2009), 2:213.

[545] Ibid., 2:208. McCune held to an unlimited in general common grace and limited in application to the elect perspective. He would agree with the Synod of Dort construction that Christ's death is sufficient for all and efficient for the only the elect. In common grace areas those realities existed because of the cosmological aspect to Christ's atonement. In salvation matters the atonement in application was designed for just the elect (p. 207). He also affirmed a sublapsarian view of the decree order (p. 218-219). He rightly questioned the logic of views that place election prior to atonement. As he stated, "Ephesians 1:4 suggests . . . . believers are 'chosen in (en, in connection with) Christ before the foundation of the world.' This seems to imply that the provision for the salvation accomplished by Christ was logically contemplated before specific individuals were purposed to have its redemptive accomplishments applied to them. The other views have God electing persons to salvation that theoretically he had not yet planned" (p. 219).

Theological Seminary.[546] This Dispensationalist provides a clear position on three key areas that give insight into his ideology on man's depravity, God's work of election, and the efficacious work of the Spirit which includes the work of God in regeneration.

First, his views concerning man's depravity reveal Enns' allegiance to the doctrine of total depravity. He does not believe man has any ability to assist or make a move towards his own regeneration because his spiritual life has died due to the ravage consequences of sin. A person's spiritual connection to God has been severed due to sin. He or she is dead in the sense of that person's spiritual condition towards God. Sin has cut the person off from the eternal life of Christ. As he says, "Ephesians 2:1 states the condition of the unsaved person: 'And you were dead in your trespasses and sins.' If the unbeliever is dead then he cannot make the initial response to God. God must make the first move."[547]

Second, Enns' affirms the doctrine of unconditional election of some to salvation. Apparently sensing that this is a tough topic, Enns opens the discussion of election by noting that the issue is not whether we can by our finite minds understand this subject. Rather, the issue is "whether or not the Bible teaches it."[548] Enns recognizes that finite minds often struggle with this subject found in Scripture. Yet he urges people to accept what God stated and not attempt to discard it based upon emotive disdain.

He then provides a definition of what he thinks is a Scriptural definition of election. His definition is as follows:

> Election may be defined as that eternal act of God whereby he, in his sovereign good pleasure, and on account of no foreseen merit in them, chooses a certain number of men to be the recipients of special grace and eternal salvation. One of the principal passages concerning election is Ephesians 1:4 in the statement "he chose us." The verb "chose" is the Greek *eklego*, which means "to call

---

[546] Paul Enns, "*Ministry: Teaching and Administration*," [online]. Accessed 13 July 2015. Available from http://paulenns.com/ministry-teaching-and-administration/; Internet.

[547] Paul Enns, *The Moody Handbook of Theology* (Chicago, IL: Moody Press, 1989), 337.

[548] Ibid., 328.

out" from among the people. The word means that God selected some individuals from out of the masses. Moreover, the word is always used in the middle voice meaning God chose for himself. This describes the purpose of the choosing—God chose believers to be in fellowship with him and to reflect his grace through their living a redeemed life. Several characteristics are to be noted in election: it took place in eternity past (Eph 1:4); it is an act of a sovereign God, and it is according to his sovereign will (Rom. 9:11; 2 Tim. 1:9); it is an expression of the love of God (Eph. 1:4); it is not conditioned on man in any way (2 Tim. 1:9; Rom. 9:11); it reflects the justice of God; there can be no charge of injustice against God in election (Rom. 9:14, 20).[549]

The definition above aligns precisely with the standard views of a Reformed soteriology position. Theologians could not properly categorize that position as semi-Pelagian or Arminian.

Third, Enns discusses two forms of grace in God's kingdom, common grace and special grace. Common grace extends to all of humanity whereas special grace extends only to the elect.[550] When describing special grace Enns resorts to the term efficacious to describe it. This type of grace causes the person who experiences it to come to faith in Christ. Efficacious grace works on a person in such a way that it changes that person's desires and affections.

He provides two definitions to this type of grace: (1) the work of the Holy Spirit which effectively moves men to believe in Jesus Christ as Savior," and (2) special grace is irresistible. . . by changing the heart it makes man perfectly willing to accept Jesus Christ unto salvation and to yield obedience to the will of God."[551] Interestingly, Enns pulls these two definitions from theologians Charles Ryrie and Louis Berkhof,[552] which again shows the unity of these two traditions with respect to these two

---

[549] Ibid., 328.

[550] Ibid., 333-335.

[551] Ibid., 335.

[552] Ibid., 342.

particular theologians as Berkhof was a Covenant Calvinist and Ryrie was a Dispensationalist.

Fourth, Enns shows that efficacious grace has certain key markers that distinguish it from other forms of grace. This special grace is "limited to the elect," it is never successfully "rejected," it always involves the work of the "Holy Spirit" and the "Word of God," it is applied "toward individuals, not to groups, nor to the church as a whole," and it is determined for the elect in "eternity past."[553]

18. Dr. Mal Couch (1938-2013)

As a personal student and disciple of Dr. Mal Couch for many years, I can testify to his strong and unwavering stance on election and predestination as well as monergism. I deeply miss Mal and the many hours of long conversations we had over various theology topics, including the doctrine of election and God's providential rule. He did not appear to ever waver in his stance or teachings that God elects, God calls, God births man unto faith in Christ. His classroom teachings, his sermons, personal conversations, and his writings have all pointed to this truth.

One of the clearest teachings he has on this subject comes from his thorough and detailed exegetical commentary on 1 and 2 Thessalonians. In this commentary he makes a clear case for the eternal elective work of God as well for the work of the Spirit in causing someone to come to faith. Dr. Couch says of 2 Thessalonians 2:13-14 this,

> Divine election is proclaimed throughout the Scriptures. God chose or decreed before the ages (1 Cor. 2:7), from the ages (Col. 1:26), and "before the foundation of the world" (Eph. 1:4). Election is clearly Pauline revelation, that is, that God had called men to a salvation to which he had before chosen them. 'This is both logical and Pauline (Rom 8:30) [NTC].[554]

---

[553] Ibid., 335-337.

[554] Mal Couch, *The Hope of Christ's Return: Premillennial Commentary on 1 & 2 Thessalonians* (Chattanooga, TN: AMG Publishers, 2001), 233.

In addition to his Calvinistic understanding of election, Dr. Couch also affirmed the teaching that God through the Holy Spirit works to convert a sinner by efficacious grace. He believes that the Holy Spirit must cause the heart to turn toward Christ. He, in the same vein as his teacher Dr. John Walvoord, affirmed the sovereign work of grace in the sovereign plan of God. He specifically said,

> The Spirit of God is the agent for this sovereign calling and redemption (John 3:5; Titus 3:5). Faith is exercised in time by the one who has been awakened by the Spirit. Faith itself is not self-generated. All humans are said to be dead in sin and children of wrath by nature (Eph. 2:1, 3) and cannot come to salvation without faith that in itself is a gift of God (Eph. 2:8) . . . . [God's calling] would indicate a once-for-all efficacious calling that brings the elect to salvation . . . . Christ taught this sovereign in salvation when he said, "No one can come to me, unless the Father who sent me draws him; and I will raise him up on the last day" (John 6:44).[555]

Dr. Couch was a direct disciple of both Dr. John Walvoord and Dr. Charles Ryrie. He studied under those men and matured in his theology under their guidance. Thus it is interesting to see that he came forth from under them with a definite Calvinistic theology. Even his doctrine of regeneration aligns with the classic Reformed position. Couch stated,

> Regeneration is the sovereign act of God. We have no act in it . . . .The Holy Spirit, according to the will of God divinely recreates in man that which was lost at the fall of man . . . . Man was dead and unable to do one thing to give himself life, either physically or spiritually. . . . If man is dead spiritually he can do nothing in the act of regeneration. By the work of the Holy Spirit in regeneration just as in the generation of man in creation, there is a divine work accomplished in man according to the will of God. Faith is a result of regeneration and not the cause of regeneration. God the Holy Spirit once again breathes the breath of life (spiritual life) into a

---

[555] Ibid., 234.

man and he is reborn spiritually. The result of this regeneration is the consciousness of God and of sin in the individual's life upon which he cries out to God for salvation. There are some who reject this notion of regeneration prior to salvation for they think this would mean that there are those who are walking around having being regenerate yet unsaved. However, the direct result of regeneration is salvation. We are born again that we will believe. The Holy Spirit regenerates us so that we are able to place our faith in Christ and his finished work.[556]

I recall once in class lectures where he told us that he went into a library at Baylor University when comparing the two doctrines of Arminianism and Calvinism and stacked on a table the books by both the Arminians and those by Calvinists. He said the books by Calvinists were large, heavy on theology, and full of substance. Dr. Paige Patterson concurred with Couch noting that the Reformed persuasion has been excellent in producing tome's to articulate their perspective of the faith. As he said, "the Reformed tradition has been nothing if not superb in the breadth of literature produced favoring its position."[557]

However, these teachers also noticed how lightweight many of the Arminian works were in comparison to the Calvinist authors. When Dr. Couch evaluated the Arminian books he noticed they were light, thin, and lacking in theological substance. Likewise, Dr. Patterson noticed that as well saying, "non-Calvinist authors have often fallen into inadequate argumentation, or positions that I found untenable, such as the possibility of the loss of salvation, open theism, and even universalism."[558]

In reflecting over my time under the discipleship of Dr. Couch, I recall that he had a deep love for the doctrine of God's absolute providence and grace. He even shared many stories to his students where

---

[556] Mal Couch, "Regeneration," in the *Tyndale Theological Seminary New Testament Doctrinal Greek Word Study*, edited by Mal Couch (no place or date of publication), 160-161.

[557] Paige Patterson, "*Foreword*," in *Salvation and Sovereignty* by Kenneth Keathley (Nashville, TN: B&H Publishing, 2010), ix.

[558] Ibid.

God spared him by providence for other work that he would later do in life. He has faithfully fathered many disciples in the precious truths of God's sovereign grace and he has been a champion for these truths in his life and teachings. As a Dispensationalist he taught with clarity that God's love for us was an unconditional love. God did not love us because we first loved God. Instead God elected to love us first and then we responded to that love. Couch taught that we did not do anything to deserve God's love, and consequently we could not do anything to lose God's love. If God elected us in eternity past that love would carry us all the way through eternity.

19. Dr. John F. MacArthur Jr. (b.1939)

For some Covenant theologians MacArthur poses an anomaly. He makes his five point Calvinist position well known (though he affirms the atonement still gives some grace to all; dual atonement view) while also affirming a Dispensational view of Scripture. Some Calvinists do not like to claim him as one of their own because he is Dispensational. Yet some Dispensationalists do not like to claim him as their own because he is so Calvinistic.

In relation to those of the Calvinist tradition, it poses such consternation that one Covenant theologian, Reginald Kimbro, tries to redefine MacArthur into something other than a Dispensationalist. Kimbro tries to claim first that MacArthur is a "moderate Dispensationalist."[559] But then he even redefines MacArthur further to apparently make an attempt to dissuade readers from thinking a Calvinist like MacArthur can really be Dispensational too. As he says, "a careful reading of MacArthur's defense of Dispensationalism reveals that the only point he defends is premillennialism."[560]

Notwithstanding the confusion of Kimbro, the position of MacArthur seems rather clear. He affirms the main markers of a

---

[559] Reginald C. Kimbro, *The Gospel According to Dispensationalism* (Toronto, Canada: Wittenburg Publications, 1995), 191.

[560] Ibid., 192.

Dispensational theology[561] as well as a Calvinistic theology. He affirms several Dispensational ages of time, the promises for both Israel and the body of Christ, the rapture of the body of Christ before the time of God's wrath (standard pre-tribulationism), a premillennial view of Christ's return to earth, and with those positions he also affirms a soteriology that aligns with the Calvinist perspective.

With respect to man's depravity, MacArthur affirms that "he is dead while he is alive."[562] According to Ephesians 2:1-3 MacArthur says that the person born into this world experiences this radical corruption to such an extent that the "person who is spiritually dead has no life by which he can respond to spiritual things, much less have spiritual life. No amount of love, care, and words of affection from God can draw a response. A spiritually dead person is alienated from God and therefore alienated from life. He has no capacity to respond."[563] By these statements he reveals he affirms the doctrine of man's total depravity as classically affirmed within the Reformed/Calvinist tradition.

Second, in regard to election and predestination MacArthur affirms the position that God alone chooses some before the foundation of the world. Commenting on Ephesians 1:4-6, he says that there are three types of election spoken of within the Bible. The first is God's election of ethnic Israel (Deut. 7:6), the second is God's election of people to some vocation (Acts 9:15; Rom. 1:5), and the third type is God's election of some to salvation which is the type being spoken of in the Ephesians 1 text.[564]

This personal eternal election means that some "belonged to God before time began" because those people had their name "written from the foundation of the world in the book of life of the Lamb who has been slain."[565] This "unmerited favor that God grants to totally depraved sinners

---

[561] John MacArthur Jr., *The MacArthur Bible Commentary* (Nashville, TN: Thomas Nelson, 2005), XVI-XIX.

[562] John MacArthur Jr., *The MacArthur New Testament Commentary: Ephesians* (Chicago, IL: Moody Press), 53.

[563] Ibid.

[564] Ibid., 10.

[565] Ibid., 14.

is not related to any initiative of their own will, but is solely of his sovereign grace and mercy (Eph. 1:4-7; Titus 3:4-7; 1 Pet. 1:2)."[566]

Additionally, MacArthur shows that the doctrine of foreknowledge does not mean merely foresight, which is the common Arminian perspective on God's method of election. In discussing God's sovereignty in election further MacArthur shows from his commentary on 1 Peter 1 that the biblical terms, "elect according to foreknowledge," means God's determination. As he says, "the word does not refer to awareness of what is going to happen; rather, it clearly means a predetermined relationship in the knowledge of God."[567] He adds, God brought the salvation relationship into existence by decreeing it into existence ahead of time. Christians are foreknown for salvation in the same way Christ was foreordained before the foundation of the world to be a sacrifice for sins (cf. Acts 2:23). Foreknowledge means that God planned before, not that he observed before . . . . Thus, God prethought and predetermined or predestined each Christian's salvation."[568]

As to the atonement, the atonement of Christ secures the redemption of the elected saints who were chosen before the foundation of the world. In explaining the atonement MacArthur says that someone limits the atonement, either God or man. In his perspective God designs the atonement to actually pay for only the sins of the elect, i.e., those who believe.[569] Specifically he says,

> the atonement is limited. Yes, it is limited to those who believe. Those who believe are limited by the sovereign electing purpose of God. In that sense, the atonement is limited. It is limited to those who believe and that limitation is established by God and not by man since man can't believe on his own. But the atonement is

---

[566] John MacArthur Jr., *The MacArthur Bible Commentary* (Nashville, TN: Thomas Nelson, 2005), XIV.

[567] Ibid., 1903.

[568] Ibid.

[569] John MacArthur Jr., "For Whom Did Christ Die?," *Grace To You*, last modified 2008, accessed July 10, 2015, http://www.gty.org/resources/sermons/90-363/For-Whom-Did-Christ-Die?Term=limited%20atonement.

unlimited in the sense of its actual power and its actual effectiveness. Jesus did actually accomplish on the cross the atonement of those who are His own. The death of Christ is not a potential, general atonement, it is an actual particular specific atonement.[570]

In regard to the efficacious or irresistible grace of God upon the elect, MacArthur affirms the Calvinist view that God moves upon the elect in such a way they must come to faith in Christ as Lord and Savior. "Faith itself is a gift from God (Eph. 2:8,9)."[571] This drawing work of God is described as "efficacious."[572] MacArthur asserts clearly this:

> Scripture indicates that no 'free will' exists in man's nature, for man is enslaved to sin (total depravity) and unable to believe apart from God's empowerment (Rom. 3:1-19; Eph. 2:1-3; 2 Cor. 4:4; 2 Tim. 1:9) . . . . The drawing here [in John 6:44] is selective and efficacious (producing the desired effect) upon those whom God has sovereignly chosen for salvation, i.e. those whom God has chosen will believe because God has sovereignly determined that result from eternity past (Eph. 1:9-11).[573]

MacArthur's positions are unmistakably clear. Examining his position on 2 Timothy 2:25 it is clear as well that he affirms faith and "repentance" are "produced by God's sovereign grace . . . and without such grace human effort to change is futile."[574] "Ultimately, it is not a man's will that produces salvation but God's will."[575]

---

[570] Ibid.

[571] John MacArthur Jr., *The MacArthur Bible Commentary* (Nashville, TN: Thomas Nelson, 2005), 1461.

[572] Ibid., 1375.

[573] Ibid.

[574] Ibid., 1809.

[575] Ibid., 1346.

Is Dispensationalism Orthodox on the Gospel?

20. Dr. Erwin Lutzer (b.1941)

Lutzer earned his Th.M. degree from Dallas Theological Seminary and has for many years served as pastor of Moody Church in Chicago Illinois. Additionally, he holds a LL.D. from Simon Greenleaf School of Law and an honorary Doctor of Divinity from Western Conservative Baptist Seminary. He is a prolific author with over thirty books to his credit.

Lutzer as a Dispensationalist also embraces a thorough Calvinistic soteriology. In his book, *The Doctrines that Divide*, he provides solid counters to the Pelagian, Semi-Pelagian, Arminian, and Wesleyan views on free will and grace. At the end he closes his work with a clear position that lands on the side of God's sovereignty with numerous Scriptures references speaking to God's meticulous providential rule over others.

In Lutzer's mind the issue of free will and predestination rises to a major issue of importance. As he says, "to the greatest minds in the history of the church, one's answer to this question determined whether or not he understood the gospel."[576] In chapters nine through twelve Lutzer examined the debate of this controversy throughout church history. Monumental figures argued about these matters. Pelagius and Augustine, Erasmus and Luther, Arminius and Calvin, and lastly Wesley and Whitefield received attention as to the vociferous debate.

Though Lutzer remains largely silent as to his own perspective through those chapters, he does at the end reveal why the Calvinist arguments seem to have the most weight their favor for biblical fidelity. Lutzer argues that God does ordain evil or suffering. He uses several examples to prove this case. When an earthquake happens and it kills vast numbers of people, could not God have used his power to prevent it from taking place? Or suppose a car jack gives away and the car it was holding falls on a man underneath it. Could not have God made the metal strong enough to last just a few more seconds before it collapsed and crushed the man under the car? Does God lack the power to restrain such events from happening?

---

[576] Erwin Lutzer, *The Doctrines that Divide: A Fresh Look at the Historic Doctrines that Separate Christians* (Grand Rapids, MI: Kregel Publications, 1998), 153.

To say God just permitted this does not resolve the issue of God ordaining evil. In explaining how God ordains permission Lutzer says, "God . . . ordains [evil] through secondary causes. Arminians say God only permits it. Nonetheless, his permission necessarily means that he bore ultimate responsibility for it. After all, he could have chosen 'not to permit' it."[577] Lutzer concludes by saying, "Calvinists pointedly admit that God ordains evil—this is consistent with both the Bible and logic."[578]

In addressing God's sovereignty in salvation and reprobation, Lutzer concurs with the Calvinists that Romans 9 teaches "the potter has power over the clay to make one vessel unto honor and another to dishonor."[579] He continues by showing how Romans 9 counters the Arminian perspective. He says, "As Paul moved through the passage, he knew that the natural response of the readers would be, 'You will say to me then, 'Why does he still find fault? For who resists his will?' (v. 19). If Arminianism were correct, we would expect Paul to answer, 'God finds fault because men have a free will and therefore could have chosen to be obedient.' Here is his opportunity to set the record straight. But Paul said nothing about free will."[580]

In explaining why God does not chose to save all of mankind Lutzer says, "God does not delight in the death of the wicked . . . . However, he has chosen to forego the desire to bring all to salvation and has chosen to elect only a remnant to eternal life. Why? More important to God than the happiness of man is the desire to display his attributes . . . .With the entire human race fallen into disobedience and sin, God, though he owed salvation to no one, elected some to eternal life, thereby showing his love and mercy."[581]

Additionally, insight into Lutzer's position on these matters may be gleaned from examining the doctrinal statement at his place of

---

[577] Ibid., 209-210.

[578] Ibid., 210.

[579] Ibid., 214.

[580] Ibid.

[581] Ibid., 221, 222.

ministerial service. Moody Church, where Lutzer has served for years as pastor, also embraces a Calvinistic soteriology according to its doctrinal statement.[582] All of the leaders in that body are required to abide by that statement. Accordingly, this too reveals Lutzer's agreement to a Calvinistic ideology.

21. Dr. Arnold G. Fruchtenbaum (b.1943)

Born from Jewish parents, Dr. Fruchtenbaum came to faith in the Messiah at age thirteen. He lost his family during the holocaust. Educated at Cedarville University, Dallas Theological Seminary, and New York University Dr. Fruchtenbaum made a monumental mark in the field of Dispensational theology with the publication of his work *Israelology*. Speaking of its development and its importance Dr. Mal Couch says of that new work,

> It was Dr. Arnold Fruchtenbaum who realized that the elements of Israelology were missing from the classical divisions of Systematic Theology. While all Dispensationalists and most premillennialists dealt with Israel in their theological volumes, still there was not a concentration of looking with close observations at what God was doing with the Jewish people in His plan of history. Fruchtenbaum's book, Israelology, began the process of focusing on the Jewish people and their role in God's historical and prophetic development through the ages. Israeology should now be considered as a logical subject and sequence for all Systematic Theology.[583]

Likewise, professor Dr. Chris Cone also tips his hat towards the pioneer work of Fruchtenbaum in this area of Israelology. He says,

---

[582] Moody Church, "What We Believe," *The Moody Church*, accessed August 23, 2015, http://www.moodychurch.org/get-to-know-us/what-we-believe/.

[583] Mal Couch, *Messianic Systematic Theology of the Old Testament* (Clifton, TX: Scofield Ministries, 2010), 39-40.

Arnold Fruchtenbaum deserves much credit for reminding us of Israel's significance in the plan of God. Fruchtenbaum rightly accurately assesses the centrality of Israel in God's plan of the ages, and observes that few systematic efforts have included the proper emphasis on Israelology. If there should be a category of study dedicated to the church, then there must be an equal amount of attention—if not greater—committed to the nation of Israel.[584]

A prolific author, as well as a successful evangelist, Dr. Fruchtenbaum has charted new ground in the field of Dispensationalism. His work Israelology is over one thousand pages. The first half of the work covers the doctrine of Israel as found in all the major traditions of theology, Covenant theology as well as even Dispensational theology. Then in the last half of the work he writes what he calls a consistent Dispensational Israelology. It is within this work that one of the more confusing elements of Dispensationalism has been clarified.

Sometimes the doctrine of Israel's election can cause confusion for the Reformed theologians. That confusion occurs because they believe Israel is just a synonym for the Church. For Reformed theologians the people of God through all eras of history are the "Israel of God," i.e., the universal church. Therefore, as they read Scripture through that lens an idea of a distinct elect nation creates trouble for their paradigm of thinking.

The Bible speaks of the nation of Israel as the elect nation. However, not all of Israel has come to faith in the Lord. How can this be if God's election is always effectual to the desired or decreed ends? Fruchtenbaum provides an answer to this dilemma from a position that retains both the role of national Israel as ethnic Israel while at the same time affirming God's sovereign election unto salvation that always comes to fruition. The answer according to Fruchtenbaum is to distinguish between *personal election* and *ethnic/national election*.

God has elected a nation, an ethnic line that runs from Jacob onward until the last Jew is born. All of these Jews are by divine design a part of the chosen nation. Yet inside of Israel there are also the personally

---

[584] Chris Cone, *Prolegomena: Introductory Notes on Bible Study & Theological Method* (Fort Worth, TX: Tyndale Seminary Press, 2009), 222.

elected Jews. These are those elected unto personal salvation. Not all of those chosen to be a part of the ethnic Jewish race are a part of the eternal chosen race. Two Israels exist in Scripture, ethnic Israel and spiritual Israel.

To be ethnically elected means a person is born of the Jewish line, and it guarantees that the Jewish race will never become extinct. *National or Ethnic election does not guarantee personal salvation.* This type of election only guarantees that the race shall continue through all generations of humanity. In other words, this election ensures that the Jewish race shall survive forever. There will forever be, as long as history runs, a Jewish people born with the DNA code stemming forth from Abraham, Isaac, and especially Jacob.

However, there is another type of election inside of Israel. There is the personal election unto salvation, spiritual election. A Jew (who is nationally elected) may also be a chosen person for salvation. Apostle Paul would be such a person, as are all other Jews in history who have embraced the Messiah. This personal or spiritual election means that not only will the person share an identity with his or her Jewishness, but the person shall also share in the eternal race, the race chosen in the Lord before the foundation of the world. This type of election guarantees that the Jew shall come to faith and be a part of the redeemed humanity.

How does this divine personal election work? Fruchtenbaum has written an entire volume on the subject of God's sovereignty and man's freedom. His positions in this work are unmistakable. No honest theologian could read this volume and miss the Calvinistic positions asserted.

First, Fruchtenbaum adopts the basic position that all people are totally depraved. Mankind is born in sin and thus because of that sin the person has no desire to will himself to God and Christ for redemption. Left in this condition man would never come to Christ. Man by nature in his or her sinful condition desires to exalt self and flee from submission to the Lordship of Christ. For Fruchtenbaum man's depravity limits his will power and ability so that in such a condition he cannot do anything that commends him towards God or grace. He defines depravity this way:

> The basic meaning is that man, when he fell into a state of sin, lost all ability to do any spiritual good. He is dead in sin. There is nothing he can do that will commend him to God in any way

insofar as salvation is concerned. There is nothing man can do that would remotely help him earn his salvation. Man basically fails the test of being able to please God. No single act of man, no matter how good, carries any merit before God. . . . [though] humanity does have free will . . . the free will is limited by his nature. Man cannot do anything towards his salvation, not even believe. . . . sin has corrupted and touched every part of man so that left to himself, he will never respond to any spiritual thing.[585]

Second, his position affirms the standard Reformed position of unconditional election. He teaches that election is not conditioned upon anything man does to gain such a status. He also denies that election is corporate instead of being personal and singular. He rejects the idea of election being based upon foresight and defines foreknowledge in such a way that it means more than simply seeing something in the advance.[586] He specifically defines election this way:

> The basic meaning of unconditional election refers to the eternal plan of God, where, on the basis only of his own good pleasure and not on the basis of foreseen faith or merit, he chose some to be saved. Out of the mass of humanity already under condemnation, already heading for Hell from the moment they are born, he chose to save some.[587]

His position on election carefully distinguishes itself from all forms of conditional, prescient, and corporate formulations of the doctrine. He discusses ten ramifications to this doctrine of election. For clarity and to avoid confusion with the above numerical order I will use an alphabetical order (A-J). The ramifications run parallel to the Reformed soteriology position even though Fruchtenbaum is one of the more foremost Dispensationalists within modern Dispensationalism. He even

---

[585] Arnold G. Fruchtenbaum, *God's Will and Man's Will: Predestination, Election, & Free Will* (San Antonio TX: Ariel Ministries, 2013), 31, 35, 38.

[586] Ibid., 38-42.

[587] Ibid., 38.

recently received the distinguished John F. Walvoord ministry award for his lifetime of ministerial service.

His understanding of election means (A) God did this by his own sovereign will and sovereign purpose (Eph. 1:4; 1 Cor. 1:27-28).[588] (B) This personal election guarantees that those elected shall certainly come to saving faith. No elected person shall die without coming to salvation (Rom. 8:29-30 & Acts 13:48).[589] (C) This election was done in eternity past, not in our historical time in which humans live (Eph. 1:4; 2 Thess. 2:13-14; 2 Tim. 1:9).[590]

(D) This election was not conditioned upon any foresight that man would exercise faith or good works (Rom. 9:11; 2 Tim. 1:9).[591] (E) God elects some to this eternal salvation but not all. Not all are chosen. Many are called but few are chosen.[592] (F) Election is grounded in the will and choice of God and not from anything within mankind. This election was done for God's own glory by his grace (Rom. 9:11, 23; 11:5-6).[593]

(G) God's election is rooted in his foreknowledge that flows from his prior decree to ordain. God knows because he preplans (Rom. 8:28-30; 1 Peter 1:2).[594] (H) Election means those people will be saved a certain way which is through the gospel being presented to them.[595] (I) Election does not conflict with human freedom. No person is forced to believe. All who believe do so because they genuinely desire to do so (Phil. 2:13).[596]

---

[588] Ibid., 39.

[589] Ibid.

[590] Ibid.

[591] Ibid., 39-40.

[592] Ibid., 40.

[593] Ibid.

[594] Ibid.

[595] Ibid.

[596] Ibid., 41.

And lastly (J), God's act to elect some means that he has chosen to pass by others not electing those. He adopts the position of passive reprobation based upon the Greek middle voice in Romans 9:22 where the vessels of wrath fit themselves for destruction.[597]

Those positions by Fruchtenbaum on unconditional election align precisely with a Reformed soteriology position. Furthermore, not only does he affirm man's depravity and unconditional election, but he also affirms the doctrine of efficacious grace. Since man will not move towards grace, Fruchtenbaum argues that this type of grace must occur if any come to Christ. As he says,

> There is . . . an effectual calling or special calling or efficacious calling, or efficacious grace or irresistible grace. This is a special call to which only the elect respond. Total depravity, defined biblically, means that man, left to himself, because he is dead in sins, will not respond to God. On his own, he will never seek God. Therefore, by unconditional election from before the foundation of the world, from the mass of humanity under condemnation because of their depravity, God chose to save some . . . . God must do something to enable the elect to respond. Irresistible grace results in divine enabling to respond to the gospel. By special, divine enabling of the elect, they are able to exercise the faith they need to receive the free gift of salvation.[598]

Fruchtenbaum uses for Scripture support the following texts: John 6:37; Acts 13:48; 16:14; Rom. 8:28-30; 9:16; 1 Cor. 1:9, 23-24; Gal. 1:15; Phil. 2:13; 1 Thess. 2:14; 5:24; 1 Tim. 1:9; Heb 3:1; and 1 Peter 2:9.[599]

---

[597] Ibid.

[598] Ibid., 70-71.

[599] Ibid., 71-72.

22. Dr. Floyd H. Barackman (d. 2007)

As a Bible college teacher for more than twenty-five years, Dr. Barackman taught both a Calvinistic and Dispensational view of theology. He taught systematic theology twenty-five years at his alma mater, Practical Bible Training School in New York (named Davis College since 2004).

As a theologian he leaned upon three Calvinistic theologians in the articulation of his position on the sovereignty of God. For example, in his discussions on God's decree he quoted W.G.T Shedd, Louis Berkhof, and Augustus H. Strong.[600] Shedd and Berkhof were well known Calvinists. Shedd was an American Presbyterian theologian. Berkhof was an American-Dutch Reformed theologian who taught for many years at Calvin Theological Seminary. Augustus H. Strong was a Reformed Baptist theologian. Late in his life he became president of Rochester Theological Seminary. These three Calvinistic theologians seem to have influenced the thinking of Barackman in how he developed his theology on God's decree.

He describes the decree of God in nine components. Of those nine, seven have significance for this issue of revealing the evidence he affirmed a Calvinistic soteriology while also being a Dispensational theologian. These seven characteristics of God's decree formed the substance of the sovereignty of God in his universe. First, God's decree did not occur in stages or in sequence. God's decree was singular (Eph. 1:11; 3:11). His decree "is one."[601]

Second, God's decree is eternal," which means for us it took place before the foundation of the world yet in God's mind it has always been determined or has always existed in God's mind (Eph. 3:11).[602] Third, this decree cannot be altered, adjusted, or affected by anything outside of himself (Heb 6:17).[603] Fourth, this decree covers all aspects of the

---

[600] Floyd H. Barackman, *Practical Christian Theology: Examining the Great Doctrines of the Bible* (Grand Rapids, MI: Kregel Publications, 1998), 69, 73, 74.

[601] Ibid., 69.

[602] Ibid.

[603] Ibid.

universe, good events, even events that seem random, and even evil events (Eph. 1:11; Rom. 11:36).[604]

Fifth, God's decree makes certain that every aspect contained within it shall come to pass (Prov. 19:21; Isa. 46:10). "His decree renders certain the actions of all creatures and all created things."[605] The omnipotence of God behind this decree means that "nothing can thwart" God's "purpose (Prov. 21:30)."[606] Sixth, the decree covers both the event and the means unto the event decreed. He uses the death of Christ as an example of this. "God determined the circumstances of his death (Acts 4:27-28) as well as its means (John 10:18)."[607]

Seventh, this decree occurs by the freedom of God (Eph. 1:5, 9, 11). This means God "was not influenced by anyone or anything outside himself" as the all-encompassing decree materialized in God's mind "freely, voluntarily, according to his own pleasure and will (Ps 135:6; Isa. 40:13, 14; Rom. 11:33-36)."[608]

In summarizing his understanding of this topic Barackman sought to place this position in between the two polar opposite ideologies, the idea of fate and the idea of chance. He said,

> God's decree is not controlled by or synonymous with fate, which is a system of undetermined, impersonal causes and effects. God's decree is personal; fate would be impersonal. God's decree is wisely planned for specific ends; fate would be the action of chance, which would produce random, uncertain results. Because of God's decree, neither fate nor chance exists.[609]

---

[604] Ibid.

[605] Ibid., 70.

[606] Ibid.

[607] Ibid.

[608] Ibid.

[609] Ibid.

Those ideas Barackman held on God's decree develop with more particularity in the area of election, calling, and conversion of sinners. He affirmed the position that "God elected those whom he would save (Rom. 28b; Eph. 1:4; 2 Thess. 2:13) . . . . [this] divine election is the sovereign act of God whereby he freely chose certain human beings for salvation."[610]

In answering objections to this doctrine of unconditional elective love, he responds to the common question of fairness. He says, "God's choice was not unfair, for all people, being sinners, deserved hell. Had they deserved heaven and were not chosen, then such discrimination would have been unjust. Moreover, the Creator, who is absolutely just, has the right to do whatever he pleases with his creatures (Rom. 9:14-24)."[611]

Additionally, he embraced the idea of two types of "divine calls to salvation: a general call and a special call."[612] The general call is for the non-elect whereas the special call is that "which God extends through the gospel to the elect and which results in their salvation (1 Cor. 1:2, 9, 24; Rom. 8:28, 30; 1 Thess. 2:12). This is sometimes identified as God's effectual call."[613]

Also, in this discussion on the special call of God for the elect, he identifies three elements of this special call. These three elements reveal his order of salvation. He specifically affirms monergism.[614] However, his monergism model places faith as the fruit of efficacious grace that results in the new birth. He does not affirm a synergistic view where man produces his own faith by just help from the Holy Spirit that results in the new birth. He specifically argues for a sovereign work of grace by saying:

> One, God sweeps away satanic blindness (2 Cor. 4:3-6) and gives understanding of the gospel (Acts 16:14; 8:30; 2 Cor. 4:6). Two, he convicts the elect of their sins (John 16:8-11). And three, imparting

---

[610] Ibid., 333.

[611] Ibid., 334.

[612] Ibid., 335.

[613] Ibid.

[614] Ibid., 342.

repentance (Acts 5:31; 11:18; 2 Tim. 2:25) and faith (2 Peter 1:1; Acts 3:16), he draws the elect person to himself (John 6:37, 44). Since this divine activity occurs below the level of human awareness, the person's desire and decision to receive the Savior are, in effect, his or her own . . . . [But] God's special call to salvation is irresistible, not in the sense that it is never resisted, but in the sense it is never resisted successfully.[615]

In anticipation that some may object to placing faith before regeneration, as is common among Reformed theologians, Barackman countered that criticism by adding, "God can give salvational faith to one who is spiritually dead as readily as he can make inanimate stones cry out (Luke 19:40). The divine gift of salvation faith itself has the inherent force to enable its recipients to trust in the Savior just as the gift of life enables one to live."[616]

23. Dr. Robert P. Lightner (1931 - 2018)

Dr. Robert P. Lightner served many years as Professor of Dallas Seminary and has also served as one of the professors for theology at Tyndale Theological Seminary. He was one of my favorite professors in seminary. One of the very first books I bought as a student of theology was written by Dr. Lightner (*Sin, the Savior, & Salvation*). I bought that book, along with two others in a local bookstore.[617] Lightner's book introduced me early to the ideas of God's unconditional elective love. His moderate Calvinistic perspective, which avoided the extremes of high Calvinism and the conditional love theologies of Arminianism, stood upon the literal and plain meaning of biblical texts. It has remained a very helpful resource in my theological pilgrimage. I sorely miss him with his recent death. He was working on writing the introduction to this work

---

[615] Ibid., 335, 336.

[616] Ibid., 335-336.

[617] The very first three books that initiated the development of my library were: The Glory of God by Dr. John MacArthur; Crucial Questions about Hell by Ajith Fernando; and Sin, the Savior, and Salvation by Dr. Robert Lightner.

when the Lord called him home to glory. He enthusiastically encouraged me in this work and believed the body of Christ needed this work.

Dr. Lightner stood in line with evangelical orthodoxy with his views of Christ saving sinners. Two works in particular reveal that Lightner embraced the view that Christ alone breaks the will of the sinner and draws the elect to faith by grace alone. Dr. Lightner rejects the Roman Catholic position that says man's will can achieve and obtain the grace of God through co-operation with the grace of God.[618] Therefore, he embraces the historic Calvinistic view that says Christ effectively draws and grants new life to the sinner.[619]

Furthermore, his works deny the views that God's election of sinners is conditioned upon what the lost sinner would do in response to God's offer.[620] He rejects prescient election. In other words, Dr. Lightner embraces a Calvinistic view that God elects sinners by his mere pleasure and not because of foreseen faith or because God learns of a person's faith.

In *Evangelical Theology: A Survey and Review*, Lightner discusses the difference between common grace, which is granted to the entire world, and the doctrine of efficacious grace, which is granted only to the elect. He says of this work of the Spirit, "This work of the Spirit in moving sinners to trust in Christ the sin-bearer has been called irresistible grace, efficacious grace, or effectual grace . . . . that work of which results in the individual's acceptance of Christ as Savior is not a process. Rather, it is an instantaneous act simultaneous with faith. Scriptural support for this effective work of the Spirit is found in those passages which speak of the call that leads to salvation (e.g. Rom 1:1; 8:28; 1 Tim. 6:12; 2 Peter 1:3,10)."[621] Lightner discussed this efficacious grace comes to those who

---

[618] Roman Catholic Council of Trent, 1547, Canons four and five.

[619] Process justification theologies violate the fundamental doctrine of salvation by grace alone.

[620] I had the benefit of taking Dr. Lightner's seminary course on the doctrine of salvation. In that course his views were a moderate Calvinistic or Amyraldian view of soteriology.

[621] Robert P. Lightner, *Evangelical Theology: A Survey and Review* (Grand Rapids, MI: Baker Books, 1986), 199.

were chosen in Christ before the foundation of the world. He writes of this:

> We often feel that everything about our salvation began when we made our decision to trust Christ as Savior. The fact is, God was at work on our behalf long before that moment of decision. We did not, we could not, initiate the salvation we enjoy in Christ. Scripture declares that we were chosen in Christ "before the foundation of the world" (Eph. 1:4). Peter told the scattered Christians they were chosen "according to the foreknowledge of God the Father" (1 Peter 1:2). Paul, the apostle to the Gentiles, put it this way: "For whom He foreknew, He also predestined to be conformed to the image of His Son" (Rom. 8:29). And again, "God from the beginning chose you for salvation through sanctification by the Spirit and faith in the truth" (2 Thess. 2:13). The Savior himself spoke of the sovereign electing work of God the Father to the multitudes who came to Him to hear Him: "All that the Father gives Me will come to Me, and the one who comes to Me I will by no means cast out, . . . No one can come to me unless the Father who sent me draws him; and I will raise him up at the last day" (John 6:37, 44) . . . . We do not understand why God has been pleased to the things He has. Why were we chosen and brought to faith in Christ and many others were not? Why were many called but only a few chosen (Matt. 22:14)? We will never know the answers to many of our queries until we see the Savior face to face.[622]

And needless to say, Lightner, adds that the Scriptures teach the "personal, pre-temporal election"[623] of sinners to salvation. This again is not based upon man for he is "utterly depraved."[624] And since the sinner is utterly depraved the Holy Spirit must move and break the stubborn will of

---

[622] Robert P. Lightner, *Sin, the Savior, and Salvation: The Theology of Everlasting Life* (Grand Rapids, MI: Kregel Publications, 1991), 148.

[623] Ibid., 149.

[624] Ibid., 41.

man and enable him to believe.[625] "Every possible human instrument in the plan of salvation is eliminated. John the apostle said it was not of blood (not of human lineage), not of the will of the flesh, not even of the will or desire of man (John 1:13). No, it is all of God."[626] God's electing and saving work does not depend upon anything in man's will as Romans 9:16 teaches.[627]

24. James Quiggle

One of the most prolific Dispensational writers in the past 25 to 50 years has been James Quiggle. For those of us who know him, we recognize he has a very keen mind devoted to precision and the fundamentals of the faith. With over 70 monographs published, he ranks in the top 10 to 20 most prolific authors in our Dispensational heritage.

Quiggle with explicit clarity embraces a Calvinistic soteriology. He references these matters on a regular basis in his articles, books, and in his public media ministry. One book in particular, *God's Choices: The Doctrines of Foreordination, Election, and Predestination* covers the doctrine of salvation in relation to God's sovereignty.

A very helpful section in his book gives the reader some definitions to the terms he uses. Even in these definitions one can see his clear Calvinistic stances. He defines election as "the choice of a sovereign God . . . to give the gift of grace-faith-salvation to effect the salvation of some sinners, and . . . to take no action, positive or negative, to either effect or deny salvation to other sinners. The decree to election includes all means necessary to effectuate salvation in those elected."[628] By this

---

[625] Robert Lightner, Seminary class lecture, "*The Doctrine of Soteriology*," 2003.

[626] Robert P. Lightner, *Sin, the Savior, and Salvation: The Theology of Everlasting Life* (Grand Rapids, MI: Kregel Publications, 1991), 145.

[627] Robert Lightner, Seminary class lecture, "*The Doctrine of Soteriology*," 2003.

[628] James D. Quiggle, *God's Choices: The Doctrines of Foreordination, Election, and Predestination* (no place of publication, 2012), 7.

definition alone, Quiggle has made his stance clear that he embraces a Calvinistic view of soteriology.

Quiggle also devotes some time to explaining the various lapsarian decrees.[629] After discussing the main options, he chose to create one he finds most satisfying to scripture instead of the various existing models. He rejects the supralapsarian models and all models that place sin in the hand of God. In his view, the supralapsarian model violates God's justice and character.[630] In the model he created (10 steps), he affirmed the view that God decreed to "permit the fall of mankind into sin."[631] This distinguishes him from the high or extreme supralapsarian Calvinism models.

Yet, he clearly rejects the idea that people choose Christ and on that basis of faith God then chooses man, a view known as foresight election. In rejecting foresight election Quiggle stated this of that view:

> There are man-made explanations of election. . . . The basis for these man-made explanations is foreknowledge: that God chose certain persons just because he knew they would believe when hearing the gospel; that certain persons were elected because God had foreseen their faith. This view eliminates the sovereignty of God . . . .[632]

Furthermore, Quiggle uses historical theology to show his continuity with the historical stream that affirmed God's eternal election of sinners. Quiggle recognizes that novel interpretations often have less credibility. He said, "I have provided" historical quotations "from various centuries of church history so the reader may understand that mine is no novel doctrine of foreordination and foreknowledge."[633] In an age where

---

[629] Ibid., 35-38.

[630] Ibid., 36-37.

[631] Ibid., 38.

[632] Ibid., 64.

[633] Ibid., 55.

misrepresentation is common among some movements against the historicity of eternal election soteriology, especially among those like Dr. Leighton Flowers and Dr. Ken Wilson and their followers, Quiggle traces history back to even Clement and then through a vast line of church history showing his view of election has historical continuity in it.

Dr. Leighton Flowers and those in his Soteriology 101 ministry commonly speak of Bezanism (omnicausality; God actively decrees all) as Calvinism (even though 2 types of Calvinism reject Bezanism), and in doing so Flowers and the ministry grossly misrepresents on a regular and habitual basis the views of lower level Calvinistic teachers. Dr. Ken Wilson, in addition to the errors of Flowers, pushes the idea the doctrine of eternal election began with Augustine and alleges Augustine developed his idea from Gnosticism and other heretical philosophies.

Neither of them, Flowers nor Wilson, correctly represents the full view of history or theology on these matters. Quiggle counters these ideas that the idea of eternal election began with Augustine and, like Dr. R.K. McGregor Wright[634] and Dr. John Gill,[635] finds support for this doctrine in the early fathers and through the history of the church. As a Dispensationalist he counters the Covenant Calvinist critics that claim Dispensationalism is inherently Arminian, and on the other hand he also counters those like Flowers and Wilson who claim sovereign election theology did not exist prior to Augustine.

Quiggle says, "from the apostolic era forward, election to salvation was the common faith of the church."[636] He then lists those he believes taught the form of election he affirms. From Clement of Rome,[637] Clement

---

[634] R.K. McGregor Wright, *No Room for Sovereignty* (Downers Grove, Ill: IVP Press, 1996), 18-42.

[635] John Gill, Cause of God and Truth, Vol. 4.

[636] James D. Quiggle, *God's Choices: The Doctrines of Foreordination, Election, and Predestination* (no place of publication, 2012), 106. In quoting this I recognize that other views of election existed in history. I think Dispensationalism has been correct in not making the doctrine of election an essential of the faith. Just as those who produced the Chicago Statement of Inerrancy were all conservative evangelicals, so too in Christianity conservative evangelicals can vary on how best to explain election and remain in common fellowship for the gospel so long as extreme views are rejected on both sides.

[637] Ibid., 106-107.

of Alexandria, Minucius Felix, Lactantius, Chrysostom, Athanasius, Augustine, down to the Reformation, and into modern day theologians and denominational confessions[638] Quiggle highlights those who have taught the eternal election view that he too affirms.

In examining Ephesians 1 on God's election, Quiggle believes that all who ever have been saved have been elected in Christ prior to creation. All sinners elected are recorded in the book of life in Christ. He said of election and effectual grace:

> Election is the eternal act of God that establishes the sinner as saved in Christ. . . . God chose us 'in Christ'. The merit of Christ is the sole ground for salvation . . . . In the timelessness of God's existence before he created, he elected those whom he would in later time create. . . . he decreed to elect a definite number of sinners to redemption in the Redeemer. . . . Jesus is, as it were, the book of life, in whom the believer is written down and acknowledged by God as his child. . . .[639]

This election then means that God in time works through his providence to move these elected ones to faith in Christ. Quiggle said:

> Only a super-natural intervention—God's gift of conviction, given by his grace, and thus infallibly leading to faith, can turn . . . into saving faith and change the state of the soul from sinner to saved. . . . the conviction-faith that I am a sinner and Jesus is my only Savior has its origin and source in God alone. That conviction is regenerative in that it restores the spiritual perception required to make a faith decision to believe on Jesus Christ for personal salvation. . . . he [the sinner] is convicted of the truth and on the basis of that conviction he personally appropriates the truth. . . . this is God's sovereignty, working through man's responsibility, to infallibly accomplish God's purposes and plans in his election of sinners in Christ to salvation, in love by grace through faith.[640]

---

[638] Ibid., 50-55, 106-109.

[639] Ibid., 82.

[640] Ibid., 168-169.

Quiggle clearly as a Dispensationalist identifies as a Calvinist. He thoroughly rejects Arminian and/or other non-Calvinist views of election. He like many others represents a long line of Reformed Calvinistic Dispensationalists.

25. Dr. Kenneth Keathley

Dr. Ken Keathley earned his Masters of Divinity degree and PhD from Southeastern Baptist Theological Seminary in North Carolina. He currently serves as the Director of the L. Russ Bush Center for Faith and Culture as well as Senior Professor of Theology, occupying the Jesse Hendley Chair of Biblical Theology at Southeastern Baptist Seminary.

As a Dispensational premillennialist, he has written widely in the field of soteriology. He is a type of Calvinistic Molinist. He affirms man's depravity, God's eternal election of sinners, and a type of monergistic effectual work of grace that moves the elect to salvation. As a professor of Southeastern he also signs the Abstract Principles of faith that the famous Calvinist James P. Boyce with Basil Manly, John Broadus, E.T Winkler, and William Williams crafted as the confession to be used for the first Southern Baptist Seminary.[641] What is confessed in the Abstract of Principles concerning election and man's depravity? The following sections reveal what Keathley affirms.

> **V. Election**
> Election is God's eternal choice of some persons unto everlasting life-not because of foreseen merit in them, but of His mere mercy in Christ-in consequence of which choice they are called, justified and glorified.
>
> **VI. The Fall of Man**
> God originally created Man in His own image, and free from sin; but, through the temptation of Satan, he transgressed the command

---

[641] https://archives.sbts.edu/the-history-of-the-sbts/our-beliefs/the-development-and-role-of-the-abstract-of principles/#:~:text=After%20the%20idea%20to%20found,necessity%20of%20such%20a%20statement .

of God, and fell from his original holiness and righteousness; whereby his posterity inherit a nature corrupt and wholly opposed to God and His law, are under condemnation, and as soon as they are capable of moral action, become actual transgressors.

Dr. Keathley as a Dispensationalist not only affirms that confession, but his teachings verify that he affirms a strong view of man's depravity, God's eternal election of sinners, and a type of monergism that moves the elect to freely believe in Christ. Of man's depravity Keathley has said: "The fall affected every aspect of our being: the mind is darkened (Rom. 3:11), the will is twisted (2 Pet. 2:19); and affections are disordered (Isa. 57:21; Titus 3:3; 1 Pet. 2:11). . . . Scriptures portray humans as morally evil . . . spiritually sick . . . and spiritually blind. . . . The lost are in bondage to sin (John 8:34; Rom. 6:6)."[642] Clearly, he confesses man's condition as "radical depravity."[643]

Furthermore, Keathley subscribes to a type of election that remains an "individual" (not corporate) as well as "unconditional."[644] He adds, "if God had not first chosen us we would not have chosen him (John 15:16)." In his view Ephesians 1:4 means we were individually chosen in eternity past. The doctrine of election "is the clear teaching of scripture."[645] In his view, "God ordains the salvation of the elect but only permits the damnation of the reprobate."[646]

Keathley argues also that God's drawing grace, or overcoming grace, effectively leads an elect sinner to faith. Because humanity walks in radical depravity the Lord must intervene so the person will believe. He stated, "All are spiritually dead (Eph. 2:1), spiritually blind (2 Cor. 4:4), and spiritually incapacitated (Rom. 8:6-8). The apostle does not say just the unconverted are lost, but that they lack the capacity to rightly

---

[642] Kenneth Keathley, *Salvation and Sovereignty: A Molinist Approach* (Nashville, TN: B&H Publishing, 2010), 63.

[643] Ibid.

[644] Ibid., 7.

[645] Ibid., 140.

[646] Ibid., 142.

comprehend the truth and that they have no desire or love for it."[647] Therefore, he continues, "before anyone can be converted . . . God must graciously invade the darkness of the person's heart."[648] In his view, what he calls the ambulatory overcoming grace model, "the call of the Holy Spirit through the gospel is effectual in those for whom it was intended (i.e, the elect)" while too a real ans sincere calls extends to "every hearer."[649]

Though Keathley has more to say on the matter, especially in how he explains God's three types of knowledge and how those operate to bring a possible world into an actual world, these positions above give enough clarity to rightly classify him as within a type of Calvinistic view on the doctrine of elective grace. He is another Dispensationalist that affirms a type of Calvinistic soteriology within a more nuanced Molinist model.

26. Dr. Tony Evans

Tony Evans is a popular Christian pastor of the large church Oak Cliff Bible Fellowship in Dallas Texas. He is also speaker, author, and a widely-syndicated radio and television **broadcaster** in the United States. He was the first African-American to earn a doctorate from Dallas Theological Seminary.

Evans as a Dispensationalist affirms a Calvinistic position in regard to man's sin, predestination, and an elect person's conversion. His positions reflect alignment with a basic Reformed soteriology. Yet he is also clearly a Dispensationalist.

First, Evans teaches that man is conceived with a sin nature that exists from birth. Every person inherits a sin nature. He calls this sin nature our inborn depravity which means "every facet of human nature has been polluted, defiled, and contaminated by sin."[650] This sin nature means

---

[647] Ibid., 129.

[648] Ibid.

[649] Ibid., 137.

[650] Tony Evans, *A Theology You Can Count On* (Chicago, IL: Moody Press, 2008), 711.

that we have been born spiritually dead to God. Humans have been "cut off from its life source and is dead."[651] Every person is therefore, "born spiritually dead."[652]

Second, he provides a position on how it is that these spiritually dead sinners come to faith. He affirms that election was based in eternity past when God chose some to salvation. He specifically says, "God's offer of salvation is valid to all, and yet those who respond do so because they are the elect of God before the foundation of the world was laid."[653] He affirms that there is a mystery to this doctrine of election and that the Bible affirms both God's sovereignty as well as man's responsibility. He uses the ministry of Paul and Barnabas to show this mysterious symmetry. They preached the gospel and "when they had finished the message, the Bible clearly says, 'As many as had been appointed to eternal life believed' (Acts 13:48)."[654] He concludes his position on predestination and election by simply affirming, "God elects some to salvation for his own sovereign purposes and because he is gracious."[655]

As often is the case, Evans expects for people to question how this doctrine can be fair. He rightly asks the popular question, "how is it fair that God has elected some sinners to salvation while passing over others . . . . If God so loves the world, how can he choose some sinners and not others?"[656] Evans response to such a question or argument is as follows:

> The Bible says that God chose or elected us in Christ "before the foundation of the world" (Eph. 1:4). Election is based on God's eternal purposes and his prerogative to choose, not on our

---

[651] Ibid., 712.

[652] Ibid.

[653] Ibid., 775.

[654] Ibid.

[655] Ibid., 775-776.

[656] Ibid., 773.

behavior. Paul confirmed in this in Romans 9 as he discussed God's choice of Jacob and rejection of Esau.[657]

Third, Evans places the work of regeneration within the Triune work of the Godhead. Yet Evans does not suggest man has any contribution to his regeneration. He says that since we have "no capacity to commune with God" and that we are "dead in our sins (Eph. 2:1)" that such truths reveal why we need the "Spirit of God" who "brings your spirit alive."[658] He calls the Spirit a "divine surgeon" whose job it is to "break open the soul by cutting into it like a skilled surgeon."[659] This cutting away seems to take place at the time of God's work of conviction and regeneration of a sinner. Evans says,

> According to James 1:18, God the Father brought us forth to new life through his word, while John 5:21 says that God the Son gives life to whomever he wishes. Regeneration is also attributed to the Holy Spirit, whose work in salvation is to renew us to the point of salvation (Titus 3:5) . . . . the new birth is the means by which we pass 'out of death into life' (1 John 3:14). This is exactly what Jesus taught in John 3, a seminal passage on the new birth.[660]

These positions by Evans reveal his agreement with the basic ideology among a Reformed soteriology. His argument leaves room for mystery, and he steers a route that seeks to balance God's sovereignty and man's freedom, but even so his basic stance aligns more with the Reformed position than with a semi-Pelagian or Arminian position.[661]

---

[657] Ibid.

[658] Ibid., 412.

[659] Ibid., 415.

[660] Ibid., 761.

[661] Evans' Bible Commentary takes a different view of election. This occurs as it seems because of multiple editors working on it, a common problem in works filtered through multiple authors and editors.

27. Dr. Danny Akin

In his own words, a spiritual child of Dr. Paige Patterson,[662] Dr. Akin studied at Criswell College (B.A.), Southwestern Baptist Theological Seminary (M.Div.), and the University of Texas at Arlington (Ph.D.). Dr. Patterson hired him to teach at Criswell College. Then Akin followed Patterson to Southeastern Baptist Theological Seminary to serve under Patterson there as a professor of Theology and Dean of Students. Akin later took a post at The Southern Baptist Theological Seminary in Louisville Kentucky as a professor, Dean over the School of Theology, and as a Senior Vice President over Administration.

After Paige Patterson accepted the presidency at Southwestern Baptist Theological Seminary, Dr. Akin became the sixth president of Southeastern Baptist Theological Seminary upon Patterson's departure. Currently in his early sixties, he continues in that position at Southeastern Baptist Theological Seminary.

I have always found it interesting that even as a protégé of Patterson, Akin retained a closer affinity to Criswell's type of Calvinism than Patterson's perspective on these matters. Patterson served as a link between Criswell and Akin, and though Patterson has expressed at times a perspective that affirms some type of unconditional or sovereign election view in salvation[663] he rejects limited atonement and irresistible grace.[664]

---

[662] Danny Akin on several past occasions has stated this publicly about Paige Patterson being his spiritual father. While at an Evangelism conference in Georgia (an Acts 1:11 conference), Danny stated that all the theology he has ever learned he learned from Paige. I took that to be a metaphorical statement, i.e., a statement of honor he attributed to how much Paige had taught him over the years in theology and life. Sadly, a recent breach of fellowship has happened between Akin and Patterson due to the unjustified allegations made against Patterson by the SWBTS seminary board that led to his termination as SWBTS President.

[663] Southern Seminary Magazine, December 1998, p. 37. See also his discussion of election in the Baptist Study Bible, edited by W.A. Criswell, page 1611. Also see his discussion on election in his Revelation Commentary, pages 324 and 384.

[664] Paige Patterson, "*Shoot-Out at the Amen Corral: Being Baptist Through Controversy*," in *Why I Am A Baptist*, eds. Tom J. Nettles and Russell Moore (Nashville TN: Broadman & Holman Publishers, 2001), 71.

Yet Dr. Akin has retained a stronger emphasis on this doctrine as a type of Dispensationalist than has Patterson.[665] Whereas Patterson has at times identified himself as affirming man's depravity, unconditional election, and preservation of the saints,[666] Akin affirms more of the markers of a Calvinistic faith. He affirms monergism, man's helpless condition in depravity, God's choice to save many through unconditional election, Christ's particular atonement limited in application (not limited in provision), and the preservation of the saints who will persevere in the faith.

Akin affirms that people suffer from total depravity. Akin stated that a recognition of "total depravity is really the proper basis for a positive approach to life."[667] Man's depravity is so real and so extensive that he affirms scripture's witness that "the corruption of sin which extends to all people and to every aspect of each person" to such a degree that nothing in an "unbeliever can commend that person to God."[668] In support of his

---

[665] I asked Patterson at an evangelism conference in Pickens South Carolina about both Criswell and Akin and their Calvinism in contrast to his. He replied, "Yes, Criswell and Danny are a little more Calvinistic than I am." In 2010, Patterson wrote the foreword to the Calvinistic-Molinist work by Dr. Kenneth Keathley, another Calvinistic Dispensationalist though more in the vein of Molinism. In that foreword Patterson said that he has become more "uncomfortable with the usual definitions of three other petals of the TULIP [referring to the T.U. & P] and the fact that in order for me to endorse them I have to be certain that the definitions are correlated with what I find on the pages of Holy Scripture." Quote in Foreword, *Salvation and Sovereignty* by Kenneth Keathley (Nashville TN: B&H Academic, 2010), viii. See next footnote on how Patterson defines election.

[666] At that evangelism conference noted above in the prior footnote, Patterson described election to me this way. "It is unconditional on what lost man does and conditioned on what God does. Lost man contributes nothing to his own election." He stated then he affirmed man's depravity, God's elective choice, and the preservation of the saints while rejecting limited atonement and irresistible grace. When asking him about his thoughts on limited atonement after his public Q&A session, Patterson stated this: "I do not find one single verse anywhere in the entire Bible that supports limited atonement."

[667] Danny Akin, *Systematic Notes: Christian Theology Part I, Book VI, Anthropology & Hamartiology* (n.d. no publisher), 68.

[668] Ibid., 64.

stance on total depravity Akin cites many verses, some of those are: Romans 1:18-3:20; Ephesians 2:1-3; 1 John 1:8; and Psalms 14:3.[669]

In regards to election Akin affirms the classical Reformed stance that God chooses people based upon his sovereign and loving will alone. God does not make his choice after a person exercises faith in Christ. He also rejects corporate election. Akin states, "before the foundation of the world, God chose particular individuals unto salvation. His selection was not based upon any foreseen response or act performed by those chosen. Faith and good works are the result, not the cause of God's choice."[670]

To support his doctrine of election, Dr. Akin uses many texts. Some of those texts he uses are: John 6:37, 44, 65; Acts 13:48; Romans 9:11-13; and 2 Timothy 1:9. These texts, as well as others, in Akin's view establish the doctrine that God chooses to place his unconditional elective love on some that will certainly result in their salvation. It not only guarantees initial salvation but it also guarantees their eternal salvation that secures them in the grace of Christ forever.[671]

The elect also experience an inward work of grace to such a degree that it certainly brings about salvation of those elected. This has been termed efficacious grace. The grace of the Lord effects or accomplishes the eternal purpose for eternal redemption of those chosen in eternity past. Identifying himself in line with the Southern Baptist Faith and Message, the confession of faith for his denomination to which he belongs, Akin states that "faith and repentance are precious gifts of God that are wrought in the soul through the regenerating work of the Holy Spirit."[672] Akin defines this more specifically in saying, the gospel invitation extends a general outward call to salvation to all who hear the message. In addition to this external call, the Holy Spirit extends a special inward call to the

---

[669] Ibid.

[670] Danny Akin, *Systematic Notes: Christian Theology Part II, Book III, Salvation* (n.d. no publisher), 49.

[671] Ibid., 124.

[672] Ibid., 55.

elect .... the special call of the Spirit will not be rejected; it will result in the conversion of those to whom it is made."[673]

28-37. Ten More Calvinistic Dispensationalists Briefly Noted

I have covered twenty seven Dispensationalists that have clearly affirmed a Calvinistic perspective of salvation. I will now conclude this section with briefly noting ten more theologians that also as Dispensationalists align with a Calvinistic view of election and grace. The evidence overwhelmingly reveals that the critics of Dispensationalism that wrongly label it as Arminian or non-Calvinistic in soteriology have at best been grossly ignorant of the actual teachings of Dispensationalism, or sadly at worst (I hope not the case) for some purposefully dishonest with the facts. It is impossible to read Dispensational literature and miss this massive portion of theologians who comprise one of the most significant streams of thought in Dispensationalism.

28. Dr. William Baker

In adding to the twenty-seven, already covered, I will briefly mention these next ten teachers who were Calvinistic Dispensationalists. Dr. William Baker taught for many years at some of the most widely recognized Dispensational academies in the United States. During that time he taught for over twenty-five years at the Moody Bible Institute. He also earned his ThD from Dallas Seminary. When writing on 1 Peter, Dr. Baker noted that those chosen according to God's foreknowledge in 1 Peter 1:1-2 reveals to us that God elected us to salvation. In his words, "this choosing or election . . . is theologically the fundamental basis for salvation. According to Romans 9:11, election is not based on anything within the chosen person but according to God's purpose.[674]

---

[673] Ibid., 56.

[674] William Baker, *The Books of James & First and Second Peter: Faith, Suffering, and Knowledge*, in the Twenty-First Century Biblical Commentary Series, eds. Mal Couch & Ed Hindson (Chattanooga, TN: AMG Publishers, 2004), 101-102.

29. Steven Ger

Steven Ger, who established and leads Sojourner Ministries, earned his ThM from Dallas Seminary. He is a fourth generation Jewish believer. He wrote a commentary on the book of Acts. One text, Acts 13:48, has very often revealed where one stands on the doctrine of election. For Ger, this text reveals God elects man unto salvation. He said of this text, "It is difficult to miss the doctrine of God's sovereign election in this verse."[675] In his view, God appointed those who would come to faith "according to his "sovereign purpose."[676]

30. Dr. Woodrow Kroll

In a Romans Commentary, the famous teacher Dr. Woodrow Kroll who served as President of Back to the Bible ministry, defended the ideas of man's total depravity and God's sovereign election to redeem many. Of depravity he said, sinners prior to being drawn to Christ are "incapable of spiritual understanding (1 Cor. 2:14). . . . because people by nature are sinful and want nothing to do with God. It is only when sinners are drawn by God to himself that they seek the Lord Jesus Christ in repentance and confession (John 6:44).[677]

Furthermore, in explaining Romans 8:28 Kroll emphasizes the effectual call of God. He said, "only those who have been effectively called by God and have embraced the Lord Jesus as Savior can expect all things to work together for their good."[678] He then expands on the doctrine of God's foreknowledge and election in verses 29-30. He explained that "the salvation provided by God, there is a link from eternity past, through

---

[675] Steven Ger, *The Book of Acts: Witnesses to the World*, in the Twenty-First Century Biblical Commentary Series, eds. Mal Couch & Ed Hindson (Chattanooga, TN: AMG Publishers, 2004), 198.

[676] Ibid.

[677] Woodrow Kroll, The Book of Romans, in the *Twenty-First Century Biblical Commentary Series*, eds. Mal Couch & Ed Hindson (Chattanooga, TN: AMG Publishers, 2002), 40-41.

[678] Ibid., 140.

the present, to eternity future. That link includes foreknowledge, predestination, calling, justification, and glorification."[679] He emphatically then explained this is not foresight election. In rejecting foresight election Dr. Kroll stated, "for God to preview history to discern our response to the gospel and then act accordingly, would make the creature sovereign over the Creator."[680] This clearly does not equal Arminian Dispensationalism.

31-32. Dr. Mike Stallard & Dr. Tom Constable

Dr. Mike Stallard, longtime professor of theology at Baptist Bible Seminary, along with Dr. Tom Constable, former director of Doctor of Ministry Studies at Dallas Seminary, both conclude that the doctrine of election exists in the book of 2nd Thessalonians. Dr. Stallard examined 2 Thessalonians 2:13 and believed that the best interpretation pointed to God's sovereign election. He said Paul wanted to his readers have assurance "that their election was no recent innovation; they were included in God's plan from the dateless past."[681] This election took place in the "pretemporal beginning of the program of redemption (1 Cor. 2:7; Eph. 1:4; 2 Tim. 1:9; Titus 1:2)."[682]

Dr. Constable discovered the same idea in 2 Thessalonians. Commenting on 2:13 he too said that this act of God in choosing some from the beginning is "not on the basis of their love for him or any merit on their part." Instead God elects and "the means God uses to effect salvation is the work of the Holy Spirit who sets aside chosen individuals for lives of holiness and separation from sin (cf. John 16:7-11)."[683]

---

[679] Ibid., 141.

[680] Ibid.

[681] Mike Stallard, *The Books of First & Second Thessalonians: Looking for Christ's Return*, in the Twenty-First Biblical Commentary Series, eds. Mal Couch & Ed Hindson (Chattanooga, TN: AMG Publishers, 2009), 186.

[682] Ibid.

[683] Thomas L. Constable, 2 Thessalonians, in the *Bible Knowledge Commentary: New Testament*, eds. John F. Walvoord & Roy B. Zuck (USA: SP Publications, 1983), 721.

33-35. Dr. Stanley Toussaint, Dr. Harold Hoehner, & Dr. Roger Raymer

Three more Dallas Seminary professors also wrote in the Dallas Seminary Faculty Commentary that God elected and effectually drew sinners to salvation. Dr. Stanley Toussaint, Dr. Harold Hoehner, and Dr. Roger Rayner all affirmed as Dispensationalists a Calvinistic view of salvation. In Acts 13:48, Dr. Toussaint recognized that God elected individuals to salvation and assigned these to salvation.[684]

Dr. Hoehner in Ephesians 1 credits salvation to the threefold functions of the Trinity. God elects, the Son dies, and the Spirit seals the ones elected. Spiritual blessings occur because we are chosen in eternity past when God sovereignly chose some to believe.[685] These elected ones were then in time effectually called to salvation. [686] Dr. Raymer arrived at these conclusions as well. In 1 Peter he noted that being elected according to God's foreknowledge does not mean foresight election. Election is a predetermined plan, not "passive foresight."[687]

36-37. Dr. Michael G. Vanlaningham & Dr. Gerald Peterman

In writing a commentary on Romans in the Moody Bible Commentary, Dr. Vanlaningham, presents the Calvinistic view of eternal election. He in his view, God freely chooses those he will save. "That he chooses to save some indicates his grace, not his unfairness."[688] From fallen humanity, metaphorically represented by the clay in Romans 9, God

---

[684] Stanley Toussaint, Acts, in the *Bible Knowledge Commentary: New Testament*, eds. John F. Walvoord & Roy B. Zuck (USA: SP Publications, 1983), 390-391.

[685] Harold Hoehner, Ephesians, in the *Bible Knowledge Commentary: New Testament*, eds. John F. Walvoord & Roy B. Zuck (USA: SP Publications, 1983), 6616-617.

[686] Ibid., 617.

[687] Roger Raymer, 1 Peter, in the *Bible Knowledge Commentary: New Testament*, eds. John F. Walvoord & Roy B. Zuck (USA: SP Publications, 1983), 840.

[688] Michael G. Vanlaningham, Romans, in *The Moody Bible Commentary*, eds. Michael Rydelnik & Michael Vanlaningham (Chicago, Ill: Moody Press, 2014), 1760.

"chooses to make a vessel for honorable use . . . and another for common use."[689]

Dr. Gerald Peterman also in this Commentary produced by Moody faculty defended the Calvinistic view of election and grace. In his view, election is an "astonishing blessing." He defined it as "God's loving choice of certain individuals to be his own." He rejected the idea God elected based on "human faith or deeds" because "election happens before the foundation of the world (cf. John 17:24; 1 Pt. 1:20; Rv. 13:8)."[690]

Chapter Summary: Dispensationalism is Clearly not an Arminian Movement

The allegations made by our Reformed Covenant friends in the faith that Dispensationalism has roots in Arminianism lack merit. Not only do such allegations lack merit, they lack historical validity. How many Dispensational Calvinists does it take to convince our Covenant Calvinist friends in the faith that some beloved theologians have erred in calling Dispensationalism an Arminian theology? These thirty-seven highlight a long span of teachers in our movement that have taught a Reformed Calvinistic view of election and salvation.

Are all Dispensationalists Calvinistic? No, and this is not the goal of this research to prove that all are Calvinistic. In our movement, we welcome those who affirm justification by faith alone in Christ alone. Many godly theologians of the ages have not always arrived at the exact same view of how election works. No doubt, in our movement we have understood that even our best efforts to explain it we remain limited in being able to satisfactorily explain all of these unsearchable judgments and unfathomable ways of God (Rom. 11:33).

Some great legendary leaders of the Lord in our movement have not been Calvinistic in their view of election. Names come to mind like D.L. Moody, Dr. H.A. Ironside, Dr. Henry Thiessen, Dr. Charles Stanley, two of my Christicommunity colleagues and friends, Dr. William F. Luck and Pastor Luke Morrison, the famous evangelist Dr. John R. Rice, Dr. Harold

---

[689] Ibid.

[690] Gerald Peterman, Ephesians, in *The Moody Bible Commentary*, eds. Michael Rydelnik & Michael Vanlaningham (Chicago, Ill: Moody Press, 2014), 1847.

Hunter, and others who have a different view of election as Dispensationalists. How we think it best to define election does not constitute a fundamental of the faith. It does not constitute an issue of orthodoxy so long as the extremes on both ends, Bezanism (God authors original sin; active omnicausality) and Open Theism (extreme Arminianism), remain excluded from the theological explanations.

Nonetheless, the false, combative, and divisive allegations made by Reformed Covenant Calvinists against their true friends in the faith who also affirm a single, holistic, family of God in Christ because of God's elective graces that the Spirit effectually applies to produce saving faith needs to end and never be uttered again. Any theologian who speaks such nonsense, and continues to allege Dispensationalism is inherently Arminian or leads to that by default brings shame on himself by denying objective reality.

One might as well make the wrong comment that Thomas Jefferson rejected the United States Declaration of Independence. To wrongly think that of Jefferson has as much validity as these old, worn out, historically invalidated, and blatantly false allegations that Dispensationalism is inherently Arminian or an anti-Calvinistic theology. Objective history shows otherwise for anyone willing to examine it and accept facts.

Anyone who makes these allegations reveals their bias, dishonesty, or historical ignorance, none of which should mark godly evangelical Bible believing, Christ loving, Spirit filled ministers of the Word, all of which I think my Reformed Covenant friends are in their souls. Therefore, because they do love the Lord and their Dispensational neighbors, it is past time to drop these allegations against their brethren in the Lord.

Chapter 4. Diversity among Dispensationalists and Covenant Theologians on the Atonement of Christ

The doctrine of Christ's substitution of himself in the place of sinners has been a hallmark doctrine for Evangelicals. This doctrine receives a significant amount of focus as well within the discussions concerning a Calvinistic soteriology. Calvinist scholar Dr. John Gerstner makes so much of the issue over the doctrine of limited atonement that he argues if a person rejects this understanding then a Calvinistic soteriology cannot exist. In his perspective, a "denial of limited atonement destroys the possibility of Calvinism."[691] Yet his position, if true, would by default place many of his own heritage in question of their orthodoxy per his definition. How a man of intellectual caliber and theological knowledge could ignore or fail to recognize the many Reformed/Calvinistic theologians who held to some form of unlimited provision in the atonement astounds me beyond words. I find it unfathomable that he made such a glaring mistake as that in the comment above.

Of course, Dispensationalists in fact do have some diversity in this area. Some, like Dr. Dr. Donald Grey Barnhouse, affirmed more of a limited atonement model. Other Dispensationalists, such as Dr. Lewis Chafer and Dr. John Walvoord, to name just two of many, affirmed more so of an unlimited atonement position. This does not mean they embraced a universal salvation view or that they adopted a view of the atonement that undermined the need for a substitution. Affirming atonement for all with some benefit to all without eternally saving all has been a long standing view among those who are Calvinistic. Luther, Calvin, and even 2/3rds of the 3 parties at Dort held to some type of atonement beyond the elect. The debate at Dort was so intense that one man was so angry about the universal atonement view being proposed that he challenged another man to a duel. It literally could be said it was like a "shootout at the Amen corral." Some academic folk will be upset I used some humor in a scholarly work. Shame on them for not having a jovial spirit ☺.

---

[691] John Gerstner, *Wrongly Dividing the Word of Truth: A Critique of Dispensationalism* (Morgan, PA: Soli Deo Gloria Publications, 2000), 128.

But the same diversity exists in the history of Covenant theology too. For example, numerous scholars have come forth in the last three decades who assert that even John Calvin himself did not support the idea of a limited only atonement as so often presented among Reformed/Calvinist circles. That alone deserves close attention when contemplating this matter. Three scholars in particular highlight this point about Calvin.

Dr. R.T. Kendall in *Calvin and English Calvinism to 1649* makes a persuasive case that Calvin did not affirm what is popularly known today as limited atonement. Instead his research of Calvin shows that this early Reformed theologian embraced a type of universal atonement. In speaking to Calvin's thoughts on Isaiah 53 and Hebrews 9:28 Kendall argues that Calvin's perspective could not be clearer. "Fundamental to doctrine of faith in John Calvin . . . is his belief that Christ died indiscriminately for all men," even though "he does not pray for all."[692] Even when Calvin disputed with the Decrees from the Council of Trent he refused to comment on the assertion they made concerning Christ's death for all men.[693]

Other scholars have come to the same conclusion as did Kendall. Dr. G. Michael Thomas earned his Ph.D. in tracing the doctrine of the atonement within the Reformed tradition. Of Calvin he noted that his teachings on the atonement of Christ did not speak directly to the question of "for whom Christ died."[694] Yet even while not addressing the question directly he says that it remains "undeniable" that he took the freedom to present "redemption in universal terms."[695] At times he had no hesitation in "repeating, without modification, the biblical statements about the possibility of some for whom Christ died perishing."[696] According to

---

[692] R.T. Kendall, *Calvin and English Calvinism to 1649* (Carlisle Cumbria, United Kingdom: Peternoster Press, 1997), 13, 14.

[693] Ibid., 14-15.

[694] G. Michael Thomas, *The Extent of the Atonement: A Dilemma for Reformed Theology from Calvin to the Consensus* (Carlisle Cumbria, United Kingdom: Paternoster Publishing, 1997), 27.

[695] Ibid.

[696] Ibid., 28.

Thomas it seems that Calvin viewed the atonement from two vantage points or through two layers of thought.[697] From one layer of thought Christ died for the elect, yet in another form of thought he died for all of the world.[698] Thomas concluded that this double layer perspective of Christ's death for the elect in one way while also for the whole world in another way left an "inherently unstable" theology for those who followed him.[699]

Dr. Kevin Kennedy arrived at similar conclusions as well in his Ph.D. research on Calvin's view of the atonement at The Southern Baptist Theological Seminary. His research too affirms that "those who claim that Calvin held the view of universal atonement are well within their rights to make that claim."[700] The reasons for that right are as follows: (1) Calvin employs many "unqualified universal statements" concerning the "atonement;"[701] (2) in many places where the word many is used Calvin expanded that term many to more than just the elect and made it apply to whole human race;[702] and (3) Calvin spoke of those who stand in judgment do so with double culpability for rejecting the Savior who died for them.[703] These key positions seem to lead properly to the conclusion that good reasons exist for affirming "Calvin held to a universal atonement."[704]

Additionally, it appears that even at the famous Calvinistic/Reformed Synod of Dort, an "international church

---

[697] Ibid., 33.

[698] Ibid.

[699] Ibid., 34.

[700] Kevin Kennedy, "*Was Calvin a Calvinist*," in *Whosoever Will: A Biblical-Theological Critique of Five-Point Calvinism*, eds. David L. Allen and Steve W. Lemke (Nashville, TN: B&H Publishing, 2010), 195.

[701] Ibid., 196.

[702] Ibid., 201-204.

[703] Ibid., 205-207.

[704] Ibid., 211.

assembly,"⁷⁰⁵ unity on the question of the extent of the atonement did not occur. As Dr. Thomas says of that historic meeting, "nothing caused greater division at the Synod of Dort than the question, 'for whom did Christ die.'"⁷⁰⁶ Several branches of the geographical body of Christ were represented at this Synod. Of those various branches several different ideas on the atonement were enunciated.

It appears that the views primarily fell into three positions: (1) the hyper-Calvinist view that Christ died only for the elect and that the gospel should not be preached to all; (2) a view that understood the atonement of Christ as both limited and universal; (3) and some type of view that represented the death of Christ for all with special application to the elect and a general application to the rest of humanity.⁷⁰⁷ Dr. Thomas notes of these divisions that "these apparent contradictions had been with the Reformed from the beginning, but appeared at Dort more obviously and embarrassingly than before."⁷⁰⁸

Those stark differences were so sharp that it seems one advocate of one view challenged another from a different perspective to "a duel."⁷⁰⁹ Such a situation highlights the seriousness of the "fundamental antagonism"⁷¹⁰ in the debate over the atonement at this Synod. The resolution to such differences was to adopt language of sufficiency for Christ's death for all and efficient for only the elect as those were the constant positions resonating through the various submissions by the representatives.⁷¹¹

---

[705] M.E. Osterhaven, "*Synod of Dort,*" in *Evangelical Dictionary of Theology*, ed. Walter A. Elwell (Grand Rapids, MI: Baker Books, 2001), 354.

[706] G. Michael Thomas, *The Extent of the Atonement: A Dilemma for Reformed Theology from Calvin to the Consensus* (Carlisle Cumbria, United Kingdom: Paternoster Publishing, 1997), 147.

[707] Ibid., 149-150.

[708] Ibid., 150.

[709] Ibid.

[710] Ibid.

[711] Ibid., 138.

Yet this language was left open to interpretation. As Thomas noted, "The distinction between the sufficiency and efficacy of the atonement was able to command the assent, if not the enthusiasm, of all participants at Dort. . . . Its acceptance enabled" the leadership of Dort to "pronounce that the Synod had achieved substantial unity. It was, however, only an apparent unity, on the basis of a formula open to very different interpretations."[712]

Other writers concur that this controversy that existed in the early era of the Reformation continues today in regards to the perspective of the extent of the atonement. Dr. Kenneth Good has well said, "considerable controversy has arisen among Calvinists themselves on the extent of redemption accomplished at Calvary."[713] He too believes that the historical documents from the Synod of Dort reveal they were divided over this subject.[714] This division has been resolved by some who believe the specific atonement texts for the elect refer to eternal or special grace where the universal statements of Scripture refer to general or common grace for all.[715]

Yet even so with these various divisions in the Calvinist/Reformed stream of thought (four point and five point Calvinists) Dr. Good posits that "those who espouse a four-point position are included in the category of Calvinist."[716] These various perspectives on this one point are to be seen as "different members of one family."[717]

This knowledge of the diversity on the question of the extent of the atonement even among the Synod of Dort ought to cause humility among those today discussing this matter. If even the strongest Calvinist/Reformed convention in the history of the world debated this one point with great vigor and passion, how is it wise or honorable to declare

---

[712] Ibid., 140.

[713] Kenneth Good, *Are Baptists Calvinists* (Rochester, NY: Backus Book Publishers, 1988), 67.

[714] Ibid., 68.

[715] Ibid., 71.

[716] Ibid.

[717] Ibid.

any particular Dispensationalist or Dispensationalism as a whole as anti-Calvinistic because of those within Dispensationalism that embrace some form of unlimited atonement that coalesces with some of the perspectives among those in the Synod of Dort? If a Covenant theologian calls Dispensationalism an Arminian movement because most in it embrace some form of benefit in the atonement for all then those same Covenant theologians, if consistent and not hypocritical, would have to label a large portion of their own Covenant Reformed movement as Arminian too because many in it have also rejected a strict limited atonement view that restricts all benefits of the atonement to only the elect.

For Whom Did Christ Die? A Proposed Solution from a Reformed Dispensational Model

Dr. Robert Lightner has properly noted that "evangelical theologians and students of Scripture have heatedly debated the question of for whom Christ died."[718] Contrary to what many "five point Calvinists" would have you to believe, not even the original Reformed theologians could agree on this point. As noted earlier, even at the strongest Calvinist Convention this side of the celestial shores of heaven, the Synod of Dort (1618-1619), this issue led to an intense debate that resulted in a synthesis view.

Dr. Lightner has also faithfully shown that it appears from the writings of the earliest church fathers that they held the "belief in an unlimited atonement."[719] Furthermore, he has noted that the "children of the reformers were not united on this matter . . . . the Lutheran branch almost without exception embraced the unlimited view."[720] Men like Luther, Melanchthon, Osiander, Brentius, Oecollampadius, Zwingli, and Bucer held to a universal or cosmological atonement view of Christ's

---

[718] Robert Lightner, *Evangelical Theology: A Survey and Review* (Grand Rapids, MI: Baker Book House, 1986), 210.

[719] Robert P. Lightner, *The Death Christ Died: A Biblical Case for Unlimited Atonement* (Grand Rapids, MI: Kregel Publications, 1998), 11.

[720] Ibid., 12.

death.[721] Additionally, it appears that the German Reformed Church in its Heidelberg Catechism of 1563 as well as the Church of England's Thirty Nine Articles embrace a universal atonement position.[722]

So where should faithful Evangelicals today stand on this matter? Is it even worth the time to study it? Or is this some esoteric debate better left to the monasteries or even the neo-monastics today who are often the seminarians who sometimes love to write and talk only among themselves? Certainly Dr. Charles Swindoll has reminded Christendom of the danger of "theological scholars" who are "notorious for talking only" among "themselves" because such language and writings as that are "woefully lacking in relevance and reality."[723]

Though the terms or vernacular in this matter might indeed stretch the mind of a younger believer, it does seem to be a debate, or rather more of an intramural dialog, among brethren who have an already existing affinity with one another. It is worth the attention of believers to do their best to ascertain how the atonement applies today. Indeed, a believer might even discover a few anomalies in his or her current views resulting in a motivation towards better acuity of thought and expression. Dr. Lightner has provided for us a clue as to why this subject is important to flesh out accurately. Like an actuary who calculates and states the risks, he shares with us what is at stake in this debate:

> This subject is of paramount importance to the ambassador for Christ. Unless Christ died for all men, the message of God's love and Christ's death must be given with tongue in cheek and with some reservation, because some may hear who are really not numbered among those whom God loved and Christ died. Consistency and honesty would demand that the one who believes in limited atonement refrain from proclaiming God's universal offer of the good news of God's love and grace in Christ to all men indiscriminately, since in that view God did not extend grace to all

---

[721] Ibid.

[722] Ibid.

[723] Charles Swindoll, *Growing Deep in the Christian Life: Returning to Our Roots* (Portland, OR: Multnomah Press, 1986), 12.

nor did Christ die for all. Therefore, to tell all men that these things are true and that salvation is available for them is to speak that which is not true if the limited view be accepted.[724]

As already noted, the strongest "Calvinist" convention in church history, the Synod of Dort, was divided over this subject and most of the Reformed theologians from that point have also been divided over this matter. My church history and systematic theology professor in undergraduate school, Dr. Chad Brand, once commented in class that it is valuable to study church history to see where God has raised up various groups to help compensate or offset a weakness or error in another group. He also commented that when we see two solid groups arriving at similar positions but still having some minor disagreements in one area that it is probably because both groups have only an element of truth. I have applied that point of what I think is true wisdom to this subject at hand.

For years the two schools of thought have been in opposition to one another over the question of the extent of the atonement. The "sufficient for all" camp says there is no room for the death to be limited except only in the application aspect of it. The "for the elect only" camp uses the logic of the substitution aspect of Christ's death to press the "all," "every," and "whole world" passages into a meaning that refers only to the elect groups or all classes of people who believe. They rely on the argument as set forth by John Own that either: (a) Christ paid for all the sins of all people and that is universalism; (b) Christ paid for some of the sins of all people and that leads to every person's condemnation; (c) Christ paid for all of the sins of the elect which means only they are saved.[725] *If these were the only options*, logic would most certainly require everyone to adopt position "c."

However, there is a better option that allows for us to follow the wisdom as set forth by Dr. John Calvin himself. Calvin stated that he agreed with the idea that Christ's death was sufficient for the whole world

---

[724] Robert P. Lightner, *The Death Christ Died: A Biblical Case for Unlimited Atonement* (Grand Rapids, MI: Kregel Publications, 1998), 15.

[725] John Owen, *The Death of Death in the Death of Christ* (Carlisle, PA: The Banner of Truth Trust, 1967), 124-178, 231-247.

but efficient only for the elect.[726] In commenting on Romans 5:15, where the word "many" is used, Calvin stated the term "many" does not apply to "any part of men," but that it "embraces the whole human race."[727]

Even clearer is Calvin's view of Romans 5:18. As noted earlier, other scholars have arrived at the same conclusion that Calvin held to a universal type of atonement. Dr. Kevin Kennedy, who earned his Ph.D. on his research upon Calvin's view of the atonement, says "when reading Calvin, one is struck with the sheer number of unqualified universal statements that he makes regarding the atonement. Many of these simply assert that Christ died for the redemption of humanity or the whole human race."[728]

Bible scholar Dr. R.T. Kendall has also concluded that Calvin taught a form of universal atonement.[729] I, as with many others, have wrestled with these various views on the atonement for some time. I have never been able to settle with a Bezanism limited atonement format due to allegiance to the Evangelical and/or Dispensational hermeneutic of applying a historical grammatical method to the atonement texts. A plain, straightforward, and literal reading of certain atonement texts reveal universality.

However, the idea as set forth by some of the Dispensationalists that the death of Christ was for each and every person in order to make them *savable* seemed to defy logic as well as some texts where Scripture says God is indeed not just a *potential savior* for all but *actually the savior of all now*. Literal interpretation demands, it seems to me, more than only a mere *potentiality*.

---

[726] John Calvin, *Calvin's Commentaries Volume XXII: 1 John* (Grand Rapids, MI: Baker Book House, 1998), 173.

[727] John Calvin, *Calvin's Commentaries Volume XVI: Harmony of Matthew, Mark, and Luke* (Grand Rapids, MI: Baker Book House, 1998), 427.

[728] Kevin Kennedy, "*Was Calvin a Calvinist? John Calvin on the Extent of the Atonement*," in *Whosoever Will: A Biblical-Theological Critique of Five-Point Calvinism*, eds. David L. Allen and Steve W. Lemke (Nashville, TN: B&H Publishing, 2010), 196.

[729] R.T. Kendall, *Calvin and Calvinism to 1649: Studies in Evangelical History and Thought* (Oxford, UK: Oxford University Press, 1997), 13-28.

For example, 1 Timothy 4:10, which is set in a Christological context (vs. 6), says that God "is the Savior of all people, especially of those who believe." To try and make this text read that he is the *"potential Savior"* seems to me to violate literal hermeneutics. At the same time to say that the words "all people" does not apply to everyone but all people groups, as many limited advocates argue, violates not only the meaning of the words but also the compare and contrast emphasis of the text. It is as if Paul is concluding that there is one group that is saved by God yet there is another group that is *especially saved* by God.

So how do we reconcile these truths from Scripture? As stated, if we apply the notion that both sides to this debate have had an element of truth I think the answer is available to us. *First*, we start with the text and allow it to speak for itself. We do not tweak the meaning of the inspired words to fit a proposed system. John Owen's argument is strong if we accept his premises, but his choice of words in the premises are in need of some adjustment. His premises were a bit hasty in that some other options existed. His statement needs to be: *"Christ eternally paid for the sins of all of the elect."*

If we make a distinction in the God-head (which involves the application aspect by the Spirit) as to the *purpose of the atonement* in regard to the elect and non-elect we can resolve this tension that has existed for too many years within equally devout evangelicals. When two persuasions of theology absolutely affirm the total sovereignty of God in unconditional election of sinners to salvation that in itself ought to cause those theologians to make a concerted effort to try and understand some point or nuance from one another that each side may be missing. Progress in historical illumination within the body of Christ may occur in greater ease when mutual respect translates into an eager heart to grasp the underlying heart motives to a particular theological strand that resides basically within the same tradition of theology.

Second, we do not add to Scripture some idea as if God were trying (implying he failed) to save the non-elect by having Christ die for them. God's sovereign purpose is not contradictory nor is it ever thwarted (Dan. 4:35). Christ did not die to "make eternally savable" a non-elect person if we are speaking of the eternal sense of salvation. *Why would God make someone eternally savable whom he has chosen in eternity past not to eternally save because of their natural refusal of Christ?* This defies logic and makes the God-head split. God chose not to elect yet Christ still died to make the non-elect savable or potentially savable? This seems to be terrible logic at best and at worst a teaching that breaks the unity and harmony of the work of the Triune God.

The key to this is to then adjust the *purpose* (not the substitution element) in the death as well as the *place* where the actual limit of the atonement is limited. It is here where the Lord Jesus and the Holy Spirit work in concert. Jesus makes a provision and in this provision he has a *dual purpose;* the Holy Spirit then applies the work and carries out the boundaries or limits to the provision made by Christ. Christ's substitution for mankind is for a *dual definite purpose* that is administered by the Holy Spirit in a *dual manner*. In both aspects the atonement accomplishes the intended purpose.

Third, let us examine a literal reading of two texts that place these two truths side by side to one another. If we apply a literal reading of Romans 5:18-19, it provides for us both truths on the benefits of Christ's death for all and for the many, the elect. The text reads:

> So then as through one transgression there resulted *condemnation to all men*, even so through one act of righteousness there resulted *justification of life to all men*. For as through the one man's disobedience the *many were made sinners*, even so through the obedience of the One *the many will be made righteous* (NASB, Italics mine).

The first set of points here in verse 18 are: (1) Adam's one sin condemned the whole human race. (2) Christ's one act as the second Adam represented the same ones who were condemned. (3) All of humanity were represented by Adam and thus by Christ's act all of humanity receives the benefit of life (not eternal life but *just life*). The second set of points is here in verse 19 as follows: (1) There is a shift from "all" to the "many" in verse 19. In the Greek it reads this way: τῆς παρακοῆς τοῦ ἑνὸς ἀνθρώπου ἁμαρτωλοὶ κατεστάθησαν οἱ πολλοί. A rough literal translation would be as follows: the disobedience of one man sinners were made many. A clearer English rendition of that would be: the disobedience of one man made the many sinners. This text moves from the all (the whole human race) to the more narrow select group, the many. It shows a specific person and specific set of people by the definite article "the" modifying the noun "many" (οἱ πολλοί). (2) Adam represented this specific group and made this group of many sinners. (3) Christ represents this same specific group and this same specific group will be made "righteous." To be righteous is to receive eternal grace and eternal redemption when the Spirit baptizes you and seals you in the faith. This many would be the elect.

The third point for observation is that there is a difference in the word "life" and the word "righteous." Paul is moving from the *general benefit of Christ's death*, which gives regular or general physical life to all, a form of physical salvation or deliverance for the temporary time of earthly life, which the Greek word soter (σωτήρ from σῴζω) can mean and then moving to the *specific benefit of righteousness*, which means the eternal or ultimate sense of soter (σωτήρ from σῴζω) for the elect, or the many. This verse in Romans connects with the theme in Paul's statement in 1 Timothy 4:10. How is it that God as Christ is the Savior of "all men," but more so in a special sense (especially) of those "who believe?"

These two verses reveal that God has used the death of Christ as the means to justify giving "life" to all people temporally. If a person has life right now, whether they have just a second of life or many years of life, this is due to the graciousness of God to justify it through the death of Christ. As Romans 5:18 says, "as one trespass led to condemnation for all men, so one act of righteousness [by Christ] there resulted *justification of life to all men*." The Greek reads this way:

Ἄρα οὖν ὡς δι' ἑνὸς παραπτώματος εἰς πάντας ἀνθρώπους εἰς κατά κριμα, οὕτως καὶ δι' ἑνὸς δικαιώματος εἰς πάντας ἀνθρώπους εἰςδι καίωσιν ζωῆς.

What does that mean for God's relationship to humanity? God is absolutely sinless and holy. Therefore, he cannot look upon any sin. Habakkuk says, *"You who are of purer eyes than to see evil and cannot look at wrong, why do you idly look at traitors and are silent when the wicked swallows up the man more righteous than he"* (1:13)? The answer as to how God can see the sinful world and allow them to have some life is apparently because God chooses to look at the world through the eyes of Christ, through the eyes of the one who shed his blood for the human race. The act of God not destroying the sinful human race is an act of mercy and grace. And as Dr. John Walvoord stated, "all grace stems from Christ's death on the cross for our sins."[730] Common grace is a part of the all; it is a portion of grace from the cross.

Therefore, any life, any goodness, any second whereby God's wrath against sin is withheld comes from the work that God did in his Son Christ on the cross and is now carried out by the Holy Spirit. The common, universal, encompassing mercy and grace of God the Father is purchased by Christ on the cross, and then applied generally and universally by the sovereign work of the Holy Spirit. This is why when we read 1 Timothy 4:10 we see both truths of Scripture in one sentence. There is the universal grace of God as well as the specific and special grace of God. Dr. John MacArthur has rightly stated:

> It seems best to understand this verse to be the teaching that God is really the Savior of all men, who actually does save them—but only in the temporal sense, while believers He saves in the eternal sense. In both cases, He is their Savior and there is a saving that He does on their behalf. In this life, all men experience to some degree the protecting, delivering, sustaining power of God. Believers will experience that to the fullest degree for time and for all eternity.[731]

Dr. MacArthur explains even further that in this Timothy passage the "use of the adverb *malista* (especially), which must mean that all men will enjoy to some extent the same kind of salvation as believers enjoy. The adverb is not adversative or contrastive, it cannot be saying that **all men** are saved in one sense, but **believers** in another. The difference is one of degree, not kind."[732] In other words, this passage does not mean that some are saved one way and then those who believe are saved a different way. The difference is that there is a general work of grace for all and a specific work of grace for the elect, i.e. those who come to believe.

---

[730] John F. Walvoord, *End Times: Understanding Today's World Events in Biblical Prophecy* (Nashville, TN: Word Publishing, 1998), 94.

[731] John MacArthur Jr., *The MacArthur New Testament Commentary: 1 Timothy* (Chicago, IL: Moody Press, 1995), 168,169.

[732] Ibid., 168.

One aspect of the grace gives a degree of life and the full aspect of grace gives the full benefit of life, namely eternal life. All receive some grace from the atonement. But not all receive eternal life from the atonement. Dr. Charles Hodge, one of the most well known Princeton Calvinists made this point. The death of Christ gives some grace to all and that gives some life to all people. He said,

> . . . it does not follow from the assertion of its having a special reference to the elect {the atonement} that it had no reference to the non-elect. Augustinians readily admit that the death of Christ had a relation to man, to the whole human family. . . . It is the ground on which salvation is offered to every creature . . . . it {also} secures to the whole race at large, and to all classes of men, innumerable blessings, both providential and religious. It was, of course, designed to produce these effects; and, therefore, Christ died to secure them . . . . it has in all ages been customary with Augustinians to say that Christ died . . . sufficiently for all, efficaciously only for the elect. There is a sense, therefore, in which he died for all, and there is a sense in which he died for the elect alone.[733]

Likewise, in the same line of thought Dr. John Calvin said of Romans 5:18, "He [Christ] makes this favour common to all, because it is propounded to all, and not because it is in reality extended to all; for though Christ suffered for the sins of the whole world, and if offered through God's benignity [goodness of disposition or heart; kindness of nature and graciousness] indiscriminately to all, yet all do not receive him."[734] It is clear that Calvin's view is that the death of Christ benefits the *whole world* and that even though in reality it does not extend to them in the eternal saving sense, it is still made for all and offered to all. Dr.

---

[733] Charles Hodge, *Systematic Theology* (Grand Rapids MI: Wm. B. Eerdmans Publishing Company, 1995), 2:545-546.

[734] John Calvin, *Calvin's Commentaries: Romans 1-16*, Vol. XIX (Grand Rapids, MI: Baker Books, 1998), 211. Brackets are mine.

Russell Moore has seemingly accurately described this view of the atonement as "Cosmic Atonement."[735]

Dr. Lewis Sperry Chafer asked one of the most difficult questions to the strict "five point Calvinist" theologians in regard to the words used by God in the Bible to describe the death of Christ. Throughout Scripture we find God's word using the words, "whole world," "all men," and "world." Chafer rightly asked, "could God" have used "any more explicit language than he used to express such an intent?"[736] What other words were available to the inspired writers of the New Testament to use had they wanted to say Christ died for everyone?

When they spoke of the universal spread of sin to the world, to all, to everyone, they used the same words in the Greek to describe that condition. If those words mean all, everyone, and whole world without exception, what would lead us to think those same terms would not be used for the benefit of Christ's death to all, to everyone, and to the whole world when Christ is the second Adam (1 Cor. 15:45)?

If the first Adam's act touched the *whole world* why does not also the second Adam's act touch the *whole world*? Without this view there seems to be no explanation as to how the universe is upheld (Hebrews 1:3) and how all people have "life and breath" and "live and move and exist" in "him [God]" (Acts 17:25, 28). It seems there must be a universal aspect to the atonement of Christ in order for God to interact with the entire world, lest he violate his own holiness.

The teachings of Scripture present a Savior who died for all of mankind; all of mankind actually does receive some benefits of this death. The non-elect have life and because of Christ's death for them they are called unto repentance (Acts 17:30). They have no excuse not to come to Christ because Christ died for them. Christ did not come to condemn the world but to save the world (John 3:17), which everyone does experience at least to some degree now (1 Tim. 4:10). We believe that the "value of Christ's death is extended to all men, but the elect alone come, by divine

---

[735] Russell D. Moore, "*Atonement*," in the *Holman Illustrated Bible Dictionary*, eds. Chad Brand, Charles Draper, Archie England (Nashville, TN: Holman Bible Publishers, 2003), 143.

[736] Lewis Sperry Chafer, *Systematic Theology* (Grand Rapids, MI: Kregel Publications, 1993), 3:205.

grace wrought by an effectual call, into its fruition, while the nonelect are not called but are those passed by."[737]

Some Evangelical Dispensationalists believe as well that due to Christ's death for the whole world this places "the whole world in a position of infinite obligation to Himself through the sacrifice of Christ."[738] The blame rests totally upon that individual for not coming. For those who do come we know that they came not of their own but due to God's sovereign grace (Eph. 1:1-11; 2:1-10). Though not a Dispensationalist Dr. Russell Moore accurately notes:

> The message of the atonement is presented in strikingly universal terms. All are invited to find refuge in the atonement of Christ (Luke 14:16-17). The apostles plead with sinners to trust in the atoning work of Jesus (Acts 2:40; 2 Cor. 5:20). All human beings are not only invited but commanded to believe the gospel (Acts 17:30-31).[739]

A literal hermeneutic, balanced with a harmonious correlation of the biblical data, seems to instruct the universal camp that the atonement does more than just make someone savable. The provision of Christ is actual and it actually does give some sufficient temporary salvific benefits to all people even if they do not believe in Christ. To the particular camp, their refusal to admit Christ's death benefits the whole world divides the work of the Triune God and splits the work of the Trinity as well as leaves the holiness of God in question since he relates to sinful humanity. Even in the O.T. the sacrifices the priest made for Israel was for the elect and non-elect, the believer and unbelievers. How can a holy God interact with that which is unholy unless there is a covering between him and the sinful universe?

---

[737] Ibid.

[738] Ibid.

[739] Russell D. Moore, "*Atonement*," in the *Holman Illustrated Bible Dictionary*, eds. Chad Brand, Charles Draper, Archie England (Nashville, TN: Holman Bible Publishers, 2003), 144.

The answer seems to be that there is a "dual" work of God in two spheres. The Father, Son, and Spirit administer *common grace to all* and *special grace to the elect*. Christ's death, designed by the Father, is a provision with two spheres to it that the Holy Spirit sovereignly administers as he pleases to whom he pleases when he pleases. As with God, the beginning and end is totally in his sovereign control. He gives grace and applies grace by sovereign discretion. Some receive common grace while others receive special grace, but both groups are at the mercy of God and owe God gratitude for whatever degree of mercy he so chooses to give. There is no need to violate literal, natural, historical, and grammatical interpretation principles to press a system onto the text of Scripture to try and force the atonement into a mold that the text does not support.

There seems to be a better way to be honest with Scripture, and that way is to see the atonement as a dual (for both elect and non-elect) and definite (which accomplishes an actual specific purpose for each) atonement. The provision is made for humanity and the Spirit applies that provision and makes it particular in accordance to his work of grace in the world. The Spirit applies the common and general benefits of the atonement universally. Some receive more common grace and some receive less, but every person who has any life whatsoever now on earth has some grace (anything short of hell is some form of grace). The Spirit also applies the eternal aspect, the particular element, and benefit of the atonement but he does so here with just the elect. The elect receive the common grace as well as the full eternal application of grace that brings internal righteousness which culminates in glorification with Christ.

Chapter 5. A Dispensational Continuity Perspective on the Godhead's Unified Work of Redemption in the O.T. & N.T.

Some of the criticism from the Covenant Calvinist tradition has been that Dispensationalism teaches two avenues or two plans of redemption, one plan of salvation for Israel and another plan of salvation for the N.T. believers, particularly for those in the church or the body of Christ. Supposedly Dispensationalists have taught Israel is saved by obedience to the law and N.T. believers in Christ are saved by grace through faith in the death and resurrection of Christ.

A vast array of literature has already been dedicated to this debate. For the purpose of this work, I have a narrow focus. The focus is to show that some Dispensationalists have clearly taught that O.T. saints as well as N.T. saints believed in the same redemptive message in all the dispensations. Dispensationalists have readily admitted that sometimes some within the tradition have made unclear statements that caused confusion.

Dr. John Feinberg, writing in the early 1980s, even stated that "it must be admitted that statements made by certain dispensationalists in the past appeared to teach multiple ways of salvation."[740] But he quickly added that those questionable statements by even some of those were clearly resolved once a person analyzed those theologians in the full context of their thinking. As he said, "such careless statements did not reflect the full thinking of those theologians . . . as [could] be seen from other statements they made."[741] Those careless statements, or unclear statements, or even isolated rudimentary statements disconnected from the holistic plan and purpose of God through all dispensations, a trans-dispensational approach, has created some confusion.

---

[740] John S. Feinberg, "Salvation in the Old Testament," in *Tradition & Testament: Essays in Honor of Charles Lee Feinberg*, eds. John S. and Paul D. Feinberg (Chicago, IL: Moody Press, 1981), 42.

[741] Ibid.

To help to clear this up, a holistic examination that honors both the doctrine of the singular plan of redemption by God's solitary decree as well as progressive revelation offers a realistic answer for systematization of divine revelation. In other words, the doctrine of the gospel of redemption is trans-dispensational though it materializes incrementally in history. Yet in this historical development a central issue of the doctrine of who is "in Christ" must receive attention as it offers an avenue for further clarification against the backdrop of some confusion among the Dispensational tradition.

One reason why the multiple plans of salvation criticism has gained some traction has been due to the vernacular used by some Dispensationalists in describing the position of O.T. saints in contrast to N.T. saints. Often it has been asserted that N.T. saints are "in Christ" whereas O.T. saints are not in Christ. That nomenclature has not been properly scrutinized for what it could mean when read apart from other balancing positions made by the theologian adopting such language. Historically, several prominent Dispensationalists have described the O.T. saints as "not in Christ" and the N.T. saints as "in Christ."

For example, one of the most formidable apologists for Dispensationalism, Dr. John Walvoord, wrote that the "in Christ" phrase "is a technical theological description of Christians" that "are baptized by the Holy Spirit at the moment of salvation."[742] This event according to Walvoord did not occur before the day of Pentecost and because. He believed the "in Christ" position "distinguishes saints of the present church age" from those of prior ages.[743] Another example of this line of thought has been stated by Dr. Thomas Constable who says, "the phrase in Christ refers exclusively to Church-Age saints."[744] Additionally, Dr. John Feinberg took that position as well stating,

---

[742] John Walvoord, "*The Order of the Resurrections*," in *Understanding Christian Theology*, eds. Charles Swindoll and Roy B. Zuck (Nashville, TN: Thomas Nelson Publishers, 2003), 1334.

[743] Ibid.

[744] Thomas L. Constable, "*1 Thessalonians*," in *The Bible Knowledge Commentary: An Exposition of the Scriptures by Dallas Seminary Faculty*, eds. John F. Walvoord and Roy B. Zuck (USA: SP Publications, 1983), 704.

The ἐν χριστῷ (en christo) relationship, union of the believer with Christ, is part and parcel of the New Testament believer's salvation, whereas that relationship does not pertain to salvation of an Old Testament saint. Such union with Christ is accomplished by means of the ministry of the Holy Spirit whereby he baptizes the believer into the Body of Christ (1 Cor. 12:13). But the Holy Spirit did not begin to perform that ministry until the day of Pentecost (Acts 2).[745]

Those types of statements seem to continue offering substance for present day criticism against Dispensationalism's view of salvation, at least in part with O.T. saints. Though other statements by Walvoord, Constable, and Feinberg would clearly show they affirm only one way of salvation (thus revealing they have an orthodox confession), there seems to be a more stable position on how to articulate the status of O.T. saints before the unique baptism of Spirit work that began in Acts 2, a key dispensational perspective related to the doctrine of progressive revelation. All fundamental evangelical conservatives realize the Bible progresses in stages of revelation. The issue is how much progress exists at each stage of history.

There seems to be a way in which a Dispensationalist can honor the essentials of Dispensationalism and progressive revelation, particularly the distinction in God's family with Israel and the body of Christ formed by the unique N.T. work of the baptism of the Spirit, while also affirming the relational position of O.T. saints with the one and only Savior of the cosmos, Jesus Christ.

This contrasting perspective, and proposed solution, may be perceived by some to be a standard difference between Classical and/or Revised Dispensationalism and more modern forms of Progressive Dispensationalism. But that does not seem to be the case. Some Dispensationalists from the Classical or Revised school of thought have taken a different perspective on this. Though they may not be as well known as someone like a John Walvoord, there is a thought among a

---

[745] John S. Feinberg, "*Salvation in the Old Testament*," in *Tradition & Testament: Essays in Honor of Charles Lee. Feinberg*, eds. John S. and Paul D. Feinberg (Chicago, IL: Moody Press, 1981), 63.

Classical or Revised Calvinist Dispensational school of thought that sees the Old Testament saints as being in a sense in Christ even while still retaining a different family position distinct from the body of Christ as well as in their distinct order for their resurrection than the New Testament saints.

That perspective might be the very aid needed to help counter the confusion created by the "in" Christ perspective of N.T. saints and the implied ideology that O.T. saints are outside of Christ and thus by default saved from sin outside of Christ. Indeed others see a need in this area. Dispensationalist Dr. Dale S. Dewitt has stated that "dispensational theology needs to do more work on salvation's meaning and extent under the old covenant."[746] Likewise, Dr. John Feinberg noted too in the 1980s that "the study of salvation in the Old Testament is more urgently needed"[747] because "the question of salvation in the Old Testament receives little or no treatment whatsoever."[748]

The Covenant Criticism Restated: Dispensationalism Denies that Old Testament Saints are in Christ & by That Teaches O.T. Works Salvation

Many Covenant theologians claim that Dispensationalism teaches multiple avenues of salvation, especially in regard to the position of Old Testament saints and New Testament saints. Though many of those criticisms are stated earlier in this work, it will suffice to reiterate one of those assertions here at this section. Grover Gunn has stated,

> Dispensationalists recognize that if Old Testament saints are in Christ as Paul used that term, then Old Testament saints are in the

---

[746] Dale S. Dewitt, *Dispensational Theology in America During the 20th Century: Theological and Cultural Context* (Grand Rapids, MI: Grace Bible College Publications, 2002), 162.

[747] John S. Feinberg, "*Salvation in the Old Testament*," in *Tradition & Testament: Essays in Honor of Charles Lee Feinberg*, eds. John S. and Paul D. Feinberg (Chicago, IL: Moody Press, 1981), 40.

[748] Ibid., 39.

church universal (1 Corinthians 12:13), and that would effectively destroy the dispensational dichotomy between Israel and the church. A salvifically unified people of God through the ages is a concept antithetical to the foundational presuppositions of Dispensationalism. This fundamental dispensational bias against the salvific unity in Christ of the people of God through the ages is, I think, the most basic weakness in the dispensational teaching on Old Testament salvation.[749]

Covenant theologians have seized upon the "in Christ" phrase and the teaching that it exclusively applies only to N.T. saints as a way to try and discredit the system of Dispensationalism. That distinction then leads to another conclusion by the Covenant theologians, which is if the O.T. saints are outside of Christ then they must be saved by some other means than Christ and his atoning grace. An example of this, reiterated here, is Dr. Clarence Bass who stated,

> The presupposition of the difference between law and grace, between Israel and the church, between the different relations of God to men in the different dispensations, when carried to its logical conclusion will inevitably result in a multiple form of salvation—that men are not saved the same way in all ages . . . . This distinction implies that there are two principles under which man has been saved—law and grace.[750]

Therefore, as an antidote to such criticisms, the following Dispensational perspective might help clarify how Dispensationalism can affirm *one elect family of God* that is "in Christ" or "in the Lord" (Yahweh), while retaining the historical divisions in the family of God by delineating a distinct period of people (in light of progressive revelation) that are "in the body of Christ" by way of the unique work of the baptism of the Spirit that only occurs in the New Covenant era. In other words,

---

[749] Curtis Crenshaw and Grover E. Gunn III, *Dispensationalism Today, Yesterday, and Tomorrow* (Memphis, TN: Footstool Publications, 1985, reprinted ed. 86, 87, 89, 94, 95), 267.

[750] Ibid., 36.

there seems to be a solid, stable, and scriptural precedent in positing that the people of God in the Old Testament were saved by grace, regenerated, adopted into the family of God, and were also in Christ," though not in "the body of Christ" because the baptism of the Holy Spirit had yet to occur. The body (family of Christ for the NT era) came to existence when the wall of partition was broken down between Jew and Gentile creating in himself one new man. As Paul said,

> ... but now (key word noting a time transition) in Christ Jesus you who used to be far away have been brought near by the blood of Christ. For he (Christ) is our peace, the one who made both groups into one and who destroyed this middle wall of partition . . . . He did this to create in himself one new man out of the two . . . to reconcile them both in one body to God through the cross. . . . so then you (Gentiles) are no longer foreigners and noncitizens, but you are fellow citizens with the saints and members of God's household (Eph. 2:13-20).

Additionally, there seems to be two ways a Dispensationalist could articulate the sense in which O.T. saints were in Christ. One is that they were baptized into Christ (the Lord) though not into the body of Christ. In that paradigm the body of Christ is only formed by the unique work of the baptism of the Spirit while the baptism of a person into the Lord at salvation occurs throughout all time and history.

A second option is that the baptism of the Spirit does not begin until the coming of the Spirit and that all O.T. saints were provisionally in Christ the Lord by their salvation but that each O.T. saints did not personally experience the baptism into Christ until Christ died and arose again sending the Spirit. In this case the O.T. saints were provisionally held in Christ in the same way that he was provisionally the atoning sacrifice before he ever came to earth.

Also, this second method or option, which is a little more on the discontinuity side of the continuum for historical development, would or could argue that the O.T. saints were held in paradise, Abraham's bosom so to speak, and did not go to heaven until Christ died and applied his work to them by the Spirit. Then after the death of Christ he then took the O.T. saints to heaven with him when he arose.

Either of those two positions could be argued from a dispensational perspective of scripture (literal hermeneutic) and from a dispensational view of progressive revelation. Neither would destroy the unique work of the Spirit in forming the historical body of Christ that began around Acts 2. Nor would it require that all O.T. saints and N.T. saints be resurrected exactly at the same time. Being in Christ for salvation does not necessitate that all who are in Christ must be the same members of the family even though they are in the same family. Various distinct family members can exist in one overall family.

Whatever view one adopts, the "in the body of Christ" phrase literally seems to be more unique to the New Testament era than the mere "in Christ" phrase. To be "in Christ" means to be bought by him through his blood. He stands as the head of the human race and he will administer justice to those who refuse to acknowledge his Lordship, or he will administer grace to those who do acknowledge him as Lord and Savior over their lives. All of humanity is in God (Acts 17:28) and in one sense in Christ (Col. 1:17) by him acting as their creator and sustainer.

The question, therefore, is not is someone in God and/or Christ. The more proper question is this, in what sense is someone in Christ? Is the person in God/Christ by mere justice, i.e., by the just act of God creating them and sustaining them in himself (a creative justice sense)? Or is the person in God/Christ by both means of being justly created and sustained as well as also in his special favor by grace? Believers are in the Lord in the eternal grace sense. Unbelievers are in the Lord in the justice sense. If they die in that state they seal themselves in the Lord's sphere of eternal justice forever.

Dispensationalism has an avenue, and precedent set forth by earlier leaders, to show that Old Testament saints were in God/Christ (Yahweh) even in the sense of grace by the work of God regenerating them based on the eternal elective decree of placing them in the grace of the Lord. The substitution of Christ (foreknown from eternity and actualized in time) forms the basis for them to experience grace from all eras of history. Christ's work of redemption was established in eternity past and realized historically on the cross of Calvary. Though not as widely recognized, nor adopted by some of the most famous and popular Dispensationalists, this path seems to provide a more solid exegetical route and overall systematic harmonization of the entire set of biblical revelation.

Truths for a Unified Trans-dispensational Family of God in Christ that also Distinguishes N.T. Saints from O.T. Saints

1. The Importance of a Literal Hermeneutic & Its Application to Colossians 1:17-18: A Foundation to a Trans-dispensational Christological (Yahweh) Focus of History & Eternity

Although not alone in the broader Evangelical community, Dispensationalism has historically sought to take the Bible in its most plain meaning. Dispensationalists affirm an originalist or ordinary approach to the Bible. They believe that what the Bible meant to the author and his original audience is the correct meaning of the text. They deplore and reject postmodern, revisionist, trajectory, allegorical, mystical, creedal, and reader-response approach methodologies[751] that place the interpreter in the role of creating the meaning of the text rather than discovering the meaning of the text. In short, Dispensationalism has categorically rejected methodologies that place the "reader as the ultimate determiner of truth."[752] This has largely been discussed under the concept of the historical grammatical hermeneutic. In short we call this proper exegesis.[753]

In a plethora of texts this has been the mantra of the Dispensational system itself. The proper science for interpretation of literature, either in a law context, biblical context, or any other genre context, remains one of the most important disciplines for an exegete. As Dispensationalist Dr. Josh McDowell says, "our task is not to create the meaning; it is simply to uncover the original intended meaning. The Apostle Peter tells us that 'no prophecy of Scripture is a matter of one's own interpretation' (2 Peter 1:20

---

[751] Christopher Cone, *Prolegomena: Introductory Notes on Bible Study & Theological Method* (Fort Worth, TX: Tyndale Seminary Press, 2009), 124-154.

[752] Robert L. Plummer, *40 Questions About Interpreting the Bible* (Grand Rapids, MI: Kregel Publications, 2010), 127.

[753] Josh McDowell, *God Breathed: The Undeniable Power and Reliability of Scripture* (Uhrichsville, OH: Shiloh Run Press, 2015), 56.

NASB). So instead of reading into a text a meaning we think might be there, we must draw out the meaning God intends for us to understand."[754]

More times than not, the first step towards an ungodly or illegitimate perspective develops due to dishonest and deceptive methodologies adopted in approaching the specific literature under study. No other honest methodology exists other than seeking to understand written or oral language through a historical and grammatical hermeneutic. People that reject this methodology and resort to unnatural exegetical endeavors reveal dishonesty in the practice of interpreting language.

When people begin with a presupposition to look beyond the actual words of the text, with a purposeful or trajectory ideology, they depart from the plain meaning explicitly stated by the words of the text. That approach produces skewed ideas that pass under the cloak of religiosity. Scripture itself shows that the Lord's people sought to communicate the Bible in a plain manner. For example, in Nehemiah's day, Ezra and the other leaders with him stood before the people and "read from the book, the Law of God, clearly, and they gave the sense, so that the people understood the reading" (Neh. 8:8). To interpret written or oral communication in any other way other than through a means to give a clear sense to the language violates the purpose of language.

Even those in the natural common grace realm realize how important the issue of a proper hermeneutic is for discovery of truth and original intent. Supreme Court Justice Antonin Scalia and jurist Bryan Garner state it this way,

> The ordinary-meaning rule is the most fundamental semantic rule of interpretation. It governs constitutions, statutes, rules, and private instruments. Interpreters should not be required to divine arcane nuances or to discover hidden meanings. . . . Some theorists deny that plain meaning or ordinary meaning ever exists. But common experience proves the contrary: In everyday life, the people to whom rules are addressed continually understand and apply them.[755]

---

[754] Ibid.

[755] Antonin Scalia and Bryan A. Garner, *Reading Law: The Interpretation of Legal Texts* (St. Paul, MN: Thomson/West Publishers, 2012), 69, 71.

This might be known as the most basic rule to the proper methodology for any and all exegesis of any written or oral form of communication. Scalia and Garner stress it so emphatically that they say this type of hermeneutic, often known as plain interpretation or originalism, "is the *only* approach to" the "text that is compatible with democracy."[756] If a Judge reading (interpreting or construing) a law, constitutional or statutory, assigns to it some new meaning that the people (Constitution) or legislators (statutory) did not assign to it then the judge has changed the law,[757] and by doing so is functioning in a "radical departure from our democratic system."[758]

An "Originalist" approach is the *only* option for those who desire to be honest people with text at hand. "Originalism, properly pursued, is not result oriented."[759] Note again, the emphasis on honesty. To interpret language in any other means other than through the historical and grammatical methodology reveals a dishonest endeavor. Those who follow such an endeavor exhibit their own dishonest nature.

Originalism, as Scalia would call it, or the literal method allows the words of the text to be the authority over the one doing the interpretation. Sometimes people think when we say literal that we do not allow for metaphorical language. That is not the proper idea behind the term literal. Though we do not take *each and every word as literal* (metaphorical language exists), we do take the Bible as a whole literally if by that it means we seek to interpret the words by seeking to understand their original or normal meaning in the historical context. To say the Bible is to be interpreted in a literal way is just another way of saying the Bible is to be interpreted in a normal, plain, or ordinary way without any special methods imposed upon it from the outside. The meaning of the text is to be found in the words of the text. That is the literal methodology. This is

---

[756] Ibid., 82.

[757] Ibid.

[758] Ibid., 83.

[759] David F. Forte, "The Originalist Perspective," in *The Heritage Guide to the Constitution*, ed. Edwin Meese III (Washington, DC: Regnery Publishing, 2005), 15.

why we sometimes call the literal method the historical grammatical method. Josh McDowell explains further:

> Language is composed of words, of course. Words are the building blocks of ideas. And when we assemble words together in sentences and paragraphs, they become the basic unit of communication. This is true of any literary work of words, sentences, and paragraphs that communicate God's truth . . . . Writers communicate their intent in specific ways that we can analyze and understand to determine meaning. . . . Though the Bible is God's communication of his truth to us, we must keep in mind that it is in the form of a work of literature (and must be, in order to communicate effectively). This means that the same linguistic principles apply to the Bible as to other writings. We can understand passages better if we allow the language to speak in ordinary ways, as it does in all works of literature, instead of imposing a special, artificial standard for language usage in the Bible. This means we cannot take every word of the Bible as literal. We must allow its metaphors, similes, and analogies to be what they are, and not force them to be anything other than metaphors, similes, and analogies.[760]

When the literal method is employed the interpretation work remains humble with no effort to dethrone the words that constitute the message in order to create some other message. In other words, when a person approaches a text with a plain, literal, original intent methodology, that person does not come to the text with an agenda to make it say whatever he or she desires for the text to say (which is what Satan desires to do with God's word). It leaves the text as the authority (God in the case of the Bible or the people and Constitution in a democratic-republic) and keeps the reader humble before the text. That method is the *only honest* method available and is to be pursued by those who seek to be honest people. Christ followers, therefore, have no other options as for a

---

[760] Ibid., 57,58.

hermeneutic. It guards against the idea the text has "no fixed meaning, subject to changing interpretations according to the spirit of the times."[761]

The fluid or multi-meaning ideology aligns with the spirit of humanistic liberalism, not with Evangelical theology in general nor Dispensationalism in particular. In the government sphere the fluidity ideology has often been articulated through the living constitution interpretive ideology. Sometimes that approach has been called the "purposive approach," as stated by Supreme Court Justice Stephen Breyer.[762] In another work he calls this interpretive methodology a "purpose-oriented approach" that is contrasted with the "purely text-oriented approach,"[763] otherwise known as literalism or originalism. It allows the reader to make the document conform to him or her (or some goal) rather than the reader conforming to the document as formed by the ideas expressed through words at the moment of codification. It allows the reader/interpreter to seek a particular consequence through inserting or expanding the text to that desired goal. As Justice Breyer says, "focus on purpose seeks to promote active liberty."[764]

By active liberty he seems to suggest that judicial interpretations need to consider the present active will of the people, i.e., the consensus of thought from the general sphere of the nation. Such an approach, however, misses the point that the "present will of the people" is established through representatives who have been elected to write laws, through a Federal Constitution and various State Constitutions, and that if those expressed laws do not reflect the present will of the people then it is the responsibility of the people, not judges, to alter those laws by persuading the representatives, replacing representatives, or through amending the respective constitution. The will of the people is codified in a word form:

---

[761] David F. Forte, *"The Originalist Perspective,"* in *The Heritage Guide to the Constitution*, ed. Edwin Meese III (Washington, DC: Regnery Publishing, 2005), 13.

[762] Stephen Breyer, *Active Liberty: Interpreting Our Democratic Constitution* (New York, USA: Vintage Publishing, 2005), 85.

[763] Stephen Breyer, *Making Our Democracy Work* (New York, USA: Vintage Books, 2010), 94.

[764] Stephen Breyer, *Active Liberty: Interpreting Our Democratic Constitution* (New York, USA: Vintage Publishing, 2005), 115.

The Calvinism of Dispensationalism

laws, statutes, and constitutions. This purpose oriented approach, in the legal world or in the religious world, leads to the departure of sound interpretive principles. Honest courts have ruled that the interpretive methodology of judges ought to retain the original sense method.[765]

The same type of radical departure from democracy that Scalia noted can be said of those who embrace some other methodology for interpreting Scripture. To adopt meanings not intended by the authors (God and the human author) is to commit a radical departure from the Holy God's intended meaning, and is to depart from the truth of Christianity just as when a judge reads laws in some other manner and by doing so departs from democracy. Both are dishonorable and dishonest approaches to the text. Dispensationalism has been a champion for the cause of single meaning to each text discovered by the application of the normal, plain, or original intent hermeneutic.

Dr. J.R. Graves, a nineteenth century Dispensationalist, stated the golden rule for literature analysis. In 1883 Graves taught this,

> The Bible was made for man in the language of men, and must be interpreted by the rules that govern human language. The literal, which is the received meaning of a word, is to be in all cases retained, unless weighty and necessary reasons require that it should be abandoned where a figurative or a secondary may be employed. If the Bible is not to be translated and interpreted by these rules, then it is not a revelation to man, unless the author of it

---

[765] Many courts in a vicissitude of jurisdictions have affirmed the golden rule of hermeneutics. For example, Bryant v. City of Charleston, 295 S.C. 408, 368 S.E. (2d) 899 (1988) affirmed that "in construing a statute, its words must be given their plain and ordinary meaning without resorting to subtle or forced construction to limit or expand the statute's operation." In Hamrick v. State Farm Mutual Auto Insurance Company, 241 S.E. (2d) 548 (1978) the court stated, "in the interpretation of statutes and insurance policies, the rule is the same. Words should be given their plain, ordinary meaning." In Lake County v. Rollins, 130 US 662, Supreme Court (1889), the court established the rule that "the framers of the Constitution employed words in their natural sense; and where they are plain and clear, resort to collateral aids to interpretation is unnecessary and cannot be indulged in to narrow or enlarge the text."

gave the race a lexicon to translate and a commentary to interpret it.[766]

Those principles, advocated for early on in the seminal days of Dispensationalism's systematization season, have been the hallmarks for honest exegetes not only within Dispensationalism but in honest Christianity overall. For example, Dr. Gordon R. Lewis and Dr. Bruce A. Demarest, neither of whom aligns with a Covenant or Dispensational theology per se, affirm that the "meaning of a biblical statement is the ordinary, or normal, meaning of the statement (usually literal with some figures of speech) in terms of its context and author's purpose . . . . the intended meaning is the one, literal, historical, grammatical, contextual meaning, not a deeper or secret meaning. Although the applications of a passage are many, the meaning in context is one."[767]

Another example, from a nondispensational tradition and from within the Covenant Calvinistic theology tradition, Dr. Charles Hodge of Princeton Seminary took the position that the *only honest* method of interpretation is the plain methodology. He noted that "the words of Scripture are to be taken in their plain historical sense. That is, they must be taken in the sense attached to them in the age and by the people to whom they were addressed. This only assumes that the *sacred writers were honest*, and meant to be understood."[768] Note again the emphasis on the issue of honesty. Dishonest people seek to add multiple meanings to the text through subversive methodologies. Honest people seek the one original meaning. Hodge aligns with others, even Justice Scalia, on the

---

[766] J.R. Graves, *The Work of Christ Consummated in Seven Dispensations* (Texarkana, TX: Bogard Press, 1928), ix.

[767] Gordon R. Lewis and Bruce A. Demarest, *Integrative Theology: Historical Biblical Systematic Apologetic Practical*, Three Volumes in One (Grand Rapids, MI: Zondervan, 1996), 1:30, 31.

[768] Charles Hodge, *Systematic Theology* (Grand Rapids MI: Wm. B. Eerdmans Publishing Company, 1995), 1:187. Italics mine. It cannot be overemphasized that the only honest approach to the interpretation of Scripture is to use the literal, ordinary, plain, and/or originalist methodology. Those who approach the Bible from a different methodology do so from a fundamentally dishonest and sinful mental position. They show their arrogance in imposing something else (often their own goals) into the text.

aspect that the plain or literal or original methodology exudes the only honest approach to the text.

Additionally, a more modern Covenant Calvinist theologian concurs with Hodge on the necessity to approach the Bible as a document to be understood through the proper scientific method of solid exegesis. Dr. Robert L. Reymond has pointedly asserted that because Scripture is inspired through words that such inspiration "binds us to the grammatical/historical method of exegesis."[769] Note how serious Reymond makes this issue to be with his word choice "binds." A person will not understand the Bible nor be able to explain its contents honestly when loosening himself or herself from those bindings because this truth functions as a fundamental axiom.

Historical grammatical exegesis is a time-tested cardinal method and most essential linguistic principle. Reymond adds that if an interpreter "is to apprehend God's self-testimony" that interpreter must "seek to put himself in the writer's linguistic, cultural, historical, and religious shoes to discover the writer's intended meaning."[770]

Additionally, noting further support from the natural or common grace disciplines, Dr. Leland Ryken, a professor of English, mentions that the proper literary study of Scripture relies upon the historical-grammatical approach to the text. As he says, "the literary approach that I describe in this book is a logical extension of what is commonly known as the grammatical-historical method of biblical interpretation . . . . we must begin with the literal meaning of the words of the Bible as determined by the historical setting in which the authors wrote."[771] A literary study of Scripture aligns with the literal, or plain, interpretive methodology because when properly interpreting a piece of literature a person will recognize the genre of that specific literature.

Scripture contains poetry, narrative, law, proverbs, parables, epistles, satire, and visionary future prophetic genres. A proper hermeneutic recognizes each genre of Scripture "has its distinctive

---

[769] Robert L. Reymond, *A New Systematic Theology of the Christian Faith* (Nashville, TN: Thomas Nelson Publishers, 1998), 49.

[770] Ibid.

[771] Leland Ryken, *How to Read the Bible as Literature* (Grand Rapids, MI: Zondervan Publishing, 1984), 12-13.

features" and this to a degree "affects how we read and interpret a work of literature."[772] A literal method recognizes such literary genres. For example, when reading poetic sections of Scripture, the interpreter will acknowledge exaggerations by the writer as "hyperbole" and accept those expressions as "a standard way of expressing emotional truth."[773] A normal or historical-grammatical method contains within it this literary analysis recognition.

Whether from the natural world, such as with legal courts that interpret constitutions and statutes, or from the supernatural revelation of Scripture, Dispensationalism has made a concerted effort to excel in the field of hermeneutics. What Dr. J.R. Graves taught as a Dispensationalist in the 1800s has been stressed by the faithful followers of Christ throughout history and other portions of Christ's body. It has continued to be stressed by twentieth and twenty-first-century Dispensationalists. Dispensationalism has indeed worked within not only the mainstream of Christianity as to how one properly interprets special revelation language, but they too find themselves in concurrence with jurists in the natural grace realm who recognize an honest approach to language analysis only occurs when a plain or literal hermeneutic is applied to documents.

In fact, due recognition must acknowledge that Dispensationalists have emphasized this matter as much if not more so than most in the various fields of thought. The normal hermeneutic is a hallmark of Dispensationalism, and even by confessional Covenantalism, and is a certain counter to the subjective methodologies of humanistic liberalism. A safe, solid, and stable hermeneutic has been a substantive essential to the Dispensational tradition as the quotes from the forthcoming Dispensationalists shall verify.

For example, Dr. Charles Ryrie says this literal, or plain, or original intent historical grammatical hermeneutic is the "second aspect of the sine qua non of Dispensationalism."[774] Likewise, Dr. Chris Cone states that the application of a consistent literal or historical grammatical

---

[772] Ibid., 25.

[773] Ibid.

[774] Charles C. Ryrie, *Dispensationalism* (Chicago, IL: Moody Press, 1993), 40.

hermeneutic is one of the four key pillars to Dispensationalism.[775] Additionally, Dr. Earl Radmacher once noted that the literal methodology of biblical interpretation comprised the very fundamental essence of Dispensationalism.[776] Furthermore, Dr. Tommy Ice has noted that many "believe only dispensationalists attempt to apply" the literal or plain or historical grammatical hermeneutic "consistently from Genesis to Revelation."[777]

Concurring with all of the above, Dr. Elliot Johnson pressed the point saying, "the literal rule of interpretation (with normal usage) is actually a provisional guide or maxim, a rule of thumb."[778] Moreover, philosopher and theologian Dr. Norman Geisler even states that within the three sets of fundamentals, number one doctrinal and number two epistemological, there is also a third, the hermeneutical fundamental which is the literal historical-grammatical method.[779] He says this methodology provides a test for "evangelical consistency."[780] Without this method he argues with great vigor one loses all sense of objectivity and shifts to a subjective standard.[781]

Dr. Mal Couch noted that even when interpreting a highly symbolic book, like the book of Revelation, he urged interpreters to accept

---

[775] Chris Cone, "*Four Pillars of Dispensationalism*," in *Dispensationalism Tomorrow & Beyond: A Theological Collection Honor of Charles C. Ryrie* (Fort Worth, TX: Tyndale Seminary Press, 2008), 24-25.

[776] Earl D. Radmacher, "The Current Status of Dispensationalism and Its Eschatology," in *Perspectives on Evangelical Theology,* eds. Kenneth S. Kantzer and Stanley N. Gundry (Grand Rapids, MI: Baker Publishing, 1979), 171.

[777] Thomas D. Ice, "*Dispensational Hermeneutics*," in *Issues in Dispensationalism*, eds. Wesley R. Willis and John R. Master (Chicago, IL: Moody Press, 1994), 45.

[778] Elliot Johnson, *Expository Hermeneutics: An Introduction* (Grand Rapids, MI: Zondervan, 1990), 268.

[779] Norman Geisler, *Systematic Theology in One Volume* (Bloomington, MN: Bethany House Publishing, 2011), 1427-1428.

[780] Ibid., 1428.

[781] Ibid., 125-131.

the literal method unless context otherwise indicated through the use of "comparative language."[782] As he suggested, "if one were on a desert island and read Revelation for the first time, how would he normally interpret the book? The answer would be 'actual and literal,' unless there was an . . . allegorist around to say, 'No' . . . .The literal meaning, with comparative language, must be accepted unless there are other indicators that require one read the verses some other way."[783]

Dr. Paige Patterson also concurs with this hermeneutic methodology. He says when approaching even a genre like Revelation it still produces far more faithful results to remain with the literal method of interpretation than to "switch to allegorical methods when the subject is eschatology."[784]

A question could be posed here. If the normal, or plain, or historical grammatical hermeneutic is to be used even in a genre such as the book of Revelation, then how much more so in all other forms of genre throughout Scripture? It appears that the only safe and honest method to linguistic analysis, the scientific method interpreting literature, is to apply a historical grammatical method of interpretation. That alone is the only honest approach to discover the meaning of the written text. Dr. Robert Lightner summarizes well this mainline Evangelical, and in this case Dispensational, position on the proper science of interpreting language. He says,

> Generally speaking, evangelicals would define their view of hermeneutics as literal or normal . . . . The literal interpretation as applied to any document is that view which adopts as the sense of the sentence the meaning of that sentence in usual or ordinary or normal conversation or writing. The literal meaning is best obtained by the grammatical historical method. When the literal, normal, or plain method is employed in seeking to understand the

---

[782] Mal Couch, "*Interpreting the Book of Revelation*," In *A Bible Handbook to Revelation*, ed. Mal Couch (Grand Rapids, MI: Kregel Publications, 2001), 48.

[783] Ibid., 49.

[784] Paige Patterson, *The New American Commentary*: Volume 39, *Revelation*, gen ed. E. Ray Clendenen (Nashville, TN: B&H Publishing, 2012), 38.

Bible, the customary meanings of the words are understood. The literal or normal method of interpretation recognizes figures of speech, parables, etc., as figurative but looks for a literal, nonfigurative meaning.[785]

The Evangelical, and of course the Dispensationalist who is an Evangelical, approaches the Bible with the belief that God desired to communicate his heart and mind to us through language. Dr. Ryrie asserts, "The purpose of language itself seems to require literal interpretation. That is, God gave man language for the purpose of being able to communicate with him."[786] One who seeks to approach the Bible with some different hermeneutic should ask, why would an all knowing and all powerful God create language if his creative tool would not be sufficient for even him to use to communicate with another portion of his creation who are created in his image?

God's creation bears his image, an image magnified through the use of language because of the rational thought processes employing that tool of God for connecting with one another and even with God. As Ryrie pointed out, "if God originated language for the purpose of communication, and if God is all-wise, then we may believe that he saw to it that the means (language) was sufficient to sustain the purpose (communication)."[787]

In addition to those points noted by Ryrie, Dispensationalist and philosopher Dr. Norman Geisler provides some fundamental philosophical reasons why the normal or plain method of interpretation is the only proper method to employ if the person is truly making an honest effort to understand God's word. He says that the laws of logic point to the idea that the words communicated by God must provide an absolute meaning. If there is an Absolute Mind who created a document, the Bible, then that document must provide for us an absolute meaning. "If there is an absolute Mind, then there can be absolute meaning. The objective basis for

---

[785] Robert P. Lightner, *Evangelical Theology: A Survey and Review* (Grand Rapids, MI: Baker House Publishing, 1986), 23-24.

[786] Charles C. Ryrie, *Basic Theology* (Chicago, IL: Moody Press, 1999), 128.

[787] Ibid.

meaning is found in the Mind of God."[788] Consequently, since God is omnipotent and infinite he is fully able to "convey meaning to finite creatures, since there is common ground between them in both the undeniable laws of thought and the similarity (analogy) between Creator and creature."[789]

Consequently, a person, who is made in the image of God, may employ proper methods to discover the absolute meaning of this absolute mind, i.e., God. To do that one must read the Bible to "look for the author's meaning, not the reader's." He must also allow the words to stand by affirming or recognizing the "what" and not per se the "why." "Purpose does not determine meaning. One can know what the author said without knowing why he said it . . . . Meaning deals with what? and significance deals with so what?"[790]

Additionally, a person ought to look for "meaning in the text, not beyond it. The meaning is not found beyond the text (in God's mind), beneath the text (in the mystic's mind), or behind the text (in the author's unexpressed intention); it is found in the text (in the author's expressed meaning). For instance, the beauty of a sculpture is not found behind, beneath, or beyond the sculpture. Rather, it is expressed in the sculpture. All textual meaning is in the text."[791]

These points made by Ryrie and Geisler seem to be summarized by Dr. Lightner who pulls all of those concepts together to explain why a literal hermeneutic remains the objective standard for discovering the true meaning of any text, especially with holy Scripture. He says,

> There are three major reasons given in support of a consistently literal hermeneutic—biblical, logical, philosophical. Of the biblical reason it has been said, 'The prophecies of the Old Testament concerning the first coming of Christ—his birth, his rearing, his ministry, his death, his resurrection—were all fulfilled literally.

---

[788] Norman Geisler, *Systematic Theology in One Volume* (Bloomington, MN: Bethany House Publishers, 2011), 126.

[789] Ibid.

[790] Ibid., 127.

[791] Ibid., 127.

There is no nonliteral fulfillment of these prophecies in the New Testament. This argues strongly for the literal method. Concerning the logical reason, it has been argued, if one does not use the plain, normal, or literal method of interpretation all objectivity is lost. What check would there be on the variety of interpretations which man's imagination could produce if there were not an objective standard which the literal principle provides? And, philosophically the purpose of language itself seems to require a literal interpretation. Language was given by God for the purpose of being able to communicate with man.[792]

Why is the prior information so important to this discussion of Colossians 1:16-18? When the literal hermeneutic is applied to this portion of the text it provides a solid antidote to the perceived or actual problems long associated with Dispensationalism in regard to O.T. saints and their position in or out of Christ. The text itself, not per se a systematic theological grid, reveals that all things, which would include O.T. Israel, exist "in Christ." A literal hermeneutic applied by the Dispensationalist can help resolve a longtime lingering issue that has unnecessarily divided the two main systems of theology and hindered their collective organization in fighting against the common antichrist ideology of humanistic liberalism.

The Greek reads:

καὶ αὐτός ἐστιν πρὸ πάντων καὶ τὰ πάντα ἐν αὐτῷ συνέστ κεν.

The wide sweeping inclusivity of context reveals the encompassing nature of the Greek term πάντα. In this text the term (a nominative, plural, neuter noun) carries the idea of all things, the "totality or the whole."[793] The question then becomes, all of what? The answer is provided in the last word: συνέστηκεν. This term (finite verb, 3rd person, singular, perfect tense, indicative, active verb) means "to stand with," to "place

---

[792] Robert P. Lightner, *Evangelical Theology: A Survey and Review* (Grand Rapids MI: Baker House Publishing, 1986), 24.

[793] Spiros Zodhiates, "πᾶς," in *The Complete Word Study Dictionary: New Testament* (Chattanooga, TN: AMG Publishers, 1992), 1124.

together."⁷⁹⁴ So the text so far states "all things, the totality stands as placed together." But where are all things, the totality of all, positioned? The text provides this answer as well. It says, ἐν αὐτῷ, i.e. in him or in Christ.

By logical deduction then the following can be asked and answered: (1) Does Israel exist as a part of God's creation? Yes, Israel is a part of the totality of God's creation mentioned in Col. 1:16. (2) Is Christ Jesus holding all of these parts, and thus the totality of all creation, together with him? Yes, the text literally says that all things, which includes Israel, is held together by Christ. (3) Is there a place or position mentioned as to where these parts that make up the total, which includes Israel in part, exists? Yes the text places all of the parts, which includes Israel, as positioned "in Christ." The same phrase, ἐν Χριστῷ of 1 Thessalonians 4:16 is the same phrase used in Colossians 1:17. However, Colossians 1:17 reveals the all encompassing scope of this "in him {Christ}" perspective. Israel, as well as all O.T. saints, would be in Christ.

Other texts of Scripture highlight this theme as well. For example, Hebrews 1:3 speaks to this universal, encompassing, wide sweeping providence of God where he "upholds the universe by the word of his power." Interestingly when reading this in the Greek the term "universe" used in the English Standard Version translates the Greek term "πάντα." That is again the same term used in Colossians 1:16-17 when describing the all-encompassing creative acts of Christ as well as the all-encompassing positioning of those same created aspects. Everything in the universe (πάντα) has been "created through him and for him and he is before all things, and in him all things hold together" (Col. 1:16-17). This concept is also highlighted by Paul's statement mentioned by Luke in Acts 17:28, "In him (Ἐν αὐτῷ) we live and move and have our being."

The entire universe, including all people, exists in God and in Christ since Christ is God, Yahweh. Dispensationalism can acknowledge this without falling into either universalism or Covenant theology's perspective that being in Christ causes all distinctions in the family of God to be erased. Living "in God/Christ" does not mean all who live in that sphere share in the covenant of eternal grace. Nor does it mean that

---

⁷⁹⁴ Spiros Zodhiates, "συνίστημι," in *The Complete Word Study Dictionary: New Testament* (Chattanooga, TN: AMG Publishers, 1992), 1344.

everyone in that sphere shares the same identity. I will discuss more on this when we examine Colossians 1:18 that relates to the headship of Christ over the redeemed body.

First, to explore the universalism idea further, the question or issue in regard to universalism is not, "are all people in Christ?" The proper question is what relationship do all of the people in Christ have to the Christ they are placed within or held together by? Is a person standing together with Christ in a position of grace (the redeemed) or is the person standing in a position of justice (the non-redeemed) to Christ? That answer establishes the safety net to guard against a failure to recognize all portions of Scripture that classify all of humanity into one or the other category when viewing them from their eternal habitation. Some texts clearly divide humanity into those two classifications. Only a liar could misrepresent the clear teachings Jesus had on some who would spend eternity in hell (see Matt. 8:12; 13:41-42; 49-50; 25:46; Mark 9:43; 48-49; Rev. 14:9-11; 19:3). Universalism is not even a serious consideration in how to understand this Colossians 1:16-18 text of Scripture.

If the entire Bible is believed, as is the case for those who follow Jesus Christ as Lord, then to try and assert this Colossian's texts leads to universalism only highlights that person's lack of respect for the full witness of biblical revelation. Such a person who attempts that from this text reveals a dishonest nature. Clearly, even some who are "in Christ" are not a part of the eternally redeemed. Only those who experience eternal redemption reside with Christ in heaven.

Second, if all are in Christ does that not mean Israelite saints and the New Covenant era saints in the body of Christ are one and the same? That is the argument Covenant theologians have tried to use. Grover Gunn argues exactly that way. He says, "to be in covenant union with Christ is to be in the Body and the Bride of Christ, and to be in the Body and Bride of Christ is to be in the church universal, and for the Old Testament saints to be in the church universal is to deny Dispensationalism."[795]

But that merging together of so many concepts fails to also take into account the full data of biblical revelation. Just like the Universalist

---

[795] Curtis Crenshaw and Grover E. Gunn III, *Dispensationalism Today, Yesterday, and Tomorrow* (Memphis, TN: Footstool Publications, 1985, reprinted ed. 86, 87, 89, 94, 95), 266.

who would argue that being "in Christ" means all are part of the redeemed, the Covenant Theologian commits the same reductionist philosophical error. Of course, the Covenant theologian would not by this error of reducing all in Christ to being the same peoples stand in the same level of an error as the Universalist. Those who embrace universalism are guilty of a first order violation worthy of breaking fellowship with by their false teaching that all will experience eternal salvation. But, even so, the Covenant theologian would still by the error follow the same methodological avenue in arriving at that conclusion as the Universalist.

A simple-natural world illustration may help highlight this point. Imagine one hundred people are standing in the Sherlin residence. Just because all of the people standing in the Sherlin's residence are standing in/with the Sherlin residence does not mean all one hundred are in a covenant relationship with Mr. Sherlin. Temporarily residing in such a position, my residence, does not automatically make all of them permanent residents. Only those who are related to me by blood or law may remain as permanent residents. The same principle applies to Christ. He may have all of humanity standing in/with him temporarily. But only those who are in covenant relations with him have a permanent residence in eternity with him.

Several errors exist in Grover Gunn's perspective. (A) To be "in Christ" is not the same as being "in a covenant union with Christ." The Bible only says all are "in Christ." The believers, pre-Israel believers, Israelite believers of the O.T., and the saints of the N.T. in the body of Christ, would of course be in *covenant relations* with the Lord Jesus. But they are believers and to believe is to be related to Christ by the covenant of grace. An unbeliever is not within or connected to the covenant of grace and therefore Gunn's argument breaks down. An unbeliever relates to Christ through the covenant or relationship of justice.

(B) The Bible speaks of being "in Christ" and also of "being in the body of Christ." More will be said of that in subsequent sections. For now it is enough to merely point out that again Gunn and those in his company commit the reductionist error. Just because one text mentions being in Christ does not per se mean all who are in Christ are also in the body of Christ. For that to be true there would need to be a text that says, "all in Christ are in the body of Christ," or "all saints in God and Christ are in the body of Christ." But no such text exists.

(C) Gunn's argument that if a person is in the Body and/or Bride of Christ then they are also in the universal church. This fails to grasp the historical progression of God's one elect family. It fails, like the prior assertions, to account for multiple peoples mentioned in Scripture who make up the one family of God.

Again, take for example a natural family. In a natural family there may be one people by one last name, yet in that one people are various members related to the patriarch by different positions and eras. For example, my dad, Bill Sherlin had a father, mother, and numerous siblings. He also had one wife, two sons, a daughter-in-law, and two grandchildren. All of them have the last name Sherlin. But in that one portion of the larger Sherlin family, that pre-dated dad and post-dates dad, different members in that family existed. One was a wife. Two were sons, one was a daughter-in-law, and two were grandchildren. Then there were Sherlin family members prior to dad's immediate family. It was one family with different members in that family who came along at different times in history.

Likewise, in God's family, just as in natural families, there is one elect family of God, that is the redeemed of all ages. Yet in that one redeemed family of all ages there are various members and historical divisions. Some of the redeemed are pre-Israelite saints. Some of the redeemed are Israelite saints who lived in the Mosaic Law era/dispensation. Some are members of the Bride of Christ who make up the body of Christ on this earth in this New Covenant era/dispensation. Some will be post-church tribulation saints. Some will be millennial saints. In other words, the specific classification of the redeemed saint who is in Christ's grace covenant occurs by what period of history God birthed that person.

A literal interpretation of Colossians 1:16-18 gives us this paradigm. There is the "all who are in Christ" through all of the ages and then there is also the "body of Christ," i.e., the church (Col. 1:18). The body of Christ, or the bride of Christ, is a distinct organization for a distinct period of time charged with a distinct purpose of taking dominion through the art and task of discipleship. That distinct people with Dispensational theology may remain distinct while not denying the place of O.T. saints in the Lord. Regrettably, Dispensationalism has apparently at times fallen prey to the fear of the accusation by the Covenant theologians that to be "in Christ" means Israel and the Church must be the same people of God. Such a fear is unjustified.

The following reasons, born out of this first reason of a literal hermeneutic applied to Colossians 1:16-18, reveals a better approach that retains continuity in the doctrine of grace and salvation while also still affirming historical divisions in the family of God. In short, there can be one family of God with various members (such as Israel and the Church) in that one family. Just as with God himself, who is Triune (one and three), so too there is one redeemed of all ages with multiple members in that family.

2. God's Single Doctrine of Election for All People Creating One Redeemed Family

Dispensationalism, as noted in prior sections of this work, has largely been within the Lactantius and Augustinian (early church era), Luther and Calvin (Reformation era), Hodge and Warfield (modern era) perspective on God's sovereignty in dispensing unconditional love in contrast to the many conditional love theologies. Dispensationalism experienced its strongest era of resurgence and formalization from within the womb of the Reformed heritage era. As a type of theology it mostly aligned with that tradition in the modern era with only some slight modifications in the areas of ecclesiology, Israelology, and eschatology.

But in regards to soteriology Dispensationalism, by and large by some of the most notable leaders, has affirmed that any person who is ever saved from any portion of history has been saved because that person was sovereignly elected by God's omniscience that he implemented by his providential omnipresence and omnipotence throughout the history of redemption.

For example, Dispensationalist Dr. Arnold G. Fruchtenbaum, from the classical or revised Dispensationalist tradition, teaches clearly that any person who is redeemed in any age or dispensation comes to such redemption only because of this sovereign elective act of God. In discussing God's elective work he mentions that the Bible speaks of national ethnic election as well as personal salvific election. Only those who are personally elected will come to Christ. Yet all who do come to Christ in any dispensation are a part of the one elect family of God. He says,

> In dealing with the concept of election, a distinction must be made between individual election and national election. The former is soteriological and results in the salvation of that individual. This type of election extends to both Jewish and Gentile individuals and any person who has ever believed, either Jew or Gentile, was the object of God's individual election. . . . National election does not guarantee the salvation of every individual within the nation since only individual election can do that.[796]

Dr. Fruchtenbaum's perspective of election highlights the unity of these people in Christ. Only the elect will come to believe in the Lord. And all who do believe are of the elect. This election was according to Fruchtenbaum done in eternity based upon texts like Ephesians 1:4 and 2 Thessalonians 2:13-14.[797] That logically means that the only ones who come to the Lord are those elected from eternity past, and that those who come constitute the one elect of God, i.e., the one redeemed family of God. "Out of the mass of humanity, already under judgment, already under condemnation, heading for its final place, the Lake of Fire, from that mass of humanity, he chose some to bring to salvation. He elected some."[798]

Other Dispensationalists have come to the same conclusion as well. The legendary Southern Baptist pastor, evangelist, and conservative stalwart Dr. W.A. Criswell taught that there was only one single elect family of God of all ages. He believed those God elected, no matter in what dispensation, were in covenant union with Christ Jesus. He spoke of a singular people, the elect of God. To refer back to Colossians 1:17, these are the ones in Christ who are elected to grace in Christ. Though all of the universe is in/with Christ due to him being the Sovereign over it, some who are in Christ are also in his elective graces. Criswell says, "God

---

[796] Arnold G. Fruchtenbaum, *Israelology: The Missing Link in Systematic Theology* (Tustin, CA: Ariel Ministries, 1989), 567.

[797] Arnold G. Fruchtenbaum, *God's Will & Man's Will: Predestination, Election, & Free Will* (San Antonio, TX: Ariel Ministries, 2013), 38, 39.

[798] Ibid., 42.

promised Jesus before creation of the world, somewhere in the courts of God's heaven above, that if he suffered and died for the sins of the fallen race, God would give him a people. He would not die in vain . . . . God would give to Christ a people after he suffered and died for the sins of the fallen race. That is election."[799]

3. The Trans-dispensational Atonement of Christ Magnified in Each Dispensation

Dispensationalists can articulate that those in Christ (Col. 1:17), and who are elected in eternity past unto grace (Eph 1:4; 2 Thess. 2:13-14) experienced faith in the atonement of Christ as so revealed in their current dispensation. In Revelation 13:8 one point of the text is that the Lamb of God "hath been slain from the disruption of the world,"[800] and in one point the author highlighted the truth about the "death of Christ" has "ever" been "known to God."[801] The death of Christ and the names related to him in the book of life were "known before the actual creation of the world."[802]

That transhistorical, out of time, decree of Christ's atonement breaks into history from the earliest of time with the pre-cross believers. God progressively unfolds the atonement of Christ from the very first segment of history with our parents Adam and Eve. As Dr. Mal Couch noted, "From Genesis 3:15 and throughout the Old Testament, the central character is the Messiah . . . . Everywhere he is to be traced in type, symbol, promise and prophecy."[803]

---

[799] W.A. Criswell, *Great Doctrines of the Bible*, Volume 5, *Soteriology*, ed. Paige Patterson (Grand Rapids, MI: Zondervan Publishing, 1985), 139.

[800] Donald Grey Barnhouse, *Revelation: An Expositional Commentary* (Grand Rapids, MI: Zondervan, 1971), 239. It seems Barnhouse used this word "disruption" because he affirmed a period of time (maybe aeviternity) where the angels sinned and disrupted the world prior to the world of humanity.

[801] Ibid.

[802] Paige Patterson, *The New American Commentary*: Volume 39, *Revelation*, gen ed. E. Ray Clendenen (Nashville, TN: B&H Publishing, 2012), 278.

[803] Mal Couch, *Messianic Systematic Theology of the Old Testament* (Clifton, TX: Scofield Ministries, 2010), 28.

Such an idea apparently is how Jesus Christ and the apostles viewed the O.T. Dr. Couch's assessment seems on target that the O.T. presented Christ throughout its pages. Dr. Michael Rydelnik concurs with Couch saying, "Consistently, the apostles contended that Jesus of Nazareth was 'the Messiah . . . the One Moses wrote about in the Law (and so did the prophets)' (John 1:41, 45). This was the perspective they learned from Jesus himself when he said that 'everything written about me in the Law of Moses, the Prophets, and the Psalms must be fulfilled' (Luke 24:44)."[804]

Of course, those animal sacrifices in the O.T. did not remove sin and guilt in the eternal sense.[805] However, because Christ was eternally slain in the mind of God, which would one day occur historically in our earthly space and time, those types and symbols were markers and objects for faith that the Old Testament saints trusted in as they rested and relied upon the promise of God for redemption from sin. That belief in God was also a belief in Christ as Christ is Yahweh. Dr. Jeff Heslop has said,

> belief in the Father and/or Son has always been the content of faith because both are called Yahweh . . . . Lord is translated from the Greek word kurios (in the LXX) which is itself a translation of the Hebrew word Yahweh (in the Hebrew OT). . . . Thus when Scripture says that Abraham believed in Yahweh and it was counted to him as righteousness, it would not be wrong to claim that he too believed in Christ (whether directly or indirectly), as Christ is Yahweh.[806]

This concept of "belief in God" is critical and has not been emphasized enough from the pens of many Dispensationalists. Too, the connective link that God is in Christ and Christ is in God, i.e. the Jesus is

---

[804] Michael Rydelnik, *The Messianic Hope: Is the Hebrew Bible Really Messianic?*, ed. E. Ray Clendenen (Nashville, TN: B&H Publishing, 2010), 8.

[805] Mal Couch, *Messianic Systematic Theology of the Old Testament* (Clifton, TX: Scofield Ministries, 2010), 156.

[806] S. Jeff Heslop, "*Content, Object & Message of Saving Faith*," in *Dispensationalism Tomorrow and Beyond: A Theological Collection in Honor of Charles C. Ryrie* (Fort Worth, TX: Tyndale Seminary Press, 2008), 238.

Lord doctrine, has not been applied proportionately to this discussion within the progression of revelation from the O.T. to the N.T. The O.T. saints did more than believe "God's testimony," they actually "believed in God himself."[807] "Scripture is very clear about this matter," a person must believe in God and his provision he offers for redemption, and in this case the "ultimate object of faith in any and every age is God himself. The ultimate issue at any given time in history is whether a man will take God at his word and exercise saving faith in the provision for salvation which God reveals."[808]

It is an act of the believer who makes an "ultimate commitment to God."[809] To believe in God in the O.T. is to then believe in Christ, and to believe in Christ to then believe in God. To refuse to believe in Christ is a rejection "of God himself."[810] To reject the God as revealed in the O.T. and his provision and promise is to also then reject Jesus Christ himself since both are Yahweh. The person, provision, and promise are all wrapped together into one message. When a person in the N.T. or O.T. committed themselves to Yahweh they were committing themselves to the person, provision, and promise of that being. Thus all of these believers are "in Yahweh." This is the O.T. and N.T. doctrine of redemption.

Dr. Fruchtenbaum has discussed it this way, "When Adam and Eve committed that first act of disobedience, sin entered and separated them from God. From that point on, the means of bridging the separation of man from God was by the means of the blood. This bridging of the gap is called redemption. In the history of God's dealing with his people, the means of redemption was always by blood."[811] In fact, Fruchtenbaum argues that the 613 Laws of Moses revolved around, or could be

---

[807] Ibid., 236.

[808] John S. Feinberg, "*Salvation in the Old Testament*," in *Tradition & Testament: Essays in Honor of Charles Lee. Feinberg*, eds. John S. and Paul D. Feinberg (Chicago, IL: Moody Press, 1981), 56.

[809] Ibid.

[810] Ibid., 57.

[811] Arnold Fruchtenbaum, *Messianic Christology* (Tustin, CA: Ariel Ministries, 1998), 129.

summarized by, the "redemptive element of blood" that "ran through the entire Law."[812] He believes that "a great summary statement for the entire Law was to be found in the third book of Moses, Leviticus 17:11... It can easily be said that all of the Law revolves around this one statement.... All [the] different sacrifices had the same purpose: that the Jew might be rightly related to God. All seven feasts of Israel—Passover, Unleavened Bread, Firstfruits, Pentecost, Trumpets, Day of Atonement, and Tabernacles—required the shedding of blood."[813]

In concert with Fruchtenbaum, Dr. John Feinberg spoke of how central this blood theme or atonement theme was within the overall package of redemption. The O.T. doctrine of redemption contained a person, a provision, and a promise. These were wrapped together. As he said, "the entire Old Testament . . . teaches that blood sacrifice is of utmost importance in order for man to maintain a right standing before God."[814] This theme begins, according to Feinberg, from the beginning in Genesis 3:15.[815] "In addition to the theme of sacrifice, there is the theme of promises . . . . in each period of the Old Testament economy, the specific content revealed for men to believe involved truths about sacrifices and promises."[816] This redemptive theme, consisting of a person (Yahweh), his provision, and promise runs through all dispensations of revelatory history.[817]

Dr. Criswell highlighted this trans-dispensational redemptive theme in his famous sermon, "The Scarlet Thread of Redemption." The death of Christ, sealed in the mind of God in eternity past and historically realized in earthly time, became a dominant symbol through the sacrificial

---

[812] Ibid.

[813] Ibid., 129-130.

[814] John S. Feinberg, "*Salvation in the Old Testament*," in *Tradition & Testament: Essays in Honor of Charles Lee. Feinberg*, eds. John S. and Paul D. Feinberg (Chicago, IL: Moody Press, 1981), 59.

[815] Ibid.

[816] Ibid., 60.

[817] Ibid.

system beginning with Adam and Eve and continuing onward through the entire pre-cross era until the actual death of Christ who served us as the one true and final sacrificial Lamb. This sacrificial system, intertwined with the promise of a redeemer to come (Gen. 3:15), set the context for the object of faith for all Old Testament saints. They placed their faith in the Lord and his promise to deliver magnified through the physical sacrifices.

Dr. Michael Rydelnik of Moody Bible Institute captures how this redemptive promise intertwines with the life and death of the promised deliverer. He says, "It seems appropriate to understand Genesis 3:15 as the first specific messianic prophecy of the Bible. . . . this text . . . does promise that Messiah will descend from humanity and he will destroy the evil force that tempted Eve, humanity's ancient enemy later revealed as Satan. Moreover, in defeating this enemy, the Messiah himself will be struck, bringing victory over the enemy of our souls through his own death."[818] Dr. Criswell elaborates further on this ideology of the doctrine of the atonement that begins in the Garden of Eden and runs the entire course of biblical revelation. He says of the garments made for Adam and Eve after they sinned,

> Covering for sin (atonement for sin) cannot be woven by human hands. Therefore, somewhere in the Garden of Eden, the Lord took an innocent animal; and before the eyes of Eve and Adam, God killed that innocent animal as the ground drank up its blood. This is the beginning of the "Scarlet Thread of Redemption." Through the slaughter of an innocent victim, God took coats of skin and covered over the shame and the nakedness of the man and his wife. This is the first sacrifice, and it was offered by the hand of the Almighty God. I have often thought that when Adam saw the gasping, spent life of that innocent creature, and when he saw the crimson stain which soiled the ground, it was his first experience of what it meant to die because of sin. Thus, the story of atonement and sacrifice begins and unfolds throughout the Word of God, until finally in glory we shall see great throngs of the saints who have

---

[818] Michael Rydelnik, *The Messianic Hope: Is the Hebrew Bible Really Messianic?* ed. E. Ray Clendenen (Nashville, TN: B&H Publishing, 2010), 145.

washed their robes and made them white in the blood of the Lamb. This is "The Scarlet Thread of Redemption."[819]

Dispensationalists have normally affirmed that Old Testament revelation does not tell the same level of detail about the God-Man Jesus Christ as does the New Testament. However, Dispensationalism does affirm that the Old Testament saints were believers in the Lord (Yahweh) and his promise to redeem. Dr. Floyd Barackman has stated, "in every age of human history, God saves people in the same way—by his grace through their salvational faith in the divine revelation about Jesus, the Savior—Redeemer (Eph. 2:8)."[820] He further emphasizes the point of Christ's atoning work by saying, "If there is any righteousness or redemption apart from the Lord Jesus that God accepts, then our Lord's atoning work was not necessary."[821]

Yet that is where it appears some Dispensationalists cause confusion which the Covenant theologians have used against the overall system. By refusing to embrace and teach that even Old Testament saints are in some sense in Christ in the pre-cross dispensation (even if only provisionally in God's mind), and actually experientially in Christ after his death and resurrection in actual time, they have given the appearance of a teaching that some are saved yet not saved "in Christ." That is problematic and can easily be avoided within a Dispensational system that honors a literal exegesis of Scripture. Barackman continues, "It is always by God's grace through faith in the divine revelation about the Savior and his atoning work, whether promised (Gen. 3:15, 21; 15:5-6; Heb. 11:41) or fulfilled (John 3:16)."[822]

---

[819] W.A. Criswell, "*The Scarlet Thread of Redemption*," in the *Holy Bible Baptist Study Edition*, eds. W.A. Criswell and Paige Paige Patterson (Nashville, TN: Thomas Nelson Publishers, 1991), 1835.

[820] Floyd Barackman, *Practical Christian Theology* (Grand Rapids, MI: Kregel Publications, 1998), 365.

[821] Ibid., 493.

[822] Ibid.

4. Pre-Cross Saints Provisionally in Christ's Grace Died and Went to Paradise until Actually Experiencing the Full Righteousness of Christ by His Death

Though all of creation is "in Christ" (Yahweh) because Christ is God and God is Christ (see John 1:1 and Acts 17:28), not all persons in Christ are those elected unto eternal grace.[823] Furthermore, it remains important to allow the historical revelation of God to progress naturally as it unfolds within the pages of Scripture. Dispensationalism has been a champion for the cause not to overstep the progressive revelation element of the historical narrative within the text.[824] God unfolds history by sovereign providence through incremental stages. Progressive revelation means the "piecemeal divine unveiling of truth throughout the ages until the completion of the Bible. God did not reveal truth about himself all at once but revealed it in many portions and 'many ways' (Heb. 1:1)."[825]

Consequently, as revelation unfolded so did the experiential history of God's people. The Old Testament saints lived under a Mosaic Law and Covenant. The New Covenant, also known as the "eternal covenant" (Heb. 13:20)[826] did not begin until after the death and resurrection of Christ. The blood sacrifices in the O.T., though ordained of God and holy, were only temporary provisions for the sins of the people. "The animal sacrifices under the Mosaic Law were intended to be of

---

[823] Some who read this may question if they are of the elect. How can one have confidence of his or her election unto grace? Apostle Peter gave us a list of the qualities of the elect. In 2 Peter 1:3-11 details are given as to what a believing elect person ought to be. By examining those traits a person can "confirm" his or her "election" (2 Peter 1:10).

[824] It is important to make sure the doctrine of progressive revelation is not confused with progressivism. Progressive revelation means that God unfolds his will and mind through history in incremental stages, progressively. Progressivism is a distinct ideological methodology rooted in humanistic liberalism that teaches people discover truth or situational truth through liberal and naturalistic means that deny universal and absolute objective norms, especially any universal norms from any supernatural being.

[825] Paul Enns, *The Moody Handbook of Theology* (Chicago, IL: Moody Press, 2008), 722.

[826] Mal Couch, *Messianic Systematic Theology of the Old Testament* (Clifton, TX: Scofield Ministries, 2010), 160.

temporary duration, a temporary measure only. God's intent was for there to be one final blood sacrifice, and that would be the sacrifice of the Messiah himself . . . . Unlike the animal sacrifices, the sacrifice of Jesus was to bring eternal redemption rather than temporary atonement."[827]

Therefore, it seems that a case can be made that the O.T. saints were provisionally in grace and then fully sealed or experientially participants in that eternal covenant of grace reality after his death and resurrection. Dr. Barackman argues this point well saying,

> While precross gospel believers . . . received divinely imputed righteousness (Gen. 15:6) and enjoyed a personal relationship with God (17:1), they did not go to heaven when they died (25:8; cf. Luke 16:22) or receive the promised inheritance (Heb. 11:13-16). These realities were not possible before our Lord's incarnation, atoning work, death, resurrection, and return to heaven (Heb. 9:15). Only then could he bring his people into union with himself and impart to them the blessings of the New Covenant. Probably the precross saints who had died were united to him at the time of his return to heaven when they were taken with him (Eph. 4:8). With this union he became their righteousness and redemption (1 Cor. 1:30), fulfilling what previously had been extended to them, as it were, on credit (Rom. 3:25; Heb. 9:15-17).[828]

---

[827] Arnold Fruchtenbaum, *Messianic Christology* (Tustin, CA: Ariel Ministries, 1998), 130, 133.

[828] Floyd Barackman, *Practical Christian Theology* (Grand Rapids, MI: Kregel Publications, 1998), 493.

5. The Holy Spirit Dwelt With but Did Not Permanently Indwell the Old Testaments Saints

Many Dispensationalists seem to also add another aspect to the distinction above concerning the precross believers going to paradise before the resurrection of Christ. The other idea associated with that is the idea related to the internal indwelling of the Spirit that only post resurrection of Christ saints experience. It seems that the precross saints experienced a form of grace but not the full application of grace that occurs in a greater proportion for today's dispensation of N.T. saints. Dr. James Hamilton takes that perspective. He says, "the Old Testament teaches that God was with his people by dwelling among them in the temple rather than in them as under the new covenant."[829] Dispensationalist Dr. Larry Pettegrew notes that Dispensationalism has had a variety of positions on this matter,[830] yet it appears that the key difference from the Old Testament to the New Testament is that no "biblical evidence" exists of a "permanent soteriological indwelling of Old Testament saints."[831]

The difference meant that the O.T. saints experienced the Spirit among and with them but the Spirit "would not be 'in' them individually and intimately (John 14:17)."[832] This again captures the concept of being "in Christ" by creative order, or in Christ because of an election unto grace. But for the O.T. saint it was a provisional experience that ran in concurrence with the progressive revelation of God in history. The O.T. saints were with Christ and were with the Spirit in a sense around them but not permanently indwelt with the Spirit until Christ resurrected. These saints were still and are now today in Christ (Yahweh) but it moved historically from a status of being provisionally in the covenant of grace (in God's mind and with regeneration but not indwelling) to fully

---

[829] James M. Hamilton Jr., *God's Indwelling Presence: The Holy Spirit in the Old and New Testaments* (Nashville, TN: B&H Publishing, 2006), 25.

[830] Larry Pettegrew, *The New Covenant Ministry of the Holy Spirit* (Grand Rapids, MI: Kregel Publications, 2001), 25.

[831] Ibid., 27.

[832] Ibid., 28.

experiencing the covenant of grace with the blessings of the indwelling of the Holy Spirit.

It is hard to miss the point made in John's writing that the indwelling of the Spirit would come only after Jesus was resurrected. "According to John 20:22, Jesus exhaled and said, 'Receive [*labete*] the Holy Spirit.' When John 7:39 speaks of 'the Spirit, whom those had believed in him were about to receive [*lambanein*],' it is natural conclude that the reception of the Spirit occurring in 20:22 is the one expected in 7:39. There is no other account of a reception of the Spirit in the Gospel."[833]

This distinction provides a clearer place to "rightly divide" the people of God. The proper division is not one of those "in Christ" (N.T. saints) and those "outside of Christ" (O.T. saints). The proper division is rather, O.T. saints who were in God/Christ saved from sin and provisionally in his grace prior to his atonement (and thus lacking the indwelling Spirit), and those who have come to enter into the covenant of grace because of his atonement and resurrection and subsequent administration of the Holy Spirit applying the atonement to the person individually in way not experienced prior to the resurrection and application of the Holy Spirit's indwelling.

This type of distinction does not relegate a portion of the redeemed as being outside of Christ whereas another portion is inside of Christ. OT saints were saved, born again, and that reality existed because of the death of Christ (still to come for them, but settled in God's eternal mind). But they did not have the same NT experience as those living after Christ's death and coming of the Holy Spirit.

In this perspective, it provides a position of one single elect family of God through all dispensations while retaining proper historical divisions whereby God places each person in relation to his progressive revelation. Precross believers are saved and a part of the single family of God although they did not experience the same fullness of blessings that they and we do now after the resurrection of Christ and the sending of the Spirit. For example of a difference of blessing, consider the sacrificial system. The OT saints had to repeat the sacrifices on a repetitive basis. NT

---

[833] James M. Hamilton Jr., *God's Indwelling Presence: The Holy Spirit in the Old and New Testaments* (Nashville, TN: B&H Publishing, 2006), 118.

saints, however, do not have to use the animal sacrificial system (see Heb. 10:1-18). Even though all believers are in the Lord through faith based on the work of the Lord for their redemption, the doctrine of progressive revelation reminds us that the experiences of the believers grew in accordance with the progress of redemptive history.

Interestingly, even Covenant, nondispensational, theologians recognize this type of differentiation in the progress of revelation. For example, Dr. Wayne Grudem argues that the precross believers did not have the resurrection power that we N.T. saints have today. He bases this on the distinction between the work of the Holy Spirit prior to Christ's resurrection and his work after his resurrection. He says, O.T. "believers, who had had an old-covenant less-powerful experience of the Holy Spirit in their lives, received on the Day of Pentecost a more-powerful new-covenant experience of the Holy Spirit working in their lives."[834]

6. Both Old and New Testament Saints Experienced Regeneration

The "in Christ" and "out of Christ" differentiation between the two testaments seems to have a connection to the question of whether the O.T. saints were born again. As noted earlier, some Dispensationalists taught that Old Testament saints were not "in Christ" (Walvoord, Constable, Feinberg to name just three). In concert with that line of thought some Dispensationalists also have taught those Old Testament saints were not born again though still rightly related to God. Dr. James Hamilton thinks

---

[834] Wayne Grudem, *Systematic Theology: An Introduction to Biblical Doctrine* (Grand Rapids, MI: Zondervan Publishing, 1994), 771. Grudem seems to believe that the Spirit did dwell within the O.T. saints (see his discussion on this on page 637). But even so while saying the Spirit did indwell the O.T. saints he arrives at a similar position with the Dispensationalists. Grudem says, "the more powerful, fuller work of the Holy Spirit that is characteristic of life after Pentecost had not yet begun in the lives of the disciples. The Holy Spirit had not come within them in the way in which God had promised to put the Holy Spirit within his people when the new covenant would come (see Ezek. 36:26, 27; 37:14), nor had the Holy Spirit been poured out in great abundance and fullness that would characterize the new covenant age (Joel 2:28-29). In this new powerful new covenant sense, the Holy Spirit was not yet at work within the disciples" (p. 637). However that language is sliced or analyzed, it seems that Grudem still admits there is a distinction in the precross people of God and the post cross people of God by the activity of the Spirit upon them.

that the question of Old Testament regeneration has plagued not only Dispensationalists but many more throughout church history. Theologians like Novatian, Martin Luther, Dispensationalist Lewis Sperry Chafer, and other Dispensationalists apparently have struggled with the question of whether or not Old Testament saints experienced the new birth.[835] This too has posed a problem for the witness of Dispensationalism.

A safer exegetical route is to accept the doctrine that the O.T. saints experienced regeneration as one aspect of the benefit of being chosen in Christ unto grace. Israel and all precross saints who believed in the person and the divine revelation concerning a promise of redemption (which included in it a faith in the atonement) experienced the circumcision of the heart. That particular vernacular, circumcision of the heart, relays the way in which the O.T. describes the doctrine of regeneration. Dr. Arnold Fruchtenbaum says that all believers who come to faith from Adam onward enter into the Spiritual Kingdom. There are not multiple avenues, multiple Spiritual Kingdoms, or an "in Christ" regeneration status only for N.T saints. From a dispensational perspective he argues for a single, all encompassing, trans-dispensational Spiritual Kingdom that covers all believers. He says.

> The Spiritual Kingdom is composed of all who have experienced the new birth in all times by the Holy Spirit. From Adam until our day and as long as men continue to be born on this earth there will be the existence of the Spiritual Kingdom. Every individual since Adam onward who has been born again by faith through the regenerating work of the Holy Spirit is a member of this kingdom.[836]

Dr. Floyd Barackaman shares a similar view as does Fruchtenbaum on this matter. He affirms that the O.T. saints had to be regenerated if they were "in Christ." I would suggest a slight qualification to that by saying that the "in the elective graces of Christ" guarantees that the person

---

[835] James M. Hamilton Jr., *God's Indwelling Presence: The Holy Spirit in the Old and New Testaments*, ed. E. Ray Clendenen (Nashville, TN: B&H Publishing, 2006), 18-24.

[836] Arnold G. Fruchtenbaum, *Israeology: The Missing Link in Systematic Theology* (Tustin, CA: Ariel Ministries, 1989), 610.

experiences regeneration. If we take Colossians 1:16-18 literally, all things (which includes O.T. saints and even the unsaved) are basically in Christ in the creative sense of the term. However, there is an "in the grace of Christ position" that some "in God/Christ" experience. Those who are in the grace of Christ (Yahweh) elective decree experience the vivifying work of the Spirit through regeneration. No matter if it is Abraham who "believed in Yahweh" or a person today who believes in Christ (Yahweh), it is a person "who believes in him" and not merely what is said about the person "independent of himself."[837] Barackman says,

> The regenerative aspect of salvation requires that one be in Christ, for this involves the deliverance of his personhood and immaterial human nature from inherent corruption (Titus 3:5; 1 Peter 1:22), their being created in righteousness and true holiness (Col. 3:10; Eph. 4:24) infused with spiritual life (Rom. 8:10; Eph. 2:1). With Christ as our life (Col. 3:4), these realities spring from our being created in him (Eph. 2:10) and our being new creatures in him (2 Cor. 5:17).[838]

7. Baptism into Christ and his Grace Occurs for All Saints; Baptism into the Body of Christ Only Occurs for those Alive from Pentecost to the Rapture

Just as there are at least two types of election in Scripture, national (ethnic) election and individual election unto eternal grace, so too there are at least two types of baptisms into Christ mentioned in Scripture. All people who come to faith in the divine revelation concerning the promise of redemption through the Lord experience a baptism of grace into Christ. These are the saints elected in the grace of Christ from eternity past (Eph. 1:4). However, these people span many different dispensations. Historically some of these are precross saints, some are saints of the N.T. dispensation, some are saints from the tribulation era, and some are saints

---

[837] S. Jeff Heslop, "*Content, Object & Message of Saving Faith*," in *Dispensationalism Tomorrow and Beyond*, ed. Chris Cone (Fort Worth, TX: Tyndale Seminary Press, 2008), 237.

[838] Floyd Barackman, *Practical Christian Theology* (Grand Rapids, MI: Kregel Publications, 1998), 493.

from the millennial age. These people make up the one family of God, i.e. the elect from all ages.

Yet within the N.C. dispensation, sometimes labeled the dispensation of grace, there are those who experience both, the baptism into the grace of Christ as well as by virtue of the time in which they live receive simultaneously the placement into the body of Christ. Those who live from Pentecost (Acts 2) until the rapture of the body of Christ (1 Thess. 4:13-18) experience the concurrent baptism of the Spirit that places them into both Christ and his historical body. Those who live prior to this time do not make up the bride and body of Christ although they do become immersed into the grace of Christ and become a part of his family. O.T. saints made up the wife and body of God the Father and were within the Triune family by way of Christ's (Yahweh) redemptive grace. O.T. Israelite saints were a distinct historical member of God's family from Christ's bride and body. Dr. Barackman explains this distinction this way,

> To be in Christ does not necessarily mean to be in his mystical body, the church, for these are distinct concepts, realities, and activities of the Holy Spirit. The baptism into Christ (Gal. 3:27) is a distinct work from the baptism into his body (1 Cor. 12:13, 17; Col. 1:18). While Church age gospel believers (those saved during this age) experience both aspects of the Holy Spirit's baptism, all other saved peoples of human history—the precross gospel believers and those of the Tribulation Age and Kingdom Age—are only baptized into him and partake of the positional blessings that are in him. There is no evidence, that I am aware of, that they are members of the Lord's church.[839]

Does an "in Christ" Trans-dispensational Position Undermine the Pre-Tribulation Rapture Doctrine for N.T. Saints?

Some might ask a question at this point concerning the common pre-tribulational rapture position espoused almost by every Dispensationalist. If all saints from the O.T. to N.T. are in Christ, does such a position alter the distinction made between the timing of the

---

[839] Ibid.

resurrection of the O.T. saints (Daniel 12:1-2) and those of the N.T. era? In other words, would it then require that all of the saints in Christ be resurrected at one moment in time? And if so is the rapture at the end of the tribulation as so clearly stated in Daniel 12:1-2?

First, in response, a contextual reading of 1 Thessalonians 4:13-18 does not require the view that Apostle Paul spoke to each and every person in Christ through all the ages. In fact, it appears he was answering a specific question about those the believers had lost to death. So it could be that Paul was specifically speaking to just those believers of this dispensation. To paraphrase it, Paul could have been saying, "I know you are grieved as you look around and see all of these loved ones you knew who have died. Do not be discouraged because those [the ones in your minds you knew] who have died in Christ will be raised with us when the Lord returns." In Paul's mind he could have been addressing the specific set of "in Christ" people and not referring to each and every single person in Christ from all of history.

Second, the burden of proof seems to be on those who say this text must mean each and every person of all historical ages. The text does not say, "And all the dead in Christ will rise first . . ." The text only says, "the dead in Christ will rise first." The definite article "the" could easily be limited to just the portion of the dead in Christ that are to be raised at this moment. Clearly there are some who were resurrected prior to this event. Matthew 27:52 reports that "many bodies of the saints who had fallen asleep were raised." If a person says that 1 Thessalonians 4:16 requires that *all of the dead in Christ* rise at this time only then a contradiction has surfaced. Clearly from the text in Matthew's gospel some were raised in a different order, prior to the time of the resurrection in 1 Thessalonians 4, or even for that matter before the Daniel 12:1-2 time of resurrection. It seems most probable that the reason Paul did not say "all the dead in Christ will be raised" is because under the inspiration of the Lord he wrote harmoniously to all other portions of prior revelation.

Paul did not say all because in his mind not all were to be raised at this one moment in time. Some had already been raised prior to this, and some would be raised after this. God has the right to order the resurrections and to determine who will be in which order as he determines as the best option. Nothing in Scripture that I know of demands every resurrection event to occur exactly at the same time with all of the people of all history in that one resurrection. Certainly Christ was resurrected as the first fruits of more to come. He and those who were raised immediately after his death do not fit within the idea of a single resurrection for all of all history.

Therefore, there is no need to see the "in Christ" phrase reference to all saints of all of history as a threat to the various orders of resurrections in God's overall program. Nothing in this weakens the pre-tribulation rapture doctrine. A Dispensationalist may honor his or her allegiance to normal, honest, plain exegesis and affirm both a rapture before the time of wrath in the Day of the Lord for N.T. saints and simultaneously affirm a different resurrection time period for O.T. saints.[840]

Conclusion: All Saints are in Christ even though Not All Saints Had Explicit Faith in Christ as We Would Today

Some Dispensationalists have presented the doctrine of salvation for Old Testament saints in such a way it has caused confusion among the people of God. The "in Christ" phrase as applied only to N.T. saints has created an apparent implication that Dispensationalism affirms two types of salvation, one for Old Testament believers and another for New Testament believers. Though numerous clarifying statements have come forth from various Dispensationalists over the years attempting to assure readers that they adhere to an orthodox soteriology, which is true when evaluating their overall theology, the "in Christ" phrase applied only to N.T. believers has hindered their confession from receiving a warm welcome from the Evangelical community, especially the Covenant theological persuasion of Evangelicalism.

The O.T. saints were in some sense in Christ because Christ is Yahweh (see Isa. 40:3 and Matt. 3:3). Either they were in Christ fully in experience, or at least provisionally (in God's mind) while alive under the Old Covenant administration, and then later before Christ ascended placed experientially into Christ and taken to heaven with Christ from paradise.

---

[840] Credit here goes to Dr. Kenneth Keathley for helping me in this section of this work. He helped me grasp how easy it was to see Christ can and does order his resurrections differently already in Scripture with the people resurrected after Christ's death. Therefore, it is not an issue for Christ to resurrect only some from a certain era of time in the rapture of 1 Thessalonians 4.

As Dr. John Feinberg stated, "God has known about Christ's death from all eternity. Since he decreed it, it was an accomplished fact in his thinking long before it was an accomplished fact in history. Because God knows that the deed will be done (since he decreed it), and because he sees all of history (including the completed work of Christ) at once, God can grant man salvation, even before the sacrifice is performed in history."[841]

The belief of the O.T. saints was in a person who by his promise would make a provision to redeem sinners from sin. This is the doctrine of redemption that runs through all dispensations from Genesis to Revelation. The O.T. saints had an "implicit" faith in Yahweh (God/Christ). This faith through the progression of revelation that developed in history "became explicit in the New Testament."[842] The Old Testament revelation, often implicit through typological elements,[843] became historical reality when that person, the Lord (Yahweh), entered into history as promised and provided atonement for the sins of the world. As Dr. Jeff Heslop summarized this matter,

> God is the object of faith, but more importantly, the content of saving faith is always Yahweh. The message that points to Yahweh, however, expands with the progress of revelation. This distinction provides an understanding of Biblical soteriology with proper focus on progressive revelation while avoiding even the appearance of introducing more than one way of salvation.[844]

From Genesis to Revelation, through all dispensations, God/Christ moves history towards final consummation. In this historical progress he

---

[841] John S. Feinberg, *"Salvation in the Old Testament,"* in *Tradition & Testament: Essays in Honor of Charles Lee. Feinberg*, eds. John S. and Paul D. Feinberg (Chicago, IL: Moody Press, 1981), 55.

[842] Norman Geisler, *Systematic Theology in One Volume* (Minneapolis, MN: Bethany House Publishers, 2011), 1970.

[843] Ibid.

[844] S. Jeff Heslop, *"Content, Object & Message of Saving Faith,"* in *Dispensationalism Tomorrow and Beyond*, ed. Chris Cone (Fort Worth, TX: Tyndale Seminary Press, 2008), 251.

is the Lord, Yahweh, who redeems mankind by himself through being faithful to his promise to provide atonement for the sins that broke humanity's relationship with their Creator. As Creator all people live and move and have their being inside of God, the Lord (Yahweh), and inside of the Lord are those who experience the elective graces of Christ/God (Yahweh). These people make up the only family of God, the redeemed of all the ages.

Yet in this one family of God are various historical members. Though all of the redeemed are in Yahweh (God/Christ) not all in Yahweh make up the body of Christ, a particular people from a particular period of history in the overall progress of revelation in God's redemptive and glorification program. Those who died in Yahweh before the unique baptism work of the Spirit, which formed the body of Christ beginning in Acts 2 onward, have a different place in the family of God than does the body and bride of Christ. The bride or body of Christ has a distinct time for their resurrection (before the time of God's wrath). Those of Israel who lived and died before Acts 2 make up another portion of the family of Yahweh. They shall be resurrected after the great tribulation, i.e. the time of Jacob's trouble.

Dispensationalists would apparently be wise to articulate the O.T. saints as being in God/Christ/Yahweh in some sense or another (see Col. 1:20). By doing so that slight nomenclature adjustment could alleviate much confusion by some who misunderstand the distinctions being made in the family of God by the idea that N.T. saints only have a position in the Lord Jesus Christ. No vital or substantive doctrine important to Dispensationalism is hindered, weakened, or jettisoned by revising this language. Furthermore, some classical or revised Dispensationalists have already historically made such a statement as this in the past.

However, those voices have been the minority voice. But their voice seems to be the voice that could rectify an issue that does not need to exist among the Dispensational tradition of theologians. Other avenues exist that honor both literal hermeneutics and the concept of progressive revelation with distinctions between Israel and the Church that avoid implications of a flawed soteriology due to an "in Christ" and "out of Christ" division between the precross and post-cross saints in God's redeemed family.

Chapter 6. A Dispensational View of Foreknowledge and a Synthesis of God's Omniscience with Man's Will

God's Eternal Foreknowledge: A Rejection of the Open Theism Perspective and the Arminian Prescient View that God Learns the Future

One of the most troubling and unbiblical movements in the circles of Christendom and within religion today has been with the new ideology that God must learn in order to make decisions about the election and salvation of his created beings. A solid, stable, and straight forward hermeneutic, as espoused by Evangelicals in general and in particular by Dispensationalism, safeguards against this severe slippage into such sin. The Bible teaches God is omniscient, but many have subverted this for the idea of God being omni-observant, i.e. God must learn in order to know how to respond to the beings he created.

It is of utmost importance to correctly define and affirm this doctrine. Catastrophic damage to the faith occurs when someone deviates from the doctrine of God's full omniscience. Those who believe that God is a being who makes educated guesses, normally called open theists, and those who believe that God looks into the distant future *outside of himself* from eternity in order to see and/or figure out the future, or better and more technically known as mere prescient foresight philosophers, violate the doctrine of God's full eternal omniscience. There is a difference in the definition of omniscience and the definition of omni-observant. Some Arminians in the classical sense affirm God's omniscience occurs from within himself and that he does not learn anything. These Arminian theologians remain within a conservative and orthodox view of God.

However, some modern theologians who claim to be Arminians have moved away from the classic Arminian stance and into a view that places God more as a spectator and observer of history in that he must look into history outside of himself in order to learn what choices people will make. The first option, full omniscience, means God knows all from eternity by his own being as the Sovereign, Sustainer, and Savior. The second option, what I call omni-observant, means that God has to engage in observation outside of himself and into future creation within historical time and space, the distant future from eternity, in order for him to be able to properly respond to what his creation does in that historical time and space. The first places God in the director's throne as King. The second places God in the audience and by doing so makes him to be a spectator of history and subservient to history.

Of course, to be fair, as already noted earlier, Dispensationalism has within it a variety of positions on the sovereignty of God in soteriology. Some who are Arminian (in the classic sense) or at least opposed to the doctrine of eternal election from eternity past embrace an "eternal now" perspective of election, also called congruent election.[845] These teachers simply believe God just knows the future because the future and past are always eternally now before the eternal God. They would not embrace the idea that God must look and learn the future. They often leave undefined the when and how God knows but do advocate for a full or simple eternal omniscience doctrine. They too remain within the conservative and orthodox view of God.

Others within Dispensationalism embrace a Molinist position on God's omniscience. There are even some Calvinistic Molinist Dispensationalists. Then some advocate for a more Calvinistic perspective on God's omniscience. Yet all of those perspectives reject the idea of Open Theism, i.e. the idea God must look into the future outside of himself and eternity to learn, and at times to even make educated guesses, in order to respond to how his creatures will act in time. Open Theism violates historic, conservative, biblical orthodoxy. They should be disciplined in local churches and denied communion for their apostate teaching and conservatives cannot justly partner with them in the Great Commission.

For those who insist that God must learn, and that he makes educated guesses, Dr. Millard J. Erickson has pointed out that such Open Theist views about God learning the future has its root in heretical theologians of the past. The term heretical is not used haphazardly or without notable reflection as to the intensity of such a stance. I only use the term heresy for a theology or doctrine that undermines a first order

---

[845] Richard Land, "Another View Of The Biblical Doctrine Of Election," *The Christian Post*, last modified 2010, accessed July 15, 2015, http://www.christianpost.com/news/another-view-of-the-biblical-doctrine-of-election-46788/.

doctrine of the faith; heresy is a denial of some direct, straight forward, absolute non-negotiable doctrine of the Christian faith. A heresy may be in some doctrinal area (such as Christ is not God in the flesh or that salvation is by human works; Jesus Christ has already returned, etc.), in some epistemological area (such as Scripture is not inspired), or in an ethical area (such as the practice of homosexuality is not a sin; murder is sometimes a holy option; adultery is acceptable, etc.).

First order doctrinal deviations either destroy the doctrine of salvation or the idea undermines a fundamental truth required for historical orthodoxy. Level one heresy falls into the categories of 1A (damnable heresy) and 1B (heresy). If one believes justification occurs through good works, or that Jesus Christ is not the Savior and only way to heaven, then these errors constitute damnable heresy. If a person believes in physicalism or that scripture has error in it, or that God did not create the universe such a person may not be in damnable heresy, but he or she would still be a form of heresy known as unorthodoxy, i.e. cut off from the historic true body of Christ and outside the boundaries of fellowship. In both cases, such people cannot be in fellowship, communion, with the body of Christ.

Anytime a person denies a plain, absolutely direct, first order truth that person has departed from the faith and aligned himself with the spirit of the anti-Christ. In this area of doctrine, Paterology, the false idea of God learning, has arisen from numerous modern-day thinkers, and this idea has not come "from the mainstream of Christianity."[846] It is a severe departure and deviation from a clear standard of the Christian faith. As the Bible so plainly says, "God knows everything" (1 John 3:20c). To assert that God makes educated guesses denies that absolute truth. To say that God must first look outside of eternity and into a future time and space to learn in order to know everything means again that there was a time in which God did not know everything. Again, that is a denial of this doctrine of full omniscience.

Numerous texts throughout Scripture directly affirm that God knows everything. Psalm 145:7 states, "Great is our Lord, and mighty in

---

[846] Millard J. Erickson, *What Does God Know and When Does He Know It? The Current Controversy over Divine Foreknowledge* (Grand Rapids, MI: Zondervan Publishing, 2003), 248.

power; His understanding is infinite" (ASV). Job said that God "sees everything under the heavens" (Job 28:24b). God described himself through Isaiah this way, "I am God, and there is none like me, declaring the end from the beginning and from ancient times things not yet done, saying 'My counsel shall stand, and I will accomplish all my purpose'" (46:9-10 ESV).

  The historical proponents of views asserting that God must look and learn or make educated guesses have not been a friend of Christ or Christianity in general. In many respects those advocates were apostate antagonists towards the view of God's absolute foreknowledge known as omniscience. People who have promoted this view have been from the likes of "Celsus" who was not a Christian "at all, or who like Marcion or the Socinians, [who] held heretical views in some other areas. Some were not theologians, but philosophers, psychologists, and scientists."[847] Not to discredit philosophers, psychologists, or scientists, it would be wise to highlight the point that those people in those fields were not those intertwining biblical theology into their chosen common grace disciplines. The problem was not they were philosophers, psychologists, or scientists. The problem was they were not theologians within those fields of thought. No better word of rebuke can be given other than this: "The fear of the LORD is the beginning of knowledge" (Prov. 1:7a).

  My perspective as an Evangelical Dispensationalist argues that many in Christendom who embrace either open theism or a type of open prescient foreknowledge (God must look outside of eternity into some future point in order to learn what will transpire), instead of the only truth of full eternal omniscience, are maybe great moral theologians or ministers of great civil virtuous philosophy, in that they often hold high moral values, sincere ethics, and are people who generally speaking express a dedication to decency in the home, church, and community. I appreciate their stance on moral issues, I respect them and praise them for their integrity in the common areas of grace and in the common areas of life, and I love them deeply as people and ministers of great morality.

  However, those philosophers stop short of embracing the true God of heaven and earth because they err on who the real God is by substituting the real God for a false god who is omni-observant instead of

---

[847] Ibid., 248.

the God who is truly omniscient. My teacher Dr. Norman Geisler said these people taught finite godism. He even once said to us that God created us in his image and these teachers returned the favor by creating a god in their own image. These teachers seem to teach something more akin to Deism than Judeo-Christianity. They often hold good morals, good virtues, but they lack stable theology rooted in an eternal God who is the Alpha and Omega (Rev. 22:13).

Many of these people are in fundamentalism, evangelicalism, and many denominations of Christianity. Many of these are very popular teachers, pastors, evangelists, and some of whom are very gifted people in their talents. They do great works of morality and are good people even though they are not following the true God as set forth in the Bible in these areas. In many cases they even present the gospel of grace when giving simple presentations from the Bible itself about the need to repent and come to faith in Christ. At times they even are avid promoters of the basic gospel message of repentance and faith in the Lord Jesus Christ for salvation. For those aspects Evangelicals may show gratitude for the areas those teachers do have right.

Though heretical and in the sin of idolatry, these ministers of morality and even sometimes ministers of the basics of the gospel, are very often great defenders of other Christian truths. Yet with all of the accolades apropos for this group, they still fall short of understanding one of the doctrines of the Christian faith about the Father God and his unconditional love. They err concerning the truth about God the Father and the manner whereby he relates to the universe. A denial that God is fully omniscient from *within himself in eternity and aeviternity* (God knows all without having to learn from earthly history) undermines a fundamental of the Christian faith. How he knows something in eternity and in aeviternity may be debated, but not that he does know all prior to and apart from earthly history, at least not if one wants to retain the confession of a Christian view of God.

The Father God governs his house-hold universe as a Father who has thought up all of history in one single comprehensive decree that is either one moment of eternity or within one successive or sequential creative wave of eternity, however that is measured and/or fathomed. That sovereign moment of creativity in the mind of God is later or subsequently historically applied through sovereign providence in time and history by active and passive works of providence within the created order. Though that may sound difficult to grasp, it seems simpler than one may realize at first. Jesus taught his disciples to pray for the "Kingdom to come, your will be done, on earth as in heaven." The orientation is the eternal Kingdom of God, his sovereign will, coming to earth, not the will of those on earth coming to be done in heaven. The Christian perspective is one of a mind oriented towards the sovereign Kingdom rule of God coming to be the reality on earth. A full omniscience doctrine aligns with that orientation. A mere prescient doctrine or Open Theism doctrine does not.

The order of creation is the fruit of the root of God's omniscience whereby he knows all because he planned all either directly or indirectly, either actively or passively. God knows all (omniscience) and thus he also controls or governs all in some sense or another (through omnipotence) as he as the Father relates to all of his created universe through him being present everywhere (omnipresence). The three "Os" so to speak, omniscience, omnipresence, and omnipotence remain the best sure standard in recognizing the God of the Bible versus fictitious, imaginary, and idolatrous gods created by the mind of man.

In those three historic terms the power and authority of God has been succinctly summarized: *omnipotence*, *omniscience*, and *omnipresence*. Through those three characteristics God rules with absolute sovereignty. Dr. J.R. Graves, an early Southern Baptist Dispensational theologian,[848] correctly realized "Unless this fundamental principle is apprehended by the student of divine truth, all must appear dark and contradictory to him. God's determinate counsel underlies all his acts."[849] Yet from my personal experiential observations, many believers seem to fear peering into this type of theological perspective of our Father God. When people do ignore contemplating this doctrine it does seem to cause people to suffer and to exhibit shallow mental acuity in understanding the sovereign providence of God in history and their lives. They do seem to exhibit confusion, as if a huge question mark hovers over their lives and

---

[848] Dr. Graves was a 19th century Dispensationalist as he lived in the 1800s. His theological writings contributed to a strand of Dispensationalism in Fundamentalism, Evangelicalism, and in particular the Southern Baptist life throughout the 1800s and 1900s, and to some degree even into this present century.

[849] James Robinson Graves, *The Work of Christ in the Covenant of Redemption: Developed in Seven Dispensations* reprint ed. (Texarkana, AR: Bogard Press, 1883), 53.

circumstances. Confidence, conviction, and courage seem lacking when the doctrines of full omniscience, full omnipresence, and full omnipotence do not take center stage in the thinking of a believer.

    Dr. J.L. Dagg, an early Evangelical Baptist theologian, stated that "in their stupidity" some "have worshipped gods of wood and stone, which having eyes, see not, and having ears, hear not; but the deity that the Bible makes known, is a God of knowledge."[850] The Lord "does not acquire knowledge" as we humans do.[851] The "extent of God's knowledge is unlimited. He knows all things; all things possible, and all things actual . . . . All events, past, present, or future, are known to God."[852]

    As to God's omnipresence, Dr. Dagg taught that God's "essence is not divided and diffused" as "the whole deity is everywhere present by his energy and operation."[853] And since God is omniscient and omnipresent he governs in those traits through his omnipotence. "God is able to do whatever he pleases" because "if he absolutely wills or desires to do anything, and fails to accomplish it" then such would mean "God is not omnipotent."[854] Indeed the Bible says this much when it says, "What God desires, that he does" (Job 22:13). Paul stated it in the N.T. this way when he said God "works all things according to the counsel of his will" (Eph. 1:11).

    What ultimate limitation exists in light of such texts other than the mind of God alone who determines what to will or to allow by his own character? Scripture does not seem to give any other ultimate limiting factor. God may indeed allow another element in creation to have a certain way (as he did with Lucifer and Adam), but even so that is still only taking

---

[850] J.L. Dagg, *Manual of Theology* (Harrisonburg VA: Gano Books, 1990), 67. Dagg is not a Dispensational theologian. I use his thoughts here as an example of an Evangelical in general whose thoughts on God's omniscience, omnipresence, and omnipotence align with Dispensational Evangelical theologians.

[851] Ibid., 68.

[852] Ibid., 70.

[853] Ibid., 61.

[854] Ibid., 74, 102. Scriptures used by Dagg to support this position included: Job 22:13; Dan. 4:35; and Eph. 1:11.

place by God's divine prerogative of permission. He is not ultimately thwarted.

All of the acts of God within historical time have some root to the eternal omniscience of God. God does not react to Creation's first move. Creation reacts to God's first move. He is the divine initiator of all history in some sense or another though without being the cause, author, or direct initiator of sin. In such a position, nothing in all of creation can ultimately or finally resist or thwart God from doing as he so well pleases (Dan. 4:35). History is the story of God's providential plan and rule. God has all that is needed within himself to execute and do as he so desires through his power. Nothing can stop, hinder, or alter God's plan and work. Everything God purposes will come to pass just as he has omnisciently known from within his mind from within eternity.

An Exegetical Study on God's Absolute Omniscience From a Literal Hermeneutic: The Bible tells us When God Knows the Future

When theologians encounter the doctrines of God's foreknowledge, omniscience, and the like, such themes naturally cause people to theologize. Though these truths remain extremely difficult to comprehend and harmonize, most likely due to some aspects God has made or declared as a mystery (see Rom. 11:33; Eph. 5:32; Col. 1:27), such matters are still not "off limits to theologize about" in regard to the "the relationships which exist between God's electing sovereignty on one hand and man's freedom and responsibility to choose on the other."[855] That assessment seems true.

Admittedly, the following section is that, an attempt to formulate a logical construct on mostly *when and how* God knows the future. This then, moves the discussion from an "A" level cardinal truth issue, which is that God does know all things past, present, and future without exception and without having to learn it (he knows it in eternity before history occurs in our time), to a "B" level issue of when and how does God indeed know all that he does know in eternity past. In the "theological triage"

---

[855] Paige Patterson, *A Pilgrim Priesthood: An Exposition of the Epistle of First Peter* (Eugene, OR: Wipf and Stock Publishers, 1982), 25.

model of theology this issue would fall within a second or third order issue. So long as a believer or person affirms that the Bible does in fact teach God knows all without exception, then the first order issue, the non-negotiable, has been settled. Open Theism and/or some form of mere prescient foresight models of theology where God has to look to learn the future would fail in the first order truths of Scripture.

But once the full omniscience of God has been affirmed the next aspect of the discussion becomes when and how does God know all without exception. So long as the when and how does not point to a God who learns in order to know (which means for a moment he did not know) then the discussion builds from implications and deductions and systematic efforts. Those extra steps in the theological method allow for more tolerance and latitude in attitude as deference is given to the various models offered by sincere believers. The exegesis forthcoming will not address those who hold to a congruent model of God's knowledge, or a classic Arminian view (God just knows from eternity), or those who affirm it is fully a mystery that we simply cannot fathom. It will, however, continue to show why if the exegesis following is true then it exposes the serious error of the idea that God must look to learn the future.

When examining Peter's preaching as told by Luke, a person can glean much concerning God's overall providence of history. Peter preached calling out the people of God to listen to the message of the cross. Luke recorded this in Acts chapter 2. Jesus Christ's death took place because of God's definite plan, predetermined plan, determined purpose, and foreknowledge (Omniscience) yet the sin was placed directly in the hands of people, not God.

A great way to see this text is by looking at how numerous English translations translate a portion of this text: *"Men of Israel, hear these words: Jesus of Nazareth, a man attested to you by God with mighty works and wonders and signs that God did through him in your midst, as you yourselves know—this Jesus, delivered up according to the definite plan and foreknowledge* (ESV) *predetermined plan and foreknowledge* (NASB) *determined purpose and foreknowledge* (NKJV) *God's set purpose and foreknowledge* (NIV) *God's prearranged plan* (NLT) *by the deliberate will and plan of God* (TNEB) *in accordance with his own plan God had already decided* (GNB) *in the predestined course of God's deliberate purpose* (Moffatt's) *by the fixed purpose and intention of God* (Goodspeed) *by the determinate counsel and foreknowledge* (KJV) *of*

God, you crucified and killed by the hands of lawless men." These texts highlight the extent of God's sovereign rule within the most horrific event in all of human history, the death of the perfect God-Man Jesus Christ at the hands of sinners.

God is not Omni-Observant but Omniscient from Himself

All of those translators, because they are honest with the actual words of the text and do not try and remove God from his director's throne, recognize that this Greek sentence, τοῦτον τῇ ὡρισμένῃ βουλῇ καὶ προγνώσει τοῦ θεοῦ ἔκδοτον διὰ χειρὸς ἀνόμων προσπήξαντες ἀνείλατε, means in some way that God *thought up and/or planned the death of Christ in his own mind before it ever was to be in history.* Nowhere throughout Scripture do you find the Bible saying God *looked to see* or *learn* in history outside of himself and eternity and then planned secondarily in accordance to what he learned from history. All of God's plans (or plan if a singular comprehensive decree with logical succession) for history to come were developed in his mind in eternity or aeviternity past (prior to actual time and space existing). He ordered the affairs of the universe in his eternal omniscience, not from within time and history as we know it.

The Bible could very easily say that God looked to learn had that been what God so desired for it to communicate. There were precise Greek words that could have been used to say such a thing had that been what God had wanted to say. For followers of Christ, who embrace the words of Scripture were divinely chosen by God himself (2 Tim. 3:16), it makes sense that God stated his mind clearly within the pages of Scripture. This is the doctrine we Dispensationalists and Evangelicals in general call the perspicuity of Scripture, or the clarity of Scripture. Christians believe in the verbal plenary inspiration of the Bible and thus because of that affirm that had God wanted to say something different, he would have chosen the precise words to communicate the difference. God desires to communicate his mind to his creation through the written word. Though man penned the words, God chose each and all of the words just as he so desired.

The Bible Does Not Say God Looked into the Future and Saw the Future so He Could then Make His Plan

If God had meant to say he made his plan after or secondarily according to what he learned from history he would or could easily have said it this way: "Men of Israel, hear these words: Jesus of Nazareth, a man attested to you by God with mighty works and wonders and signs that God did through him in your midst, as you yourselves know—this Jesus, in accordance to what God looked (αναβλέψαςto visually look at, observe) and saw (εἶδεν [aorist/past tense version]-which comes from the main Greek word ὁράω which means to see, perceive, to look at such as with the eyes, seeing to the point of perceiving to the point of knowing it) delivered Jesus up to be crucified and killed by the hands of lawless men."

God Did not Choose the Greek Words for Look and See. Luke Used These Words in Other Places but not in Describing God's Foreknowledge

Luke, who wrote the book of Acts, wrote under the inspiration of God. In Acts he chose the exact words to show that God does not look and see the future but that he purposed the future, and because of that he therefore knew the future from within himself. However, in certain places in the Bible we see that Luke did use the terms that mean to look or to see, i.e. to learn from observation from historical surroundings. So this reveals to us that had Luke wanted to communicate this about God, he would have said this in the book of Acts on God's knowledge. However, Luke did not use the words for *look and see* but instead used definite terms that prove God's absolute omniscience. God knows all from *within himself* and *from his own creative or providential act(s)*. The brief study of the terms in Luke's other writing will help us.

Luke 21:1: Jesus Looked and Saw/Observed

In Luke 21:1 God says that "Jesus looked up [αναβλέψας] and saw [εἶδεν] the rich putting their gifts into the offering box and he saw [εἶδεν] a poor widow put in two small copper coins." Jesus we see in this text functioning in his normal human state whereby to know or to figure out what was going on around him he used his normal human faculties to observe and see the events around him by looking at the events in time.

Luke 17:14: Jesus Responds After Looking and Seeing Their Actions

Luke 17:14 says: "And when he [Jesus] saw (ἰδὼν) them he said to them, 'Go and show yourselves to the priests.' And as they went they were cleansed." Here again we can glean that Jesus responded, or made his choice or directive after he saw, perceived, looked and learned from his historical surroundings. The Greek word here is again precise in that it shows a human action or a response to what has been observed, learned, or seen.

What Then Does the Difference Between the Words Look and See and Foreknow Mean?

There is a difference between know/ginosko (γινώσκει πάντα knows all-present tense; see 1 John 3:20) and foreknow/pro-ginosei (προγνώσει or προώρισεν to know before the time because of a prior [πρό=a prefix to the word] inner determination of omniscience for that to be, either passively or actively; see Acts 2:23 & 1 Peter 1:2) from the words look (αναβλέψας) and see/observe (εἶδεν). God does know everything in the present and he also foreknows everything from eternity. However, he foreknows from eternity as God the Father because he thought up (created from his own mind) all of time and history in one single thought (or wave of thoughts) in eternity. He did so without looking into any form of time and history to see or observe.

Omniscience means that in some way or another God thought up in eternity within himself the history of the universe. It does not mean that God observed, looked into history so as to learn, or saw what would be and then made his decisions and plans based upon that. Such a thought is the human transplanting the way he learns and sees things onto God the Father. An infinite God knows because he knows himself and all that his created beings designed by him will certainly do or not do in relation to the providential circumstances they shall exist in when actually living in earthly time and space. God perfectly knows himself and what his providence will accomplish. He looks to himself, not to man, and from his own knowledge he fashions history through active or permissive providence.

God does see and watch all things presently. Genesis 1:31 and 6:5 teaches us this. Just like a director will see and watch his own play, drama, or production, God as the Father presently sees and watches his own story (history). But God does not see and watch to know or learn because God is omniscient before history ever took place or before he ever saw it. God thought out the universe by his own will and mind. He thought up (the omni/infinite aspect of God) every single moment of time (knowledge that would come to fruition in time and space). To say anything less is an improper view of the Tri-unity of God and how he knows himself and his providential acts.

A Biblical Diagram of God's Mind/Knowledge in Contrast to a False View of God's Mind/Knowledge from the Open Theist and Mere Foresight View

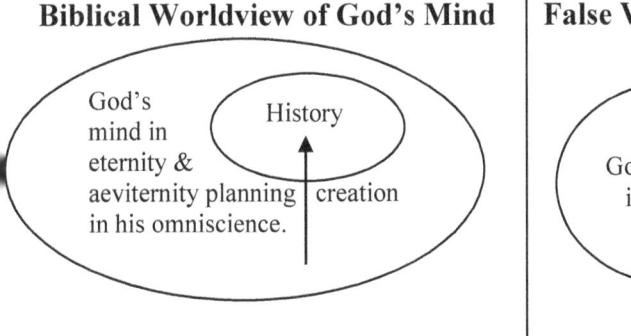

Biblical Worldview of God's Mind	False Worldview of God's Mind
God's mind in eternity & aeviternity planning creation in his omniscience. / History	God's mind in eternity — Looks To See → History in time / Learns/Foresees/Guesses
See Acts 17:28=History is inside of God's Mind	

This diagram captures the biblical teaching. God does not look, observe, learn, or grow in what he understands about the future. God foreknows, and the word foreknows means that he thinks up all or is aware of what he will providentially accomplish or allow and this reality occurs in his mind without reference to any effort on his part to learn, see, or observe anything outside of himself and outside of eternity. History does not occur independently of God. History exists in some way or another within the mind of God. God is responsible and takes responsibility for his own knowledge. Nothing outside of God determines or influences him in what he knows. He knows because he thinks up (creative order) his knowledge or understands his creation and providence from within himself in eternity past.

He plans and understands his own knowledge, he determines his own knowledge because he knows himself perfectly, he purposes his own knowledge, he decrees from his own knowledge, he sets in place his own knowledge, he understands his own actions of providence to come in the earthly historical future before there is a time and history in motion by the human perspective. Once that was set in his mind, he governed the universe as the Father of the house-hold universe that he providentially created to make sure that every detail that he has determined and foreknown in his mind comes to play inside of time and history. Every molecule and every second of history moves according to the precise, perfect, and predetermined plan of God's mind, yet he does so without ever violating his holiness or ever condoning or agreeing or participating in any sin or unholy thought, attitude, or act.

Nothing moves in God's universe without his omniscient providential oversight. God's omniscience and providence negates any idea of random forces or random chances ruling over history. In fact, chance has sometimes been redefined into an actual element instead of a mere formal mathematical abstraction. God, however, rules over his universe in providence and he does this too without ever violating mankind who is made in his image with a will and mind capable of making decisions.

Addressing the issue of chance briefly, it needs to be said that this term has caused a lot of confusion in the modern era because of new ideas assigned to that term. The word chance, defined herein as "a formal word with no material content . . . a pure abstraction,"[856] does not exist as a power or entity in God's universe. Though mathematical possibilities exist (the abstract concept of chance), that does not make it an actual element with power to cause or influence. Dr. R.C. Sproul rightly says, "Chance is not an entity. It is not a thing that has power to affect other things. It is no

---

[856] R.C. Sproul, *Not a Chance: The Myth of Chance in Modern Science and Cosmology* (Grand Rapids, MI: Baker Books, 1994), 5.

thing. To be more precise, it is nothing. Nothing cannot do something. Nothing is not. It has no 'isness.' Chance has no 'isness.'"[857]

If chance is a mere abstraction (not an element) without a power that causes or influences something else, then to say chance determines something is to give it causative power free from any other element acting upon it. It redefines chance into an actuality or into some element. If defined in that way chance is defined as a causative element totally independent from God or any other law of the universe. In such a case God and chance "cannot coexist."[858] The "two are mutually exclusive."[859]

A Proposed Dispensational Synthesis of God's Infallible Omniscience & Foreknowledge with Man's Responsibility

Theologians of all shades in Evangelicalism have wrestled with how to harmonize a view of God's omnipotence, omniscience, and infallible foreknowledge with man's will and responsibility. Theologians are not alone either. The best and most astute philosophers of history have wrestled with this tough subject. It has created general controversy among both theologians and philosophers for ages.[860] But the debate has even had those within the hard sciences mystified. Dr. Erwin Schrodinger, a physicist, sees the tension on this in the theological realm comparable to the free will of man issue in the laws of nature.[861] The universal law of cause and effect in science is like the spiritual laws of God's omniscience and omnipotence. This subject, therefore according to the physicist Schrodinger, leaves us "with a deep mystery into which we cannot penetrate."[862]

---

[857] Ibid., 6.

[858] Ibid., 3.

[859] Ibid.

[860] Mortimer J. Adler, *The Idea of Freedom*, Vol. 2 (Garden City, NY: Doubleday & Company, 1961), 464-487.

[861] Ibid., 473.

[862] Erwin Schrodinger, *Science and Humanism* (Cambridge, United Kingdom: Cambridge University Press, 1951), 59-60.

Dispensationalism joins in that discussion and debate with similar determinations. Dispensationalists are historically and in many cases presently more along the Reformed/Calvinistic stream of thought. Yet Dispensationalism does not deny the apparent tensions in these twin truths of God's sovereignty and man's responsibility. As Dr. Mortimer J. Adler properly noted of the finest minds in world history, "some accept the apparent irreconcilability of man's free choice with God's omniscience and omnipotence as a mystery beyond human comprehension."[863]

In fact, numerous Dispensationalists seem to affirm with tenacity God's sovereignty in salvation while specifically asserting that even after a thorough examination of all data on the subject we must recognize some mystery to the subject. They often sing in concert with philosopher Rene Descartes who said, "how the freedom of the will may be reconciled with Divine pre-ordination" remains a mystery and not fully answerable in our present finite minds.[864]

Indeed, there appears to be some mystery to how God's sovereignty (omniscience and omnipotence) works in concurrence or in a "compatibilist" manner within human freedom, or even within a liberty view of freedom. This debate of God's will and man's will has been a hot topic throughout most all periods of Christendom. The position herein is in contrast to some versions of "simple indeterminism" and "libertarian" human freedom,[865] or what I call hard libertarianism, which seems to deny an abundant amount of biblical data to the contrary.

Yet it is also in contrast to hard determinism and hard compatibilism which also seems to run into problems biblically, especially when viewed from the angle that all things, including sin, are caused by the Lord. Supralapsarian forms of determinism appear to step outside the boundaries of orthodoxy and impugn the good nature of God. The manner in which God determines all matters remains a major issue that if not

---

[863] Mortimer J. Adler, *The Idea of Freedom*, Vol. 2 (Garden City, NY: Doubleday & Company, 1961), 466.

[864] Rene Descartes, *Philosophical Works of Descartes*, Vol. 1, editor and translator Haldane and Ross (Cambridge, United Kingdom: Cambridge University Press, 1931-1934), 234-235.

[865] Norman Geisler and Paul D. Feinberg, *Introduction to Philosophy: A Christian Perspective* (Grand Rapids, MI: Baker Books, 1980), 199-205.

correctly handled can tarnish the holiness of the Lord. Orthodoxy affirms God actively ordains some realities and passively ordains some realities. These distinctions remain essential. God allowing sin by determining to allow created beings who exercise liberty to create sin remains a very different worldview than the view that God actively decrees and causes through providence original sin.

When speaking of salvation the work of the Lord leads a sinner to such a place under drawing grace that the person can rest in faith and experience the eternal grace of Christ for eternal redemption. Though a person *can* and *sometimes does* choose otherwise or against one's strongest set of desires (liberty of the will, soft libertarianism; Adam chose against God in Eden with a good inward nature), when under the operation of the efficacious grace of the LORD the person designed and called in grace *will not* fully, finally, and invariably choose otherwise if the efficacious work of the Lord in his pursuit through his established means remains upon that person. I have sometimes considered the idea of us using the term combinationalism to merge together the two aspects of compatibilism and libertarianism. But, for now we will skip the conversation on what term should we use or create to best describe this.

However, keep in mind too, the Lord may choose to allow one to escape and miss the efficacious elective work of grace and condemn oneself, often through the neglect of his people failing to obey the Great Commission that leaves blood on their hands (see Ezekiel 3:18; Acts 20:26). Believers can commit something in the spirit world that resembles the legal world where we speak of being an accessory to a crime. When a person commits a crime of "accessory" it often means they share guilt in the principle crime. When believers fail to witness and carry out their assigned tasks for the Great Commission the Lord may allow this to serve as the means to someone being turned over to sin and not elected unto conversion.

By aiding a sinner by a failure to witness, pray, serve, live righteously, etc., the saint aids the lost sinner in establishing oneself as a non-elect person by the refusal of the levels of grace present around the sinner. Adding to the definition above, a generic definition of this libertarian type of freedom is important to state. Mortimer Adler's definition is one of the best. This type of freedom is defined as the following: "a man is free who has in himself the ability or power to make what he does his own action and what he achieves his own property."[866]

Yet even in such a position of freedom, with due recognition of extensive corruption due to man's depravity, such a position still leaves room for the grace of the Lord that overcomes the person's sin to such a degree of primacy that such persons "find the drawing irresistible."[867] Though humanity has the resources and liberty to freely obey the law and/or embrace Christ they never would unless the grace of the Lord overcomes their sin in such a way they succumb to the Savior's drawing power of love in grace. Acts 16:14 speaks of this. The Lord opened Lydia's heart and she then responded. Her response happened because of a prior work of grace that was sufficient and efficient for her to respond in faith.

An illustration may help in this matter. It is like when a man pursues a woman properly and by his efforts he creates in her such an overwhelming desire that she freely consents to his advances and succumbs to his love and affection. Though the woman chooses to concur with the man she does so while under the intoxicating allurement of love and passion. Her surrender is natural, freely given, and yet no less compelling inwardly to such a degree she feels as if she were drawn to the man with an uncontrollable wave of emotion and reason that overcame her.

Though not a perfect illustration, this is a very rudimentary analogy. Just as a man by his love and grace pursues a woman and by that love draws the woman to himself, so too Christ draws his chosen bride to himself in a similar manner of love and grace. His efficacious work operates on and in a person in such a way that person is overwhelmed with an inward pleasure and sense of love for Christ that the person succumbs to the drawing love of Christ and naturally concurs with Christ claiming him as Lord and Savior. Though both the woman experiencing the intoxicating allurement from a man winning her over and the person with Christ that he pursues and wins over *could* say no (they have a will, a

---

[866] Mortimer J. Adler, *The Idea of Freedom* (Garden City NY: Doubleday & Company, 1961), 2:35.

[867] Kenneth Keathley, *Salvation and Sovereignty: A Molinist Approach* (Nashville TN: B&H Publishing, 2010), 107.

mind, and the faculty of knowing the other option exists) neither person in such a scenario *will* say no. Though other options exist, such a person in these conditions will concur and gladly receive the love they inwardly experience. They could choose otherwise to their desires (people are more than their collective sum of desires). But being able to do so and actually doing so are not the same.

Yet, too, the man pursuing the woman and Christ pursuing the lost sinner may choose to stop and let that person reject and exit the sphere of pursuit. A man may after pursuing a woman and experiencing her rejections may choose to halt efforts. Likewise, Christ can after pursuing a sinner at some point halt and let that sinner have his or her own way leading to damnation. The one pursuing may justly cease pursuit once the person crosses a line that justifies letting that one walk away.

In this infallible sense what God knows will occur shall happen in one sense of certainty because of "causal primacy."[868] This efficacious work of God upon someone is not from an unjustified external or internal coercion. Nor is the move of God upon someone in such a way or manner that it robs man of "causal initiative on the plane of finite or natural causes, even though it is dependent for its being and operation on the finite causal power of God, which extends to everything that is or happens."[869]

Rather, the inward work of grace with the outward graces moves upon the elect (the one who can be righteously moved to believe and has been chosen to come to faith) in such a way they naturally and freely concur with the compelling love that captures them. God, who made their will and mind, has the right to interact inwardly with them in such a way that they will surrender to his will. Though they have a will their will is no match for the grace of Christ that is radically intoxicating to the chosen ones who experience this level of drawing that creates in them an

---

[868] Mortimer J. Adler, *The Idea of Freedom* (Garden City NY: Doubleday & Company, 1961), 2:228.

[869] Ibid. Adler notes that one key to this discussion is an understanding of efficient causes, formal causes, and final causes. Additionally, he categorizes the different types of freedoms: (1) circumstantial freedom of self-realization; (2) an acquired freedom of self-perfection; (3) a natural freedom of self-determination; (4) political liberty, a special variant of circumstantial self-realization; and (5) collective freedom, a special variant of acquired self-perception (p. 4-50).

insatiable desire for Christ Jesus. They do not put forth any effort to gain Christ. Instead, they experience Christ and in that experience they quench their thirst and, unlike the ones who defiantly refuse and who by their refusal of graces establish themselves as the non-elect, they willingly remain in the gracious drawing graces of the Lord and relax by faith in the graces of their beloved Savior for all of earthly history and eternity.

However, the ones who the Lord has allowed to establish themselves as the non-elect, though convicted and drawn to a status of awareness and life, do as did Adam (who had awareness and life) who before and in the presence of God opted out of his gracious position. Those non-elect (the ones the Lord justifiably allows to walk away after initial pursuit) will invariably with ultimate finality at some point totally choose their own way that leads to eternal damnation. Though they have the resources to choose Christ, are offered Christ, and even experience the grace of Christ, they mature out their own condemnation (see Matt. 13:18-21).

Dr. Kenneth Keathley's illustration of an ambulatory model is helpful here. Consider a person who wrecks and is on the side of the road from a catastrophic car crash. The medics in the ambulance find the person bleeding and without any respiration. The medics give initial care by placing the person in an ambulance. Then while inside the ambulance the person experiences medical grace, and yet at some point after resuscitation the person refuses this grace and exits the presence of grace which ultimately seals the person's own demise and doom.[870]

Now consider this scenario. A person who is found unresponsive on the side of the road from a severe car wreck may be picked up by an ambulance and driven to the hospital for emergency surgery. If in route to the hospital the person awakes from initial care, and yet does "nothing" then that person is "delivered to the hospital" and rescued.[871] The rescued one remains in the medical graces and experiences full healing.

But if along the way a person awakes and makes a "demand to be let out" the medical staff "will comply" while expressing "regret," even

---

[870] Kenneth Keathley, *Salvation and Sovereignty: A Molinist Approach* (Nashville, TN: B&H Publishing, 2010), 104.

[871] Ibid.

giving "warnings" as to the danger of getting out of the ambulance.[872] But these people have the permission to exit and when they do they "incur the blame for refusing the services of the ambulance."[873]

So it is with God who rescues the elect, who do nothing and experience eternal redemption, whereas in his effort with others who refuse grace they at some point choose to exit the spiritual ambulance of grace in order to choose their own way, even in spite of all of the pleadings and warnings not to do so. These who refuse and who the Lord grants the freedom to such refusal by letting the one do so through an act of justice, such ones experience justice and establish themselves as the non-elect as the Lord lets them go, passively allowing them to condemn themselves. This is passive reprobation.

Why do these people choose to reject God's grace and die in their sins? That too is a mystery in this subject, a mystery of *their minds*, not God's mind in this case. Their love for themselves and their own desires for self-justification remains a mystery. "The evil of unbelief remains a mystery, but" in this aspect the mystery is "with the unbeliever" and not with "God."[874]

One key to this is the understanding of *perspective*. This point goes back to something Dr. W.A. Criswell taught. As a Dispensationalist, he taught that we can only see one perspective at a time in this subject, not both perspectives at the same time. From the infinite perspective all things are known in God's ordered mind and thus established with certainty in one way or the other (direct or indirect causes; active causation or passive causation; efficient causes, formal causes, yet not final causes). From the finite perspective the experiential decision is unknown, unpredictable with absolute certainty, and chronologically developing. Man may have his nature altered and drawn in another direction while still in liberty willing to a certain position that is in agreement with the redirected nature (compatibility with new desires and nature). This means man is free but not autonomous. God can be sovereign and man can be free without a

---

[872] Ibid.

[873] Ibid.

[874] Ibid., 106.

contradiction because that is an issue of mere primacy.[875] These are two lines of mysterious reality; both are true but to the human perspective in tension.

The question is not really one of an "either or" but one of how it is a "both and." There is a way, it seems, that both theories of the will harmonize once we move beyond the question of does a human act in both ways (compatible views and libertarian views) and move to the issue of primacy of the will, i.e., can God work in and through a person's mind to accomplish something through that person (making his nature compatible with his providence) while still granting a degree of libertarian freedom.

One will has to have primacy while still not violating the other will in the equation since man is created in the image of God with rational thought processing capabilities, albeit terribly debilitated and corrupted thoroughly by sin from the fall (total depravity). In this case God's will has primacy over man's will (because God created it), and consequently God is in a way able to govern man's will (utilizing his wisdom and instrumental means of his people in that process too) while still doing so without violating man's will and freedom or responsibility.

It is true that the one who is elected will certainly, fully, and finally freely act or choose in accordance with the inward nature (John 3:3-8; Acts 16:14) if the degree of grace applied to someone tilts the scales more so for the Lord over and against the power of sin in that one's heart and mind. That level of grace, applied through the Lord and the means unto that end, captures a soul and delivers it from sin. God and his people carrying forth the task of evangelism, education, and edification act as the source and sequences to God's elective choice of those who will come, and the ones chosen did nothing to awaken themselves, position themselves, or merit for themselves that overcoming grace that the Spirit uses in God's elective purposes through sanctification unto obedience (1 Peter 1:2).

In other words, election is conditioned on what God does but unconditional on what lost man does.[876] A lost person makes no

---

[875] R.C. Sproul, *The Invisible Hand: Do All Things Really Work for Good?* (Phillipsburg, NJ: P&R Publishing, 2003), 81.

[876] I have found E.Y. Mullins explanation on this somewhat helpful, though rudimentary. His view of a sequenced unconditional election has not been developed very well in the Evangelical tradition, if at all. Some, like Leighton Flowers, deny that Mullins held to a

contribution to his or her own election unto eternal salvation. But one who remains lost forever did so by contributing to his or her removal from grace and the fruit of that rejection and removal yields damnation by rejecting the Lord's elective gracious efforts. God reserves the right to withdraw his pursuit and to allow one to choose his or her own damnation, i.e., to remove oneself from a current level of sustaining grace in Jesus (John 1:9; Col. 1:17). A life of full and final resistance to the Lord leads to one being "erased from the book of life."[877]

In the case of those who have not experienced the completed drawing and regeneration of the Lord it is not that these lost people lack the resources to choose Christ or obey his laws. They could choose to obey God's law (or even man's law code) and/or call on Christ as Lord and Savior (as they have a mind and a will), but they *will never will to do so apart from the efficacious grace of the LORD* (Rom. 3:10-18; 1 Cor. 2:14; 2 Cor. 4:4).[878] The willingness, a necessary component to the act

---

sequenced view of eternal election view. Also, Dr. Adam Harwood of New Orleans Baptist Seminary wrongly places Mullins in the view of conditional election. Mullins rejected conditional election. He taught a form of unconditional election. The evidence and scholarship reviewing Mullins disagrees with Flowers and Harwood. Dr. Paige Patterson, Dr. Arnold Fruchtenbaum, Dr. Chris Cone, Dr. Al Mohler, and I all think that Mullins held to a type of unconditional sequenced election. One can read of his view on this in his work *"The Christian Religion in Its Doctrinal Expression"* (p. 347). See also Al Mohler's explanation of this about Mullins' view in *"E.Y. Mullins: The Axioms of Religion"* (compiled by R. Albert Mohler, eds. Timothy and Denise George, p.14).This type of view Mullins had seems to align with how the Calvinist C.H. Spurgeon saw election when he said, "Lord, call out your elect, and then elect some more" (Lewis Drummond, "Charles Haddon Spurgeon," in *Theologians of the Baptist Tradition*, eds. Timothy George and David S. Dockery, p. 122).

[877] Robert L. Thomas, *Revelation 1-7: An Exegetical Commentary*, ed. Kenneth Barker (Chicago, IL: Moody Press, 1992), 263.

[878] Mal Couch's manuscript, *An Essential Doctrinal Statement for Restoring Biblical Integrity in the Local Church*, handles these tensions well. Man is not free in an absolute sense because of sin. As Mal said, "in this sinfulness, no man seeks God of himself." He is "certainly not free" due to the corruption of sin, though Scripture "often speaks of his responsibility" (p. 41). Pure or original freedom was lost in the Garden of Eden when Adam and Eve stood in a sinless condition. When describing the effectual grace and calling by the Spirit Mal uses both terms "would" and "could" to cover this matter. He says, "We know for certain, because no one seeks God on his own, that God must draw individuals to Christ by the Holy Spirit. No one would or could come to Jesus without

being done free from coercion, does not ever exist in someone who rejects fully and finally Christ and his grace. A person who affirms a compatible view of man's will does not have to deny that "God has granted at least some type of libertarian choice to the moral agents he created."[879] Yet at the same time it is certainly biblical to also believe that "everything" that occurs happens "by God's will or by his permission."[880]

As Dr. Couch stated of that issue, "Nothing has or ever will happen that is not included under the umbrella of this all inclusive decree."[881] He adds further, "the Bible proclaims the God of Scripture as an absolute Monarch who has planned all things and is now executing all things."[882] Dr. Kenneth Keathley, a Calvinistic Molinist Dispensationalist, and Dr. Couch, a Calvinistic Dispensationalist, both explain further, in saying God "directly wills and accomplishes all that is good by his grace but permissively allows the evil that occurs"[883] even though such "sin is within the scope of [God's] all inclusive decree."[884] "Sin did not sneak up

---

this sovereign calling. This is called efficacious grace and it absolutely brings one to the Lord" (p. 43, italics mine). Too, Mal shows humility with these truths as he said this work is a "mysterious grace" (p. 43) and that God's sovereign decree in an "unexplainable way" included "sin" in the "all inclusive Decree." He added, "while no theologian fully understands, we know sin did not 'sneak up on God,'" yet even so God is still "not the author of sin" even though "sin is within the scope of his all inclusive Decree" (p. 21). Learning to walk these divine tensions in Scripture requires maturity and skill. Mal exemplified that.

[879] Kenneth Keathley, *Salvation and Sovereignty: A Molinist Approach* (Nashville TN: B&H Publishing, 2010), 149.

[880] Ibid., 40.

[881] Mal Couch, *An Essential Doctrinal Statement for Restoring Biblical Integrity in the Local Church*, edited by ArlynKantz (Fort Worth, TX: Tyndale Theological Seminary, No date of publication), 21.

[882] Mal Couch, *The Sovereignty of God* (Clifton, TX: Scofield Ministries, 2013), 1.

[883] Kenneth Keathley, *Salvation and Sovereignty: A Molinist Approach* (Nashville, TN: B&H Publishing, 2010), 40.

[884] Mal Couch, *An Essential Doctrinal Statement for Restoring Biblical Integrity in the Local Church*, edited by Arlyn Kantz (Fort Worth, TX, Tyndale Theological Seminary, No date of publication), 21.

on God. He was not caught off guard or helpless."[885] God "is sovereign and his control is meticulous."[886] Yet God "is not the author, origin, or cause of sin."[887] Consequently, in light of God's sovereignty and man's sinfulness "man is incapable of contributing to his salvation or of even desiring to be saved" and so due to that "individual election is unconditional."[888] Yet too, "God genuinely desires for the salvation of all humanity."[889]

These truths are in tension but not in contradiction. In some ways this truth has a mysterious depth to it. Dr. Couch properly noted, "No one on earth can explain how God can be sovereign and yet man be responsible but this is what the Bible clearly teaches from Genesis to Revelation."[890] But, of course, we do our best to explain the essential elements of this truth for God's glory while painfully acknowledging our own inadequacies in thought and speech to fully communicate something so infinite and divine. Dispensationalist Dr. Paige Patterson urges biblical interpreters in light of this "apparent paradox" of Scripture and the "failure of 2,000 years of theological reflection to crack the mysteries of God's electing providence" such ought to lead believers to a position of "humility rather than hubris."[891] As he says more extensively,

> The doctrine of election in Holy Scripture is referenced repeatedly in one way or another. That God acted to choose some to salvation is beyond dispute for anyone who takes the Scriptures to be the

---

[885] Ibid.

[886] Kenneth Keathley, *Salvation and Sovereignty: A Molinist Approach* (Nashville, TN: B&H Publishing, 2010), 7.

[887] Ibid.

[888] Ibid.

[889] Ibid.

[890] Mal Couch, *The Sovereignty of God* (Clifton, TX: Scofield Ministries, 2013), 1. Couch preferred the term "responsibility" rather than "free will" (see p. 11).

[891] Paige Patterson, "Eight Theses On Election," *SBC Today*, last modified 2010, accessed July 23, 2015, http://sbctoday.com/tuesday-post/.

infallible Word of God. However, exactly what this means and how it is to be understood in view of the responsibility assigned to humans to respond to God in the ways mandated in Scripture is beyond present human comprehension . . . . All efforts to explain this achieve only limited success.[892]

Dispensationalists like Patterson, who does not classify himself as a Calvinist, and Criswell, who is admittedly more Calvinistic than Patterson, do not stand alone. They along with Covenant Calvinists recognize that within this doctrine some mystery remains.

Covenant Calvinists recognize there is a mystery to this doctrine as well. For example, Calvinist Dr. R.C. Sproul admits that this truth reveals numerous "mysteries"[893] though without contradiction. When examining these twin truths, he says this mystery is "inescapable."[894] Yet he distinguishes between mystery and contradiction. There can be no contradictions in God's mind or in Scripture if we claim Scripture is fully inspired and inerrant. God does not author contradictory truths. Sproul reminds us that to claim contradictory truths is "fatal to Christianity. If real contradictions can be resolved in the mind of God, then it would mean that anything God has ever spoken or revealed is now suspect."[895] The faith of Christianity cannot exist if two or more truths can contradict with each other. "If God can hold to contradictions, then perhaps in his mind there is no difference between Christ and Antichrist, between obedience and disobedience, between good and evil."[896]

Another Covenant Calvinist, Dr. J.I. Packer, concurs that this issue reveals a mystery. Of God's sovereignty he says, "the assertion of God's absolute sovereignty in creation, providence, and grace *is basic to biblical*

---

[892] Paige Patterson, *The New American Commentary: Revelation*, Vol. 39 (Nashville, TN: B&H Publishing, 2012), 324.

[893] R.C. Sproul, *The Invisible Hand: Do All Things Really Work for Good?* (Philipsburg, NJ: P&R Publishing, 2003), 85.

[894] Ibid., 83.

[895] Ibid., 84.

[896] Ibid.

belief and biblical praise."[897] Take note to his assertion of it being a basic truth. To deny that God is omnipotent equals a serious error. Many desire to ignore this truth of Scripture. But it is a basic reality if one reads Scripture with a careful eye. God's sovereignty permeates the Bible. Yet Packer realizes the sovereignty of God and man's responsibility are a difficult set of truths to mentally comprehend. God being sovereign and man's "free agency confronts us with a mystery."[898] Packer affirms that God's control over our will "is as complete as it is over anything else," but how this is precisely so "we do not know."[899]

These quotes show us that Dispensationalists are not alone in recognizing that some level of mystery exists in these doctrines. This subject is to theology like what neuroscience and neurosurgery is to the medical field. We must humbly recognize our limitations when we gaze upon such magnanimous truths as these. Dr. Norman Geisler[900] describes this matter by saying:

> Classical theists in the tradition of the medieval Fathers—the early Augustine, Anselm, and Aquinas—point out that there is no contradiction involved in claiming that (1) a future free act is determined from the relationship of God's infallible foreknowledge, and yet (2) also free when viewed from the relationship of our free choice (in the sense of the power to do otherwise). Thus, infallible foreknowledge and free choice are not contradictory, for the law of noncontradiction demands that to be

---

[897] J.I. Packer, *Concise Theology: A Guide to Historic Christian Beliefs* (Wheaton, IL: Tyndale House Publishers, 1993), 33. Italics mine.

[898] Ibid., 34.

[899] Ibid.

[900] I earned a PhD degree after this dissertation and it related to Geisler. My 3rd PhD degree was with North-West University, and there I explored Amyraldianism and Dr. Geisler's form of Calvinism. Some, like James White, allege he is an Arminian and that he held a non-Calvinistic view of election. They are wrong. Geisler taught that man does not contribute to his own election. He affirmed a unique Amyraldian model within a Thomas Aquinas paradigm. Yet even so, he embraced both unconditional election and a form of efficacious grace.

contradictory, two propositions must be affirm and deny the same thing at the same time and in the same relationship. . . . This infallible knowledge does not diminish the freedom of the creature, since God knew for sure (i.e., determined) what they would freely do (i.e., by free acts). Consequently, no contradiction is involved with God's complete control of the world in advance; He has absolute certainty of how everything will turn out, including our free choices.[901]

These issues for sure have a huge degree of importance and cannot be disregarded as an unimportant issue. As Dr. Geisler and Dr. Feinberg properly stated: "One of the most important and yet controversial philosophical questions we must face is the issue of free will. Again, it should be emphasized that morality, law, religion, as well as metaphysics, all have a stake in our answer."[902] In fact, as they have also said, this issue is a "theological question more than purely a philosophical one."[903] Believers must be careful because the compatible and libertarian views, if not kept in proper tension to one another, can lead both sides on a dangerous and disastrous trajectory. Extreme positions on either side create deadly theological, philosophical, and even legal and/or political views.

Hard compatibilism and determinism can sometimes lead to the idea that God causes sin, authors sin, or agrees with sin and is ultimately himself unholy (a harsh fatalism or even material determinism; often supralapsarian Bezanism). On the other hand, hard libertarianism and indeterminism can lead to a view that God makes educated guesses, is sometimes wrong, and impotent and unable to accomplish his desired ends

---

[901] Norman Geisler, *Systematic Theology in One Volume* (Minneapolis, MN: Bethany House Publishers, 2011), 685, 687.

[902] Norman Geisler and Paul D. Feinberg, *Introduction to Philosophy: A Christian Perspective* (Grand Rapids, MI: Baker Books, 1980), 193.

[903] Ibid., 205.

(Open Theism, Process theology).[904] Both sides destroy the idea of a biblical God and are the fruits of satanic roots.

Therefore, I urge the reader, and especially upcoming younger theologians, do not be afraid to hold two truths in divine tension. As Dr. Hayne Griffin (one of my undergraduate NGU theology professors) and Dr. Couch taught me, truth is found in the tension at times (as with the Trinity-God is One yet also three persons/members, Christ is fully the God-Man, God wrote the Bible and humans wrote the Bible, God is sovereign and man is responsible, etc.). We need to hold some truths in proper tension to rightly exercise the spirit muscles of believers. Releasing one side of the theological exercise spring can lead to anemic faith-muscles for the believers.

Dispensationalist Dr. W.A. Criswell, who referred to himself as a Calvinist,[905] describes this matter by saying, "it is a mystery we cannot explain."[906] There is, as the legendary and beloved Dispensationalist forefather Criswell said, a "language of heaven" and also a "language of earth."[907] If we keep these truths in distinction we will not "have any trouble"[908] because we cannot see the entire house of God all at the same time.[909] As Criswell said of these two divine truths by quoting Spurgeon, "I cannot make them meet, but you cannot make them cross."[910]

---

[904] Clark H Pinnock, *The Openness Of God* (Downers Grove, Ill: InterVarsity Press, 1994).

[905] Paige Patterson, *"An Interview with W.A. Criswell,"* in *The Church at the Dawn of the 21st Century: Essays in Honor of W.A. Criswell*, edited by Paige Patterson, John Pretlove, and Luis Pantoja Jr. (Dallas, TX: Criswell Publications, 1989), 6.

[906] W.A. Criswell, *"The Doctrine of Predestination,"* in *We Believe*, edited by Paige Patterson and Luis Pantoja Jr. (Dallas, TX: Criswell publications, 1977), 86.

[907] Paige Patterson, *"An Interview with W.A. Criswell,"* in *The Church at the Dawn of the 21st Century: Essays in Honor of W.A. Criswell*, edited by Paige Patterson, John Pretlove, and Luis Pantoja Jr (Dallas, TX: Criswell Publications, 1989), 6.

[908] Ibid.

[909] W.A. Criswell, *"The Doctrine of Predestination,"* in *We Believe*, edited by Paige Patterson and Luis Pantoja Jr. (Dallas, TX: Criswell publications, 1977), 86.

[910] Ibid.

In this case it is like a spring. If we let either side loose, divine absolute sovereignty and providence or man's responsibility and freedom, we lose the tension and thus the truth of God. Think of it like an exercise spring used to build your muscles. If you pull the spring outward by using both arms stretching the spring so as long as you hold to both sides you will build muscle strength. If you let one side go the spring collapses and the exercise is over and the spring is useless to your exercise regimen.

The theological spring in tension is that God is absolutely sovereign and providentially in control over every element of his universe (heavenly language; one side of the house). Man is also free and/or responsible (earthly language; the other side of the house). We must teach both clearly without making it so philosophical that no one can understand it or so one sided that one truth is neglected in contrast to the other.

Chapter 7. Conclusion: Dispensationalism and Covenant Reformed Theology Can Harmonize as a "Hand in a Glove" Union

Many truths acknowledged within Dispensationalism can naturally coalesce with the Reformed doctrinal heritage. These are doctrines that Dispensationalists would naturally affirm, at least those within the more Calvinistic Dispensational stream of thought, when theologians apply the literal methodology in interpretation of Scripture. The historical-grammatical method of biblical interpretation leads a faithful exegete to conclusions that highlight key aspects within both of the main Evangelical systems of theology.

A Final Plea: The Evidence Proves Dispensationalism Offers a Calvinistic and Practical Soteriology

Thus, it is fair to say that when you examine the totality of evidence Dispensationalism is indeed a system that aligns with the absolute sovereignty of God in salvation, even over all. I sincerely encourage and ask that my Reformed Continuity Covenant Calvinist partners in the body of Christ rethink how they portray the Calvinistic stream of Dispensationalists in their communications. Jesus Christ, our precious Lord and Savior who bled and died to save and establish us inside of his body, stated: "blessed are the peacemakers" (Matt. 5:9). He longed and prayed for us to experience peace, unity, and harmony in the faith (John 17:21). We have *some* differences that remain. Both sides acknowledge that. But in regard to the view of the gospel and how the Lord saves, we have a strong and substantive stream of unity that emphasizes the precious and amazing grace of our Lord. We do not need to create unnecessary division when we can unify in our hearts and minds around the greatest essentials.

The Dispensational forefathers who originally systematized and led the movement embraced the absolute sovereignty of God. Furthermore, those forefathers and many of the disciples from them rejected the Arminian, free will, Semi-Pelagian versions of theology that made man's will the emphatic key to the work of redemption. The Continuity Calvinists can rest assured that a substantive stream of

Dispensationalism has and continues to exist that magnifies the sovereign providential grace of the Lord as applied through the solitary covenant of redemption that places every person inside one family of God, the family of the redeemed.

Dispensationalism has been a movement that has made its stand on the literal interpretation of Scripture. As a matter of integrity, it should be requested that those who write about Dispensationalism apply the *literal method of interpretation to the Dispensationalist's writings*. When that is done the evidence is clear. Dispensationalists are normally a group of theologians who embrace a continuity model of redemption that originates in eternity within the mind of God.

Dispensationalists are often a group of theologians that find their theological kin within the Reformation heritage. Those who do not have a general affinity in that stream are not in concert with the overall thrust and emphasis that the forefathers of the Dispensational tradition established in the foundational days. Those who chart a different course have chosen an alternative theological path than the original heritage of Dispensationalism. We remain friendly with them and partner with them for the cause of the gospel, as we ought to do with all believers in the body of Christ who affirm the essentials as found in the ancient and patristic confessions of faith, yet we also recognize the value of this particular stream of Dispensationalism.

But is there more to this than mere substantiation of what Dispensationalism has stood for historically? How does an understanding of a Dispensational soteriology model with an emphasis on the sovereignty of God, while also recognizing man's responsibility, apply within a ministerial context? I would offer to the reader that Dispensationalism, because of its hermeneutic, retains a methodology that allows just enough mystery to this doctrine that unwarranted ends and dangerous conclusions are not drawn. It leaves enough room for some mystery to this to allow the minister to apply either the sovereignty of God to a person when needed or the admonition for human and/or moral responsibility when needed.

Numerous times Dispensational writers or those affiliated within Dispensationalism make it clear that even after all effort has been given to try and harmonize the biblical data on this subject that some mystery remains. Though different terms have been used, and at times with probably nontechnical definitions leaving the reader with a variety of terms that represent a similar if not identical definition, numerous theologians recognize that this doctrine of God's sovereign decree to save the unconditionally loved ones, while also recognizing man's responsibility/freedom, remains some type of mystery and/or paradox.

For example, Dr. H. Leo Eddleman, writing then at the Criswell Center for Biblical Studies, stated, "Christianity is known for its paradoxes and for its scandals. Its paradoxes are those elements of revelational truth with two facets, which seem to contradict each other. Predestination on the part of God and the free will of men appeared to contradict each other. The first church believed in them both (Acts 4:28; John 8:32). We simply cannot understand them, at the human level, but one day we shall see them from heaven's vantage point and understand how it can be true that God predestined and yet he did not take from man his individual freedom."[911]

Others join that chorus as well. Dr. W.A. Criswell, who classified himself as a Calvinist and who affirmed a Dispensational model of theology too, clearly expressed how within this doctrine, even after all our best and most gifted intellectual endeavors to cogently harmonize the biblical data, we are left to the fact God's providence highlights itself to us as a mystery. In following the lead of Dr. John A. Broadus and Dr. E.Y. Mullins, Criswell affirmed this truth remains a mystery. He said examining this truth is

> like looking at a house . . .You can never see more than half of it at a time. I can stand and see two corners, but I cannot see the other two. I can walk around the house and see two sides at a time but two are hidden from me. I cannot see all four sides of the house at the same time. But someone above me could look down on that house and see all four sides at once. So it is with us. We cannot see but alternately one half of the house at a time. But the Creator who presides above us can see all of it at once . . . . the problems of the freedom of man and the sovereignty of God have been problems that philosophers have wrestled with from the beginning of

---

[911] H. Leo Eddleman, "*The Living Word of God*," in *We Believe: Pisteuomen Series*, Vol. 1, eds. Paige Patterson and Luis Pantoja, Jr. (Dallas, TX: Criswell Publications, 1977), 14.

intelligence, but no philosopher yet has ever risen who can reconcile them. It is a mystery into we cannot enter.[912]

Other Dispensationalists of the modern era join that chorus as well. Dr. Mal Couch explicitly affirmed the absolute sovereignty of God yet he too agreed with the likes of Eddleman and Criswell that "No one on earth can explain how God can be sovereign and yet man be responsible but this is what the Bible clearly teaches from Genesis to Revelation."[913] Dr. Tony Evans concurs too that though God elects from eternity past those who come to faith it remains a mystery[914] as to how he precisely does this while not violating man's will. As he says, "God's offer to salvation is valid to all, and yet those who respond do so because they are the elect of God before the foundation of the world was laid."[915]

This extends to also the nonelect. "Those who do not come to Christ are blameworthy because the Bible never says that people are lost because they are nonelect. The lost are lost because they refuse to believe."[916] Dr. Evans recognizes that to our human minds they appear "mutually exclusive," yet he affirms the Bible "teaches both" God's sovereign election of some and the permission of others to condemn themselves by refusing grace.[917] For Evans the Bible teaches these twin truths "in perfect balance."[918]

Dispensationalist Dr. Paige Patterson has reminded those who study this doctrine that it is likely this side of heaven the subject cannot be

---

[912] W.A. Criswell, *"The Doctrine of Predestination,"* in *We Believe: Pisteuomen Series,* Vol. 1, eds. Paige Patterson and Luis Pantoja, Jr. (Dallas, TX: Criswell Publications, 1977), 86.

[913] Mal Couch, *The Sovereignty of God* (Clifton, TX: Scofield Ministries, 2013), 1. Mal preferred the term "responsibility" rather than "free will" (see p. 11).

[914] Tony Evans, *Theology You Can Count On* (Chicago, IL: Moody Press, 2008), 775.

[915] Ibid.

[916] Ibid.

[917] Ibid.

[918] Ibid.

absolutely resolved, and because of that this tension in the two doctrines remains a "paradox."[919] Yet he does not desire for believers only to ponder the mysterious nature of it. He urges believers to move further than the due recognition of the mystery and move to ask how this truth revealed in Scripture can conform people to be more like Christ. He suggests we ask, "why is the doctrine of election given in Scripture?"[920]

He offers several practical truths to help guide a believer when contemplating these ideas of Scripture. (1) The doctrine of election reminds believers that "salvation" is "an act of God from beginning to end, eliminating human works altogether in the pursuit of salvation (see Rom. 8:30)."[921] (2) The doctrine reminds believers that if they are of the elect then it is impossible for the elect to experience "apostasy or falling from salvation. How could one of God's elect fall (see Rom. 8:35)?"[922] (3) This doctrine also helps to remind believers that there is a "providential intervention of God in behalf of his children (see Rom. 8:28)."[923] (4) This doctrine of God's sovereignty also reminds the believer that "God's hand rests upon the nations of the world, guiding history to the climax which God has determined for it (see Rom. 8:21-22)."[924]

Those are wise ministerial truths offered. I would add to that list two more. Two sins often beset believers, pride and procrastination. The Bible has severe warnings in the book of Proverbs on both of those sins. I would suggest that a teacher also use these truths in a proper cultural context of ministry. When a believer or person you minister unto exhibits arrogance, pride, and a spirit focused on self the minister could use the sovereignty of God principles of Scripture to remind that believer that nothing is ever owned by any person in this world as God owns it all and

---

[919] Paige Patterson, *A Pilgrim Priesthood: An Exposition of the Epistle of First Peter* (Eugene, OR: Wipf and Stock Publishers, 1982), 25.

[920] Ibid.

[921] Ibid.

[922] Ibid.

[923] Ibid.

[924] Ibid.

governs it all for his ultimate glory and pleasure. Too, no circumstance arrives in a person's life by chance. What many may think is a random matter of chance, traffic jams and delays, an unpleasant meeting with someone, or whatever occurs in one's day, such events come to the person by some type of divine plan and intent. These events, often frustrating and agitating to a person, can be better handled with confidence, courage, conviction, and cordiality by the person when he or she realizes that God authors directly or indirectly the event as a trial designed to help shape the character of the one experiencing it.

On the other hand, when a believer is complacent, lazy, or abdicating his responsibility the minister could use the admonitions of Scripture in an effort and work as a means to stimulate that believer out of idleness. Sometimes people fall into a fatalistic attitude. They in a sense act as if life controls them and they are unable to contribute, alter, or develop their own place in this world. Such struggles could be mitigated if a believer grasps his purpose in life under the broad umbrella of living for the sole purpose of bringing glory to God daily by loving God and people and the Great Commission. Yet to funnel one's entire life and resources under that banner requires diligence, determination, decisiveness, and deliberateness. Those traits do not occur when someone becomes unbalanced and focused too much on God's sovereignty to the neglect of human responsibility.

Therefore, a wise and mature believer could move beyond the mere debate of this matter and move to real practical scenarios where the minister learns how, when, and to whom to apply which truth found in Scripture. For those who need a solid dose of sovereignty or a dose of responsibility the balanced minister who can rest in the mystery or paradox, while contextually affirming both truths with force in a situational context, will likely edify the believers better than those who emphasize one truth to the neglect of another or remain polarized in the mystery with trepidation and timidity so much that it paralyzes the person from serving a brother or sister in need with a sure Word from God.

However, some may desire to explore this matter further, especially those with a love for philosophy within the theological field. If so, this study may provide a field that a person could glean new insights beyond the historical conclusions offered herein. A trajectory for new study might develop from this point that recognizes Dispensationalism does contain a significant Calvinist stream within it.

Further Options for Exploration: A Calvinistic Molinistic Dispensationalism?

In summary, it would make sense for Dispensationalism to recognize their holy heritage while refusing to remain stagnate or statically committed to a singular soteriology stream. Biblical theology must guide the system; the system must not guide the biblical exegesis. Dispensationalism certainly has developed from the heritage of the Calvinistic or Reformed womb. As Notre Dame history professor Dr. George Marsden has said, the Dispensational movement "had strong Calvinistic ties" as one of its forefathers who led the early systematic expression of it, J.N. Darby, remained an "unrelenting Calvinist."[925] From that primary systematic leader (but certainly not the first Dispensationalist in history) to the broader "prophetic movement in America" Dispensationalism remained a movement of "predominately Calvinists."[926]

However, Dispensationalists have not been so rigid in their expressions of Calvinism to follow only one ideology or strand of Calvinism. Dispensationalism, due to its goal and allegiance to apply the historical-grammatical hermeneutic to every text of scripture from Genesis to Revelation, has been more inclined to make modifications to itself along the theological developmental journey. Two of those modifications in particular ought to receive serious focus by more Dispensationalists.

First, overall Dispensationalists have apparently retained a more faithful allegiance to the atonement texts that allow for some type of universal atonement benefit for all, even beyond the elect. In this way they seem to identify more so with the original founders of the Protestant Reformation as both Luther and Calvin held to some type of universal benefit or provision in the atonement. They certainly identify with a portion of the Synod of Dort participants who affirmed in some sense an unlimited or universal atonement view. Other noted Calvinists have taught this as well. Dr. Charles Hodge, the great Princeton Calvinist, has also taught that the atonement has benefit beyond just the elect. Specifically

---

[925] George M. Marsden, *Fundamentalism and American Culture* (Oxford, NY: Oxford University Press, 2006), 46.

[926] Ibid.

The Calvinism of Dispensationalism

Dr. Hodge stated of the dual and universal benefit of the atonement to all this:

> It does not follow from the assertion of Christ's atonement having a special reference to the elect that it had no reference to the non-elect. Augustinians readily admit that the death of Christ had a relation to man, to the whole human family, which it had not to fallen angels. It is the ground on which salvation is offered to every creature under heaven who hears the gospel . . . . moreover, it secures to the whole race at large, and to all classes of men, innumerable blessings, both providential and religious. It was, of course, designed to produce these effects; and, therefore, he died to secure them. . . . There is a sense, therefore, in which Christ died for all, and there is a sense in which he died for the elect alone.[927]

The Dispensationalist Dr. Paige Patterson once asked one of the most poignant questions on this matter. "What could be any plainer than the teaching of Scripture that Jesus Christ died for all people?"[928] Likewise, the Calvinist Dispensationalist Dr. Lewis Sperry Chafer asked what other words could have God used to say that Christ died for all people other than the words he inspired the authors to use that exist in scripture. If the words all, every man, and whole world were used, what other words did the biblical writers have at their disposal to use if they had wanted to say Christ died for each and every person in the human race? If no other words were available than these terms used why should we not accept those words in their ordinary and plain meaning?

The number of Dispensationalists who embrace a strict limited atonement view has been marginal and a minority among the tradition. But, of course, those do exist and the Covenant Calvinists must recognize that our heritage has housed both forms just as theirs has too. Most Dispensationalists have, however, seemed to think that accurate biblical exegesis requires some sort of atonement benefit to the entire world or even universe. Five point limited atonement Calvinistic Dispensationalists

---

[927] Charles Hodge, *Systematic Theology*, (Grand Rapids MI: Wm. B. Eerdmans Publishing Company, 1995), 2:545-546.

[928] Personal conversation at an evangelism conference in Pickens South Carolina.

have and continue to exist in the movement. These usually agree with the Calvinists like Jonathan Edwards and Charles Hodge that the atonement has a particular benefit to the elect and a common grace benefit to the non-elect, i.e. a dual definite atonement model. Dispensationalism has largely housed both four and five point Calvinists throughout its history. The five point limited atonement teachers, however, have not been the majority as it seems. In short, that means most have thought a literal hermeneutic applied in biblical exegesis prohibits the systematic effort from concluding the death of Christ texts must conform or yield to the logic of the doctrine of selective unconditional election.

Second, and more importantly for this study, Dispensationalists for the most part have been at peace to recognize the apparent paradox within the two streams of biblical evidence on God's sovereignty and man's responsibility. Whereas it seems Covenantal Calvinists sometimes deplore any deviation from their confessional doctrinal codes, Dispensationalism has been more interested in allegiance to or openness to theological development within the confines of the text of Scripture more so than the historical confessions. Interestingly, that spirit seems to this theologian to better align with the first maxim of Reformed theology, sola Scriptura, than the Reformed theologians who seem more reluctant to reconsider the accuracy of their confessions in light of better textual allegiance that forms the system.

So what might a better Calvinistic form of Dispensationalism look like? Though it goes beyond the scope of this study, a closing preview of where this study could properly lead in theological reflection might help set that educational trajectory. One of the fundamental principles for historical and modern Dispensationalism has been allegiance to Scripture as the supreme authority when properly interpreted. Dr. Charles C. Ryrie, a connecting representative to the historical early era (a student of Chafer) and modern era (having died in 2016), argued that a literal hermeneutic constituted one of the most essential foundations for Dispensationalism.[929] How does the application of a literal hermeneutic, a key fundamental for Dispensationalism, promote a systematic soteriology that harmonizes data from the text of Scripture, laws of logic and philosophy, and competing emphases of God's sovereignty and man's responsibility?

---

[929] Charles C. Ryrie, *Dispensationalism* (Chicago, IL: Moody Press, 1995), 40-41.

Though Dispensationalists may rightly rest in a paradox of Scripture (not a contradiction; sometimes also called a mystery), and in doing so properly emphasize the practical aspects as noted above, some Dispensationalists, such as those more philosophically and systematically oriented, may want to dive deeper into the underlying philosophical presuppositions and ideas that form the heart of God's omniscience and omnipotence in relation to his decree in history with mankind.

The question of *how does God form his own knowledge from within himself* is the fundamental key to this debate. More work could be done in study of the lapsarian decrees to offer a more holistic and healthy formulation. A fuller delineation of the sublapsarian decree model (a popular model among Dispensationalists) that recognizes both eternity as well as aeviternity could bring great clarity to the doctrine of soteriology.

Such examinations must, however, avoid process theology, modern open theism theology, as well as avoid any articulation that presents God as the author and cause of sin and consequently violating the doctrine of God's holiness and justice. The theological boundaries for heresy are clear. Yet there is room within those boundaries to formulate more precise formulations of God's omniscience.

One modern Dispensationalist has indeed attempted to forge this new route. Dr. Kenneth Keathley, a professor of Southeastern Baptist Theological Seminary, has initiated a newer proposal. As a Dispensational theologian he asserts a modern Molinist version of how God's omniscience works in history. He seems to retain more of the original views of Luis de Molina. Keathley says, he affirms the doctrines of total depravity, unconditional election, and perseverance of the saints.[930] Additionally, he affirms a type of effectual or overcoming grace view of God's omnipotence.[931] He adheres to this model within a Molinist paradigm as he affirms also God's "natural knowledge, middle knowledge, and free knowledge."[932]

---

[930] Kenneth Keathley, *Salvation and Sovereignty: A Molinist Approach* (Nashville TN: B&H Publishing, 2010), 1, 7.

[931] Ibid., 126-137.

[932] Ibid., 16, 17-41.

Those proposals, from a Dispensationalist, refer back to the ideas popularized by Anabaptist theologian Balthasar Hubmaier (1480-1528), philosopher Pedro da Fonseca (1528-1599), and the fuller systematic developer Luis de Molina (1535-1600).[933] Is it possible for Dispensationalists, especially Calvinistic Dispensationalists, to construct the doctrine of *how God thinks out history from within himself* (a position articulated in brevity earlier in this dissertation) within an unconditional election model derived at through an emphasis foremost on omniscience similar to how Molina espoused the doctrine?

How might a view of aeviternity, the period of time prior to earthly history yet not eternity, impact one's view of how God elects in an unconditional manner? These are questions that need more attention in a modern soteriology study. Could a sequenced knowledge model of God in aeviternity provide a more holistic model for a soteriology that avoids concerns that arise in Higher Calvinistic models and still avoid the concerns some have with Molinism, Arminianism, & Open Theism? Could a combination of a layered or sequenced knowledge model (Molina's view) within an aeviternity model resolve the issues that have vexed the minds of various theologians on this matter?

Dispensationalist and Molinist Dr. Kenneth Keathley and Anabaptist and Molinist scholar Dr. Kirk MacGregor both believe the most faithful interpretation of Molinist views represent a more Calvinistic version of soteriology. For example Dr. MacGregor asserts Molina rejected a foresight and/or conditional corporate election[934] and instead embraced a personal, pre-temporal, and unconditional election of *particular persons* as specifically spelled out in Scripture like Romans 9.[935] As he says, "for Molina" this "cause and ground of any person's election or reprobation is God's sovereign will."[936] Such data leads MacGregor to conclude that Molina interpreted Romans 9 "as teaching

---

[933] Kirk R. MacGregor, *A Molinist-Anabaptist Systematic Theology* (Lanham, MD: University Press, 2007), 63.

[934] Ibid., 66.

[935] Ibid., 67.

[936] Ibid.

both individual predestination . . . and unconditional election, as God elects purely according to his pleasure without regard to any foreseen faith or merits and reprobates without regard to foreseen unbelief or sins."[937]

Furthermore, as MacGregor teaches, when one embraces the "grammatico-historical" hermeneutic that methodology argues strongly against Arminian "exegesis."[938] Dispensationalists because of their emphasis on the historical-grammatical hermeneutic could potentially find a theological and philosophical synthetic home in a Calvinistic Molinist theological paradigm that even acknowledges the period of aeviternity. These ideas could be established and built principally upon the literal hermeneutic. As MacGregor says, "Molina vehemently denies that *scientia media* is in any way dependent on the future existence of free persons, but affirms that it stems entirely from the divine nature."[939] This knowledge is grounded not in the persons but instead in "God's cognitive ability to perfectly comprehend his own aptitude and power."[940] In conclusion, MacGregor offers a plausible place for Dispensationalists to work to harmonize their conclusions of the literal hermeneutic with philosophical conclusions sustainable to the laws of logic. He says:

> Unlike Arminius, Molina both interpreted Scripture (especially Romans 9) as teaching and constructed a theological system emphasizing the complete sovereignty of God to consign each individual he creates to salvation or damnation, irrespective of that person's merits or demerits in any conceivable set of circumstances but depending solely upon his good pleasure. Hence Molina concurred with Calvin on the sovereignty of God and his unconditional election of individuals. However, unlike Calvinism, in Molina's system God is completely sovereign over the eternal destinies of a world of libertarian free creatures who have in, in Augustinian terminology, 'free choice' and not merely 'free will.'

---

[937] Ibid., 68.

[938] Ibid., 69.

[939] Ibid., 73.

[940] Ibid., 75.

Remarkably, therefore, Molina's God is actually more sovereign than Calvin's, since a God who can infallibly determine the salvation and damnation of all individuals (and, in fact, providentially plan all of their actions down to the last detail) without compromising their libertarian freedom in any way is obviously superior to a God who can only determine the eternal destinies of created persons if they lack libertarian freedom and if he, in turn, premoves their bound wills toward his foreordained ends . . . . Molina's series of divine cognitive events between God's scientia media and his creative decree . . . is flexible enough to accommodate a host of insights stemming from contemporary philosophy of religion.[941]

That summary statement by MacGregor on original historical Molinism aligns well with the Dispensational Calvinistic Molinist Keathley who articulates his view this way: "God controls all things" but "God is not the author of sin. Man does not contribute to his salvation" and "God desires the salvation of all." He continues, "God is the Author and Completer of salvation" which coincides with the universal view that "Christ died for all people." Yet, "individual election is unconditional" while some forms of "God's grace is resistible." And lastly, the elect will persevere and remain "secure" even though "at crucial times" people "have the ability to choose."[942]

In his effort to balance these competing emphases of Scripture Keathley argues that the art of theology is to balance these "six pairs of twin truths: (1) God is both good and great. (2) Human freedom is both derived and genuinely ours. (3) God's grace is both monergistic and resistible. (4) God's election is both unconditional and according to foreknowledge. (5) The saved are both preserved and will persevere. (6) Christ's atonement is both unlimited in its provision and limited in its application."[943]

---

[941] Ibid., 84-85.

[942] Kenneth Keathley, *Salvation and Sovereignty: A Molinist Approach* (Nashville, TN: B&H Publishing, 2010), 7.

[943] Ibid., 9.

Maybe younger generations, especially Dispensationalists, will find this field of thought a plausible place to build a holistic theology with sufficient boundaries that protect both orthodoxy as well as orthopraxy in the field of soteriology. Prior generations of Dispensationalists seem to have remained in this field, a field that acknowledges God's absolute sovereignty in election and salvation (contrary to the inaccurate criticisms of some in the Reformed Covenant tradition), while allowing for some mystery within the overall system. For some they may want to rest in that mystery without much further exploration. As Dr. Donald G. Bloesch has well stated, "truth and faith cannot be translated into a finalized, coherent system which denies the mystery and paradox in faith. This is because this truth is suprarational as well as rational."[944]

Of course, others may indeed want to labor further in a holy effort to explain more precisely "how God can sovereignly elect and at the same time maintain sovereign justice in those actions" he undertakes "that are known to him in eternity."[945] God's theological field has enough room for both types of theologians to work together as they labor for the harvest of souls.

---

[944] Donald G. Bloesch, *Essentials of Evangelical Theology: Volume One: God, Authority, & Salvation* (Peabody, MA: Hendrickson Publishers, 1998), 18.

[945] Paige Patterson, "*Foreword*," in *Salvation and Sovereignty: A Molinist Approach* by Kenneth Keathley (Nashville, TN: B&H Publishing, 2010), x.

Appendix A: The Widespread Influence and Global Permeation of Dispensationalism

Dispensational theology has made a clear mark on the history of the church from its early seed forms, to its rise of prominence in the 1800s, and down to the current day.[946] It has made invaluable contributions to Christianity at large in various denominations and local churches.[947] Gary Demar, a non-dispensationalist writing in 2001, has noted that the eschatological views of Dispensationalism through the writings of popular author Tim LaHaye have surpassed in sales the greatest pieces of literature in history. Demar noted that the *Pilgrim's Progress* (1678), authored by John Bunyan, *Ben-Hur: A Tale of the Christ* (1880) authored by General Lew Wallace, and the modern Charles M. Sheldon's work *In His Steps*, which sold approximately two million copies in America and four million abroad, have all been surpassed by LaHaye's *Left Behind* series, which had sold "more than forty million copies."[948] David Brog, writing in 2003, revealed that LaHaye's works have at that time sold "more than fifty-five million copies."[949] This means that the Dispensationalist ideology has permeated and spread to more people than the ideas of the most popular books ever sold in literature's previous history.

Some may question or reject the words chosen above, "invaluable contributions," but the words have been chosen in light of at least one or two highly respected non-dispensational theologians that hold Dispensational theology in high esteem. Dr. O. Palmer Robertson and

---

[946] Doros Zachariades, "*Dispensation,*" in the *Holman Illustrated Bible Dictionary* (Nashville, TN: Broadman and Holman Publishers, 2003), 432.

[947] Elmer Towns and Thomas Ice, "*Dispensationalism,*" in *The Popular Encyclopedia of Bible Prophecy*, eds. Tim LaHaye and Ed Hindson (Eugene, OR: Harvest House Publishers, 2004), 81.

[948] Gary Demar, *End Times Fiction: A Biblical Consideration of the Left Behind Theology* (Nashville, TN: Thomas Nelson Publishers, 2001), xii.

[949] David Brog, *Standing With Israel: Why Christians Support the Jewish State* (Lake Mary, FL: Frontline Publishing, 2003), 59.

Ronald M. Henzel, who are both Covenant Theologians, express appreciation for the Dispensational movement. The quotes immediately below from O. Palmer Robertson, and one quote from Ronald M. Henzel, provide evangelical recognition for the orthodoxy of Dispensationalism.

Though criticized by some, (normally those from the Covenant/Reformed persuasion of Christianity and of course by most all who reject the inspiration of Scripture), and probably misunderstood by more (such as those whom have had little Bible or theological training), these two Covenant Reformed theologians have offered a sincere word of commendation for the benefits to Christianity at large from the Dispensational tradition of theology. The non-dispensational Reformed theologian O. Palmer Robertson, writing in his work *The Christ of the Covenants*, stated this of Dispensational theology:

> As the dispensational perspective is being evaluated, it should not be forgotten that covenant theologians and dispensationalists stand side by side in affirming the essentials of the Christian faith. Very often these two groups within Christendom stand alone in opposition to the inroads of modernism, neo-evangelicalism, and emotionalism. Covenant theologians and dispensationalists should hold in highest regard the scholarly and evangelical productivity of one another. It may be hoped that continuing interchange may be based on love and respect.[950]

Historically speaking, Palmer's assessment has proven correct. In a class lecture at Tyndale Theological Seminary on Inspiration and Inerrancy of Scripture, Dr. Paige Patterson attributed the conservative resurgence in the then massive liberal leaning Southern Baptist Denomination to the influence of the Dispensational School Dallas Theological Seminary and to the writings of the fundamental Baptist Dispensationalist Dr. John R. Rice. Certainly some of the main leaders of the conservative resurgent movement, such as Dr. W.A. Criswell, Dr. Paige Patterson, Dr. Adrian Rogers, Dr. Jerry Vines, and Dr. Charles Stanley, embraced key aspects of Dispensational theology. "In addition,

---

[950] O. Palmer Robertson, *The Christ of the Covenants* (Phillipsburg, NJ: Presbyterian and Reformed Publishing, 1980), 201-202.

some of the most famous evangelists, including Billy Graham, have affirmed and taught dispensational views."[951] Dr. Graham was or many years been a member of First Baptist Dallas Texas and then afterwards until his death a member of First Baptist Spartanburg South Carolina.

Ronald M. Henzel, also a Covenant Theologian, has stated that Dispensationalism has strengths that all should recognize and honor. He praises the system of theology in several areas that should help remind all Covenant Theologians to show appreciation and respect for the movement. He said,

> In many respects, as a powerful movement within the 19th and 20th century Church, Dispensationalism is not to be despised. As Richard J. Mouw reminds us, the influence of individual Dispensationalists has extended far beyond wall-charts and has triumphed over some unfair stereotypes on the part of non-Dispensationalists. Their fervent commitment to evangelism, dedication to addressing social concerns, and accurate grasp of the nature of human history rebuke those who accuse them of insulating themselves from the present world out of preoccupation with the next. And we owe them a debt of gratitude for standing in the gap as the authority of Scripture was challenged in many American seminaries in the 20th century . . . .[952]

I wish all Covenant Theologians would show this type of respect and appreciation for the Dispensational movement. Sadly, what I have seen in some cases of the time is Covenant Theologians barring the Dispensational brethren from their circles. Certainly, that happened when in the early 1900s the Presbyterians booted out many Dispensationalists from their circles. Surprisingly, many of those Dispensational scholars were devoted to the same gospel and same view of the sovereign grace of God as the Covenant Theologians. To be sure, Dispensationalists have

---

[951] Craig Blaising, *"The Extent and Varieties of Dispensationalism,"* in *Progressive Dispensatioanlism*, by Craig Blaising and Darrell L. Bock (Grand Rapids, MI: Baker Books, 1993), 12.

[952] Ronald M. Henzel, *Darby, Dualism and the Decline of Dispensationalism: Reassessing the Nineteenth-Century Roots of a Twentieth-Century Prophetic Movement for the Twenty-First Century* (Tucson, AR: Fenestra Books, 2003), 197-198.

The Calvinism of Dispensationalism

been on the attack at times and they too have acted in ways toward the Covenant brethren that have been unfair and disrespectful. But, if a Dispensationalist and Covenantal believer share the same understanding of the gospel and the sovereign grace of God,[953] then those two have so much more in common that it seems unwise to reject one another and to work in such ways as to ostracize one or the other from roles of service.

For example, I know one situation recently where a Covenant theologian refused to allow a Dispensational theologian to join and serve in the fellowship because of the different stances taken upon the doctrine of Israel and End Times. Though both agree on other essentials, especially the gospel in the Reformed tradition (emphasis on sovereignty and salvation by grace alone), the Covenant leader will not allow the Dispensationalist to use his gifts to serve in the particular body of Christ. Yet the Covenant leader says, "Here at this fellowship the gospel and Christ is the main focus, not the many other peripheral doctrines." Yet still what is spoken in word is not acted upon by allowing someone from a Calvinist and Dispensational tradition to join with the opportunity to use his gifts in service in the body of Christ.

It is these types of situations that lead me to believe that the bias among the Covenant tradition still remains in enough strength in some areas that it divides mature, godly, and evangelical believers from one another who should otherwise be able to work together in many ways for the higher cause of the gospel. In this situation I am familiar with, the Dispensationalist is in an area whereby the pure gospel is almost non-existent within the other organized fellowships. Thus, this believer desires to be a part of a fellowship where the gospel is honored and cherished but due to the bias of the Covenant leader he is excluded and rejected. The words of Dr. Ryrie seem appropriate here:

> Unfortunately, the representation of the dispensational viewpoint has not always been with integrity. . . . Neither the older nor the newer dispensationalists teach two ways of salvation, and it is not fair to attempt to make them appear so to teach. After all, a man

---

[953] Usually, but not always, the most essential litmus test to determine if agreement exists in that area relates to how one defines the doctrine of election (eternal based or faith based) and whether the new birth is synergistic (actualized because of man's will) or monergistic (actualized because God effected the movement of the person unto faith).

has to be taken at his word or all means of communication break down. It is certainly fair to attempt to prove a position illogical, but it is never fair to attempt to misrepresent that position either by misquoting or selective quoting. Straw men are easy to create, but the huff and puff it takes to demolish them are only huff and puff . . . . A sense or priority is also important. The temptation for any Christian preacher or writer to get off on a tangent or to ride a hobby horse is a very great one. That is true in doctrine, and it is true in matters of living . . . . Knowing and proclaiming this <u>whole counsel of God is our desire</u>, yet we all need priorities in our proclamation of doctrine. <u>Some doctrines in the Bible are more central than others. Paul placed a high priority on the right understanding of the gospel (Gal. 1:8-9). He placed a low priority on the doctrine of the observance of particular days (Col. 2:16-17).</u> Some doctrines should be given priority over others. We who are dispensationalists would do well to remember this. "Dispensational truth" is not necessarily the most important thing in the Bible. Even prophecy, though a major theme, should not constitute the whole of one's preaching. The spiritual life, which is without question a high priority doctrine, can be overdone . . . . It may [also] help to be reminded of some of the important doctrines to which dispensationalists subscribe wholeheartedly. After all, dispensationalists are conservatives and affirm complete allegiance to the doctrines of verbal, plenary inspiration, the virgin birth and deity of Christ, the substitutionary atonement, eternal salvation by grace through faith, the importance of godly living and the ministry of the Holy Spirit, the future coming of Christ, and the eternal damnation of the lost. Those who are divided from us in the matter of dispensationalism or premillennialism may remember the areas in which they [Covenant theologians] are united with us. As already noted, some doctrines are more important than others, so it particularly behooves us not to cut off our fellowship from those who share similar views about these important doctrines. There are few enough these days who believe in the fundamentals of the faith, and to ignore those who have declared themselves on the side of the truth of God is unwise. Something is wrong with our circles of fellowship, sense of priority, or doctrine of unity when conservatives view fellow conservatives as the opposition party and then find their theological friends among those who are teaching and promoting error.[954]

I agree with Dr. Ryrie here wholeheartedly. This principle he speaks of here applies to both the Dispensationalist and Covenant believer. I think we have grossly misunderstood the main emphases of faith, hope, and love when we who share many evangelical essentials bar the doors against one another when we differ in these other areas of doctrine. Though I am a dispensationalist and will be glad to explain and show why I am, I find it prideful for me to bar the door for ministerial service of those who may not align with me in this area exactly as I do. The graded scale of truth, or as sometimes stated, Theological Triage, is an important doctrine,[955] and learning when and where to apply what doctrine is vitally important for the body of Christ to experience and live out the faith in love.

---

[954] Charles C. Ryrie, *Dispensationalism* (Chicago, IL: Moody Press, 1995), 210, 212.

[955] Graded Absolutism in doctrine (theological triage) is more of an Evangelical position whereas Unqualified Absolutism in doctrine is a position more often associated with modern Fundamentalism. Dispensationalism has historically embraced the Graded Absolutism scale (consciously or unconsciously) since we see from a literal interpretation of Scripture that some laws or truths of God are higher or lower on the scale of importance by the very words used in the text of Scripture. Dr. Danny Akin (a dispensationalist) and Dr. Al Mohler (a Covenantalist) call this the "Theological Triage." We Evangelical Dispensationalists see higher and lower laws or doctrines, primary and secondary doctrines. Dispensationalism in the version of fundamentalism in some senses seems to embrace the Unqualified Absolutism position on the scale of doctrinal importance, i.e. all doctrine is equal in weight. Often those of that persuasion will ask, "who are we to say one law of God is more or less important than another? All of it is important." Though true that all of Scripture is important, it was God himself and biblical authors that stated some laws, doctrines, or virtues were more important than other laws and virtues and that some sins were worse than other sins (see Matt. 23:23; John 19:11; 1 Cor. 13:13). This graded scale of doctrine does not per se mean all that agree here agree with a graded scale of ethics. Some who affirm a theological triage do not affirm a graded scale to ethical laws. If that is consistent or not is another debate in itself.

Dispensationalism's Global Evangelistic Emphasis

Speaking further about the point of evangelism, Dispensationalism has also contributed to an active missionary ministry throughout the world. They have "participated in and encouraged the founding of faith missions (such as Central American Mission founded by C.I. Scofield) and parachurch ministries (such as Young Life, founded by Jim Rayburn). Dispensationalists have ministered with Campus Crusade for Christ, the Navigators, Youth for Christ, and InterVarsity Christian Fellowship."[956]

Such active evangelism efforts ought not to surprise the astute student of Dispensationalism for one of the most famous leaders of the movement itself, Dr. Lewis Sperry Chafer, who founded Dallas Theological Seminary, led an active evangelistic ministry[957] and even published a major work on the art of evangelism entitled *True Evangelism: Winning Souls by Prayer*. According to Dr. Hannah, the primary emphasis of Chafer's ministry revolved around God's grace, the centrality of Christ, and the cross of Calvary, all of which created a legacy that certainly built a longstanding heritage among Dispensationalism.[958] Such themes are commonly associated with great missionary efforts. Yet more importantly than the practical missionary activity, those themes constitute the heart of love expressed within the gospel itself.

Dispensationalism's Submission to Scripture as the Supreme Authority

Consequently, dispensational theology has been a champion for biblical study and fidelity to the nature, authority, and teaching of Scripture. The movement "has been known as a Bible exposition movement. It has produced a number of popular expositors of Scripture

---

[956] Craig Blaising, "*The Extent and Varieties of Dispensationalism*," in *Progressive Dispensatioanlism*, by Craig Blaising and Darrell L. Bock (Grand Rapids, MI: Baker Books, 1993), 13.

[957] John D. Hannah, "*Lewis Sperry Chafer,*" in *The Premillennial Dictionary of Theology* (Grand Rapids, MI: Kregel Publications, 1996), 68.

[958] Ibid., 70.

who not only helped spread dispensationalism but have impacted large portions of evangelicalism. Dispensationalists have upheld the belief that the Bible is the sole, inerrant, verbal, revelation of God available to the church today and that it provides a sure foundation for Christian life and faith."[959] The spread of Dispensational views have been enormous throughout the modern Christian faith. Dr. Craig Blaising has noted: "If you are an evangelical Christian, it is most likely that you know some who call themselves dispensationalists. And it is just as likely that you have certain beliefs and interpretations of Scripture that have been shaped in some way by dispensationalism."[960]

Dispensationalism has permeated the Christian world at large. It has in many respects called people back to the Bible alone as the standard to determine truth. Some have rightly even termed this movement as "the Bible Conference Movement."[961] This movement has spread from the early days of the Brethren churches into mainstream evangelicalism throughout the 20th and now the 21st century. Many denominations even adopted Dispensationalism as the main confession for the movement. "The General Association of Regular Baptist Churches, The Conservative Baptist Association, The Fellowship of Grace Brethren Churches, and the Independent Fundamentalist Churches of America" adopted dispensational theology.[962]

Furthermore, other denominations such as the Evangelical Free Church of America, the Christian and Missionary Alliance, and even the holiness and Pentecostal persuasions of Christianity benefited and adopted

---

[959] Craig Blaising, "*The Extent and Varieties of Dispensationalism*," in *Progressive Dispensationalism*, by Craig Blaising and Darrell L. Bock (Grand Rapids, MI: Baker Books, 1993), 13-14. Though I agree here with Dr. Blaising I would not classify myself as a "Progressive Dispensationalist" due to other areas where we would disagree, primarily in the area of hermeneutics.

[960] Craig Blaising, "*The Extent and Varieties of Dispensationalism*," in *Progressive Dispensationalism*, by Craig Blaising and Darrell L. Bock (Grand Rapids, MI: Baker Books, 1993), 9.

[961] Ibid., 10

[962] Ibid., 11.

forms of Dispensationalism.[963] Such historical testimony reveals that at the heart of Dispensational theology has been the desire to promote *unity around the Lord Jesus Christ* as revealed in his word. Some critics have charged Dispensationalism with a schismatic spirit. Such a criticism may be true of some who hold to Dispensational theology, but more than likely it is a product of some other influence on their theology.[964] Dispensationalism, through the Bible Conference Movement, sought to "make the Bible a sure basis for evangelical ecumenicity—an ecumenicity

---

[963] Ibid., 12.

[964] Schismatic spirits inside of Fundamentalism have often arisen due to the neo-monastic spirit and ascetical spirit in several versions of fundamentalism. Many have interpreted the ideas of being "separate" to mean "spatial separation" instead of mind/heart separation, which is what the Bible means in most of the cases. There are times when people need to physically run from sinful situations or places. Joseph was an OT example of that in his situation with Potiphar's wife (Gen. 39). But the call to be holy is a call to mind/heart separation first and foremost. Those who say God calls us to be holy and that means to be physically away from areas where sin exists violate the methodology of God as revealed in his omnipresence as well in the incarnation of Christ. God is omnipresent and thus he is around and seeing sin everywhere in the universe. So why is God not sinful? God is separate in spirit, mind, and heart even though he is present everywhere. Likewise, Christ left the holiest place in the universe, heaven, and came to the cesspool place known as earth that was corrupt and sinful. He never sinned, yet Christ was around sinners and people doing sinful things. One can read John 2 and see that Christ was even at a wedding where the people were intoxicated. I am not encouraging everyone to purposefully go into sinful establishments. But what I am saying is that when we embrace the false idea that separation unto holiness means spatial separation we have rejected the approach of God, Christ, and the Holy Spirit who all three are present around sin yet mature enough to not embrace the sin. And since we are to be conformed into God's image in Christ, that is the test of true maturity. Jesus Christ was actually in the most sinful place in the entire universe and he was led there by God himself. He stood in the **presence** of Satan himself (Matt. 3). How much worse can it get than in the immediate presence of Satan? Also, fundamentalism has at times embraced an "Unqualified Absolutism," doctrinal grid, and such as that naturally produces a personality type where conflict is inevitable because that viewpoint does not see a graded scale of truth or a graded scale of sin. Every truth is equally important and every sin is equally as bad, despite the fact that Christ said there were higher laws and lower laws (Matt. 22:34-40; 23:23) and greater sins (John 19:11).

that was not seen as structural, administrative, or denominational, but an ecumenicity of faith, hope, and love."[965]

The Heart & Essential Emphasis of Dispensationalism: God's Glory and Grace in Christ for Faith, Hope, and Love

The very fact that Dispensationalists have permeated the many different denominations as well as launched new churches, colleges, and other Christian organizations reveals that the movement's intent is not to destroy the unity of the God's people in history but to provide a sure basis for unity. Mature Dispensationalists, who understand the heart of Dispensational theology with its emphasis on God's glory and grace, the centrality of Christ, and the cross of Calvary (as emphasized by Dr. Chafer), promote faith, hope, love, and unity in all areas of life and faith through a common confession rooted in the Bible alone which the early church embraced, the Reformation spirit recovered, and the Dispensational movement matured. Dr. Blaising again has well stated:

> Interdenominational schools and ministries have attempted to carry on that vision to varying degrees, a vision which has helped contribute to the sense of evangelical identity in some quarters of evangelicalism. Dispensationalists, of course, were not the only evangelicals to emphasize the authority of the Bible. But their transdenominational vision and their practical orientation to expositional ministry made an emphasis on Scripture a hallmark of the movement, one that continues today as well.[966]

This spirit has been made known through the movement's ability to interact with so many persuasions of theology, even with and within different denominations. Dispensationalism, if true to its roots, has the ability to work with many when there may be significant disagreement in certain doctrinal areas so long as the Bible is the chief focus of all matters

---

[965] Craig Blaising, "*The Extent and Varieties of Dispensationalism*," in *Progressive Dispensationalism*, by Craig Blaising and Darrell L. Bock (Grand Rapids, MI: Baker Books, 1993), 14.

[966] Ibid.

of interpretations. This transdenominational element makes the Dispensational movement more of a grace centered, encouraging, optimistic movement in that it seeks to first and foremost make Scripture, not creed nor denominations, the ultimate authority in all matters of faith and practice. So long as the Bible is adopted as the sole or supreme standard for truth, then Dispensationalists normally seek to work with others for higher causes than against those with whom there are minor variations in doctrine. Such efforts exist because the Dispensationalist takes a literal reading of Scripture and thus understands that in God's household-universe, just like any rightly governed home, some truths take precedence over others and some truths are the most important for the particular moment in time and history. As Dispensationalist Dr. Norman Geisler has noted, "Not all moral laws are of equal weight. Jesus spoke of the 'weightier' matters of the law (Matt. 23:23) and of the 'least' (Matt. 5:19) and the 'greatest' commandment (Matt. 22:36)."[967] The Dispensationalist takes this teaching from Scripture literally and it leads him or her to make the grace, love, and cross of Christ the preeminent theme in his or her ministry as did Dr. Lewis Sperry Chafer.

Dispensationalism's Love for Education Has Birthed Major Educational Centers

The Bible Conference Movement has also produced a love for education among the people. Where Dispensational theology spread, so did the work to organize schools to educate the minds of the believers. Schools, seminaries, Bible Institutes, colleges, and universities were established from the Bible Conference Movement. Some of these included Moody Bible Institute, BIOLA (formerly the Bible Institute of Los Angeles) which produced Talbot Theological Seminary, Philadelphia College of the Bible, and Dallas Theological Seminary.[968] Countless numbers of churches have been founded by Dispensationalists from the

---

[967] Norman Geisler, *Christian Ethics: Options and Issues* (Grand Rapids, MI: Baker Book House, 1989), 116.

[968] Craig Blaising, "*The Extent and Varieties of Dispensationalism,*" in *Progressive Dispensationalism*, by Craig Blaising and Darrell L. Bock (Grand Rapids, MI: Baker Books, 1993), 12.

Bible Conference Movement. This even led to many schools associating with the churches to teach Dispensational theology in schools like "Grace College and Grace Theological Seminary, Northwestern College, Grand Rapids Baptist Seminary, Western Conservative Baptist Seminary (now Western Seminary). Dispensationalism has also been taught (though not exclusively) at Denver Seminary (formerly Denver Conservative Baptist Seminary)."[969] Currently one of the larger evangelical freestanding seminaries in regard to active students was founded by a Dispensationalist teacher in 1969. Dr. John Brooke, the founder of Trinity Theological Seminary in Evansville Indiana, held firmly to a Dispensational view of Israel and Christ's coming.[970] Additionally, Dispensationalist Dr. Norman Geisler founded both Southern Evangelical Seminary in North Carolina and Veritas University in California.

Such evidences as this reveal the Reformation spirit within Dispensationalism. That Reformation spirit birthed many of the early schools in America such as Harvard, Yale, Princeton, and Brown University. Reformed scholar Boettner noted that the "three American Universities of greatest historical importance, Harvard, Yale, and Princeton, were originally founded by Calvinists."[971] Reformed scholar Dr. D. James Kennedy has boldly stated that the "idea of education for everybody grew directly out of the Reformation."[972]

When the Bible "became the focal point of Christianity again" it led to "education for the masses."[973] Kennedy concurs with Dr. Samuel Blumenfeld that "the roots of education for the masses goes back to the Reformation and, especially to John Calvin. The Reformers believed that the only way the Protestant Reformation would hold would be for people

---

[969] Ibid.

[970] Personal conversation with Dr. Harold Hunter, then President of Trinity Theological Seminary, 4/21/07.

[971] Loraine Boettner, *The Reformed Doctrine of Predestination* (Phillipsburg, NJ: Presbyterian and Reformed Publishing Co., 1932), 397.

[972] D. James Kennedy and Jerry Newcombe, *What if Jesus Had Never Been Born?* (Nashville, TN: Thomas Nelson Publishers, 1994), 43.

[973] Ibid., 43.

themselves—laypeople—to read the Bible."[974] "Harvard, Yale, William and Mary, Brown, Princeton, New York University, Northwestern University, and other schools have thoroughly Christian roots"[975] that developed in the wake of the Reformation movement that spread to America from the lives of the Puritans.[976] The Princeton scholar Loraine Boettner has shown that when the true spirit of the Reformation exists it leads to a love for education. He has specifically noted:

> Wherever Calvinism has gone it has carried the school with it and has given a powerful impulse to popular education. It is a system which demands intellectual manhood. In fact, we may say that its very existence is tied up with education of the people. Mental training is required to master the system and to trace out all that it involves. It makes the strongest possible appeal to the human reason and insists that man must love God not only with his whole heart but also with his whole mind. Calvin held that a 'true faith must be an intelligent faith'; and experience has shown that piety without learning is in the long run about as dangerous as learning without piety. He saw clearly that the acceptance and diffusion of his scheme of doctrine was dependent not only upon the training of the men who were to expound it, but also upon the intelligence of the great masses of humanity who were to accept it. Calvin crowned his work in Geneva in the establishment of the Academy. Thousands of pilgrim pupils from Continental Europe and from the British Isles sat at his feet and then carried his doctrines into every corner of Christendom. Knox returned from Geneva fully convinced that the education of the masses was the strongest bulwark of Protestantism and the surest foundation of the State. 'With Romanism goes the priest; with Calvinism goes the teacher,' is an old saying, the truthfulness of which will not be denied by anyone who has examined the facts. This Calvinistic love for

---

[974] Ibid.

[975] Ibid., 52.

[976] Perry Miller, "*Puritans and Puritanism*," in the *Dictionary of American History*, rev. ed. (New York, NY: Charles Scriber's Sons, 1976), 5:468-469.

learning, putting mind above money, has inspired countless numbers of Calvinistic families in Scotland, in England, in Holland, and in America, to pinch themselves to the bone in order to educate their children .... Calvinists have not been the builders of great cathedrals, but they have been the builders of schools, colleges, and universities. When the Puritans from England, the

Covenanters from Scotland, and the Reformed from Holland and Germany, came to America they brought with them not only the Bible and the Westminster Confession but also the school.[977]

Therefore, the rise of schools, colleges, universities, Bible Institutes, and seminaries from the Dispensational tradition reveals that it too builds from the same spirit that the Calvinist Puritan and Pilgrims brought to America. Wherever pure Dispensationalism has flourished, so has the school. Dispensationalism carries the seeds of the Reformation through its emphasis on the Word of God and its emphasis on understanding the systematic household universe of God,[978] all of which requires an intelligent study of the Bible.

Dispensationalism's Influence in Global Politics

Furthermore, Dispensationalism has impacted the political world. It has not simply influenced academic, personal, or Christian denominations and churches. The movement has actually altered the *entire world politically* as well, which speaks volumes for the power in and behind this movement. Dispensationalism may very well be the main (or at least a main) reason why Israel has a homeland today. Harvard Law School graduate and former Chief of Staff for a United States Senator, David Brog has noted that "Dispensationalism has inspired millions of Christians to stand with the Jews and with the Jewish State of Israel."[979]

---

[977] Loraine Boettner, *The Reformed Doctrine of Predestination* (Phillipsburg, NJ: Presbyterian and Reformed Publishing Co., 1932), 396-397.

[978] Charles C. Ryrie, *Dispensationalism* (Chicago, IL: Moody Press, 1995), 29.

[979] David Brog, *Standing With Israel: Why Christians Support the Jewish State* (Lake Mary, FL: Frontline Publishing, 2003), 63.

The Calvinism of Dispensationalism

The love for the Jewish people led to deep political activity whereby Dispensationalism prepared the way for the birth of the Jewish state in 1948. One of the forerunners and leaders of the Zionist cause, William Blackstone, adopted "premillennial dispensationalism."[980] From that theological base, "he did more to spread and popularize dispensational theology than any other American with the exception of C.I. Scofield."[981] He worked for years to find a way to help Russian Jews find a place back home in the holy land. His "work provided a long-term benefit to the Zionist cause by preparing the ground for what would follow later. Blackstone planted the idea of a Jewish return to Palestine, and an American role in that return, in the American political consciousness."[982]

Blackstone's groundwork eventually produced fruit. In time, the ideas promoted by Blackstone would take a deep root in the heart of the 33rd President of the United States, Harry S. Truman (1884-1972). With President Roosevelt's death on April 12th, 1945, Truman was sworn into office, and after this ceremony he "fervently kissed the Bible upon which his hand rested."[983] As one writer noted, "Truman made some of the most crucial decisions in history,"[984] and one of those crucial history altering decisions revolved around a set of promises in the Bible concerning the nation of Israel and the Jewish people. The central question remained at that time of where the displaced Jews would live after escaping from the persecution of the Holocaust.

---

[980] Ibid.., 98.

[981] Ibid.

[982] Ibid.., 101.

[983] David Brog, *Standing With Israel: Why Christians Support the Jewish State* (Lake Mary, FL: Frontline Publishing, 2003), 118.

[984] Frank Freidel, *The Presidents of the United States of America* (Washington, DC: White House Historical Association, 1981), 71.

A Brief Historical Journey to President Truman's Stand for the Israel State

Politically there had been an agreement made through what has been termed the "Balfour declaration." This declaration developed under the leadership of President Woodrow Wilson with the help of William Blackstone's petition signed by leadership from the Baptists, Methodists, and Presbyterian denominations.[985] The petition, carried by the close

friend of Wilson and leading Zionist of the day Lois Brandeis,[986] led the way in moving President Wilson to sign the declaration that produced a homeland for the Jews. David Brog has recounted this grand historical event:

> On June 30, 1917, the Blackstone Memorial was presented to Wilson. On October 13, 1917, Wilson permitted Brandeis to convey to Lord Balfour and the British cabinet President Wilson's "entire sympathy" with the proposal to create a homeland for the Jews. The Balfour Declaration followed in November. Brandeis later attributed his success in winning Wilson over to the Zionist cause to his ability to appeal to Wilson's deep Christian faith. . . . Woodrow Wilson played a crucial role in securing the Balfour Declaration and all that followed. As Wilson himself later marveled, "To think that I, the son of a manse, should be able to help restore the Holy Land to its people."[987]

However, this declaration eventually collapsed, costing Israel once again any place of refuge. During Hitler's evil rise to power in 1933 and his evil campaign to rid the world of the Jews through his Satanic and anti-Semitic assault on God's Jewish people, many of the Jews began to immigrate in mass numbers to the land designated for them by the Balfour

---

[985] David Brog, *Standing With Israel: Why Christians Support the Jewish State* (Lake Mary, FL: Frontline Publishing, 2003), 116-118.

[986] Ibid., 116.

[987] Ibid., 118.

Declaration. This mass immigration, however, led to the Arab Revolt whereby they demanded the dismissal of the Balfour Declaration. In this effort, they as a people banned Jews from immigrating to the area and even forbid any land sales to the Jewish people attempting to immigrate into the area.[988] The demands led to the British rescinding the agreement and giving in to the pressure of the Arabs. In effect, the Jews lost their homeland which the British government had created in connection with the support and guidance of President Woodrow Wilson. The Princeton and Harvard scholar David Brog provides a detailed picture of what took place in this horrible time for the Jewish people.

> The Arab Revolt ended with the British capitulation to almost all of the Arabs' demands. In 1939, the British issued the notorious White Paper, which effectively canceled further Jewish immigration and land purchases in Palestine. Upon issuance of the White Paper, Winston Churchill declared, 'This is the breach, this is the violation of the pledge, this is the abandonment of the Balfour Declaration, this is the end of the vision, of the hope, of the dream." The British had closed the doors of Palestine to Jewish immigration just as Hitler was opening the doors of Auschwitz. The generation of British leaders that walked away from the Balfour Declaration was different from the generation that had promulgated it. By and large, this new generation was raised outside of British evangelical tradition that had so captivated earlier generations and therefore lacked their Christian affinity for the Jews and their dreams of a homeland. Without a Christian Zionist motive, and now without any convincing strategic motive, there remained little to bind Britain to its earlier embrace of Zionism. As Britain turned its back, the Zionists looked increasingly toward the United States to be their new champion and protector. After World War II, they would find support from a new president who shared the Bible-based sympathy for their cause that had animated the prior generation of British leaders. The seat of Christian Zionism would cross the Atlantic.[989]

---

[988] Ibid., 119.

[989] Ibid., 119-120.

With the fall of the Balfour Declaration, the Jewish people were in danger. The homeland doors were shut. Yet the Zionist cause did not die with the death of the Balfour Declaration. Though temporally interrupted, the sovereign work of the Almighty God still had a providential plan to provide a place for the Jewish people to live. God raised up Harry Truman to once again reinstitute a homeland for the Jewish people.

Truman, who in light of Franklin D. Roosevelt's death, took office in April 1945. He "moved decisively in those early months, presiding over the climatic events of World War II and dealing with other Allied leaders. His decision to drop the atomic bombs on Japan, though much criticized in later years, was an action which ended the war."[990] After World War II another wave of "effective American support for the establishment of the state of Israel"[991] developed, and it led to the creation of the nation of Israel under Truman's Presidency.

Throughout both terms President Truman accomplished many noble endeavors,[992] and his overall life and leadership "virtually attained" him the "status of a twentieth-century legend."[993] Yet Truman held one act of his in an emotional light that seems to differ from all of his other feats. His decision to support the creation of the Israeli homeland for the Jewish people has been a subject of much review.

At this point in history, the Dispensationalist movement in America was maturing and gaining a stronghold over Christianity in America. Dallas Seminary, founded in 1924 by Lewis Sperry Chafer in Texas, and Moody Bible Institute in Chicago governed by the Reformed/Calvinistic Dispensationalist Episcopalian Dr. James Martin Gray in the early 1900s, and C.I. Scofield's schools and his Scofield Study Bible, which had spread throughout the land of America from its first

---

[990] John Bowman, *The History of the American Presidency* (North Dighton, MA: World Publications Group, 2005), 140.

[991] Robert I. Wiener, "*Israeli-American Relations,*" in *The Dictionary of American History* (New York, NY: Charles Scribner's Sons, 1976), 481.

[992] John Bowman, *The History of the American Presidency* (North Dighton, MA: World Publications Group, 2005), 142.

[993] Ibid., 143.

publication by Oxford University Press in 1909, produced a *strong, broad movement* in the early part of the twentieth century.

Dispensationalism's love for the ethnic people, the Jews, and their Zionist support for the ethnically chosen people produced a mental viewpoint, a frame of mind and interpretive grid, for understanding what the Bible meant concerning the people called the Jews. Dr. L. Sale Harrison in 1934 stated: "Whatever may be our belief in the supernatural, when we see a Jew we must exclaim that he is a living miracle; and is, in himself, a wonderful fulfillment of God's prophetic Word."[994] In Truman's day many people had to wrestle with idea of the prophecies concerning the nation Israel.

It was a Dispensational interpretation of the Bible that Truman held when he determined to endorse and recognize Israel as a State in 1948. President Truman's personal friend and early business partner Eddie Jacobsen, a Jew from Kansas City, had asked for a special meeting between the President and his Zionist friend Chaim Weizmann. The President turned down this meeting which led to Jacobsen flying to Washington D.C and entering the Oval Office to make a strong emotional appeal to his friend Truman for the purpose of getting him and Zionist leader Weizmann together.[995] In this eternally divine moment that carried significant implications for the world at large, Truman succumb to the pleading of his friend Jacobsen and agreed to have a meeting with this Zionist leader. "On March 18, 1948, Chaim Weizmann was ushered into the White House through a back door for a secret meeting with President Truman.

As Jacobsen and the Zionists had hoped, Weizmann's power of persuasion, and the great mutual affection that had developed between Weizmann and Truman, won the President over. Truman assured Weizmann that the United States would abandon the trusteeship idea and continue to support the partition of Palestine into two independent states."[996] In that same year, the fruit of this meeting came to realization when at midnight on May 14th, 1948 Israel declared Independence and a

---

[994] L. Sale Harrison, *The Remarkable Jew* (Wheaton, IL: Van Kampen Press, 1934), 6-7.

[995] David Brog, *Standing With Israel: Why Christians Support the Jewish State* (Lake Mary, FL: Frontline Publishing, 2003), 122-123.

[996] Ibid., 123.

mere eleven minutes later President Truman recognized the new Jewish State by signing the following statement: "This government has been informed that a Jewish State has been proclaimed in Palestine, and recognition has been requested by the provisional government thereof. The United States recognizes the provisional government as the de facto authority of the State of Israel."[997]

As Brog recounts, "The United States was the first country to recognize Israel. President Truman had acted so quickly, in fact, that he had to write the name Israel by hand on his statement. The document had been typed before anyone even knew the name of the new Jewish State."[998] What reason led Truman to act with such decisive support for the creation of the State of Israel? What motivated Truman, what ideological viewpoint did he have that led to this decision? What presuppositions led him to support Israel?

President Truman Embraced a Literal Reading of the Bible's Promise to Israel

A key difference between infant Reformation theology and mature Reformation theology has been the consistent application of the literal hermeneutic, especially in regards to the term Israel throughout the Bible. The return to historical grammatical (literal) hermeneutics by Dr. Martin Luther and Dr. John Calvin in the Reformation era "ignited the sixteenth-century Protestant Reformation."[999] The consistent application to apply that hermeneutic to all texts concerning the word Israel led to the rise of the Dispensationalists' understanding of the continued land promises to the Jewish people. As Dr. Fruchtenbaum has stated, "there is no need to conclude that the New Testament changes or reinterprets the Old Testament."[1000] Furthermore, in applying this literal hermeneutic to the

---

[997] Ibid., 123-124.

[998] Ibid., 124.

[999] Gordon H. Johnston, "*Reformation Hermeneutics*," in the *Dictionary of Premillennial Theology* (Grand Rapids, MI: Krgel Publications 1996), 163.

[1000] Arnold Fruchtenbaum, *Israelology* (Tustin, CA: Ariel Ministries, 1996), 845.

terms Israel, Jews, and land, it leads to the belief that God still has promises to fulfill with this ethnic people.

How does that directly apply to Truman's decision to support Israel? Truman took the Bible's plain, literal, and natural meaning when he read the OT. He adopted, consciously or unconsciously, the mature Reformation ideology, Dispensationalism's view, that when the Bible promised a specific land to Israel in the area of Palestine that it meant to the ethnic people the Jews. Had he took the non-dispensational viewpoint, it would have been taken non-literally and applied to some other people other than the original recipients of the promise, namely the ethnic Jews.

Truman realized the need to honor the original promise made first and foremost in the Bible and then also by the Balfour Declaration, which developed in light of the Zionist movement. Additionally, Truman was a devout believer in the value of the Bible. Clark Clifford has shown that Truman

> was a student and believer in the Bible since his youth. From his reading of the Old Testament he felt the Jews derived a legitimate historical right to Palestine, and he sometimes cited such biblical lines as Deuteronomy 1:8 "Behold, I have given up the land before you; go in and take possession of the land which the Lord has sworn unto your fathers, to Abraham, to Isaac and to Jacob."[1001]

Truman's devotion to Scripture moved him to support Israel. He did not allegorize or transfer the promises of Israel to any other group but to the original audience. Thus he opted to support a Jewish state. Because he wore glasses growing up Truman did not play sports but became a book lover instead. Among his favorite books was the Bible.[1002] This love for the book and his love for the promises of God to Israel led Truman to make what may be the greatest or at least one of the greatest decisions in worldwide history since the events of the New Testament era. Truman realized in some way that as each time this issue surfaced, he became

---

[1001] Clark Clifford, *Counsel to the President* (New York, NY: Anchor Books, 1992), 7-8.

[1002] David Brog, *Standing With Israel: Why Christians Support the Jewish State* (Lake Mary, FL: Frontline Publishing, 2003), 126-127.

more emotional than over any other political decision made in his tenure as President. Brog mentioned that

> Like most men of his generation, Harry Truman avoided public displays of emotion. Truman made a series of tough decisions—including ordering American warplanes to drop atomic bombs on two Japanese cities—without shedding public tears of sorrow. Likewise Truman won the wars in Europe and in the Pacific and brought the troops triumphantly home without shedding public tears of joy. Yet there were a handful of occasions on which Truman was so overcome with emotion that he was unable to contain himself. According to Truman biographer David McCullough: "I have about three instances where Truman cried in public. They are very few and they are always real." Although McCullough doesn't discuss these three instances, other accounts go into greater detail. In fact, other observers describe no less than four instances in which Truman shed public tears. All four occasions were in response to expressions of appreciation for his decision to recognize Israel.[1003]

The nation of Israel stands today because the Dispensational viewpoint rose to prominence concerning who is Israel. From the earliest days of church history when the disciples of the apostles embraced a premillennial coming of Christ, to the infant days of the birth of the Reformation with its desire to return to a literal reading of Scripture, until the maturation of that movement in the ideology of Dispensationalism, God has been working in history to fulfill his ancient promise to the Jewish people concerning the land of Israel. As Apostle Paul said of these promises made to Israel: "For the gifts and the calling of God are irrevocable" (Romans 11:29).

The promises for Israel are based upon the absolute sovereignty of God to fulfill his promises. The entire process of Truman initiating this divine moment has nothing really to do with Truman but more to do with the omnipotent, providential, sovereign, and omniscient plan of the grand God who rules his universe. Even the very decisions of Presidents are

---

[1003] Ibid., 128.

ruled by the hand of God. As Proverbs 21:1 says: "The king's heart is a stream of water in the hand of the LORD; he turns it wherever he will." God owns his universe and he and he governs it through his omnipotent omniscience.

Summary of an Introductory Analysis of Dispensationalism

Hardly can anyone with any degree of honesty fail to see the power and purity of this movement on an overall basis. Sure, as with any movement, there are those who hold to incorrect views, and even some who from within Dispensationalism's own tradition have hurt the movement by some of their actions, teachings, and unbiblical stances in history. But the movement is larger than any one person. The movement is an ideological viewpoint that transcends any one denomination, any one church, and any one person no matter how well known and popular.

Overall the movement has extended the seeds of the Reformation movement into full blossom in the 20th and 21st century, and as Dr. Ryrie liked to say, "The Best is Yet to Come"[1004] because Dispensationalism is not dying.[1005] People, whether friend or foe, must recognize the benefits and blessings from this persuasion of theology. Certainly others who are honest have indeed realized this. Though no longer a dispensationalist, theologian Ronald M. Henzel has also stated the debt people owe to the system known as Dispensationalism.[1006]

Of course, just to be sure, this does not imply nor mean Dispensationalists hold the market on truth. Dispensationalists as well as Dispensationalism as a whole movement have their share of errors over the years. Yet, such an admission should not, unless previously biased or embittered against the system from the onset, lead one to dismiss or discard Dispensationalism all together. What system on earth and this side

---

[1004] Charles C. Ryrie, *The Best is Yet to Come* (Chicago, IL: Moody Press, 1981), 134.

[1005] Charles C. Ryrie, *Issues in Dispensationalism*, eds. Wesley R. Willis and John R. Master (Chicago, IL: Moody Press, 1994), 9.

[1006] Ronald M. Henzel, *Darby, Dualism, and the Decline of Dispensationalism: Reassessing the Nineteenth-Century Roots of a Twentieth-Century Prophetic Movement for the Twenty-First Century* (Tucson, AR: Fenestra Books, 2003), 197-198.

of eternity does not have some weaknesses? No person or system shall see everything it could or needs to see. As Paul said, "For now we see in a mirror dimly, but then face to face. Now I know in part; then I shall know fully, even as I have been fully known" (1 Cor. 13:12).[1007]

Sadly, not all have had such high regard for dispensational theology. To be sure, theologians from both sides of the theological spectrum have seemingly been guilty of failing to show love and respect towards one another. What God revealed to the Apostles has gradually grown in the universal church as God brought forth throughout church history a pure understanding of how he rules as the Father of his Household Universe.

[1007] Scripture references in this appendix are from the English Standard Version (ESV) unless otherwise noted.

Appendix B: Evangelical Dispensationalism: A Christ Centered Stream of Theology that Differs from Fundamentalism

Introduction: Multiple Streams Feeding One Body of Holy Water

I love my heritage. Gratitude graces my veins for the glorious God who gave me faithful teachers to help guide, grow, and govern my educational endeavors. I have received an education from a plethora of theologians from numerous traditions. In my undergraduate education I studied under my beloved Baptists. Though I would not per se call myself a Baptist today (for one example, I affirm elder rule where most Baptists adhere to congregationalism), I received from those wonderful scholars a solid education that stressed the importance of Scripture, salvation for souls, and service for the Savior. Later in one of my graduate degrees I studied under some of the most well-known Dispensational teachers within Christendom, even going on to complete a doctorate in systematic theology under a well-known Dispensational theologian in the 20th and 21st century.

Then on the other hand, I studied in a second graduate degree program that led to a second doctoral degree in theology from a vicissitude of scholars that varied widely on theological matters. Many of these theologians were not dispensationalists, or as I would say more precisely, they were more in line with the system known as continuity theology than discontinuity theology. These scholars stretched me, challenged me, and made me think in greater depth as to why I affirmed what I did from my heritage. Though I remained a Dispensationalist by conviction more so after the challenges, I gained a new appreciation for not only my tradition but their tradition as well making me more thoroughly educated in both systems of theology, even seeing how the two (Reformed and Dispensational systems) really work as a hand in glove manner (or should).

And in this journey I discovered that within my beloved heritage that I came to identify with, often named or given the term Dispensationalism, that two beneficent streams feed the tributary that I travel. Dispensationalism as a body of theology has within it many rivers, and/or smaller streams, that service this vast lake of the Lord. I love them all. All the streams have various strengths that help people find the Savior for salvation and sanctification. So I write this not in any way to discredit, denigrate, or devalue one particular stream of Dispensationalism. Though I do have a more particular stream that I find more palatable, profitable, and pleasing to the pulse of Scripture in my opinion, I share this article with due awareness that not all of the Dispensationalist scholars, saints, and servants will agree, like, or even understand this article.

The differences that I highlight in this article do not mean in any way that I think the other streams of theology within Dispensationalism constitute heresy or ungodly theologies. I do not believe that. In fact, I from my perspective of Evangelical theology have great joy and delight in working with other streams of theology not only in Dispensationalism but within even the larger body of Christ beyond Dispensationalism. Though I am an Evangelical Dispensationalist and not a Fundamentalist (of any persuasion), that does not mean I fail to appreciate those from the other streams of thought. I have physical bloodline family members that are Fundamentalists. I applaud and appreciate them in more ways than I can count. And, of course, I have great affinity for my spiritual family of Fundamentalists that fight for the faith. I will gladly minister with them for the gospel and for all of the essentials of the faith.

Nonetheless, I write this article to highlight the difference with one stream of Dispensationalism from another form of Dispensationalism (or even in theology in general). In fact, this article just as easily could even apply to the larger body of Christ as a whole as it focuses on the difference between an Evangelical and Fundamentalist. Evangelicalism and modern Fundamentalism are two distinct streams of Christian theology and methodology that exist within the overall body of Christ. Original fundamentalism as expressed in the 1900s and historic evangelicalism were virtually synonyms prior to the rise of the more modern fundamentalism movement. And these two streams of theology (Evangelicalism and modern Fundamentalism) also exist within the body of theology known as Dispensationalism. I, therefore, recognize that some of what I write here does not apply only to just Dispensationalism. It applies to the two broader versions of theology known as Evangelicalism and Fundamentalism.

Does Dispensationalism Cause Disunity? Defining Evangelicalism in Contrast to Fundamentalism

I write from the Evangelical model of Dispensationalism. Therefore, I would like to show why certainly one stream of Dispensationalism does not promote disunity in the body of Christ. One stream of theology within Dispensationalism actually works with due diligence to help bring the body of Christ together on the essentials of the faith while working together for the gospel and God's glory (glory defined as his character magnified) through the supreme standard of Scripture. Evangelical Dispensationalists do this through three key aspects to their theology: (1) their specific view of how God communicates his love to his creation, (2) a holistic theology versus a dissected (separatist) theology where special revelation theology remains disconnected to natural revelation, and (3) through a theological triage methodology where some biblical doctrines rank as more important than other doctrines.

Those three aspects of theology differ from the modern Fundamentalism models that exist in all shades or sectors of the body of Christ. Even Dispensationalism has, along with some Covenantalism forms of theology, functioned with many Fundamentalists within its ranks. Dr. Clarence Bass noted this in his work on the history of Dispensationalism. Separatism builds its theology from the following three points: (1) a theology built from its own unique order to how God communicates his love that has (2) dissected special revelation from common/natural revelation, (3) and a theology practiced methodologically through defending all doctrine as equally essential. That type of theological model we call Fundamentalism teaches that when "there is no agreement in theology and practice there could be no fellowship. Supposed doctrinal impurities in others demands complete separation of fellowship from them."[1008] This model of theology is known for its history of emphasizing a "separatistic"[1009] worldview.

[1008] Clarence B. Bass, *Backgrounds to Dispensationalism: Its Historical Genesis and Ecclesiastical Implications* (Grand Rapids, MI: Baker Books, 1960), 99.

[1009] Bruce L. Shelley, "*Fundamentalism*," in *The New International Dictionary of the Christian Church*, ed. J.D. Douglas (Grand Rapids, MI: Zondervan Publishing, 1978), 397.

Writing from within his own tradition, Dr. David O. Beale defines modern Fundamentalism as a strong separatist theology. Fundamentalism emphasizes strongly that "the Scriptures clearly teach certain criteria for true Christian fellowship. They now regard the doctrine of biblical fellowship as fundamental, inherently part of the doctrine of God's absolute holiness—separation (sanctification) from the world, from false religion, and from *every practice of disobedience* to the Scriptures."[1010] Fundamentalism functions with a central governing principle of spatial separation based upon their theological model. They so emphasize holiness as separation that it in some versions exalts that element over and beyond the incarnation principle of God's holiness coming into the world through Jesus in the flesh (John 1:14).

Dr. Earnest Pickering affirms this governing principle when he says, "separatists believe that the *governing attribute of God is his holiness*," and because "God is separate from evil, he expects his people to be so."[1011] Even more pointedly, Pickering properly explains the difference between a Fundamentalist and an Evangelical. He says Fundamentalists see God exercising his "love in holiness" whereas evangelicals see God as exercising "his holiness in love."[1012]

That presentation by Pickering highlights the differences well. Fundamentalism emphasizes God's love through spatial separation from sin, their definition of holiness. Evangelicals emphasize God's holiness coming to us through love relationally in the Lord. Fundamentalism emphasizes special revelation over and apart from general revelation and applies that emphasis through spatially separating from those they differ with by emphasizing all doctrine as equally important to such a degree differences require spatial separation from the ones they perceive as walking in disobedience to some particular doctrine or set of doctrines.

Just as Pickering writes from within the stream of Fundamentalism so I write without reservation from the Evangelical stream of theology. In my perspective Fundamentalism fails to present the best and most proper

---

[1010] David O. Beale, *In Pursuit of Purity: American Fundamentalism Since 1850* (Greenville, SC: Unusual Publications, 1986), 6. Italics mine.

[1011] Earnest D. Pickering, *Biblical Separation: The Struggle for a Pure Church* (Shaumburg, IL: Regular Baptist Press, 1979), 166, 167. Italics mine.

[1012] Ibid., 166.

version of God's love in Christ to the lost and even to the saints. I do not say that to imply or mean that my Fundamentalist friends are a failure in the work of God's kingdom. I do not think that. I ask that no one present my article in that light either. I do, however, think their approach does not best reflect the biblical model (and they think the same of our model too). They do have great success in many ways and for those I am eternally grateful. However, I think their way that has good elements in it is not the best way. I see Evangelicalism as the best and more honorable, holy, and helpful model as it highlights God's holiness in all three members of the Godhead who descended down to us in holiness through love as the Lord connects, communicates, comforts, and corrects us.

Jesus Christ's Incarnation Establishes the Evangelical Principle

The key and defining point is that Jesus Christ, who was perfect, holy, sinless and spatially separate, left his position in glory to come dwell with us relationally on earth. John 1:14 is the model for Evangelicalism. "And the Word became flesh and dwelt among us, and we have seen his glory, glory as of the only Son from the Father, full of grace and truth." God brings his holiness to us through grace and truth by relating to us in love through a person, the God-Man. God's methodology is not in love calling us to holiness by remaining spatially separate from us, as emphasized in Fundamentalism. God's ideology and methodology is Jesus Christ dwelling with us in the flesh (John 1:14) and in us by his Spirit (John 14:15-17).

Evangelicalism's idea of separation is not primarily a spatial one as much as it is a heart and mind separation. Evangelicals believe that we function as does God in being separate as he is separate though omnipresent. We see separatism more so as one of the mind thinking and acting differently not primarily as one of a presence being removed. Evangelicals are not as quick, not as eager, and not as driven to withdraw spatially from another due to our relational drive to connect, communicate, comfort, correct, and cultivate faithfulness in whatever area God has placed us. We see God's holiness in terms of maintaining mind and heart distinction from anything sinful, not as a calling to spatially separate from one who is in our opinion in error in some area or areas, especially when not related to fundamental doctrines of the faith. We do embrace the fundamentals of the faith, like our Fundamentalist friends, but we establish boundaries around the most important fundamentals while allowing for unity amidst diversity in other areas while not violating those core fundamentals.

Oddly, to us it is strange a Fundamentalist would have an issue with this because originally Fundamentalism as a historical movement in the early 1900s began with a defense of a small select set of core doctrines that they thought were the highest essentials to defend. *The original Fundamentalists in that sense were functioning like Evangelicals.* It is why I sometimes describe historic fundamentalists in today's era as *fundamental evangelicals*.

Modern evangelicals who will still unite with other evangelicals over the fundamentals of the faith, and yes even still fight for those, represent more precisely the original historic fundamentalists than the newer modern separatist fundamentalists (maybe they are neo-fundamentalists). Yet through time the Fundamentalists morphed into a new form of Fundamentalism, what I now call modern Fundamentalism (neo-fundamentalism), which made spatial separation such an emphatic point of their theology it led the movement in a direction that seems to have undermined its very foundation purpose of trying to create unity in the body of Christ.

On our end we usually associate theologies in a stream allowing unity amidst diversity with Evangelicalism in contrast to that of Fundamentalism that so heavily stresses and defines holiness as spatial separation that it fights for "separation (sanctification) . . . from every practice of disobedience."[1013] Such a theory when applied produces schism, sectarianism, and strife among the saints. And consequently, I argue that for those who think Dispensationalism breeds strife and schism in the body of Christ that such a conclusion misses the larger point of the differences between Evangelicalism and Fundamentalism. Fundamentalism in any model of theology, Dispensationalism or Covenantalism (or any denomination), produces that type of climate.

In fact, our adherents of Dispensationalism were excommunicated from the Covenantalism circles because of that Fundamentalism

---

[1013] David O. Beale, *In Pursuit of Purity: American Fundamentalism Since 1850* (Greenville, SC: Unusual Publications, 1986), 6.

methodology in the 1940s. Dispensationalism was birthed within the Reformed circles, as Dr. Tommy Ice has properly shown.[1014] Many early Dispensationalists were Reformed/Calvinists as well as Dispensationalists. Dispensationalism matured from within the womb of Reformation theology. In fact, as I have argued in other places, Dispensationalism is the fruit of the Reformation root. I made this argument under Dr. Mal Couch in my first systematic theology doctoral dissertation. He agreed with my analysis. They worked harmoniously together until the rise of the more modern Fundamentalism in the 1900s and more specifically until the 1940s when the Covenantalists excommunicated the Dispensationalists from their circles of fellowship.[1015]

That such a fracture took place in the 1940s from non-dispensational theologians against Dispensationalists ought to cause anyone accusing Dispensationalism as causing disunity in the body of Christ to pause for some serious historical reflection. From my perspective, the Evangelical body of Dispensationalism does not dissect, destroy, or dissolve the unity of the body of Christ. In fact, it seems to me Evangelical Dispensationalism through those three facets, (1) God communicating his holiness through love to us relationally (as modeled in the God-Man), (2) a holistic theology that is integrated, and (3) a theology promoted through a triage methodology (more of an incarnation of Christ model) offers an antidote to aggressive, antagonistic, and anemic versions of theology that lack full power and navigational wisdom through cultural permeation.

Had Fundamentalism not surfaced as it did in some sense in the early 1900s the trajectory with Covenantalists and Dispensationalists might have been much different today than the scene we currently have in the body of Christ between these two godly theological systems. Christians, therefore, should not see Dispensationalism itself as the cause to schism in the body of Christ. Something deeper, something behind, and

---

[1014] Tommy Ice, *The Calvinistic Heritage of Dispensationalism*, http://www.pre-trib.org/articles/view/calvinistic-heritage-of-dispensationalism

[1015] R. Todd Mangum, The Dispensational-Covenantal Rift: The Fissuring of American Evangelical Theology from 1936 to 1944 (Eugene, OR: Wipf Stock Publishers, 2007), 125-173.

something more central to a person's ideology promotes that mindset, not Dispensationalism itself. And for that matter, I do not think Covenantalism in and of itself promotes schism and disunity in the body of Christ. The ideology within modern Fundamentalism, in my opinion, promotes that problem and that ideology touches all shades of continuity and discontinuity theologies in the myriad of denominations.

Evangelical Dispensationalism on a Holistic Theology

Two men, both born in the 1800s, I think provide the symbol for the two streams of Dispensationalism. Dr. J.R. Graves, a Calvinist Dispensationalist and father of the separatist Landmarkism movement,[1016] and Dr. Lewis Sperry Chafer, another Calvinist Dispensationalist and father of Dallas Theological Seminary, modeled two distinct types of theology that still exist within the Dispensational body of theology today. Graves, more of a separatist Fundamentalist, and Chafer, an Evangelical, modeled two different types of theology. Chafer's theology laid the foundation for an Evangelical model of Dispensationalism. This can be seen in how Chafer defined systematic theology. Chafer embraced a holistic, non-separatist, integrated Evangelical model of theology.

Dr. Chafer defined systematic theology as "the collecting, scientifically arranging, comparing, exhibiting, and defending of all facts from *any and every source concerning God* and His works. It is thetic in that it follows a humanly devised thesis form and presents and verifies truth as *truth.*"[1017] This is an excellent definition that apparently was carefully thought out by Dr. Chafer from the examination he did of so many other definitions offered before him. His definition would ensure that we systematic theologians do not neglect any area of God's revelation (special or general). His definition in essence provided a succinct element that can be one of the keys to the difference between Evangelical

---

[1016] H. Leon McBeth, *The Baptist Heritage: Four Centuries of Baptist Witness* (Nashville, TN: Broadman Press, 1987), 447-456.

[1017] Lewis Sperry Chafer, *Systematic Theology* (Grand Rapids, MI: Kregel Publications, 1993), 6. Italics mine.

theologies and some Fundamentalist versions of theology. He was even more specific saying:

> Theology is . . . a discourse upon one specific, namely God. However, since no consideration of God will be complete His works and ways in the universe which He has created, as well as His Person, theology may be extended properly to include all material and immaterial realities that exist and the facts concerning them and contained in them. Though it is highly impractical to encumber the science of theology with extended discourse covering all the 'ologies' of the universe, it remains true, nevertheless, that the basic fact underlying each and every science is its relation to the Creator of all things and His purpose in creation. Though not usually included in the science of theology, the other sciences which engage the thoughts of men would be both sanctified and exalted were they to be approached, as they should be, with that awe and reverence which recognizes in them the presence, power, and purpose of the Creator. Great injury has resulted, it is obvious, from the modern tendency to divorce all subjects which border on the natural from every divine relationship when, in reality, there is no basis upon which these other 'ologies' can rest other than the original purpose of the Creator.[1018]

God has certainly and fundamentally revealed himself in Scripture. Dispensationalism has been very clear that the Bible and the Bible alone is the ultimate authority! But we should not use that in an unbalanced way and claim that it is the *only* authority. God's sovereignty and his glory have been spread throughout the entire universe. Though sinful man will not give unto God glory in these areas, he or she may still discover truths in these areas. Evangelical theology embraces the entire spectrum of God's revelation, both special and general revelation.

[1018] Ibid., 3.

All Truth is God's Truth & Is Useful in Evangelical Models of Theology: Avoiding the Sacred & Secular Ideology

Of course, sinful man will not, without the supernatural power of the Spirit, appropriate any discovery of truth to move towards God in salvation, but this does not mean that God's truth is not in and within even the natural spheres that we would call common revelation discovered and appropriated by common grace. God has revealed himself through special revelation, which is ultimate in priority, and he has also revealed himself through common revelation, which is subservient to the Bible yet still an area that requires study for harmonious correlation and synthesis. As the Evangelical Dispensationalist Dr. Norman Geisler said,

> While the Bible is all true, God has not revealed all truth in the Bible. Whereas the Bible is only truth, the Bible is not the only truth; some truth lies outside of it. Said in another way, all truth is God's truth, but not all God's truth is in the Bible . . . . General revelation, then, plays an important role in God's plan, and as such it has several unique roles . . . . General revelation encompasses much more than special revelation. Most of the truths of science, history, mathematics, and the arts are not in God's Word; the bulk of truth in all these areas is found only in God's general revelation. While the Bible is scientifically accurate, it is not a textbook on science. The mandate for doing science is not a *redemption* mandate but a creation mandate; right after God created Adam He commanded him to 'fill the earth and subdue it' (Gen. 1:28). Likewise, there are no mathematical errors in God's inerrant Word, but then again there is very little geometry or algebra and no calculus in it either. Similarly, the Bible records accurately much of the history of Israel, but has little on the history of the world, except as it bears on Israel. The same is true of most every area of the arts and science. Whenever the Bible speaks in these areas, it speaks authoritatively, but God has largely left the discoveries of His truths in these areas to a study of general revelation."[1019]

[1019] Norman Geisler, *Systematic Theology: Introduction Bible*, vol. 1 (Minneapolis, MN: Bethany House Publishers, 2002), 70-71.

To divorce these two realms is to do an injustice to theology as the *whole universe* declares the glory of God. The whole universe speaks of God and God can be found in every element of the universe. Certain versions of fundamentalism, which is distinct from evangelicalism in this area, have divorced the two sciences from one another.

I believe Dr. Chafer at the time of his writings saw or foresaw the emerging differences between one form of Fundamentalism and Evangelicalism. Sometimes a Fundamentalist and Evangelical may not differ in any substantive sense of the term. I tend to think, however, by the way Chafer defined theology, that he saw some differences between at least some types of Fundamentalism and that of Evangelicals. The first name of Dallas Theological Seminary was actually Evangelical Theological College. He established the school in 1924. The term and movement of Fundamentalism was coined around 1910 to 1915 when the books titled "The Fundamentals" were produced and distributed throughout the world.

Fundamentalism arose to prominence in the 1920s and did so in opposition to liberalism or modernism. With all of this developing around the time of Chafer's plant of Dallas Seminary he may have seen some differences or concerns in the idea or spirit of fundamentalism. My thinking is supported by Dr. John Hannah's assessment of Chafer. In his work: "*An Uncommon Union: Dallas Theological Seminary and American Evangelicalism*" Hannah noted that "since Chafer participated in the founding of the National Association of Evangelicals, it would suggest that the school is not considered a Fundamentalist institution because NAE has not been associated with an 'anti-intellectualism, combativeness, extremism, and what was viewed by many as a paranoid style'"[1020]

Dr. Hannah added even further that "Chafer shared many of the convictions of Riley and J.F. Norris, but not their attitudes and methods"[1021] In my analysis Hannah is right about Chafer. At least two key elements to Chafer's theology led him away from Fundamentalism. He held to a graded scale of truth, or what has been lately termed a

---

[1020] John D. Hannah, *An Uncommon Union: Dallas Theological Seminary and American Evangelicalism* (Grand Rapids, MI: Zondervan Publishing, 2009), 77.

[1021] Ibid.

theological triage, where love was the preeminent trait, instead of theology models without a triage. He also embraced a system of theology that sought harmony between natural revelation and special revelation in a systematic theology and apologetics. When either of those two positions are embraced one will lean towards Evangelicalism whereas if rejected one will align more with the spirit of Fundamentalism with its emphasis on spatial separation and monastic tendencies.

Having said that above, Evangelicalism and an Evangelical Dispensationalist gladly welcome the idea that every very molecule moving on earth speaks of God, and every word in the Bible speaks of God. The two sciences do not compete against each other. Instead the two fields, if understood rightly, are *complementary to one another*. Some have called this approach to theology the concordian view of theology, i.e., theology and science concur or are in concert with each other since God authors both those. Just like a wife is the complementary mate to her husband, so too are common grace spheres complementary to her mate special revelation.

Dispensationalist Dr. Paul Enns recognizes that Dr. Chafer's view differs from some views inside Christendom where knowledge of God and formulation of truth is supposedly only to be developed from direct biblical sources. Yet Dr. Enns notes that Dr. Chafer's view is a "suitable definition of systematic theology."[1022] Dr. Enns recognizes that Dr. Chafer's view differs from others, such as Dr. Charles Hodge, who places the idea of systematic theology within the confines of only direct biblical revelation.[1023] Dr. Enns noted that,

> It is apparent in these two contrasting definitions of systematic theology that Chafer holds to a wider view, emphasizing that systematic theology assimilates information about God from 'any and every source'—including information outside of the Bible. Hodge restricts his definition about systematic theology to information gained from the Bible alone.[1024]

[1022] Paul Enns, *The Moody Handbook of Theology* (Chicago, IL: Moody Press, 1989), 147.

[1023] Ibid.

[1024] Ibid.

Not All Truth is as Equally as Important; Some Truths Rank Higher than Other Truths in Evangelicalism

Dr. Enns' conclusion on this matter is a balanced view of this matter. He agrees with Chafer and adds more to the definition following the lead of an Evangelical theologian Dr. Millard J. Erickson. Dr. Erickson (who is not a Dispensationalist) provides for a stratification view of authority (a graded or triage scale view of doctrinal authority; see the next section of this article). For now I will quote the summary that Dr. Enns provides from Dr. Millard J. Erickson's model that systematic theology would be holistic:

> (1) Theology is biblical, utilizing the tools and methods of biblical research (as well as employing insights from other areas of truth). (2) Theology is systematic, drawing on the entirety of Scripture and relating the various portions to each other. (3) Theology is relevant to culture and learning, drawing from cosmology, psychology, and philosophy of history. (4) Theology must be contemporary, relating God's truth to the questions and challenges of today. (5) Theology must be practical, not merely declaring objective doctrine, but relating to life itself.[1025]

This ideology aligns very well with Dispensationalism's literal hermeneutic in that we see God's universe as the declaration of his glory (glory defined as God's character highlighted). As Dispensationalists we also see grades of authority in the various realms or spheres of the universe. The Bible for us *is the ultimate source of all truth*, but it is *not the only source of truth*. There are grades of truth as well as grades of sin. Certain laws in God's house-hold are weightier and higher. Certain sins are greater than others. There are different degrees of reward in heaven and different degrees of punishment in hell (see next section for fuller discussion on this). This is a theological concept that applies even in this subject herein. The ultimate truth is without a doubt the Bible. The Bible is the supreme and the ultimate authority in all matters, even above and over common grace or natural grace areas. Yet that does not mean we

---

[1025] Ibid., 147-148.

should not study those areas where science and fruits of study in those common areas agree or complements or illuminates something in principle form in scripture. We ought to rejoice and praise God who is the God of both special and common revelation. As Dr. Enns, states,

> The Scriptures provide a primary source of theology in their revelation of God and man's relationship to Him. If God has revealed Himself (and He has), and if that self-revelation is accurately encoded in the sixty-six books of Scripture (and it is), then the Scriptures are the primary source of man's knowledge of God. Nature is also a primary source of a knowledge of God (Ps. 19). Nature, in its harmonious revelation, is a constant witness concerning God's attributes, eternal power, and divine nature (Rom. 1:20).[1026]

Within Dispensationalism there has been this idea that God's truth is holistic. By the term holistic I mean that there are many of us who believe that God's truth is to be found in every area of life, not just in the Bible and only in the Bible. Dispensationalists Dr. Paul D. Feinberg and Dr. Norman L. Geisler also agree that God's truth is discovered in all areas of the universe, not just within Scripture. For example, when commenting on the natural studies of philosophy the two scholars say that "all truth is God's truth, and since philosophy is a quest for truth, then philosophy will contribute to our understanding of God and His world."[1027]

Dispensationalist Dr. Paige Patterson, one of the most respected Evangelical leaders within Southern Baptist life, also joins the ranks of theologians that believe that the study of all areas of the universe is important to understand God. In line with Chafer, Fienberg, and Geisler, he states:

> All truth is God's truth. The discovery of truth, whether scientific, mathematical, philosophical, historical, or theological, is the

---

[1026] Ibid., 150-151.

[1027] Norman L. Geisler and Paul D. Feinberg, *Introduction to Philosophy: A Christian Perspective* (Grand Rapids, MI: Baker Books, 1980), 22.

discovery of the ways and orderings of an omnipotent, omniscient, and benevolent God.[1028]

This definition as articulated by Chafer and affirmed by other leading Dispensationalists is also one that can help to resolve the war that has taken place inside conservative circles of Christianity. Some versions of Fundamentalism have erred by asserting an almost monastic or neo-monastic type view of Christianity. I have no doubt their goal of defending the Bible is one, if not maybe even the strongest, motive. Sometimes it is the drive to be "purely biblical" and totally holy that drives people to a study of only the Bible. Both quests are well intentioned efforts when so much of Christendom has abandoned holiness, biblical authority, and objective truth.

Nonetheless, even though these people are well intentioned, it does not change the fact that such thinking as this leads people to the "sacred-secular dichotomy."[1029] Dr. Taylor Jones, professor of Chemistry within a Dispensational college and seminary, has stated that when this sacred versus secular ideology flourishes it leads people to "considering non-theological disciplines to be less worthy of study."[1030] This divorce of the grace realms has led to people isolating themselves from an intellectual study of the so-called secular fields of thought.[1031] Yet as Dr. Taylor notes, this ideology is very common in "many Bible-believing churches today."[1032]

We must not allow for a separation between the two fields of grace. As Dispensationalists it is better to make a distinction between the two instead of attempting to separate the two. Just as the Trinity is one yet has three distinct members, and just as Israel and the Church are within the

---

[1028] Paige Patterson, *Johnny's Teacher—The Problem and the Solution* (Wake Forest, NC: Magnolia Hill Papers, 1997), 9.

[1029] Taylor B. Jones, *"Why a Scriptural View of Science,"* in *Think Biblically: Recovering a Christian Worldview*, gen. ed. John MacArthur and Master's College Faculty (Wheaton, IL: Crossway Books, 2003), 231.

[1030] Ibid., 232.

[1031] Ibid.

[1032] Ibid.

one family of God yet are still clearly distinct peoples in the overall family of God, so to there is only one Truth and all truth is a part of that Truth. Yet inside truth there are clear distinctions, levels, and functional roles. Truth in the sense of special revelation (special grace realm) is the highest authority and most **universal authority**. There is also, however, lower level truth (common, natural grace realm) and this lower level truth functions below the authority of Scripture but is still authoritative. Dr. Taylor again explains that we are to place Scripture as the *highest* authority while also seeking to see God in the natural science areas as well. He says,

> The Bible . . . is the only source of tangible, eternal Truth on earth (Isa. 40:8). This understanding ensures the total sufficiency of Scripture when applied to every issue addressed therein (Ps. 19:7-14). Having embraced this view, a scientist looking at the universe recognizes that the entire creation is the handiwork of a sovereign God (John 1:3). His/her subsequent observations and explanations will be consistent with this perspective. Any observations that appear to be at odds with this declaration . . . will be reassessed in a way that does not deny the Truth of what God has clearly and unambiguously said He has done. . . . [the scientist] will never seek to distort the Truth of the clearer teaching of Scripture so that it conforms to some current theory of science. . . . science can be of great value to society and can contribute to a wonderful, correct, and true understanding of the universe that, in turn, can be used for the benefit of all mankind. To say otherwise is to deny the essence of science. There is also built into this conclusion an appreciation for the fact that *true* does not mean *True*. The distinction between the truth of science that is subject to change and the Truth of Scripture that is a reflection of the immutability of God is also a part of this view. The adoption of the 'One Book' worldview of science retraces the errant steps of contemporary science, begun centuries ago, and begins anew to tread the harmonious and compatible path it enjoys with the Scriptures. Knowledge from the scientific realm has been returned to its proper perspective as valuable, important, a source of logically, self-consistent learning, but in submission to the Word of God. The rightful place of the divine author's authority has been acknowledged. The proper use

of Scripture where it impinges on science has been reestablished. This understanding alone allows science to resume its correct place in epistemology.[1033]

Dr. Taylor as a scientist does make the necessary and important distinction that the hard sciences (biology, physics, chemistry) are often more reliable than the soft sciences (anthropology, psychology) because in the hard sciences a person can function within the concept of scientific "reproducibility."[1034] This distinction between the hard sciences and the soft sciences does not "mean that such studies [soft sciences] are without merit or that one cannot use the results of such studies; it does mean, however, that one is less certain about the significance of the correlation . . . . . one cannot be as nearly as confident in the conclusions one draws in areas like sociology and anthropology compared with those in chemistry or physics."[1035]

In contrast though some, who have seen some of the errors coming from the soft science and even hard science spheres whereby clear biblical truth is denied for the sake of science, have gone to the *extreme* of rejecting the natural or common grace spheres of study all together. They have reacted to the grave error with a valiant and clarion call to return to the Bible! Such a clarion call is in one sense the right directional move. Yet in another sense it is wrong in its ultimate answer by splitting the fields of truth or knowledge into a sacred field and a secular field.

Sometimes reactionary movements, as found within some versions of Fundamentalism, are just as bad as the original error the reaction seeks to fight against. Just because science and the natural studies of the late 19th and 20th century went astray in some areas, such as with evolution, secular antichristian psychology, radical and secular philosophy which undermined supernatural revelation, that does not mean that we ought to divorce biblical theology from her mate of natural theology and philosophy which arises from the common grace or the natural grace realm. Some have run so far in the opposite direction of natural or

---

[1033] Ibid., 236, 237.

[1034] Ibid., 223.

[1035] Ibid., 223, 222.

common grace study that they have even come to believe that even philosophy is an unholy and unprofitable discipline to study. Dr. Geisler and Feinberg mention this noting that:

> Some Christians are suspicious of philosophy because they have heard stories of others who have lost their faith through the study of philosophy. They have been advised to avoid philosophy like the plague. Upon serious reflection it is clear that this is not wise advice.[1036]

Theologian Dr. R.C. Sproul suffered from those who believed that common grace studies were dangerous and unbiblical. While in seminary he switched from a Bible major to a philosophy major and he was sharply criticized by other students for this move. Dr. Sproul wrote of this saying:

> I decided to change my academic major from Bible to philosophy. When I made that change I was all but drummed out of the evangelical corps on our campus. My friends were horrified at my apparent apostasy. The Bible verse quoted too many times to count was 'Beware lest anyone cheat you through philosophy and empty deceit' (Col. 2:8). I was both confused and hurt by the reactions of my friends. I had turned to philosophy to strengthen my understanding of God, not to weaken it. Though I was no longer a Bible major, by no means had I rejected the Bible or the study of it. I couldn't figure out how one could 'beware' of something without first being 'aware of it. My study of secular philosophy only increased my appreciation for the depths and riches of things revealed in Scripture. It also provided me with an understanding of those issues crucial to the Christian task of apologetics. It never occurred to me that we were to abandon the world to pagans. Neo-monasticism breeds ignorance—ignorance not only of culture and the ideas that shape culture, but ignorance of theology as well. It displays more lack of faith than strength of faith. The effects of neo-monasticism are catastrophic. By retreating from engagement

---

[1036] Norman L. Geisler and Paul D. Feinberg, *Introduction to Philosophy: A Christian Perspective* (Grand Rapids, MI: Baker Books, 1980), 21-22.

with the world we have suffered defeat by default. We wring our hands at the secularization of America culture and wonder how it could have happened.[1037]

Dr. R.C. Sproul, a theologian who is in the Reformed line of the Princeton scholars, does not follow the chief of systematic theologians of Princeton, Dr. Charles Hodge. Hodge's definition of systematic theology restricted systematic study only to biblical revelation. He seemingly is critical of those who believe we should divorce the two realms of study (special grace and common grace realms). R.C. Sproul is actually more in line with Dr. Chafer's definition in this area. He has realized that the split between the two sciences, theology and natural sciences (special and common revelation), has led to a serious error in Christianity. Commenting on this issue has stated that there is a need for both a natural and special theology. Dr. Sproul says,

> As I enter the twilight years of my life, I am convinced that Gilson is fundamentally right. We need to reconstruct the classical synthesis by which a natural theology bridges the special revelation of Scripture and the general revelation of nature. Such a reconstruction could end the war between science and theology. The thinking person could embrace nature without embracing naturalism. All of life, in its unity and diversity, could be lived coram Deo, before the face of God, under his authority and to his glory.[1038]

A Theological Triage: A Biblical Methodology of Wisdom

I love how one of my pastors describes this matter. Pastor Brannon Poore (a nondispensationalist) likes to say on these matters: "*Some truths are closed handed truths and other truths are open handed truths.*" Evangelical Dispensationalists understand this theological triage model or biblical methodology. However, modern Fundamentalists (which grew from the earlier seminal leaders like J. Frank Norris) do not understand it

---

[1037] R.C. Sproul, *Essential Truths of the Christian Faith* (Wheaton, IL: Tyndale House Publishers, 1992), xiv.

[1038] R.C. Sproul, The *Consequences of Ideas* (Wheaton, IL: Crossway Books, 2000), 203.

(the historic fundamentalists seem to have affirmed this), have overlooked it, or have rejected it for a different biblical methodology. I think for those who have done so, however, they have done so against the witness of wisdom. Jesus Christ taught us to walk in wisdom. He said, "I am sending you out as sheep in the midst of wolves, so be wise as serpents and innocent as doves" (Matt. 10:16). Solomon taught this too in the Old Covenant era. He stated that wisdom is "more precious than jewels, and nothing you desire can compare with her" (Prov. 3:15).

Evangelical forms of Dispensationalism have permeated the many different denominations as well as launched new churches, colleges, and other Christian organizations throughout Christendom. The movement's intent is not to destroy the unity of the God's people in history but to provide a sure basis for unity. Mature Dispensationalists, who understand the heart of Dispensational theology with its emphasis on God's glory and grace, the centrality of Christ, and the cross of Calvary (as emphasized by Dr. Lewis Sperry Chafer), promote love, hope, faith and unity in all areas of life and faith through a common confession rooted in the Bible alone. That spirit evident in the early church, rediscovered in the Reformation era, and uniquely applied in this era within Dispensational movement has produced a distinct Evangelical methodology.

By methodology I am speaking of how a theology is applied in actual concrete life situations and even in more particular through relationships in the body of Christ. Evangelical Dispensationalism, a unique stream within the larger Dispensational umbrella, has through its methodology, derived from a literal hermeneutic, sought to build bonds among the brethren in the overall the body of Christ. In contrast to some versions of Fundamentalism, which has a different methodology, Evangelical Dispensationalism has sought to build bridges with the larger body of Christ as it promotes the love, light, and law of the Lord. Through its unique methodology Evangelical Dispensationalism has remained well suited for not only cultural permeation but also interdenominational and transdenominational ministerial permeation. The chief focus on Scripture, not creed, has given them a fluidity that allows them great latitude in ministry contexts. Dr. Blaising, professor of theology at Southwestern Baptist Theological Seminary (and former professor at The Southern Baptist Theological Seminary as well as Dallas Theological Seminary) has well stated:

Interdenominational schools and ministries have attempted to carry on that vision to varying degrees, a vision which has helped contribute to the sense of evangelical identity in some quarters of evangelicalism. Dispensationalists, of course, were not the only evangelicals to emphasize the authority of the Bible. But their transdenominational vision and their practical orientation to expositional ministry made an emphasis on Scripture a hallmark of the movement, one that continues today as well.[1039]

This methodological spirit has been made known through the movement's ability to interact with so many persuasions of theology, even with and within different denominations. Dispensationalism, if true to its roots, has the ability to work with many when there may be significant disagreement in certain doctrinal areas so long as the Bible is the chief focus of all matters of interpretations. This transdenominational element makes the Dispensational movement more of a grace centered, encouraging, optimistic movement in that it seeks to first and foremost make Scripture, not creed nor denominations, the ultimate authority in all matters of faith and practice.

So long as the Bible is adopted as the sole or supreme standard for truth, then Dispensationalists normally seek to work with others for higher causes than against those with whom there are minor variations in doctrine. Such efforts exist because the Dispensationalist takes a literal reading of Scripture and thus understands that in God's household-universe, just like any rightly governed home, some truths take precedence over others and some truths are the most important for the particular moment in time and history. As Dispensationalist Dr. Norman Geisler has noted, "Not all moral laws are of equal weight. Jesus spoke of the 'weightier' matters of the law (Matt. 23:23) and of the 'least' (Matt. 5:19) and the 'greatest' commandment (Matt. 22:36)."[1040] The Dispensationalist takes this teaching from Scripture literally and it leads him or her to make

---

[1039] Craig Blaising, *"The Extent and Varieties of Dispensationalism,"* in *Progressive Dispensationalism*, by Craig Blaising and Darrell L. Bock (Grand Rapids, MI: Baker Books, 1993), 14.

[1040] Norman Geisler, *Christian Ethics: Options and Issues* (Grand Rapids, MI: Baker Book House, 1989), 116.

the grace, love, and cross of Christ the preeminent theme in his or her ministry as did Dr. Lewis Sperry Chafer.

Dispensationalist Dr. Charles C. Ryrie on a Theological Triage

One Evangelical Dispensationalist, Dr. Charles C. Ryrie understood this truth as well. He valued the stratification methodology of theology. Unlike some versions of Fundamentalism that make each and every doctrine of Scripture equal in importance (leading to many schisms and much strife), Ryrie recognized the wisdom that God gave us in Scripture concerning variation of degrees in doctrinal importance. In answering his critics that have made unwarranted accusations about Dispensationalism teaching two ways of salvation Ryrie provided the Evangelical Dispensational triage methodology.

> Unfortunately, the representation of the dispensational viewpoint has not always been with integrity. . . . Neither the older nor the newer dispensationalists teach two ways of salvation, and it is not fair to attempt to make them appear so to teach. After all, a man has to be taken at his word or all means of communication breakdown. It is certainly fair to attempt to prove a position illogical, but it is never fair to attempt to misrepresent that position either by misquoting or selective quoting. Straw men are easy to create, but the huff and puff it takes to demolish them are only huff and puff. . . . A sense or priority is also important. The temptation for any Christian preacher or writer to get off on a tangent or to ride a hobby horse is a very great one. That is true in doctrine, and it is true in matters of living . . . . Knowing and proclaiming this whole counsel of God is our desire, yet we all need priorities in our proclamation of doctrine. Some doctrines in the Bible are more central than others. Paul placed a high priority on the right understanding of the gospel (Gal. 1:8-9). He placed a low priority on the doctrine of the observance of particular days (Col. 2:16-17). Some doctrines should be given priority over others. We who are dispensationalists would do well to remember this. 'Dispensational truth' is not necessarily the most important thing in the Bible. Even prophecy, though a major theme, should not constitute the whole of one's preaching. The spiritual life, which is without question a

high priority doctrine, can be overdone .... It may [also] help to be reminded of some of the important doctrines to which dispensationalists subscribe wholeheartedly. After all, dispensationalists are conservatives and affirm complete allegiance to the doctrines of verbal, plenary inspiration, the virgin birth and deity of Christ, the substitutionary atonement, eternal salvation by grace through faith, the importance of godly living and the ministry of the Holy Spirit, the future coming of Christ, and the eternal damnation of the lost. Those who are divided from us in the matter of dispensationalism or premillennialism may remember the areas in which they [Covenant theologians] are united with us. As already noted, some doctrines are more important than others, so it particularly behooves us not to cut off our fellowship from those who share similar views about these important doctrines. There are few enough these days who believe in the fundamentals of the faith, and to ignore those who have declared themselves on the side of the truth of God is unwise. Something is wrong with our circles of fellowship, sense of priority, or doctrine of unity when conservatives view fellow conservatives as the opposition party and then find their theological friends among those who are teaching and promoting error.[1041]

Such efforts exist because the Dispensationalist adopts and applies a literal (normal, originalism, standard, or plain) reading of Scripture and thus understands that in God's household-universe, just like any rightly governed home, some truths take precedence over others and some truths are the most important for the particular moment in time and history. If I had to explain what may be one of the most major differences between a Calvinistic Evangelical Dispensational theology versus other conservative versions of theology (such as Fundamentalism), even other Dispensational or Calvinist versions of theology, I would have to say is that Dispensationalism in the Evangelical version recognizes that though all truth is God's truth, and that God has placed degrees of authority and degrees of importance on each truth. Not every truth is as important as the next truth in a particular era, circumstance, or context.

[1041] Charles C. Ryrie, *Dispensationalism* (Chicago, IL: Moody Press, 1995), 210, 212.

Some levels of truth are higher and others are lower. Some, of course are so high that it may be hard to determine as a human what is more important, but in any case it is recognized that there are grades or degrees of truth in God's house-hold universe. Dr. Erickson calls this step the "stratification of topics."[1042] By this he means that "we need to know what the major issues are. And we need to know what can be treated as subtopics, that is, which issues, while important, are not quite so crucial and indispensable as are the major divisions."[1043]

Dr. Erickson even provides a helpful set of levels for how to determine authority within our interpretive systems. He says there are first "direct statements of Scripture" and these provide the clearest and most weighted "degree of authority." Second, there are "direct implications of Scripture" that also lead us to focus upon with a "high priority." But these, because it requires the extra step of "logical inference," the interpreter must realize more room for "interpretational error" exists. Third, "probable implications of Scripture" lead us to conclusions based upon "inferences" and therefore "less authoritative than direct implications." Fourth, interpreters build ideas from "inductive conclusions from Scripture" that ought to cause the humble interpreter to realize more likely error might exist in those conclusions. Fifth, "conclusions inferred from general revelation" means there is sometimes less clarity and accordingly the interpreter must always keep an eye on "clearer and more explicit statements of the Bible. And lastly, sixth, "outright speculations" that often rely upon "hypotheses based upon a single statement in Scripture, or derived from somewhat obscure or unclear parts of the Bible" can be "utilized" by "theologians" so long as it is not done "with the same degree of authoritativeness attributed to statements of the first category listed above."[1044]

[1042] Ibid., 78.

[1043] Ibid., 78-79.

[1044] Millard J. Erickson, *Christian Theology* (Grand Rapids, MI: Baker Books, 1985), 79-80.

Summary: Evangelicalism Embraces an Incarnational & Holistic Integrated Theology within a Theological Triage Methodology

The doctrine of Christ becoming incarnate, the God-Man, highlights the entire premise of this article. Jesus Christ communicated God's holiness by bringing God to us relationally through the act of him becoming a man (John 1:14). We Evangelical Dispensationalists, in contrast to our Fundamentalist Dispensational first cousins in the faith and second cousins in the faith with the broader Fundamentalists in larger body of Christ, see the incarnation of Christ as the paramount doctrine defining our theological substance and how that translates into pragmatic service.

Jesus Christ, the sinless and holy God, did not withdraw and isolate himself from the culture. No more should we withdraw from our beloved brethren in the faith for any and every error than a spouse ought to withdraw from his or covenanted partner for any and every error. Not all error is as equally as offensive to God or to us. Not all error in a marriage justifies a divorce. Likewise, not all error in another's life or in the body of Christ justifies spatial separation from those believers. An emphatic focus on spatial separation in the body of Christ, or even in a marriage, leads to schism and sectarianism that severs beloved bonds in the body of Christ. Jesus modeled a better way. He instead loved us, related to us, and as he did so he connected to us, communicated to us, comforted us, corrected us, and cultivated faith in us as he converted and commissioned us into his Great Commission service.

Furthermore, we believe as he did that the God-Man in his essence modeled supernatural special revelation being wed to common revelation by the act of his divine nature being wrapped into and intertwined with his human nature. He is both God (divine) and Man (natural). That alone teaches us that special revelation should not be divorced, split, or separated from general/natural revelation. We are to make those two aspects function in perfect harmony as Jesus' nature is both divine and human while still being one person. Furthermore, we believe that Jesus Christ modeled wisdom in knowing what truths ranked above others. He spoke of greater sins, implying lesser sins, and the greatest truths, implying lesser important truths, and by doing so he modeled for us the theological triage that helps build bridges for the gospel to take root. For these reasons we Evangelical Dispensationalists think this model reflects the best witness of Scripture for the Savior's service of seeking out souls to experience his sacred salvation.

BIBLIOGRAPHY

Books and Articles

Adler, Mortimer J. *Aristotle for Everybody: Difficult Thought Made Easy*. New York, NY: MacMillan Publishing, 1978.

_____. *Desires, Right and Wrong: The Ethics of Enough*. Mount Jackson, VA: Axios Press, 1991.

_____. *Ten Philosophical Mistakes*. New York, NY: MacMillan Publishing, 1985.

_____. *The Idea of Freedom*, Vol. 2. Garden City, NY: Doubleday & Company, 1961.

_____. *We Hold These Truths: Understanding the Ideas and Ideals of the Constitution*. New York, NY: MacMillan Publishing Company, 1987.

Akin, Daniel L, David P Nelson, and Peter R Schemm. *A Theology For The Church*. Nashville, TN: B & H Academic, 2007.

Alcorn, Randy. *Heaven*. Wheaton, IL: Tyndale House Publishing, 2004.

Allsion, Gregg R. *Historical Theology: An Introduction to Christian Doctrine*. Grand Rapids, MI: Zondervan, 2011.

Ames, William. *The Marrow of Theology*. Edited by John Eusden. Grand Rapids, MI: Baker Books, 1968.

Anderson, Ryan T. *Truth Overruled: The Future of Marriage and Religious Freedom*. Washington, DC: Regnery Publishing, 2015.

Ankerberg, John and John Weldon. *Fast Facts on Defending Your Faith*. Eugene, OR: Harvest House Publishers. 2002.

_____. *One World: Bible Prophecy and the New World Order*. Chicago, IL: Moody Press, 1991.

Anton SzandorLaVey, Anton Szandor. *The Satanic Bible*. HarperCollins Publishers, 1969.

Archer, Gleason L. *Encyclopedia of Bible Difficulties*. Grand Rapids, MI: Zondervan, 1982.

Arminius, Jacobus, James Nichols, William Nichols, and Carl Bangs. *The Works of James Arminius*. Grand Rapids, MI: Baker Book House, 1986.

Ashton, John F. *In Six Days*. Green Forest, AR: Master Books, 2001.

Baker, William. *The Books of James & First and Second Peter: Faith, Suffering, and Knowledge. Twenty-First Century Commentary Series*. Edited by Mal Couch and Ed Hindson. Chattanooga, TN: AMG Publishers, 2004.

Barackman, Floyd H. *Practical Christian Theology*. Grand Rapids, MI: Kregel Publications, 1998.

Barnhouse, Donald Grey. *Revelation: An Expositional Commentary*. Grand Rapids, MI: Zondervan, 1971.

_____. *Romans: God's Grace*, Vol. III. Grand Rapids, MI: Wm. B. Eerdmans Publishing Company, 1959.

_____. *The Invisible War: The Panorama of the Continuing Conflict Between Good & Evil*. Grand Rapids, MI: Zondervan, 1965.

Bass, Clarence B. *Backgrounds to Dispensationalism: Its Historical Genesis and Ecclesiastical Implications*. Grand Rapids, MI: Baker Book House, 1960.

Bateman, Herbert W. IV. *Three Central Issues in Contemporary Dispensationalism: A Comparison of Traditional and Progressive Views*. Grand Rapids, MI: Kregel Publications, 1999.

Beale, G. K and D. A Carson. *Commentary On The New Testament Use of The Old Testament*. Grand Rapids, MI: Baker Academic, 2007.

Blaising, Craig A. *Progressive Dispensationalism*. Grand Rapids, MI: Baker Books, 1993.

Blaising, Craig A. and Darrell L. Bock. *Dispensationalism, Israel And The Church*. Grand Rapids, MI: Zondervan, 1992.

Bloesch, Donald G. *Essentials of Evangelical Theology: Volume One: God, Authority, & Salvation*. Peabody, MA: Hendrickson Publishers, 1998.

Boaz, David. *The Libertarian Mind: A Manifesto for Freedom*. New York, NY: Simon & Schuster, 2015.

Brand, Chad O. *Perspectives on Election: Five Views*. Nashville, TN: B&H Publishing Group, 2006.

Brand, Chad O. and Tom Pratt Jr. *Perspectives on Israel and the Church: 4 Views*. Edited by Chad Brand. Nashville, TN: B&H Publishing Group, 2015.

Breyer, Stephen. *Active Liberty: Interpreting Our Democratic Constitution*. New York, USA: Vintage Publishing, 2005.

_____. *Making Our Democracy Work*. New York, USA: Vintage Books, 2010.

_____. *The Court and the World: American Law and the New Global Realities*. New York: Alfred A. Knopf, 2015.

Brog, David. *Standing With Israel: Why Christians Support the Jewish State*. Lake Mary, FL: Frontline Publishing, 2003.

Buswell, James Oliver. *A Systematic Theology of the Christian Religion*. Grand Rapids, MI: 1962.

Calvin, John. *Calvin's Commentaries*. Grand Rapids, MI: Baker Book House, 1998.

Cairns, Alan. "Augustinianism." In *Dictionary of Theological Terms*. Greenville, SC: Ambassador Emerald International Publishing, 2002.

Chafer, Lewis Sperry. *Grace: An Exposition of God's Marvelous Gift*. Grand Rapids, MI: Kregel Publications, 1922.

_____. *Systematic Theology*. Grand Rapids, MI: Kregel Publications, 1993.

_____. *The Ephesian Letter: Doctrinally Considered*. New York, New York: Loizeaux Brothers, 1935.

Cone, Chris. *An Introduction to the New Covenant*. Hurst, TX: Tyndale Seminary Press, 2013.

_____. "Four Pillars of Dispensationalism." In *Dispensationalism Tomorrow & Beyond: A Theological Collection Honor of Charles C. Ryrie*. Fort Worth, TX: Tyndale Seminary Press, 2008.

_____. *Prolegomena: Introductory Notes on Bible Study & Theological Method*. Fort Worth, TX: Tyndale Seminary Press, 2009.

_____. *The Bible in Government and Society*. Hurst, TX: Tyndale Seminary Press, 2012.

Constable, Thomas L. "1 Thessalonians." In *The Bible Knowledge Commentary: An Exposition of the Scriptures by Dallas Seminary Faculty*. Edited by John F. Walvoord and Roy B. Zuck. USA: SP Publications, 1983.

Couch, Mal. *An Essential Doctrinal Statement for Restoring Biblical Integrity in the Local Church*. Edited by Arlyn Kantz. Fort Worth, TX: Tyndale Theological Seminary, No date of publication.

_____. "Interpreting the Book of Revelation." In *A Bible Handbook to Revelation*. Edited by Mal Couch Grand Rapids, MI: Kregel Publications, 2001.

_____. *Messianic Systematic Theology of the Old Testament*. Clifton, TX: Scofield Ministries, 2010.

_____. "Regeneration." In the *Tyndale Theological Seminary New Testament Doctrinal Greek Word Study*. Edited by Mal Couch. No place or date of publication.

_____. *The Hope of Christ's Return: Premillennial Commentary on 1 & 2 Thessalonians*. Chattanooga, TN: AMG Publishers, 2001.

_____. *The Sovereignty of God*. Clifton, TX: Scofield Ministries, 2013.

Cloud, Henry and John Townsend. *Boundaries Face to Face: How to Have that Difficult Conversation You've Been Avoiding*. Grand Rapids, MI: Zondervan, 2003.

Clouse, Robert G. "Pentecostal Churches." In *The New International Dictionary of the Christian Church*. Edited by J.D. Douglas. Grand Rapids, MI: Zondervan, 1978.

Crenshaw, Curtis and Grover E. Gunn III. *Dispensationalism Today, Yesterday, and Tomorrow*. Memphis Tennessee, Footstool Publications, 1985.

Criswell, W.A. *Great Doctrines of the Bible, Volume 5, Soteriology*. Edited by Paige Patterson. Grand Rapids, MI: Zondervan Publishing, 1985.

_____. "The Doctrine of Predestination." In *We Believe*. Edited by

Paige Patterson and Luis Pantoja Jr. Dallas, TX: Criswell publications, 1977.

_____."*The Scarlet Thread of Redemption.*" In the *Holy Bible Baptist Study Edition*. Edited by W.A. Criswell and Paige Paige Patterson. Nashville, TN: Thomas Nelson Publishers, 1991.

Crutchfield, Larry V. *The Origins of Dispensationalism: The Darby Factor*. Lanham, MD: University Press of America, 1992.

Dagg, J.L. *Manual of Theology*. Harrisonburg, VA: Gano Books, 1990.

Demar, Gary. *End Times Fiction: A Biblical Consideration of the Left Behind Theology*. Nashville, TN: Thomas Nelson Publishers, 2001.

Demy, Timothy. "James Hall Brookes." In the *Dictionary of Premillennial Theology*. Edited by Mal Couch. Grand Rapids, MI: Kregel Publications, 1996.

Descartes, Rene. *Philosophical Works of Descartes*. Volume 1. Edited and translated by Haldane and Ross Cambridge, United Kingdom: Cambridge University Press, 1931-1934.

Dewitt, Dale S. *Dispensational Theology in America During the 20th Century: Theological and Cultural Context*. Grand Rapids, MI: Grace Bible College Publications, 2002.

Douglas, J.D. *New 20th Century Encyclopedia of Religious Knowledge*. Grand Rapids, MI: Baker Books, 1991.

_____. *The New International Dictionary of the Christian Church*. Grand Rapids, MI: Zondervan, 1978.

Drummond, Lewis A. *The Canvas Cathedral*. Nashville, TN: Thomas Nelson Publishers, 2003.

Dzugan, Ken. *How to Prove There is a God: Mortimer J. Adler's Writings and Thoughts about God*. Chicago, IL: Open Court Publishing,

2011.

Eddleman, H. Leo. "The Living Word of God." In *We Believe: Pisteuomen Series*, Volume 1. Edited by Paige Patterson and Luis Pantoja, Jr. Dallas, TX: Criswell Publications, 1977.

Eidsmoe, John. *Christianity and the Constitution: The Faith of our Founding Fathers*. Grand Rapids, MI: Baker Books, 1987.

_____. *Historical and Theological Foundations of Law Volume I: Ancient Wisdom*. Powder Springs, GA: American Vision Press and Tolle Lege Press, 2011.

Ellis, Jenna. *The Legal Basis for a Moral Constitution: A Guide for Christians to Understand America's Constitutional Crisis*. Bloomington, IN: Westbow Press, 2015.

Erickson, Millard J. *The Postmodern World*. Wheaton, IL: Crossway, 2002.

_____. *What Does God Know and When Does He Know It? The Current Controversy over Divine Foreknowledge*. Grand Rapids, MI: Zondervan Publishing, 2003.

Evans, Tony. *Theology You Can Count On*. Chicago, IL: Moody Press, 2008.

Faderman, Lillian. *The Gay Revolution: The Story of the Struggle*. New York, NY: Simon & Schuster, 2015.

Farris, Michael. *The History of Religious Liberty*. Green Forest, AR: Master Books, 2015.

Feinberg, John S. *Continuity and Discontinuity: Perspectives on the Relationship Between the Old and New Testaments*. Edited by John S. Feinberg. Wheaton, Ill: Crossway Books, 1988.

_____. "*Salvation in the Old Testament.*" In *Tradition & Testament: Essays in Honor of Charles Lee Feinberg*. Edited by John S. and Paul D. Feinberg. Chicago, IL: Moody Press, 1981.

Forte, David F. "The Originalist Perspective." In *The Heritage Guide to the Constitution*. Edited by Edwin Meese III. Washington, DC: Regnery Publishing, 2005.

Fruchtenbaum, Arnold G. *Faith Alone: The Condition of Our Salvation*. San Antonio, TX: Ariel Ministries, 2014.

_____. *Israelology: The Missing Link in Systematic Theology*. Tustin, CA: Ariel Ministries, 1989.

_____. *Messianic Christology*. Tustin, CA: Ariel Ministries, 1998.

_____. *God's Will & Man's Will: Predestination, Election, & Free Will*. San Antonio, TX: Ariel Ministries, 2013.

Gagnon, Robert A.J. *The Bible and Homosexual Practice: Texts and Hermeneutics*. Nashville, TN: Abingdon Press, 2001.

Garner, Bryan A. "Natural Law." In *Black's Law Dictionary*. Edited by Bryan A. Garner. St. Paul, MN: West Publishing, 2009.

Garrison, Tim Alan. *The Legal Ideology of Removal: The Southern Judiciary and the Sovereignty of American Nations*. Athens, GA: University of Georgia Press, 2002.

Geisler, Norman. *Christian Ethics: Options and Issues*. Grand Rapids, MI: Baker Book House, 1989.

_____. *Systematic Theology in One Volume*. Bloomington, MN: Bethany House Publishing, 2011.

Geisler, Norman and Jason Jimenez. *The Bible's Answers to 100 of Life's Biggest Questions*. Grand Rapids, MI: Baker Books, 2015.

Geisler, Norman and Paul D. Feinberg. *Introduction to Philosophy: A Christian Perspective*. Grand Rapids, MI: Baker Books, 1980.

Gilmore, Peter H. *The Satanic Scriptures*. Baltimore, MD: ScapeGoat Publishing, 2007.

George, Timothy. "Martin Luther." In *Biographical Dictionary of Evangelicals*. Edited by Timothy Larsen. Downers Grove, IL: Inter-Varsity Press, 2003.

Ger, Steven. *The Book of Acts: Witnesses to the World. Twenty-First Century Commentary Series*. Chattanooga, TN: AMG Publishers, 2004.

Gerstner, John. *Wrongly Dividing the Word of Truth: A Critique of Dispensationalism*. Morgan, PA: Soli Deo Gloria Publications, 2000.

Goldenberg, Naomi. *Changing of the Gods: Feminism and the End of Traditional Religions*. Boston, MA: Beacon Press, 1979.

Good, Kenneth. *Are Baptists Calvinists*. Rochester, NY: Backus Book Publishers, 1988.

Graves, James Robinson. *The Work of Christ in the Covenant of Redemption: Developed in Seven Dispensations.* Reprint edition. Texarkana, AR: Bogard Press, 1883.

Grudem, Wayne. *Systematic Theology: An Introduction to Biblical Doctrine*. Grand Rapids, MI: Zondervan Publishing, 1994.

Gundry, Robert. *Commentary on the New Testament: Verse-by-Verse Explanations with a Literal Translation*. Peabody, MA: Hendrickson Publishers, 2010.

Halamandaris, Bill. *The Heart Of America: Ten Core Values That Make Our Country Great*. Dearfield Beach, FL: Health Publications, 2004.

Hamilton, James M. Jr., *God's Indwelling Presence: The Holy Spirit in the Old and New Testaments*. Nashville, TN: B&H Publishing, 2006.

Hannah, John. *An Uncommon Union: Dallas Theological Seminary and American Evangelicalism*. Grand Rapids, MI: Zondervan, 2009.

_____. "John Walvoord." In *Dictionary of Premillennial Theology*. Edited by Mal Couch. Grand Rapids, MI: Kregel Publications, 1996.

Hefley, James C. *The Truth In Crisis*. Dallas, TX: Criterion Publications, 1986.

Heimbach, Daniel R. *True Sexual Morality: Recovering Biblical Standards for a Culture in Crisis*. Wheaton, IL: Crossway Books, 2004.

Heslop, S. Jeff. "Content, Object & Message of Saving Faith." In *Dispensationalism Tomorrow and Beyond: A Theological Collection in Honor of Charles C. Ryrie*. Fort Worth, TX: Tyndale Seminary Press, 2008.

Hill, Wesley. *Washed And Waiting*. Grand Rapids, MI: Zondervan, 2010.

Hodge, Charles. *Systematic Theology*. Philadelphia: [publisher not identified], 1865.

Hobbes, Thomas. *Human Nature and De Corpore Politico*. Edited by J.C.A. Gaskin. Oxford, NY: Oxford University Press, 1994.

Horton, Michael. *For Calvinism*. Grand Rapids, MI: Zondervan, 2011.

_____. *The Christian Faith: A Systematic Theology for Pilgrims On the Way*. Grand Rapids, MI: Zondervan, 2011.

Ice, Thomas D. "Dispensational Hermeneutics." In *Issues in Dispensationalism*. Edited by Wesley R. Willis and John R. Master. Chicago, IL: Moody Press, 1994.

Jennings, Fennis Dake. *God's Plan for Man*. Lawrenceville, GA: Dake Bible Sales, 1977.

Johnson, Elliot. *Expository Hermeneutics: An Introduction*. Grand Rapids, MI: Zondervan, 1990.

Jong, Norman De. *Education in Truth*. Philipsburg, NJ: P&R Publishing, 1969.

Keathley, Kenneth. *Salvation and Sovereignty*. Nashville, TN: B&H Publishing, 2010.

Kendall, R.T. *Calvin and English Calvinism to 1649*. Carlisle Cumbria, United Kingdom: Paternoster Press, 1997.

Kennedy, Kevin. "*Was Calvin a Calvinist*." In *Whosoever Will: A Biblical-Theological Critique of Five-Point Calvinism*. Edited by David L. Allen and Steve W. Lemke. Nashville, TN: B&H Publishing, 2010.

Kerr, Hugh T. *Positive Protestantism: A Return to First Principles*. Englewood Cliff, NJ: Prentice Hall Publishers, 1963.

Kimbro, Reginald C. *The Gospel According to Dispensationalism:* Toronto, Canada: Wittenburg Publications, 1995.

Kraus, Norman C. *Dispensationalism in America: Its Rise and Development* . Richmond, VA: John Knox Press, 1958.

Kreft, Peter and Ronald K. Tacelli. *Handbook of Christian Apologetics*. Downers Grove, IL: InterVarsity Press, 1994.

Kurtz, Paul. *Humanist Manifesto I and II*. Amherst, NY: Prometheus Books, 1973.

_____. *Humanist Manifesto 2000: A Call for a New Planetary Humanism*. Amherst, NY: Prometheus Books, 2000.

_____. *What is Secular Humanism*. Amherst, NY: Prometheus Books, 2007.

LaHaye, Tim F. and Edward E Hindson. *Global Warning*. Eugene, OR: Harvest House Publishers, 2007.

Levin, Mark R. *Liberty and Tyranny: A Conservative Manifesto*. New York, NY: Threshold Editions, 2009.

Lewis, Gordon R. and Bruce A. Demarest. *Integrative Theology*. Grand Rapids, MI: Zondervan, 1996.

Lightner, Robert P. *Evangelical Theology: A Survey and Review*. Grand Rapids, MI: Baker Book House, 1986.

_____. *Sin, the Savior, and Salvation: The Theology of Everlasting Life*. Grand Rapids, MI: Kregel Publications, 1991.

_____. *The Death Christ Died: A Biblical Case for Unlimited Atonement*. Grand Rapids, MI: Kregel Publications, 1998.

Lockyer, Herbert. *All the Doctrines of the Bible*. Grand Rapids, MI: Zondervan, 1964.

Long, Edward LeRoy Jr. *A Survey of Christian Ethics*. New York: Oxford University Press, 1967.

Lutzer, Erwin. *The Doctrines that Divide: A Fresh Look at the Historic Doctrines that Separate Christians*. Grand Rapids, MI: Kregel Publications, 1998.

MacArthur, John Jr., *The MacArthur Bible Commentary*. Nashville, TN: Thomas Nelson, 2005.

_____. *The MacArthur New Testament Commentary: Acts 13-28*. Chicago, IL: Moody Press, 1996.

_____. *The MacArthur New Testament Commentary: Ephesians*. Chicago, IL: Moody Press, 1986.

_____. *The MacArthur New Testament Commentary: 1 Timothy*. Chicago, IL: Moody Press, 1995.

MacDonald, William. *Believer's Bible Commentary*. Edited by Art Farstad. Nashville, TN: Thomas Nelson Publishing, 1990.

Madsen, David. *Successful Dissertations and Theses: A Guide to Graduate Student Research from Proposal to Completion*. San Francisco, CA: Jossey-Bass Inc., Publishers, 1992.

MacGregor, Kirk R. *A Molinist-Anabaptist Systematic Theology*. Lanham, MD: University Press, 2007.

Mack, Maynard. "The Leiden Hymns." In *The Norton Anthology of World Masterpieces*. General Editor Maynard Mack. New York, NY: W.W. Norton & Company, Inc., 1997.

Mangum, R. Todd. *The Dispensational-Covenantal Rift: The Fissuring of an American Evangelical Theology from 1936 to 1944*. Eugene, OR: Wipf Stock and Publishers, 2007.

Marsden, George M. *Fundamentalism and American Culture*. Oxford, NY: Oxford University Press, 2006.

_____ *The Soul of the American University: Form Protestant Establishment to Established Nonbelief*. Oxford, NY: Oxford University Press, 1994.

Mathison, Keith A. *Dispensationalism: Rightly Dividing the People of God*. Phillipsburg, NJ: Presbyterian and Reformed Publishing Company, 1995.

McAvoy, Steven L. "James Martin Gray." In the *Dictionary of Premillennial Theology*. Edited by Mal Couch Grand Rapids, MI: Kregel Publications, 1996.

_____. "John Charles Ryle." In the *Dictionary of Premillennial Theology*. Edited by Mal Couch. Grand Rapids, MI: Kregel Publications, 1996.

McBeth, H. Leon. *The Baptist Heritage: Four Centuries of Baptist Witness*. Nashville, TN: Broadman Press, 1987.

McDowell, Josh. *God Breathed: The Undeniable Power and Reliability of Scripture*. Uhrichsville, OH: Shiloh Run Press, 2015.

Merriam, Sharan B. and Edwin L. Simpson. *A Guide to Research for Educators and Trainers of Adults*. Malabar, FL: Krieger Publishing Company, 2000.

Miller, Keith B. *Perspectives On An Evolving Creation*. Grand Rapids, MI: Eerdmans, 2003.

Mohler, R. Albert Jr., "The Pastor as Theologian." In *A Theology for the Church*. Edited by Daniel L. Akin. Nashville, TN: B&H Publishing, 2007.

Moore, Russell D. "Atonement." In the *Holman Illustrated Bible Dictionary*. Edited by Chad Brand, Charles Draper, Archie England. Nashville, TN: Holman Bible Publishers, 2003.

_____. *The Kingdom of Christ: The New Evangelical Perspective*. Wheaton, IL: Crossway Books, 2004.

Morris, Henry M and John D Morris. *Modern Creation Trilogy, The*. Green Forest, AR: New Leaf Publishing Group, Inc., 1996.

Morris, Henry M. *The Biblical Basis for Modern Science*. Green Forest, AR: Master Books, 2002.

Myra, Harold and Marshall Shelley. *The Leadership Secrets of Billy Graham*. Grand Rapids, MI: Zondervan, 2005.

Nash, Ronald H. *Is Jesus the Only Savior?*. Grand Rapids, MI: Zondervan, 1994.

Noebel, David. *Understanding The Times*. Manitou Springs, CO: Summit Press, 1991.

Osterhaven, M.E. "Synod of Dort." In *Evangelical Dictionary of Theology*. Edited by Walter A. Elwell. Grand Rapids, MI: Baker Books, 2001.

Ostrowski, James. *Progressivism: A Primer on the Idea Destroying America*. Buffalo, NY: Cazenovia Books, 2014.

Owen, John. *The Death of Death in the Death of Christ*. Carlisle, PA: The Banner of Truth Trust, 1959.

Packer, J.I. *Concise Theology: A Guide to Historic Christian Beliefs*. Wheaton, IL: Tyndale House Publishers, 1993.

Paine, Thomas. "Common Sense." In *Common Sense and Other Writings*, ed. George Stade. New York, NY: Barnes and Noble Books, 2005.

Palmer, Edwin H. *The Five Points of Calvinism*. Grand Rapids, MI: Baker Books, 1972.

Pinnock, Clark H. *The Openness of God*. Downers Grove, IL: InterVarsity Press, 1994.

Patterson, Paige. *Anatomy Of A Reformation*, 1994.

_____."An Interview with W.A. Criswell." In *The Church at the Dawn of the 21st Century: Essays in Honor of W.A. Criswell*. Edited by Paige Patterson, John Pretlove, and Luis Pantoja Jr. Dallas, TX: Criswell Publications, 1989.

_____. *A Pilgrim Priesthood: An Exposition of the Epistle of First Peter*. Eugene, OR: Wipf and Stock Publishers, 1982.

_____. *Johnny's Teacher—The Problem and the Solution*. Wake Forest, NC: Magnolia Hill Papers II, 1997

_____. *The New American Commentary*: Volume 39, *Revelation*. General editor E. Ray Clendenen. Nashville, TN: B&H Publishing, 2012.

_____. "W.A. Criswell." In *Theologians of the Baptist Tradition*. Edited by Timothy George and David S. Dockery. Nashville, TN: Broadman and Holman Publishers, 2001.

Paul, Ron. *Liberty Defined: 50 Essential Issues that Affect our Freedom*. New York, NY: Grand Central Publishing, 2011.

Pentecost, J. Dwight. *Designed to Be Like Him*. Grand Rapids, MI: Kregel Publications, 1966.

_____. *Design for Discipleship: Discovering God's Blueprint for the Christian Life*. Grand Rapids, MI: Kregel Publications, 1996.

_____. *Things Which Become Sound Doctrine*. Grand Rapids, MI: Zondervan Publishing, 1969.

Pettegrew, Larry. *The New Covenant Ministry of the Holy Spirit*. Grand Rapids, MI: Kregel Publications, 2001.

Pierard, R.V. "*Theological Liberalism*." In *Evangelical Dictionary of Theology*, 2nd edition. Edited by Walter A. Elwell. Grand Rapids, MI: 2001.

Pink, A.W. *A Study on Dispensationalism*. Editor's *Biography of A.W. Pink*. No place of publication, Gideon House Books, 2015.

Plummer, Robert L. *40 Questions About Interpreting the Bible*. Grand Rapids, MI: Kregel Publications, 2010.

Pyne, Robert. "The Effect of Sin on Human Nature." In *Understanding a Christian Theology*. Edited by Charles R. Swindoll and Roy B. Zuck. Nashville, TN: Thomas Nelson Publishers, 2003.

Radmacher, Earl D. "The Current Status of Dispensationalism and Its Eschatology." In *Perspectives on Evangelical Theology*. Edited by Kenneth S. Kantzer and Stanley N. Gundry. Grand Rapids, MI: Baker Publishing, 1979.

Radmacher, Earl. "What Does Salvation Mean." In *Understanding a Christian Theology*. Edited by Charles R. Swindoll and Roy B. Zuck. Nashville, TN: Thomas Nelson Publishers, 2003.

Reisinger, Ernest C. *Lord and Christ: The Implications of Lordship for Faith and Life*. Phillipsburg, NJ: P&R Publishing, 1994.

Reymond, Robert L. *A New Systematic Theology of the Christian Faith*. Nashville, TN: Thomas Nelson Inc., 1998.

Rhodes, Kenny. *The One Who Is*. Bloomington, IN: WestBow Press, 2015.

Richards, Lawrence O. *The Bible Reader's Companion*. Baltimore, MD: Halo Press, 1991.

Ringenberg, W.C. "*Donald Grey Barnhouse*." In the *Evangelical Dictionary of Theology*. Edited by Walter A. Elwell. Grand Rapids, MI: Baker Books, 2001.

Roberts, Bob Jr. *Transformation: How Glocal Churches Transform Lives and the World*. Grand Rapids, MI: Zondervan, 2006.

Robertson, O. Palmer. *The Christ of the Covenants*. Phillipsburg, NJ: Presbyterians and Reformed Publishing, 1980.

Rushdoony, Rousas John and Herbert W Titus. *The Institutes of Biblical Law*. Vallecito, CA: Ross House Books, 1986.

Rydelnik, Miachel. *The Messianic Hope: Is the Hebrew Bible Really Messianic?*. Editor E. Ray Clendenen. Nashville, TN: B&H Publishing, 2010.

Rydelnik, Michael and Michael Vanlaningham. *The Moody Bible Commentary*. Chicago, IL: Moody Press, 2014.

Ryken, Leland. *How to Read the Bible as Literature*. Grand Rapids, MI: Zondervan Publishing, 1984.

Rymph, Catherine E. "Equal Rights Amendment." In *The Oxford Companion to American Law*. Edited by Kermit L. Hall. New York, NY: Oxford University Press, 2002.

Ryrie, Charles C. *Basic Theology: A Popular Systematic Guide to Understanding Biblical Truth*. Colorado Springs, CO: Chariot Victor Publishing, 1996.

_____. *Biblical Theology of the New Testament*. Chicago, IL: Moody Press, 1959.

_____. *Dispensationalism*. Chicago, IL: Moody Press, 1995.

_____. *What You Should Know About Inerrancy*. Chicago, IL: Moody Press, 1981.

Sandel, Michael J. *Justice: What's The Right Thing To Do*. New York: USA Farrar, Straus and Giroux, 2009.

Scalia, Antonin and Bryan A. Garner. *Reading Law: The Interpretation of Legal Texts*. St. Paul, MN: Thomson/West Publishers, 2012.

Schlink, Edmund. *Theology Of The Lutheran Confessions*. Philadelphia, PA: Muhlenberg Press, 1961.

Schreiner, Thomas R. and Bruce Ware. *Still Sovereign: Contemporary Perspectives on Election, Foreknowledge, and Grace*. Grand Rapids, MI: Baker Books, 2000.

Schrodinger, Erwin. *Science and Humanism*. Cambridge, United Kingdom: Cambridge University Press, 1951.

Sheppard, Stephen Michael. "Legal Positivism." *The Wolters Kluwer Bouvier Law Dictionary*. Fredrick, MD: Wolters Kluwer Law & Business Publishers, 2011.

Sherlin, Keith. *Satan's Strategy to Curse Christ's Congregation: An Analysis of How Anarchy and Apostasy Develop in Christian Congregations & Elderships*. Bloomington, IN: AuthorHouse Publishing, 2010.

Smith, Carter. *Presidents: Every Question Answered*. Heatherton Victoria, Australia: Hinkler Books, 2014.

Sommers, Christina Hoff. *Who Stole Feminism?* New York: Simon & Schuster, 1994.

Spencer, Stephen R. "Reformed Theology, Covenant Theology, and Dispensationalism." In *Integrity of Heart, Skillfulness of Hands: Biblical and Leadership Studies in Honor of Donald K. Campbell*. Edited by Charles Dyer and Roy B. Zuck. Grand Rapids, MI: Baker Books, 1994.

Spencer, Duane Edward. *Tulip: The Five Points of Calvinism in the Light of Scripture*. Grand Rapids, MI: Baker Books, 1979.

Sproul, R.C. *Chosen By God*. Wheaton, IL: Tyndale House Publishers, 1986.

_____. *Everyone's a Theologian: An Introduction to Systematic Theology*. Sanford, FL: Reformation Trust Publishing, 2014.

_____. *Grace Unknown: The Heart of Reformed Theology*. Grand Rapids, MI: Baker Book House, 1997.

_____. *Not a Chance: The Myth of Chance in Modern Science & Cosmology*. Grand Rapids, MI: Baker Books, 1994.

_____. *The Consequences of Ideas: Understanding the Concepts that Shaped Our World*. Wheaton, IL: Crossway Books, 2000.

_____. *The Invisible Hand: Do All Things Really Work for Good?* Phillipsburg, NJ: P&R Publishing, 2003.

_____. *Willing to Believe: The Controversy over Free Will*. Grand Rapids, MI: Baker Books, 1997.

Stallard, Michael D. *The Early Twentieth-Century Dispensationalism of Arno C. Gaebelein*. Lewiston, NY: The Edwin Mellen Press, 2002.

Steele, David N., Curtis C. Thomas, and S. Lance Quinn. *The Five Points of Calvinism: Defined, Defended, and Documented*. Phillipsburg, NJ: P&R Publishing Company, 2004.

Stormer, John A. *None Dare Call It Education*. Florissant, MO: Liberty Bell Press, 1998.

Swindoll, Charles. *Growing Deep in the Christian Life: Returning to Our Roots*. Portland, OR: Multnomah Press, 1986.

Thomas, G. Michael. *The Extent of the Atonement: A Dilemma for Reformed Theology from Calvin to the Consensus*. Carlisle Cumbria, United Kingdom: Paternoster Publishing, 1997.

Towns, Elmer and Thomas Ice. "Dispensationalism." In *The Popular Encyclopedia of Bible Prophecy*. Edited by Tim Lahaye and Ed Hindson. Eugene, OR: Harvest House Publishers, 2004.

Unger, M.F. *Unger's Commentary on the Gospels*. Chattanooga, TN: AMG Publishers, 2014.

_____."Satan." In the *Evangelical Dictionary of Theology*. Edited by Walter A. Elwell. Grand Rapids, MI: Baker Book House, 2001.

Vlach, Michael. *Has the Church Replaced Israel: A Theological Evaluation*. Nashville, TN: B&H Publishing, 2010.

Walvoord, John. *End Times: Understanding Today's World Events in Biblical Prophecy*. Edited by Charles Swindoll. Nashville, TN: Word Publishing, 1998.

_____. *The Holy Spirit.* Grand Rapids, MI: Zondervan Publishing, 1958.

_____. "The Order of the Resurrections." In *Understanding Christian Theology*. Edited by Charles Swindoll and Roy B. Zuck. Nashville, TN: Thomas Nelson Publishers, 2003.

Washington, George. *Maxims of George Washington*. Collected and arranged by John Frederick Schroeder. Mount Vernon, VA: The Mount Vernon Ladies' Association, 1989.

Watson, William C. *Dispensationalism Before Darby: Seventeenth-Century and Eighteenth-Century English Apocalypticism*. Silverton, OR: Lampion Press, 2015.

Wills, Gregory A. *Southern Baptist Theological Seminary 1859-2009*. Oxford, NY: Oxford University Press, 2009.

Wood, Gordon S. *One Day in History: July 4, 1776*. New York, NY: HarperCollins Publishers, 2006.

Wright, D.F. "John Calvin." *Biographical Dictionary of Evangelicals.* Edited by Timothy Larsen. Downers Grove, IL: Inter-Varsity Press, 2003.

Zachariades, Doros. "Dispensation." In the *Holman Illustrated Bible Dictionary.* Edited by Chad Brand, Charlie Draper, and Archie England. Nashville, TN: Broadman and Holman Publishers, 2003.

Zodhiates, Spiros. "πᾶς." In *The Complete Word Study Dictionary: New Testament.* Chattanooga TN: AMG Publishers, 1992.

_____. "συνίστημι." In *The Complete Word Study Dictionary: New Testament.* Chattanooga TN: AMG Publishers, 1992.

Internet Articles

Bhonsle, Rajan. "Homosexuality: A Doctor's Perspective - Complete Wellbeing." *Complete Wellbeing.* http://completewellbeing.com/article/homosexuality-is-it-worth-the-risk/(accessed 25 June 2016).

Busnaina, Ibrahim. "How to Decide between an M.D. and D.O." *U.S. News and World Report* http://www.usnews.com/education/blogs/medical-school-admissions- doctor/2012/04/23/how-to-decide-between-an-md-and-a-do (accessed 25 June 2016).

Couch, Mal. *The Fall Of Evangelical Seminaries: A Lesson From The Past.* http://www.galaxie.com/article/ctj04-12-07 (accessed 25 June 2016).

Enns, Paul. "Ministry: Teaching and Administration." *Paulenns.com.* http://paulenns.com/ministry-teaching-and-administration/ (accessed 25 June 2016).

Feminists For Life. "Women Deserve Better® Than Abortion." *Feministsforlife.Org.*

http://feministsforlife.org/-taf/2005/PWA2005.pdf (accessed 25 June 2016).

George, Robert P. *Bernard Nathanson: A Life Transformed by Truth*, http://www.thepublicdiscourse.com/2011/02/2806/ (accessed 25 June 2016).

Hill, Catherine. *The Simple Truth About the Gender Pay Gap*.http://www.aauw.org/research/the-simple-truth-about-the-gender-pay-gap/ (accessed 25 June 2016).

Ice, Thomas. "The Calvinistic Heritage of Dispensationalism." *Pre-Trib Research Center*. http://www.pretrib.org/data/pdf/IceTheCalvinisticHeritag.pdf (accessed 25 June 2016).

Infographic. "Do Men Really Earn More Than Women?"*Payscale*. http://www.payscale.com/gender-lifetime-earnings-gap (accessed 25 June 2016).

Kim, Christine and Jennifer Marshall. "New Research On Children Of Same-Sex Parents Suggests Differences Matter." *The Daily Signal*. http://dailysignal.com/2012/06/11/new- research-on-children-of-same-sex-parents-suggests-differences-matter/ (accessed 25 June 2016).

Land, Richard. "Another View Of The Biblical Doctrine Of Election." *The Christian Post*. http://www.christianpost.com/news/another-view-of-the-biblical-doctrine-of-election- 46788/.

Lange, Hersch and Shawn Lazar. "A Tribute To Earl Radmacher." *Grace Evangelical Society*, http://www.faithalone.org/magazine/y2014/A-Tribute-to-Dr-Radmacher.pdf (accessed 25 June 2016).

MacArthur, John. "For Whom Did Christ Die?," *Grace To You.* http://www.gty.org/resources/sermons/90-363/For-Whom-Did-Christ- Die?Term=limited%20atonement (accessed 25 June 2016).

Macdonald, William. "William-Macdonald." William-Macdonald.Org. http://www.william-macdonald.org/index.php?page=211 (accessed 25 June 2016).

_____. "My Heart, My Life, My All." *William-Macdonald.Org.* (accessed 25 June 2016).

Mcardle, Mairead. "Trending: More College Students Supporting Post Birth Abortion."*The College Fix.* http://www.thecollegefix.com/post/19896/ (accessed 25 June 2016).

Moody Church. "What We Believe." *The Moody Church.* http://www.moodychurch.org/get-to-know-us/what-we-believe/ (accessed 25 June 2016).

New York Editorial Board. "Women Still Earn a Lot Less Than Men." *New York Times.* http://www.nytimes.com/2015/04/14/opinion/women-still-earn-a-lot-less-than- men.html?_r=0(accessed 25 June 2016).

Parental Rights. "20 Things You Need to Know About the UN Convention on the Rights of the Child." *Parentalrights.Org.*http://www.parentalrights.org/index.asp?Type= B_BASIC&SEC=%7BB56D7393-E583-4658-85E6-C1974B1A57F8%7D (accessed 25 June 2016).

Patterson, Paige. "Eight Theses on Election." *SBC Today.* http://sbctoday.com/tuesday-post/ (accessed 25 June 2016).

Philip, Mark. "Thomas Paine." *The Stanford Encyclopedia of Philosophy.* Winter 2013 Edition. Edited by Edward N. Zalta. http://plato.stanford.edu/archives/win2013/entries/paine/> (accessed 25 June 2016).

Spiering, Charlie. "31 Of Supreme Court Justice Antonin Scalia's Greatest Quotes – Breitbart." *Breitbart*. http://www.breitbart.com/big-government/2016/02/13/supereme-court-justice- antonin-scalias-greatest-quotes (accessed 25 June 2016).

Trustees of Princeton University. *ThePresidents of Princeton University: Woodrow Wilson*. https://www.princeton.edu/pub/presidents/wilson (accessed 25 June 2016).

Warren, Michael. *Thomas Hobbs*. http://www.americassurvivalguide.com/thomas_hobbes.php (accessed 25 June 2016).

Wilson, Wooodrow. "Conservapedia." *Conservapedia.Com*. http://www.conservapedia.com/Woodrow_Wilson. United Nations of Human Rights."ConventionOnThe Rights Of The Child." *Ohchr.Org*. http://www.ohchr.org/en/professionalinterest/pages/crc.aspx (accessed 25 June 2016).

About the Author

Dr. Keith Sherlin has earned degrees from North Greenville University (BA; Christian/Theological Studies), Tyndale Theological Seminary (MTS), Trinity Seminary (MA & PhD with honors; dissertation in historical theology), Scofield Theological Seminary under the guidance of his mentor Dr. Mal Couch (ThD in Systematic Theology), and a PhD in Dogmatics from North West University & Greenwich School of Theology (England & South Africa). He also graduated from the South Carolina Criminal Justice Academy and has served as a law enforcement officer and local magistrate judge in SC. Furthermore, he has taught in over 5 Seminaries as well as served as a pastor, teacher, and elder in several churches. Dr. Sherlin has authored numerous books and has participated in formal debates related to biblical theology. He is now President of Christicommunity (www.christicommunity.org), a global missions organization devoted to education, evangelism, and encouragement of Christlike discipleship. Christicommunity currently has ministers in 7 different countries with schools and churches training missionaries, evangelists, pastors, and teachers for the Great Commission.

www.ingramcontent.com/pod-product-compliance
Lightning Source LLC
Chambersburg PA
CBHW020654060526
44119CB00069B/63